The Broadcast

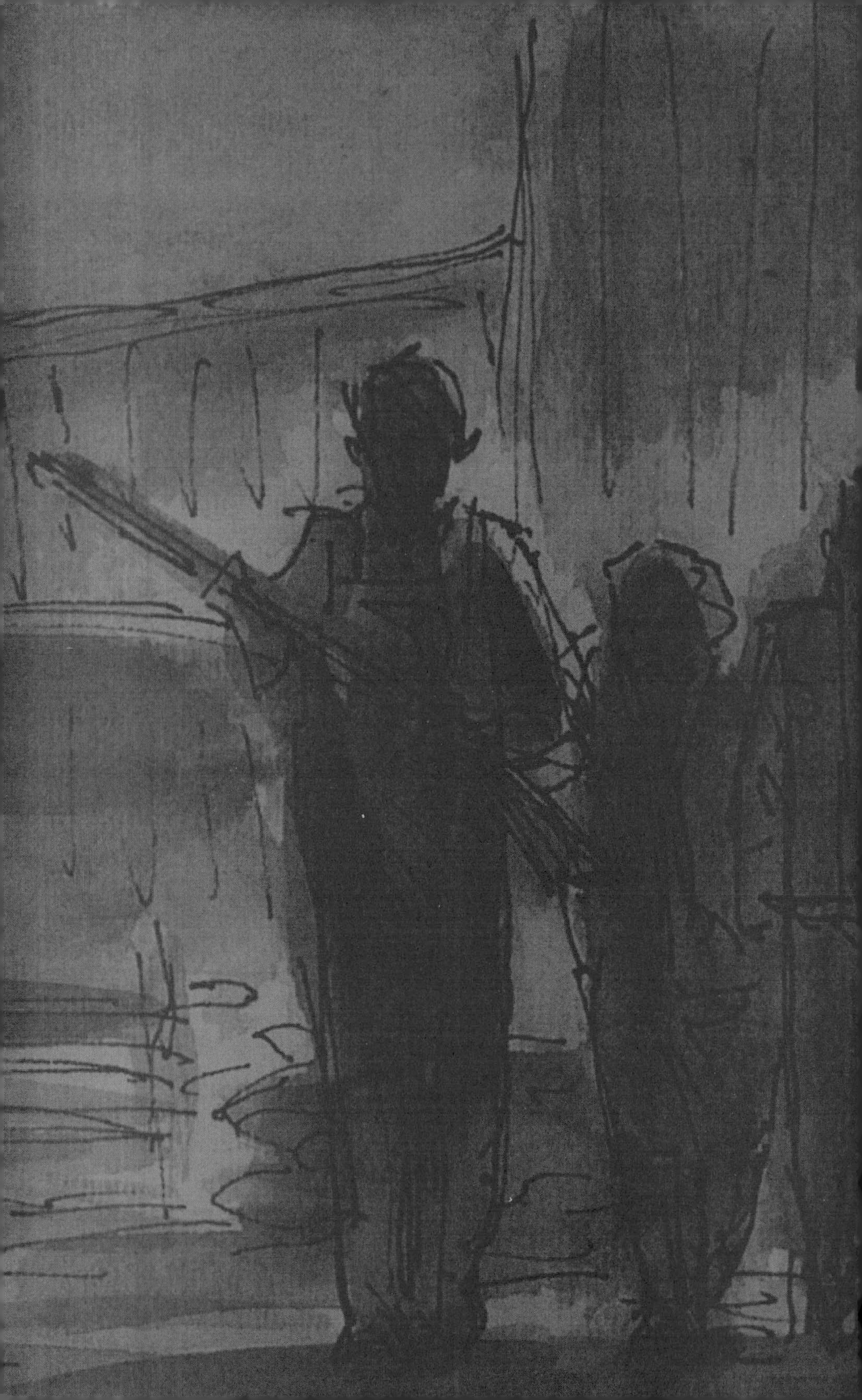

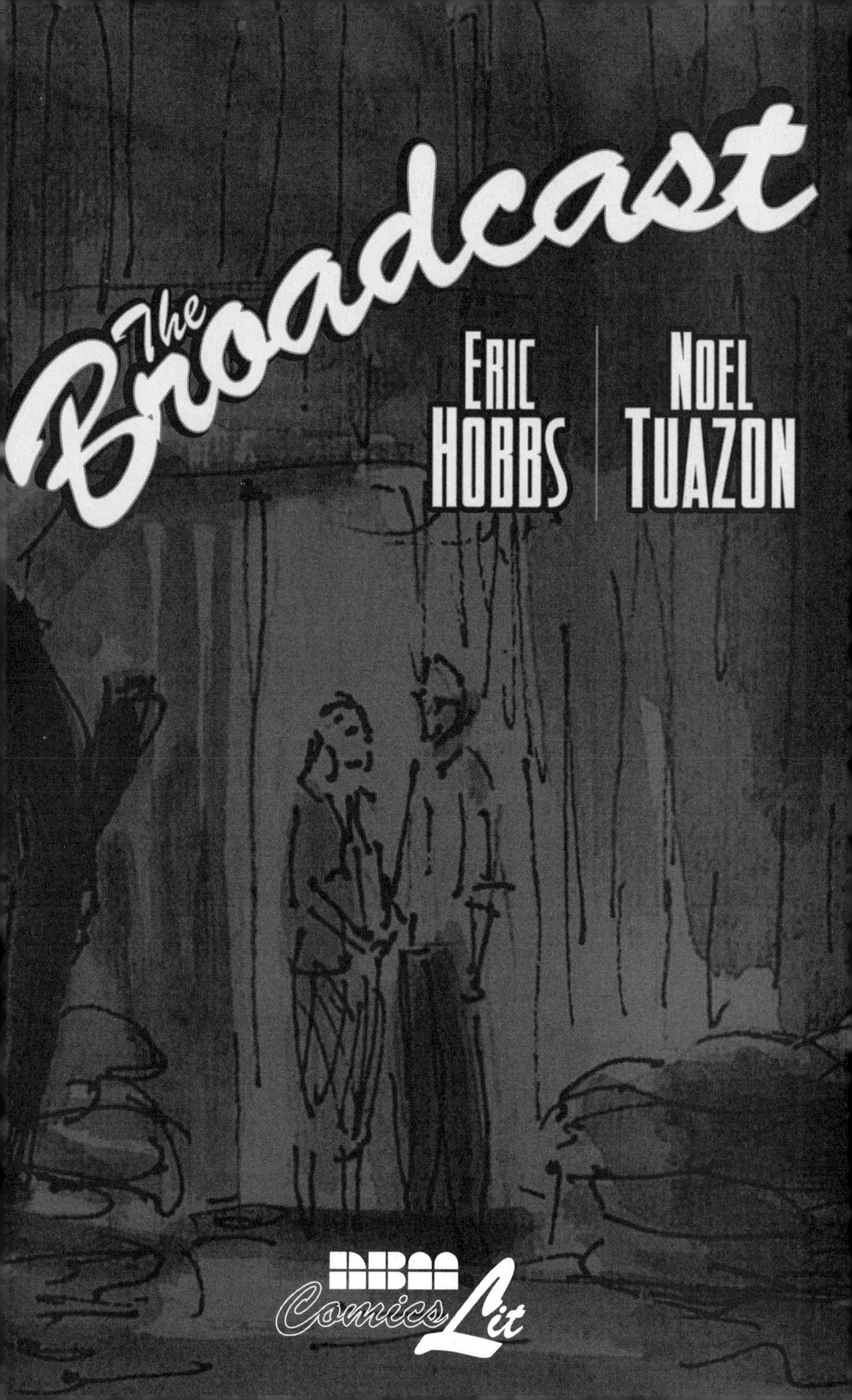
The Broadcast
Eric Hobbs
Noel Tuazon
NBM ComicsLit

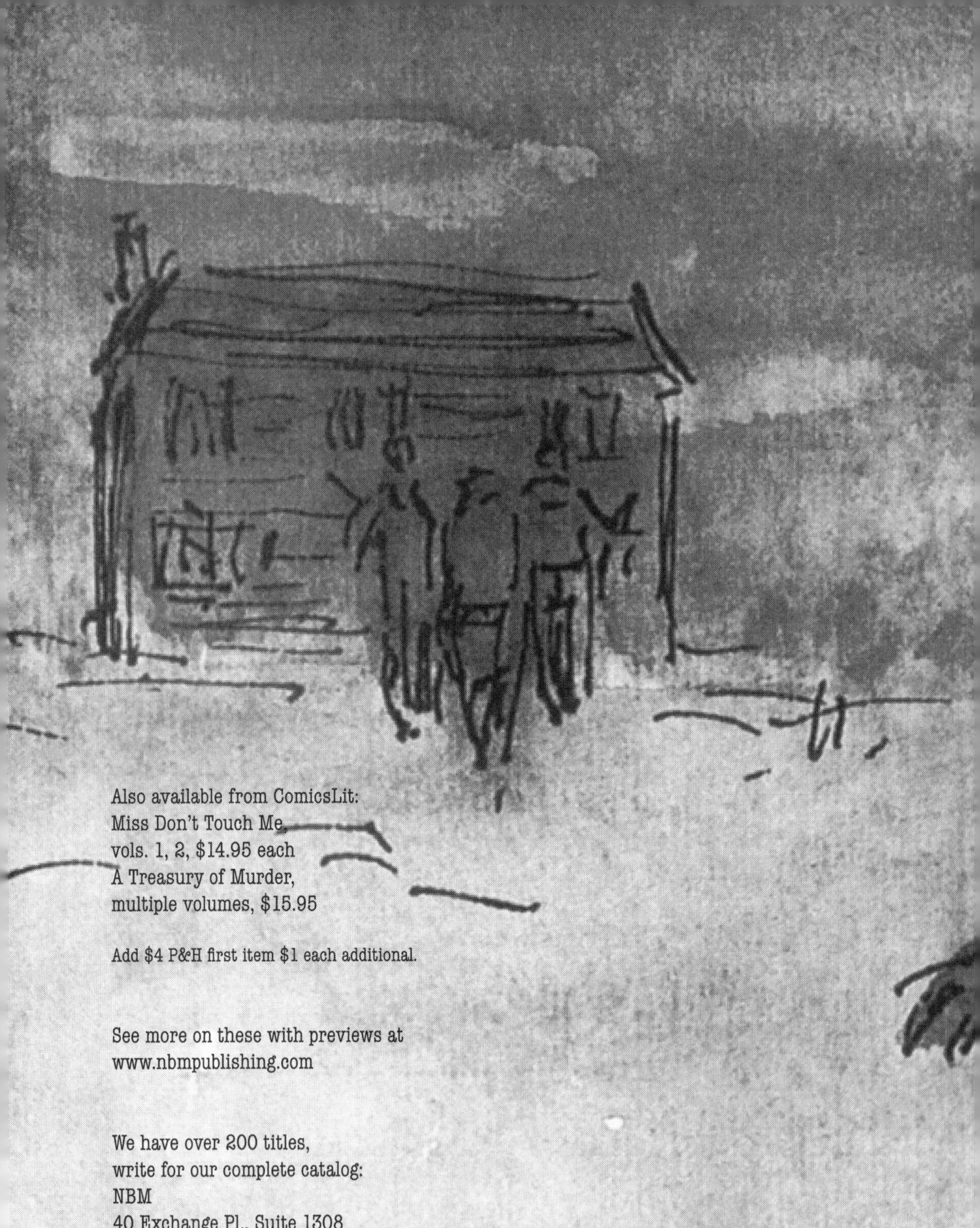

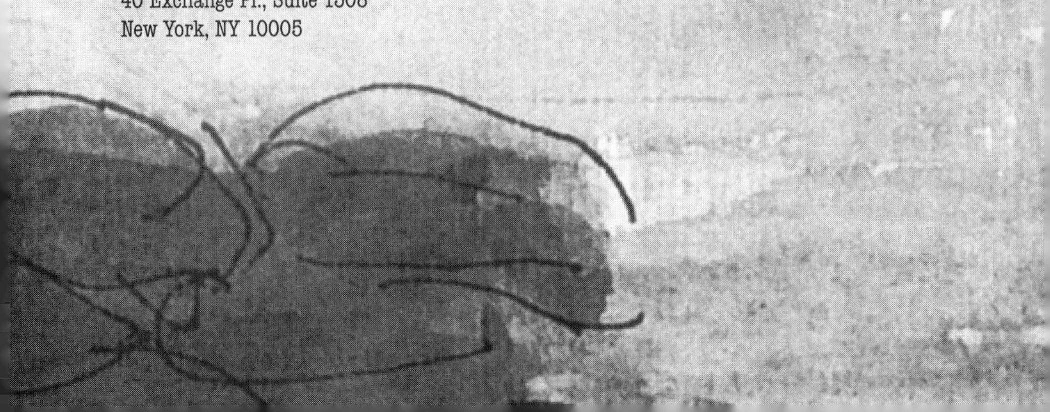

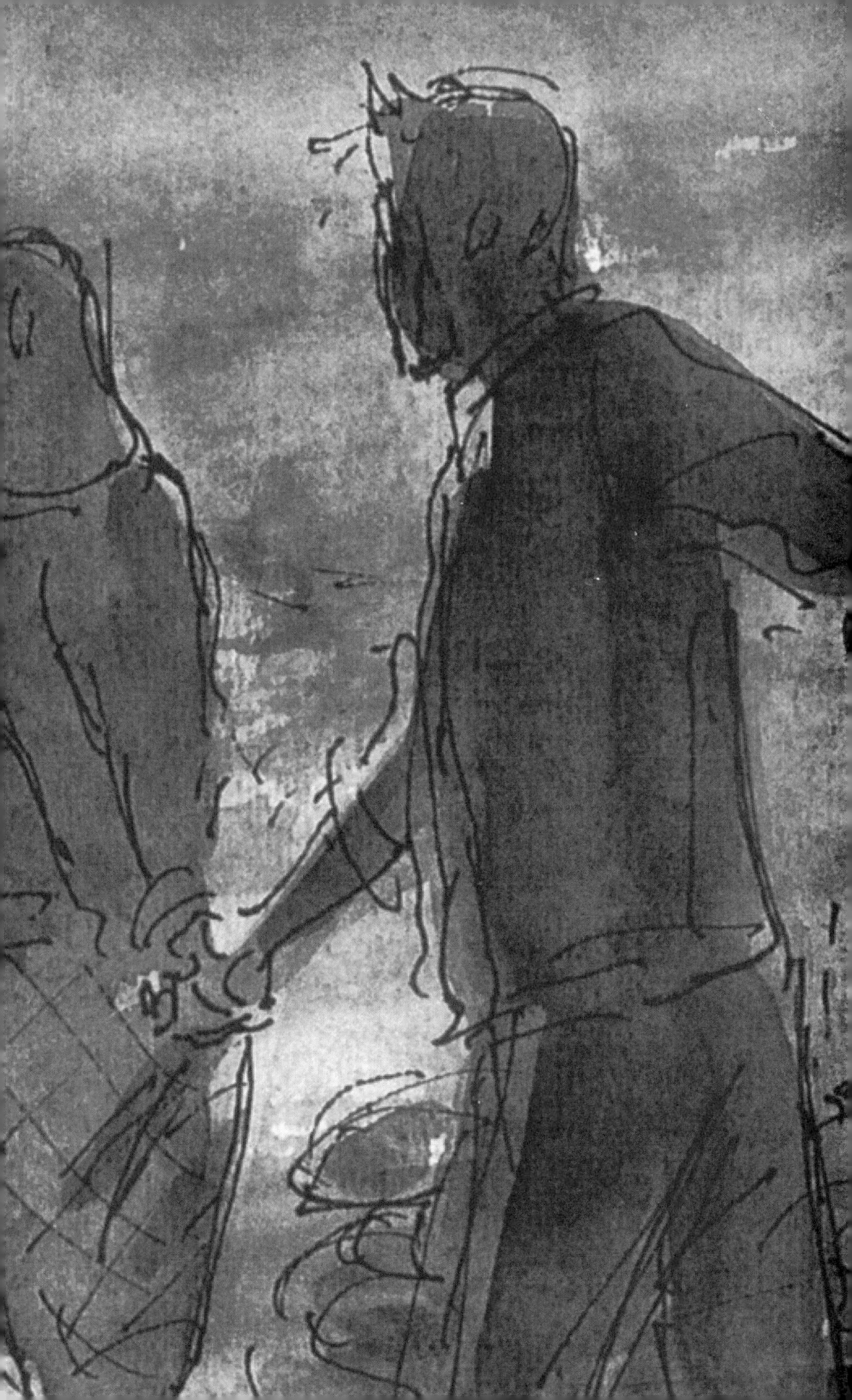

ISBN: 978-1-56163-590-0
© 2010 Eric Hobbs
Printed in Canada
Library of Congress Control Number: 2010932751
1st printing August 2010

Comicslit is an imprint
and trademark of

NANTIER · BEALL · MINOUSTCHINE
Publishing inc.
new york

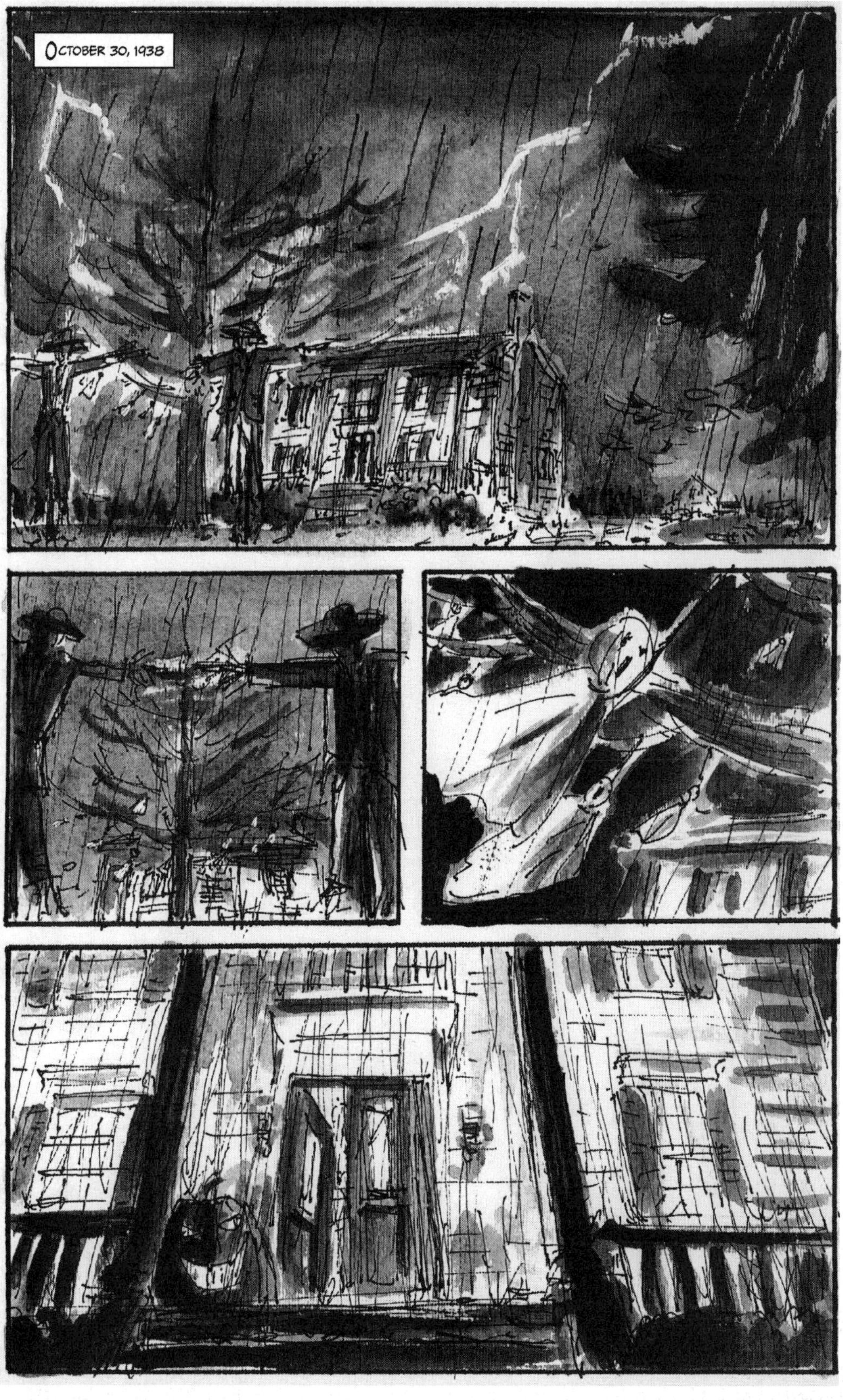
October 30, 1938

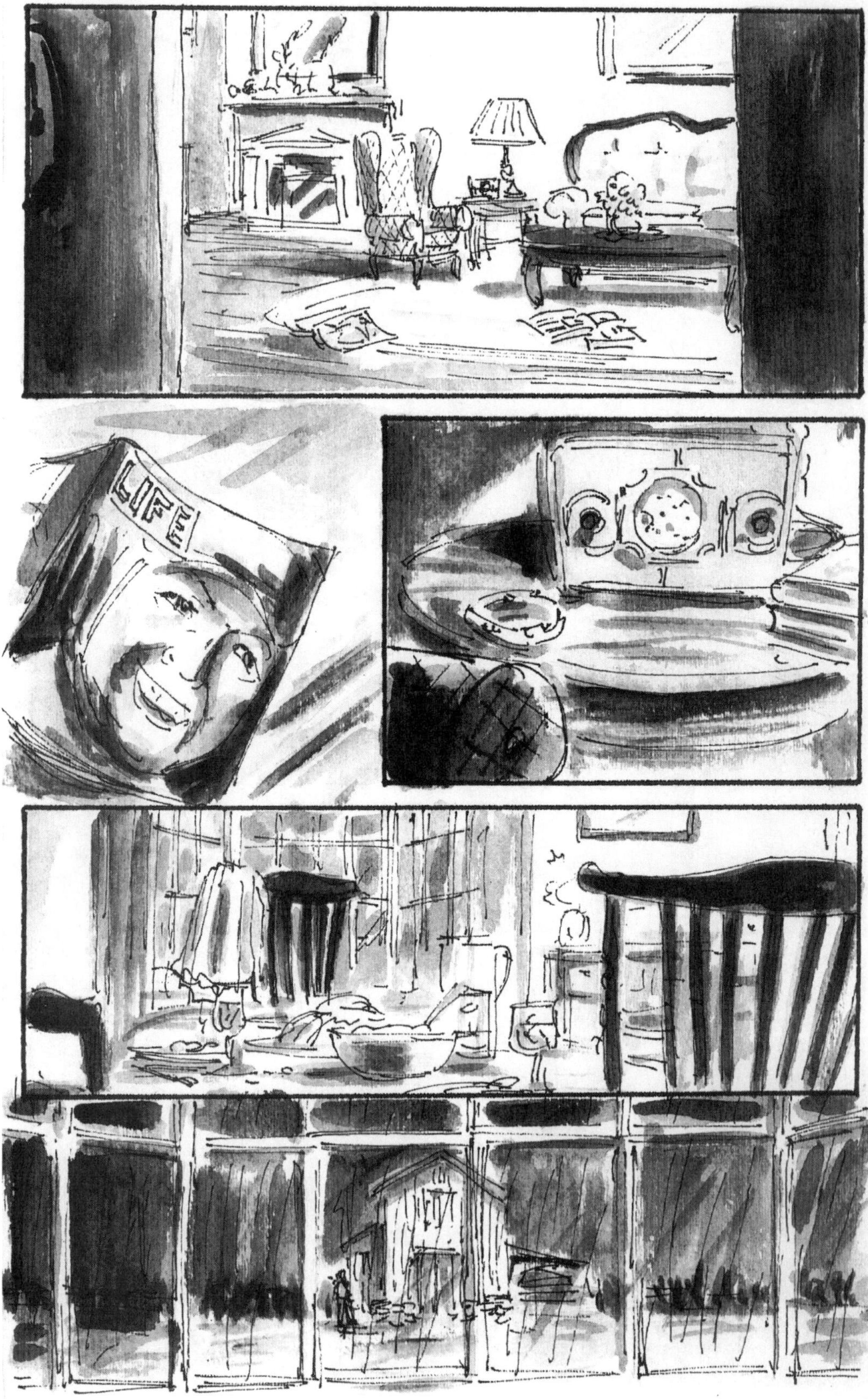
LIFE

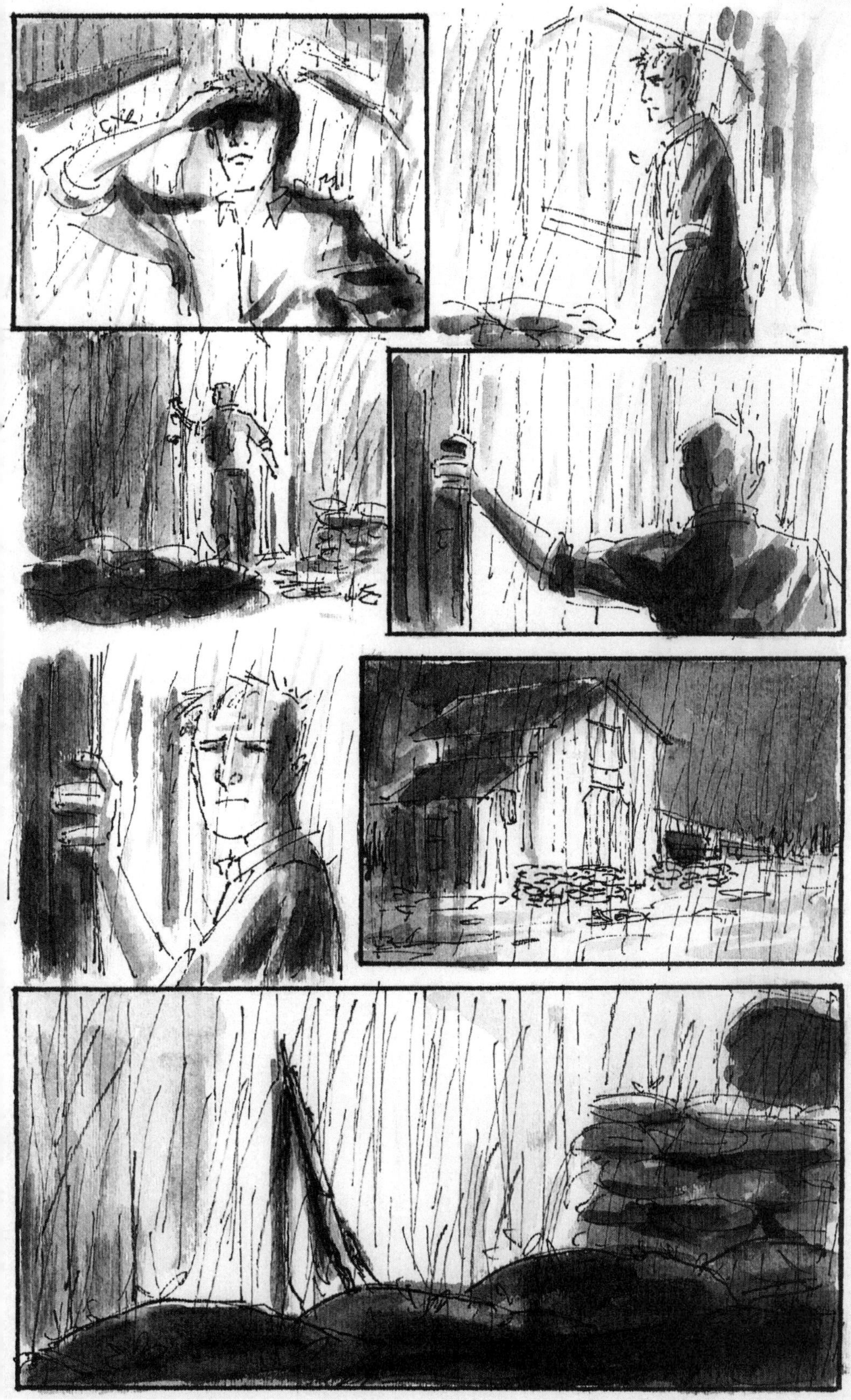

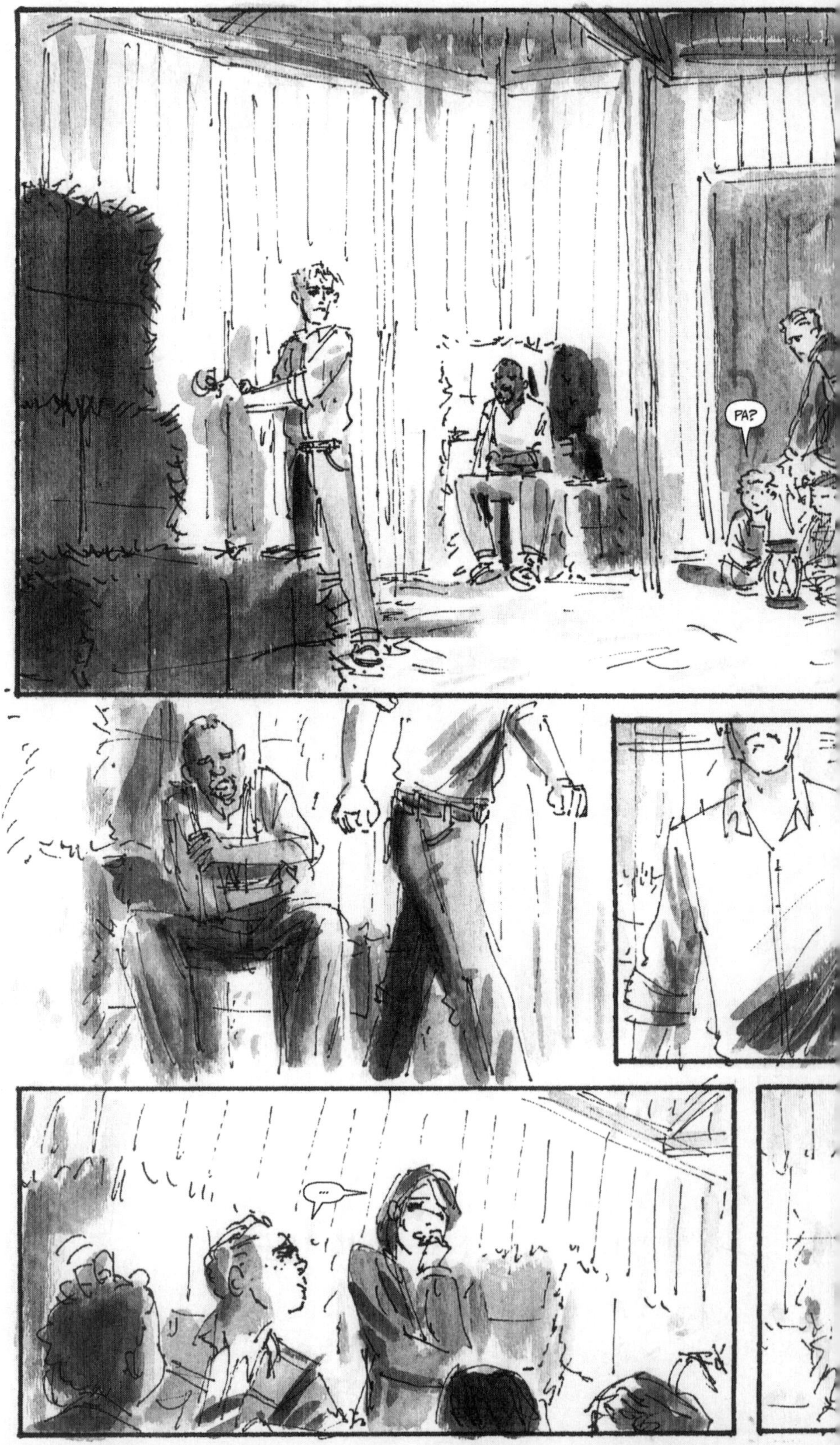
PA?
...

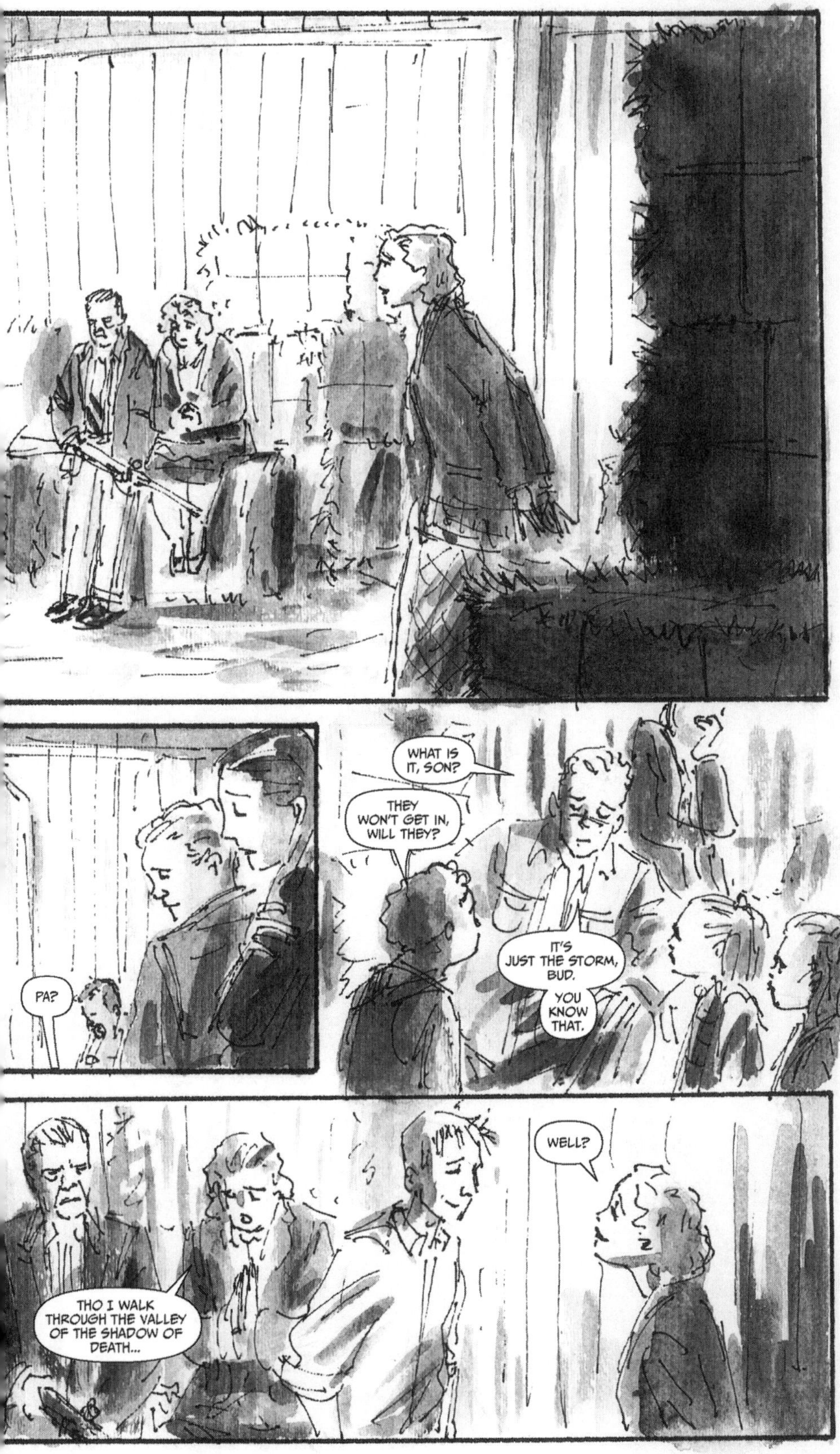
WHAT IS IT, SON?
THEY WON'T GET IN, WILL THEY?
PA?
IT'S JUST THE STORM, BUD.
YOU KNOW THAT.
THO I WALK THROUGH THE VALLEY OF THE SHADOW OF DEATH...
WELL?

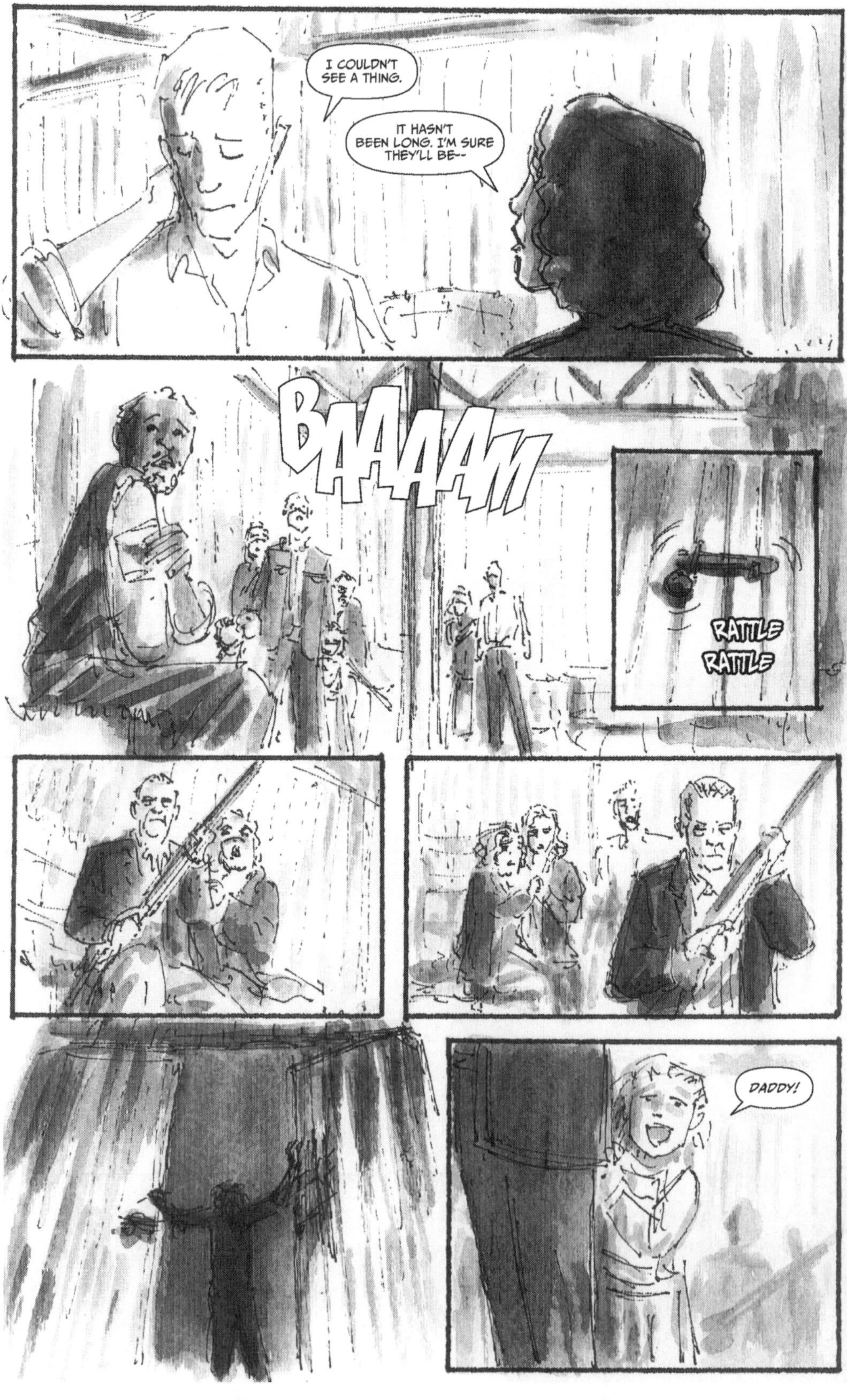
I COULDN'T SEE A THING.
IT HASN'T BEEN LONG. I'M SURE THEY'LL BE--
BAAAAAM
RATTLE RATTLE
DADDY!

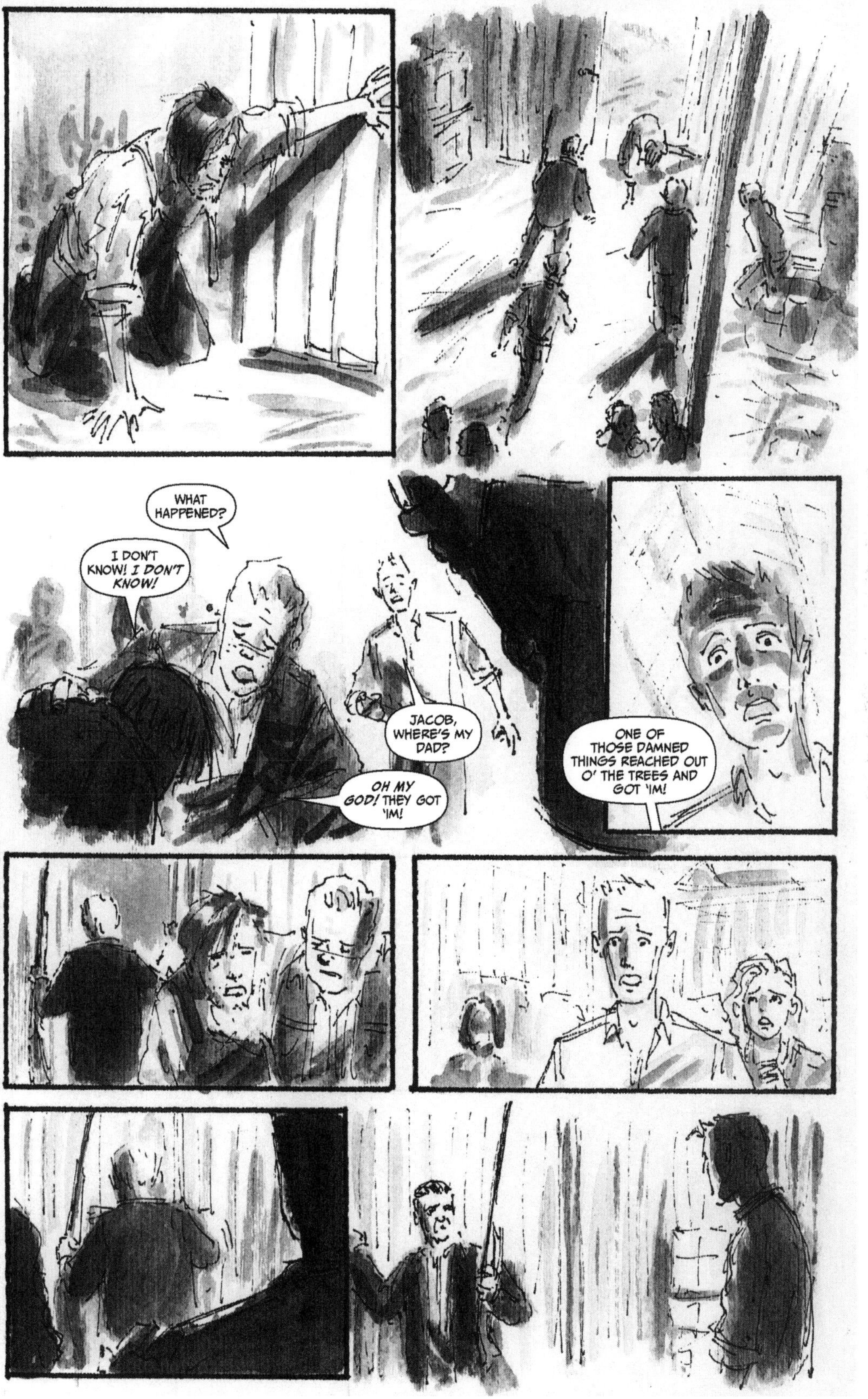
WHAT HAPPENED?
I DON'T KNOW! I DON'T KNOW!
JACOB, WHERE'S MY DAD?
OH MY GOD! THEY GOT 'IM!
ONE OF THOSE DAMNED THINGS REACHED OUT O' THE TREES AND GOT 'IM!

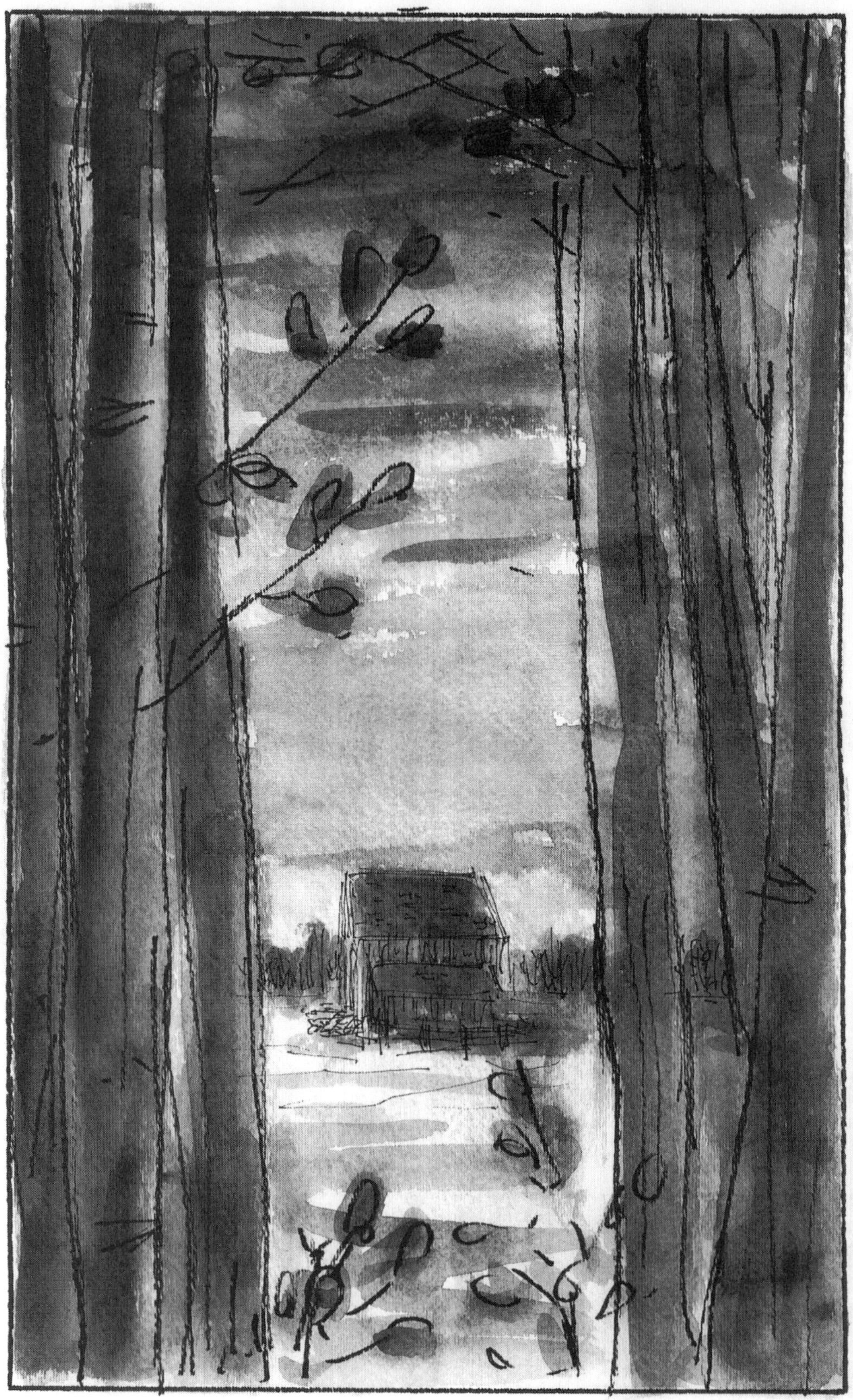

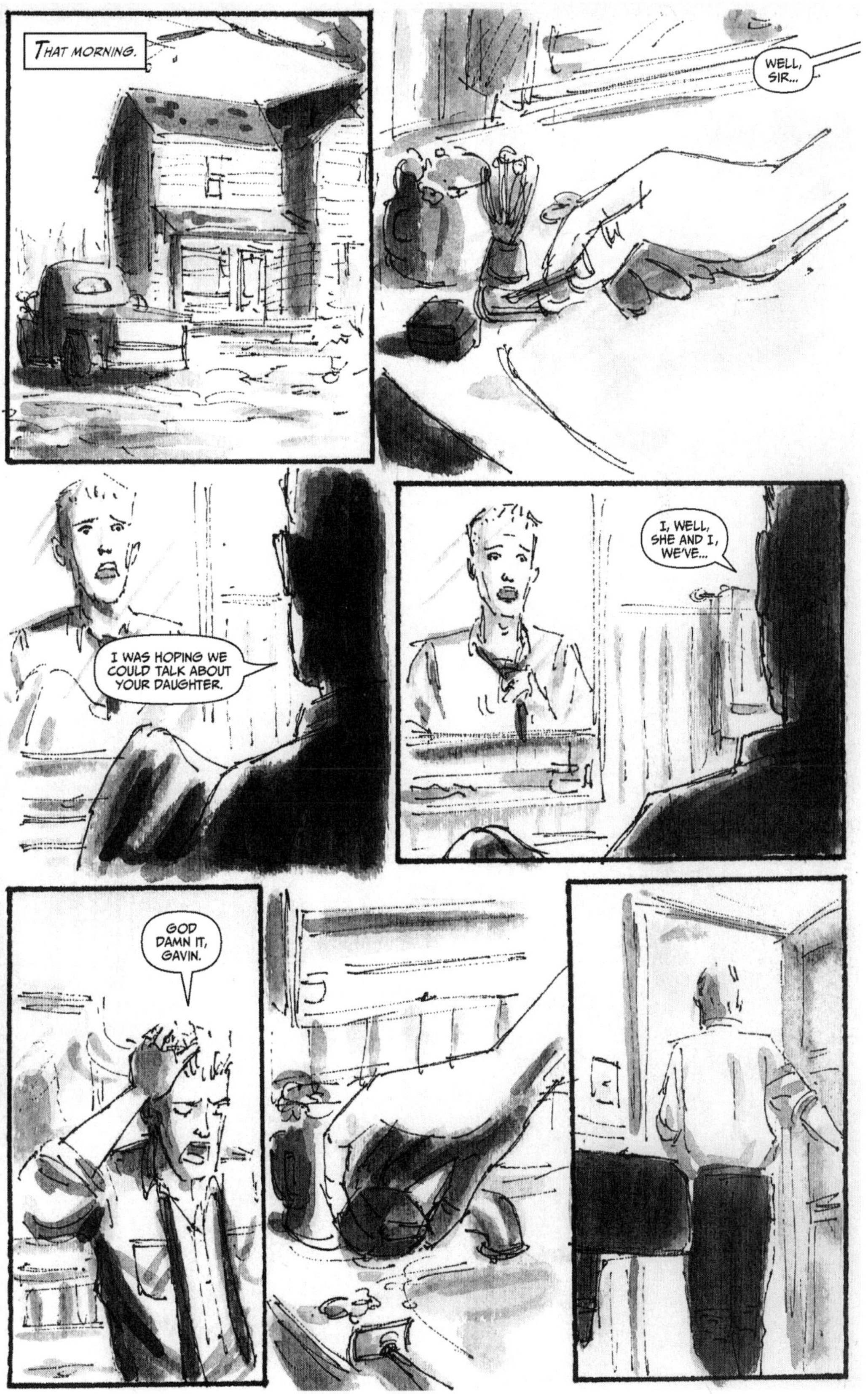
THAT MORNING.
WELL, SIR...
I WAS HOPING WE COULD TALK ABOUT YOUR DAUGHTER.
I, WELL, SHE AND I, WE'VE...
GOD DAMN IT, GAVIN.

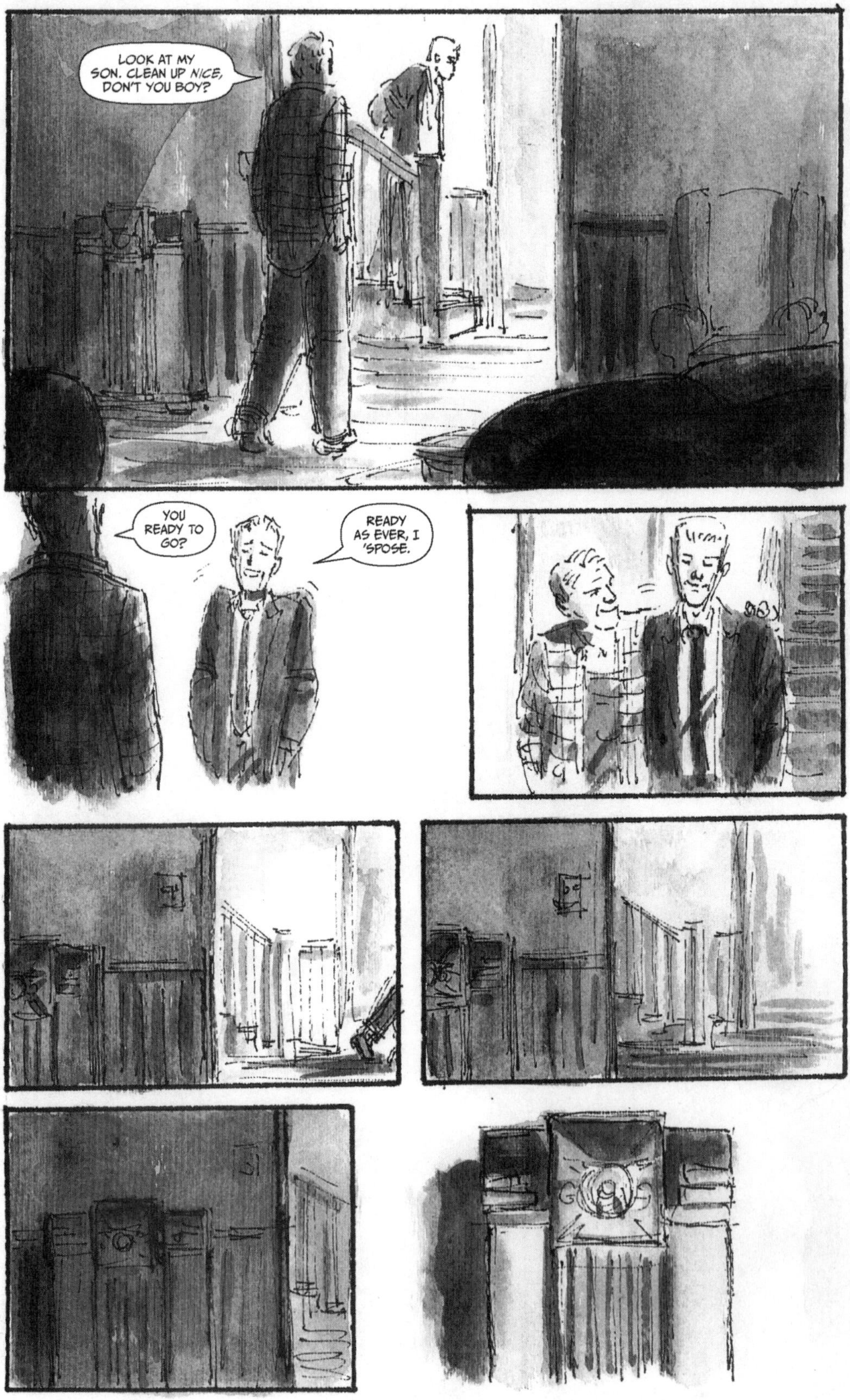
LOOK AT MY SON. CLEAN UP NICE, DON'T YOU BOY?
YOU READY TO GO?
READY AS EVER, I 'SPOSE.

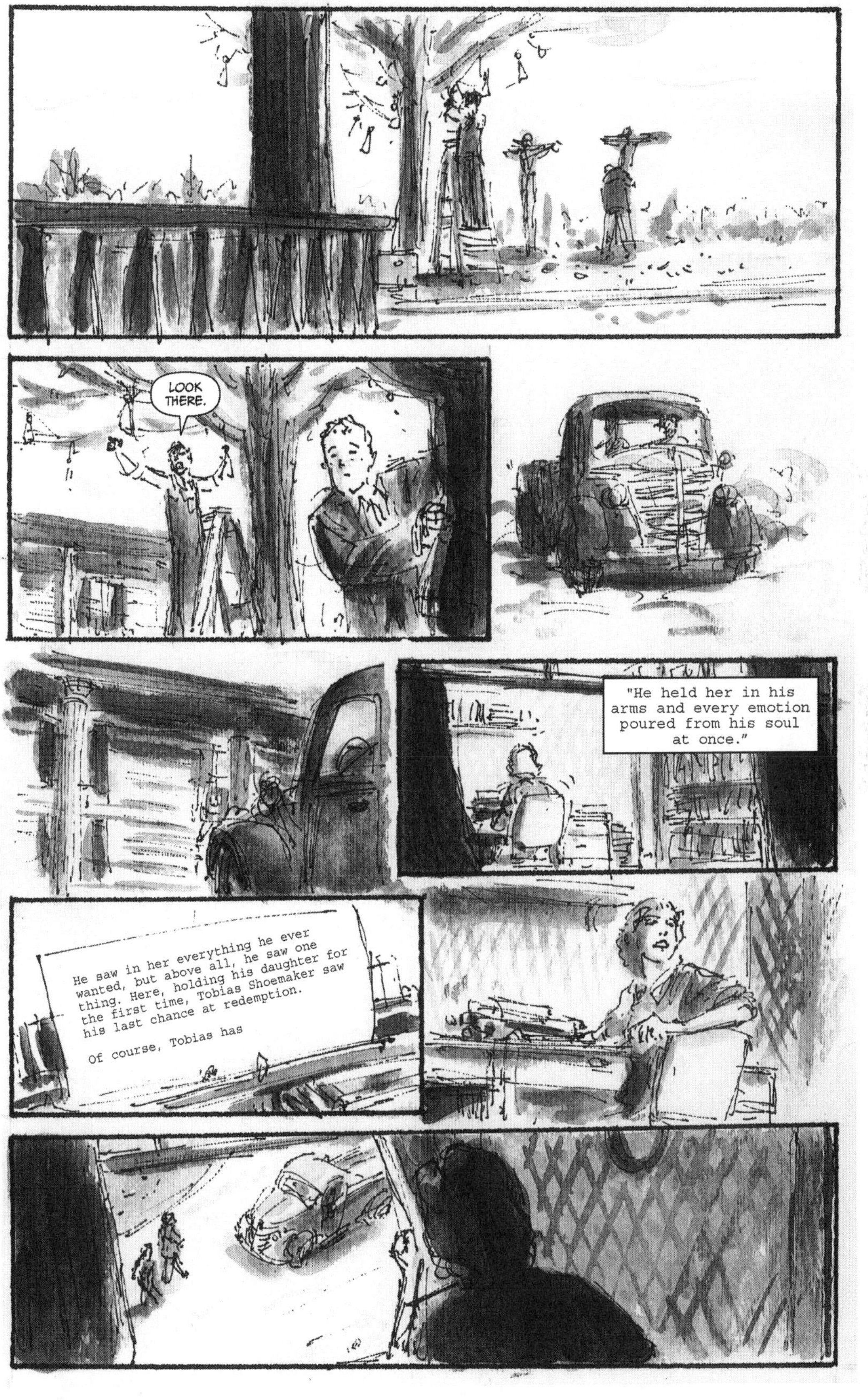
LOOK THERE.
"He held her in his arms and every emotion poured from his soul at once."
He saw in her everything he ever wanted, but above all, he saw one thing. Here, holding his daughter for the first time, Tobias Shoemaker saw his last chance at redemption.
Of course, Tobias has

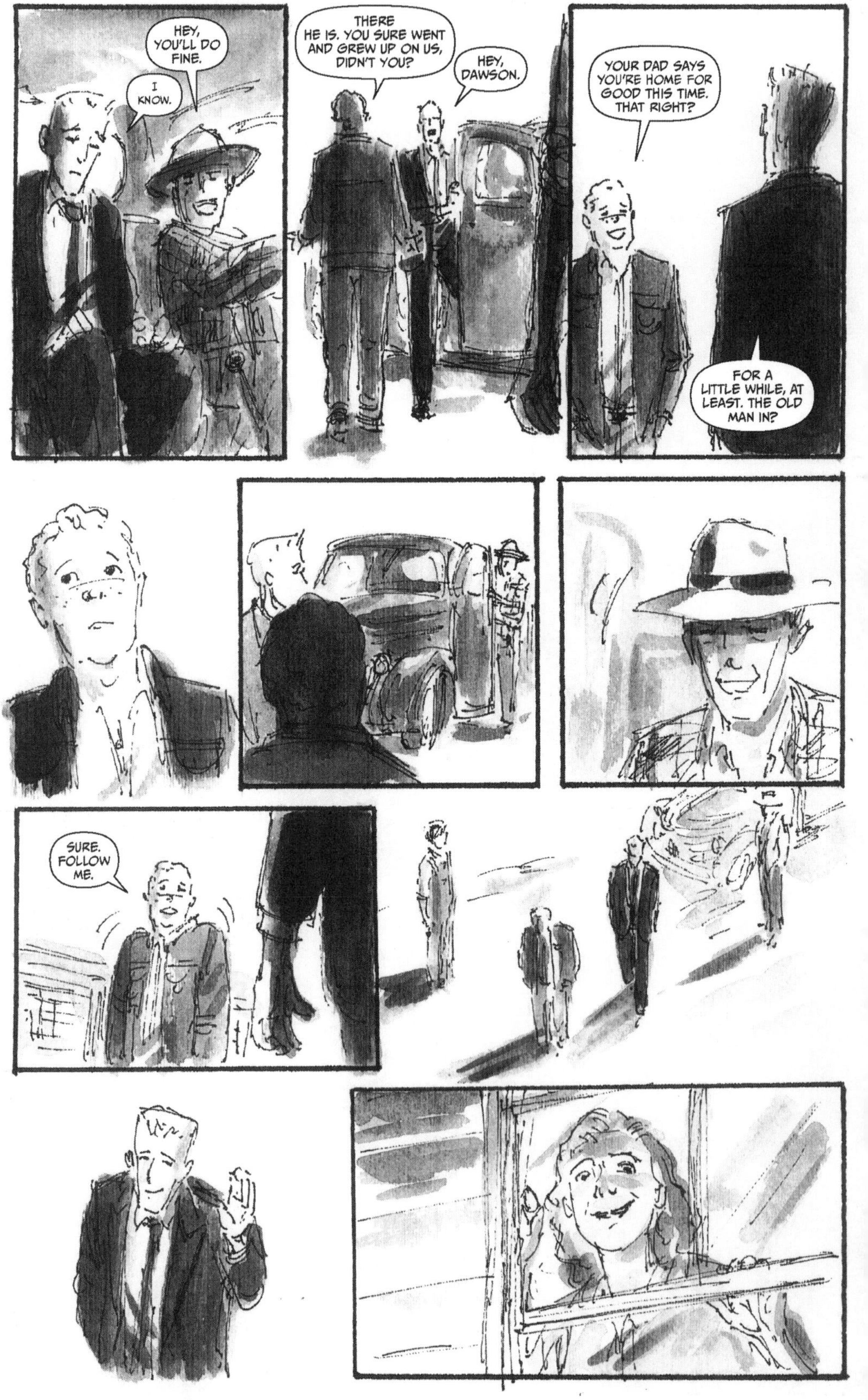
HEY, YOU'LL DO FINE.
I KNOW.
THERE HE IS. YOU SURE WENT AND GREW UP ON US, DIDN'T YOU?
HEY, DAWSON.
YOUR DAD SAYS YOU'RE HOME FOR GOOD THIS TIME. THAT RIGHT?
FOR A LITTLE WHILE, AT LEAST. THE OLD MAN IN?
SURE. FOLLOW ME.

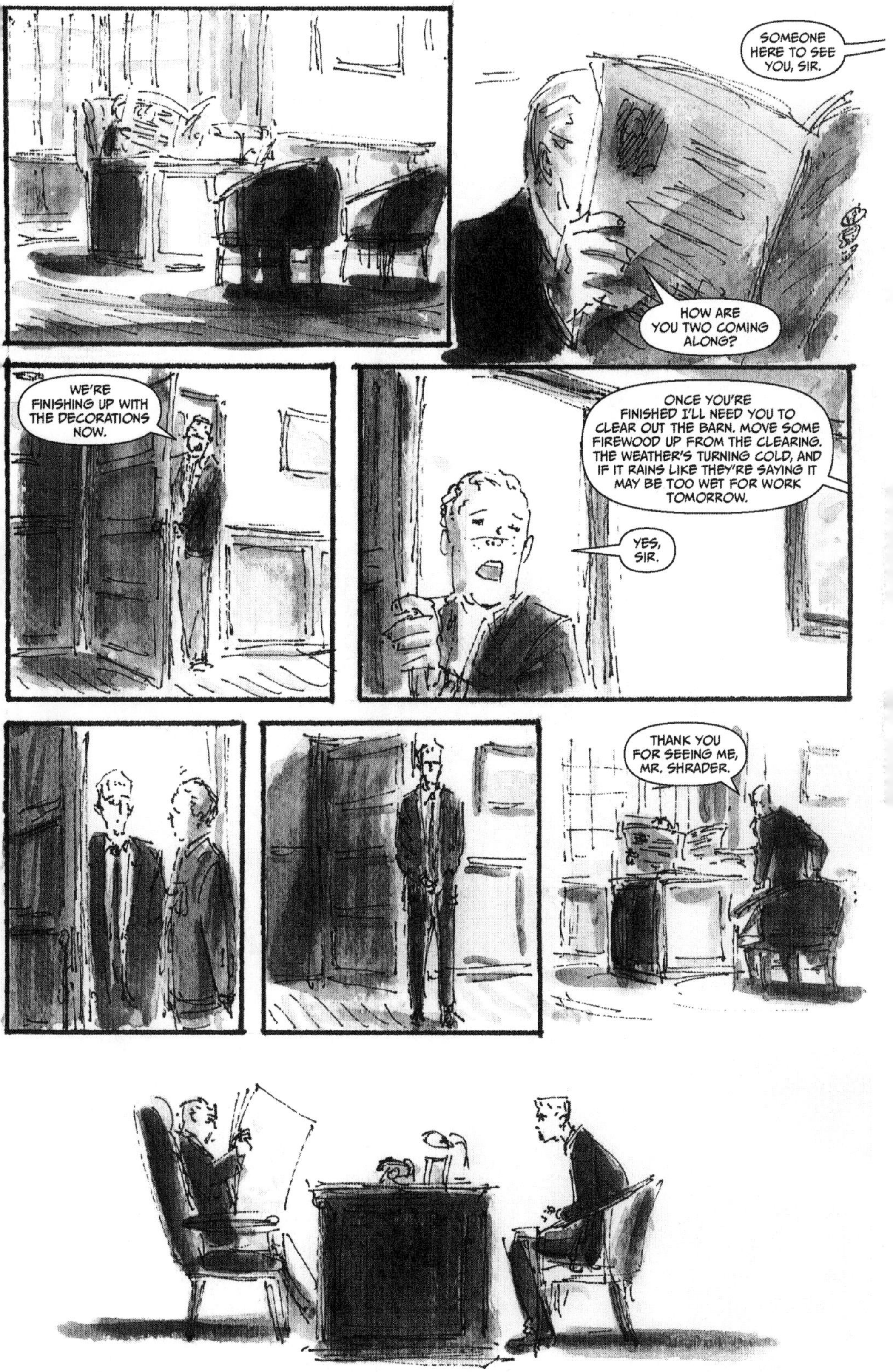
SOMEONE HERE TO SEE YOU, SIR.
HOW ARE YOU TWO COMING ALONG?
WE'RE FINISHING UP WITH THE DECORATIONS NOW.
ONCE YOU'RE FINISHED I'LL NEED YOU TO CLEAR OUT THE BARN. MOVE SOME FIREWOOD UP FROM THE CLEARING. THE WEATHER'S TURNING COLD, AND IF IT RAINS LIKE THEY'RE SAYING IT MAY BE TOO WET FOR WORK TOMORROW.
YES, SIR.
THANK YOU FOR SEEING ME, MR. SHRADER.

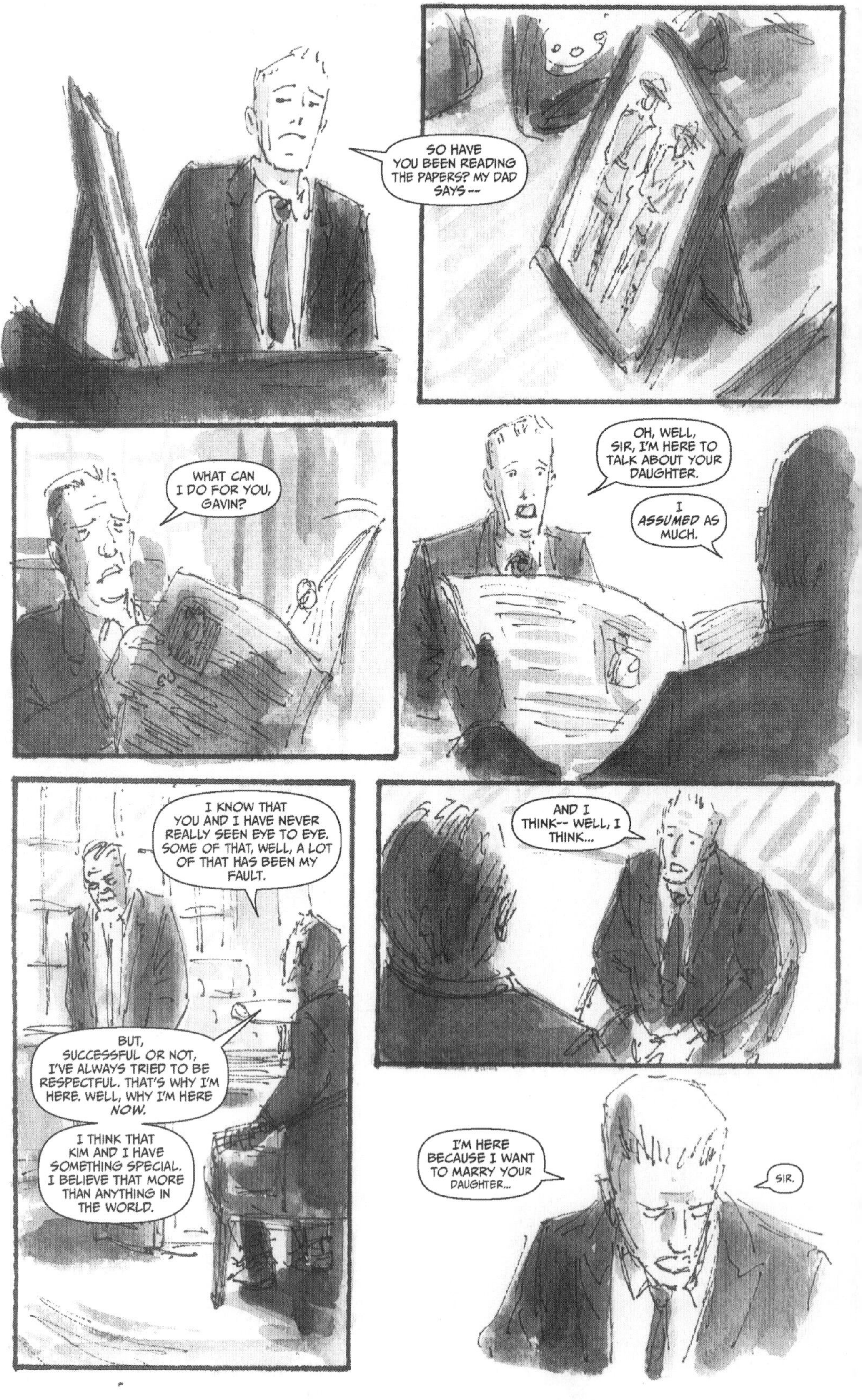
SO HAVE YOU BEEN READING THE PAPERS? MY DAD SAYS --
WHAT CAN I DO FOR YOU, GAVIN?
OH, WELL, SIR, I'M HERE TO TALK ABOUT YOUR DAUGHTER.
I *ASSUMED* AS MUCH.
I KNOW THAT YOU AND I HAVE NEVER REALLY SEEN EYE TO EYE. SOME OF THAT, WELL, A LOT OF THAT HAS BEEN MY FAULT.
BUT, SUCCESSFUL OR NOT, I'VE ALWAYS TRIED TO BE RESPECTFUL. THAT'S WHY I'M HERE. WELL, WHY I'M HERE *NOW*.
I THINK THAT KIM AND I HAVE SOMETHING SPECIAL. I BELIEVE THAT MORE THAN ANYTHING IN THE WORLD.
AND I THINK-- WELL, I THINK...
I'M HERE BECAUSE I WANT TO MARRY YOUR DAUGHTER...
SIR.

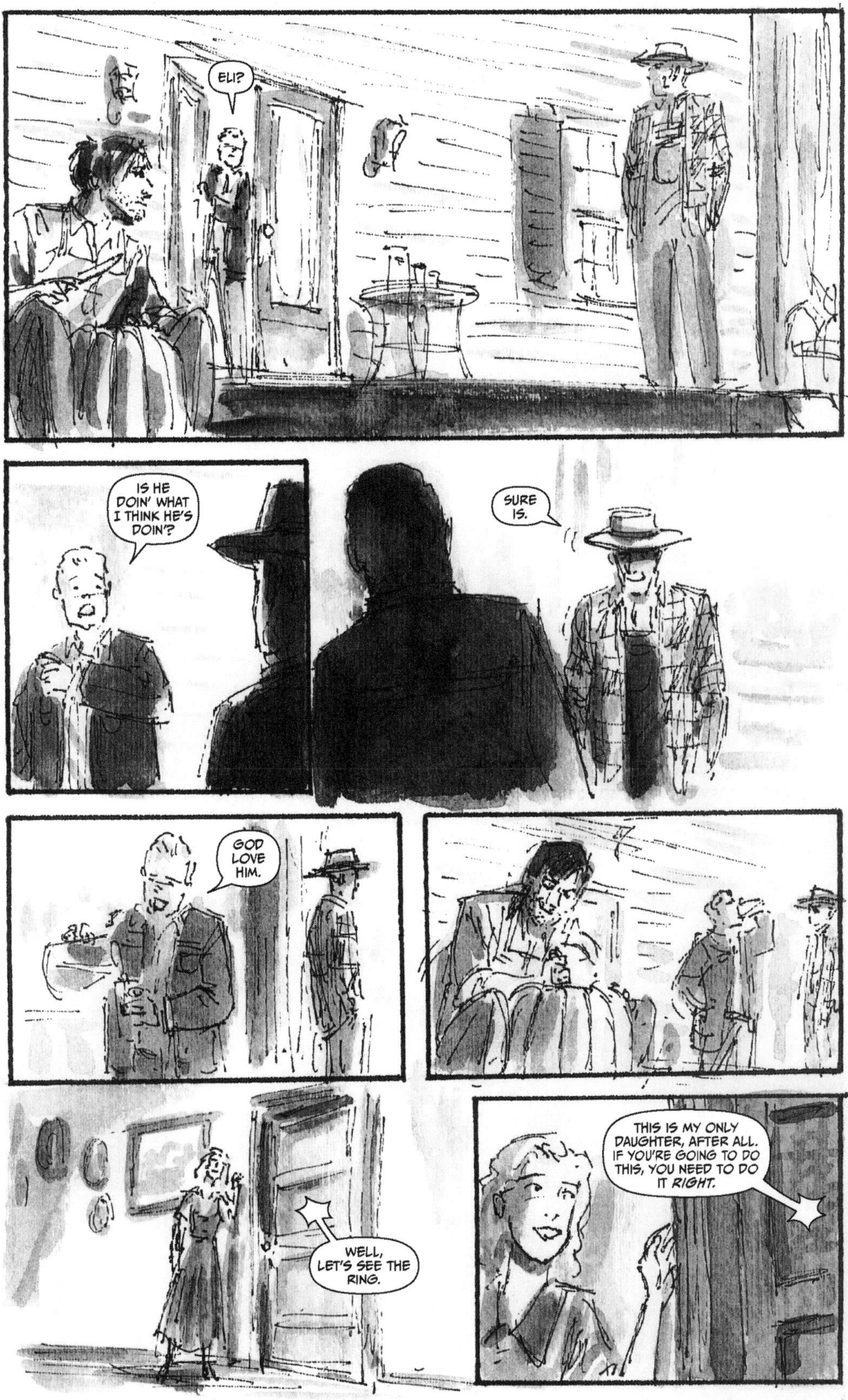
ELI?
IS HE DOIN' WHAT I THINK HE'S DOIN'?
SURE IS.
GOD LOVE HIM.
WELL, LET'S SEE THE RING.
THIS IS MY ONLY DAUGHTER, AFTER ALL. IF YOU'RE GOING TO DO THIS, YOU NEED TO DO IT RIGHT.

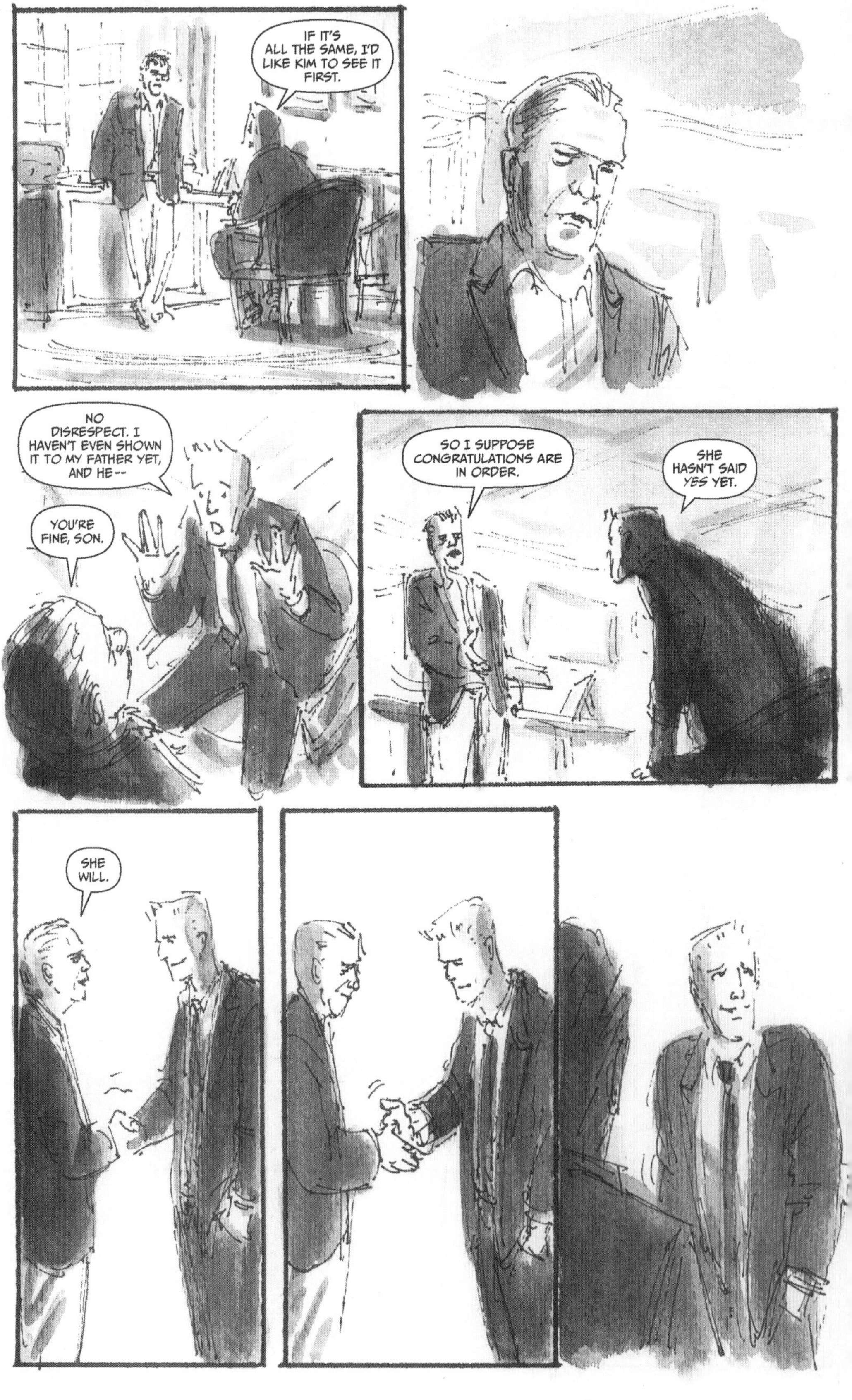
IF IT'S ALL THE SAME, I'D LIKE KIM TO SEE IT FIRST.
NO DISRESPECT. I HAVEN'T EVEN SHOWN IT TO MY FATHER YET, AND HE--
YOU'RE FINE, SON.
SO I SUPPOSE CONGRATULATIONS ARE IN ORDER.
SHE HASN'T SAID *YES* YET.
SHE WILL.

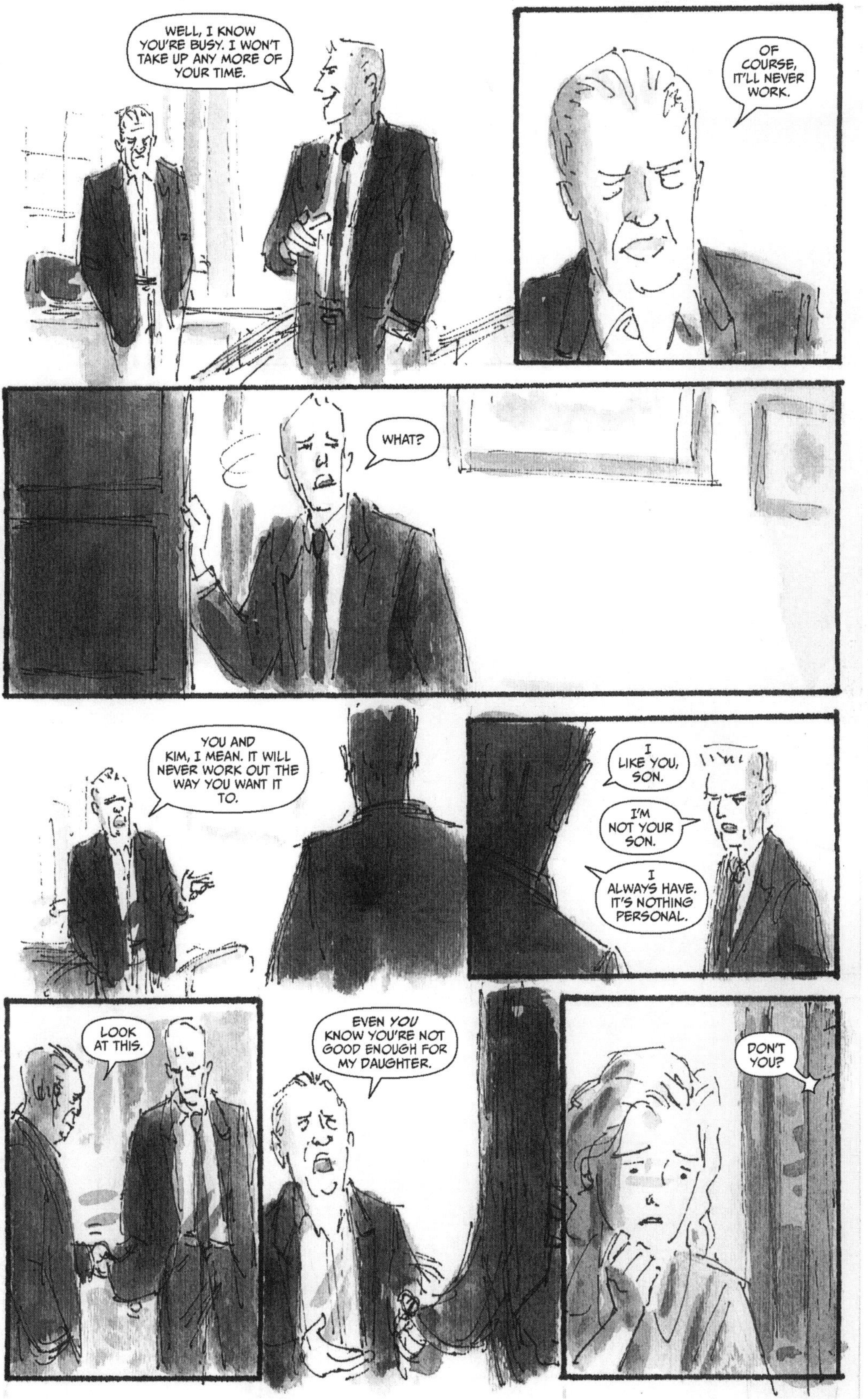
WELL, I KNOW YOU'RE BUSY. I WON'T TAKE UP ANY MORE OF YOUR TIME.
OF COURSE, IT'LL NEVER WORK.
WHAT?
YOU AND KIM, I MEAN. IT WILL NEVER WORK OUT THE WAY YOU WANT IT TO.
I LIKE YOU, SON.
I'M NOT YOUR SON.
I ALWAYS HAVE. IT'S NOTHING PERSONAL.
LOOK AT THIS.
EVEN *YOU* KNOW YOU'RE NOT GOOD ENOUGH FOR MY DAUGHTER.
DON'T YOU?

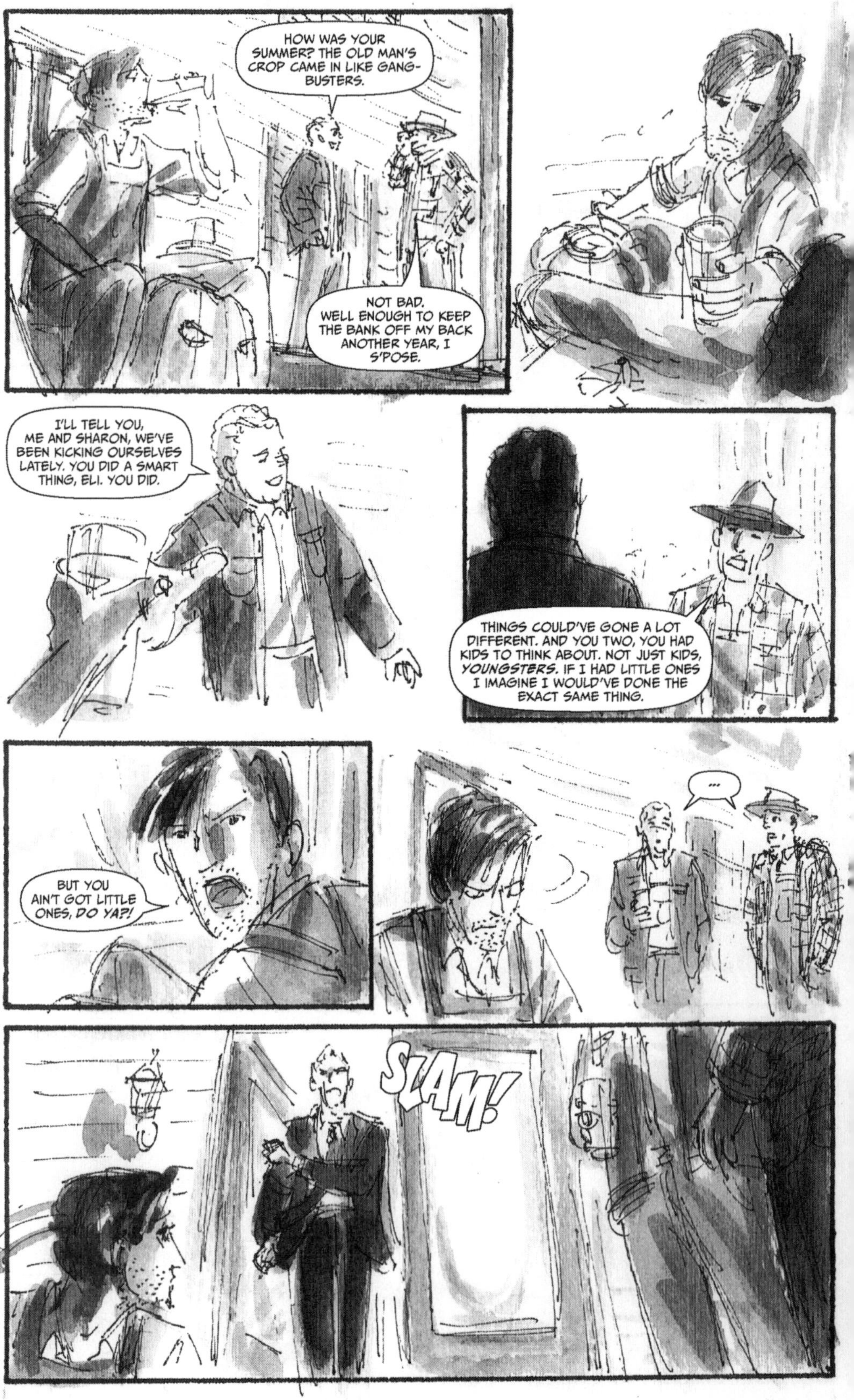
HOW WAS YOUR SUMMER? THE OLD MAN'S CROP CAME IN LIKE GANG-BUSTERS.
NOT BAD. WELL ENOUGH TO KEEP THE BANK OFF MY BACK ANOTHER YEAR, I S'POSE.
I'LL TELL YOU, ME AND SHARON, WE'VE BEEN KICKING OURSELVES LATELY. YOU DID A SMART THING, ELI. YOU DID.
THINGS COULD'VE GONE A LOT DIFFERENT. AND YOU TWO, YOU HAD KIDS TO THINK ABOUT. NOT JUST KIDS, *YOUNGSTERS.* IF I HAD LITTLE ONES I IMAGINE I WOULD'VE DONE THE EXACT SAME THING.
BUT YOU AIN'T GOT LITTLE ONES, *DO YA?!*
...
SLAM!

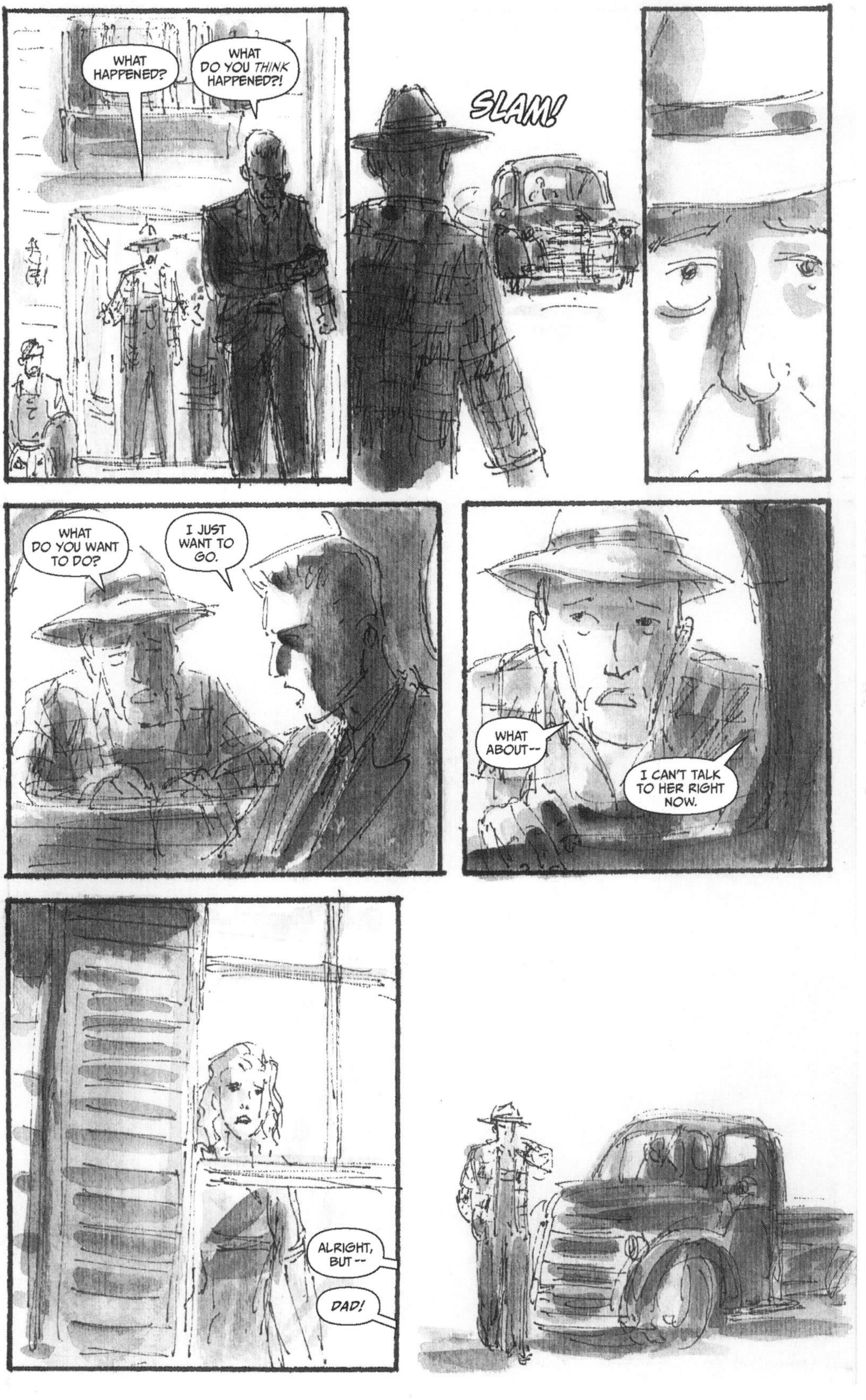

WHAT HAPPENED?
WHAT DO YOU *THINK* HAPPENED?!
SLAM!
WHAT DO YOU WANT TO DO?
I JUST WANT TO GO.
WHAT ABOUT--
I CAN'T TALK TO HER RIGHT NOW.
ALRIGHT, BUT --
DAD!

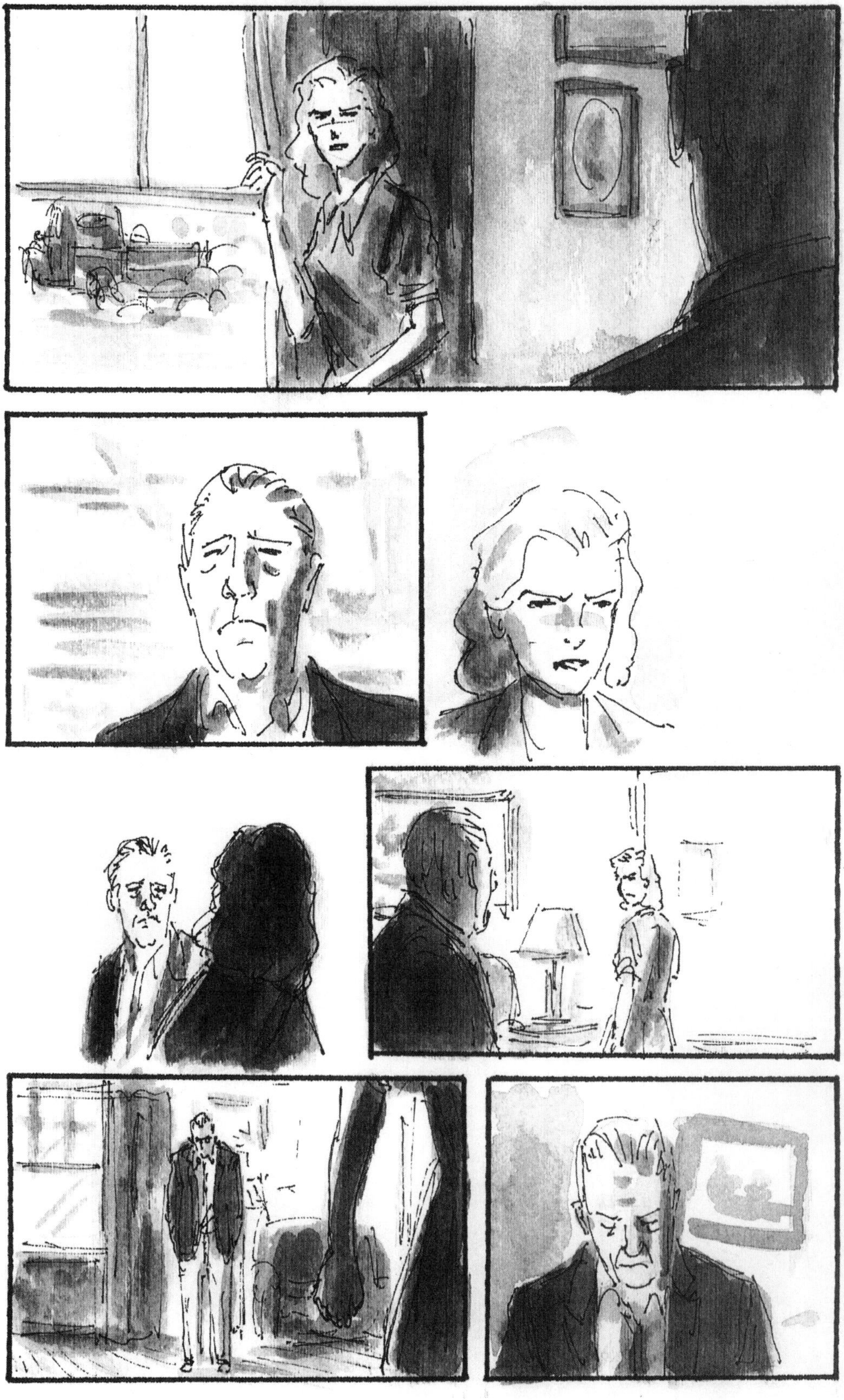

NEW YORK.

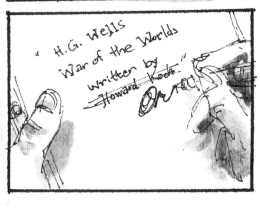

"H.G. Wells
War of the Worlds
Written by
~~Howard Koch~~"

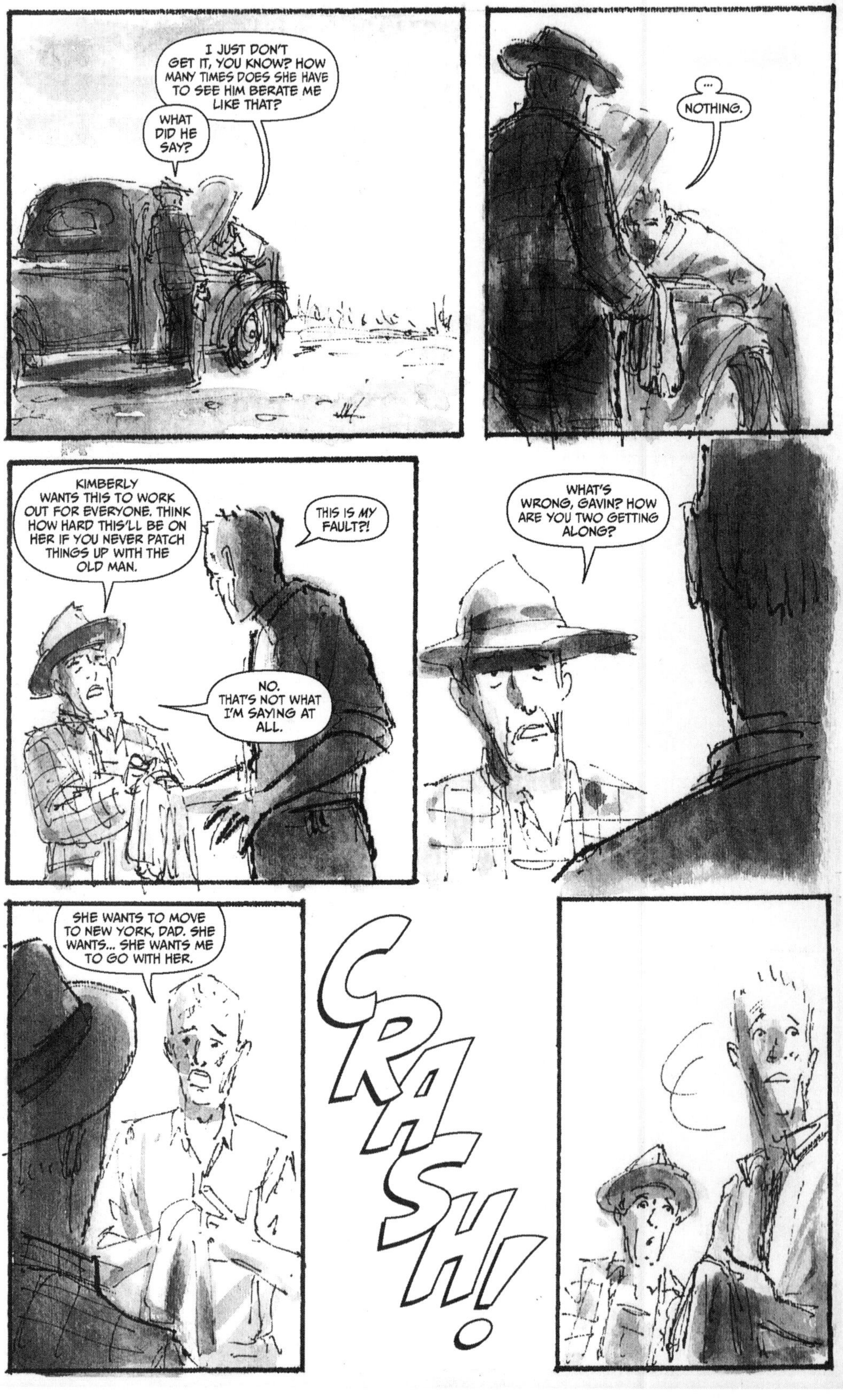
I JUST DON'T GET IT, YOU KNOW? HOW MANY TIMES DOES SHE HAVE TO SEE HIM BERATE ME LIKE THAT?
WHAT DID HE SAY?
...
NOTHING.
KIMBERLY WANTS THIS TO WORK OUT FOR EVERYONE. THINK HOW HARD THIS'LL BE ON HER IF YOU NEVER PATCH THINGS UP WITH THE OLD MAN.
THIS IS *MY* FAULT?!
NO. THAT'S NOT WHAT I'M SAYING AT ALL.
WHAT'S WRONG, GAVIN? HOW ARE YOU TWO GETTING ALONG?
SHE WANTS TO MOVE TO NEW YORK, DAD. SHE WANTS... SHE WANTS ME TO GO WITH HER.
CRASH!

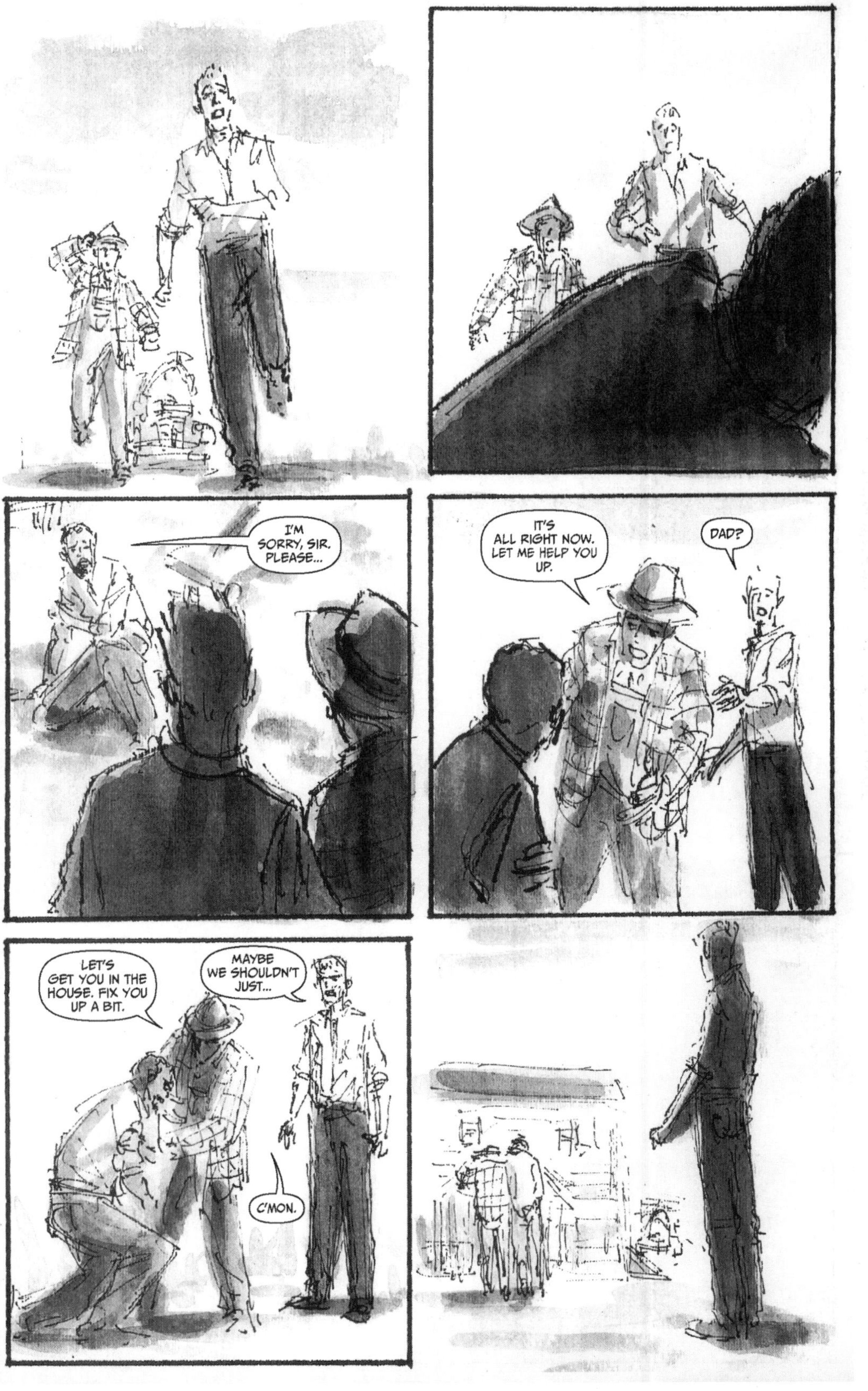
I'M SORRY, SIR. PLEASE...
IT'S ALL RIGHT NOW. LET ME HELP YOU UP.
DAD?
LET'S GET YOU IN THE HOUSE. FIX YOU UP A BIT.
MAYBE WE SHOULDN'T JUST...
C'MON.

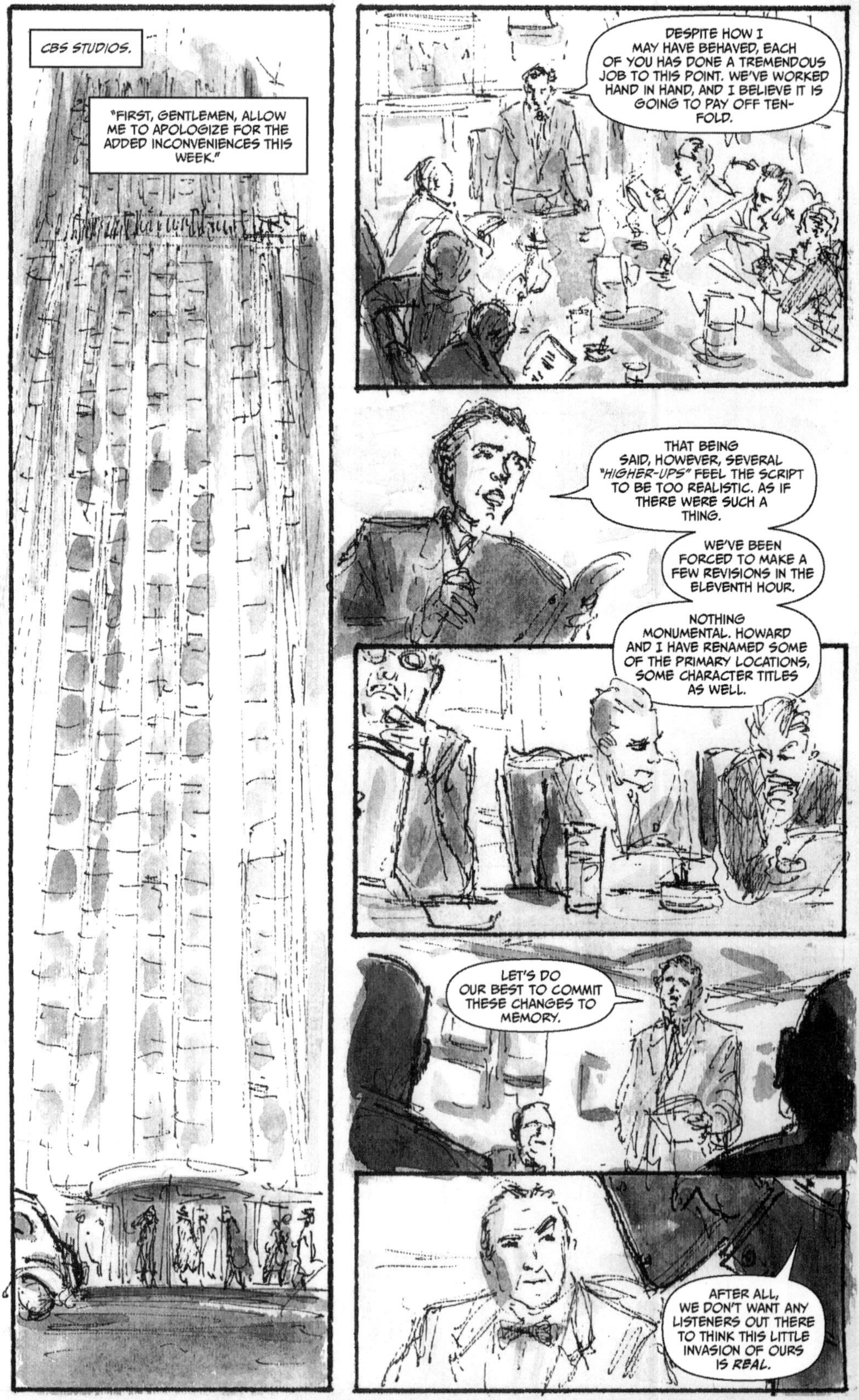
CBS STUDIOS.
"FIRST, GENTLEMEN, ALLOW ME TO APOLOGIZE FOR THE ADDED INCONVENIENCES THIS WEEK."
DESPITE HOW I MAY HAVE BEHAVED, EACH OF YOU HAS DONE A TREMENDOUS JOB TO THIS POINT. WE'VE WORKED HAND IN HAND, AND I BELIEVE IT IS GOING TO PAY OFF TEN-FOLD.
THAT BEING SAID, HOWEVER, SEVERAL *"HIGHER-UPS"* FEEL THE SCRIPT TO BE TOO REALISTIC. AS IF THERE WERE SUCH A THING.
WE'VE BEEN FORCED TO MAKE A FEW REVISIONS IN THE ELEVENTH HOUR.
NOTHING MONUMENTAL. HOWARD AND I HAVE RENAMED SOME OF THE PRIMARY LOCATIONS, SOME CHARACTER TITLES AS WELL.
LET'S DO OUR BEST TO COMMIT THESE CHANGES TO MEMORY.
AFTER ALL, WE DON'T WANT ANY LISTENERS OUT THERE TO THINK THIS LITTLE INVASION OF OURS IS *REAL*.

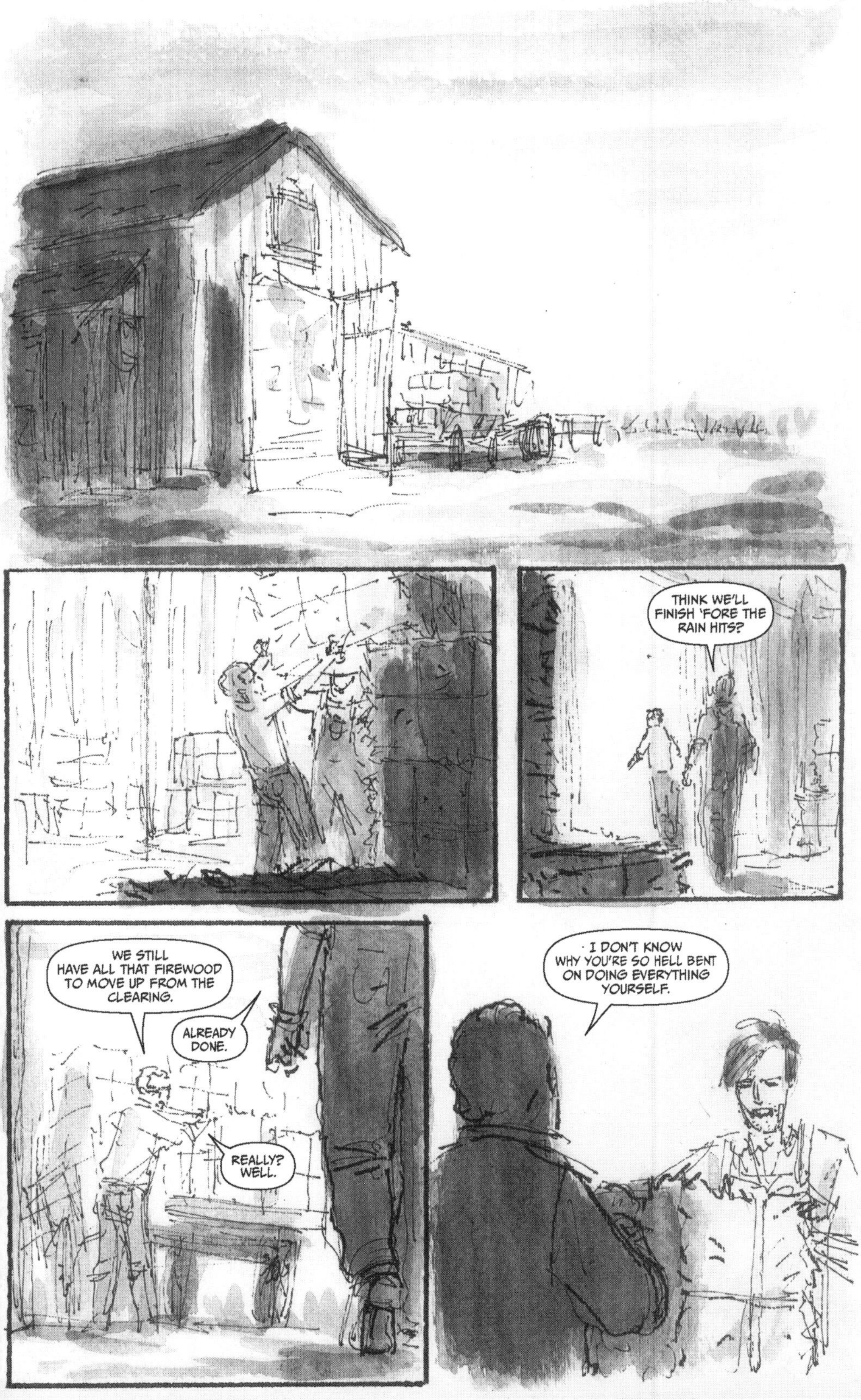
THINK WE'LL FINISH 'FORE THE RAIN HITS?
WE STILL HAVE ALL THAT FIREWOOD TO MOVE UP FROM THE CLEARING.
ALREADY DONE.
REALLY? WELL.
I DON'T KNOW WHY YOU'RE SO HELL BENT ON DOING EVERYTHING YOURSELF.

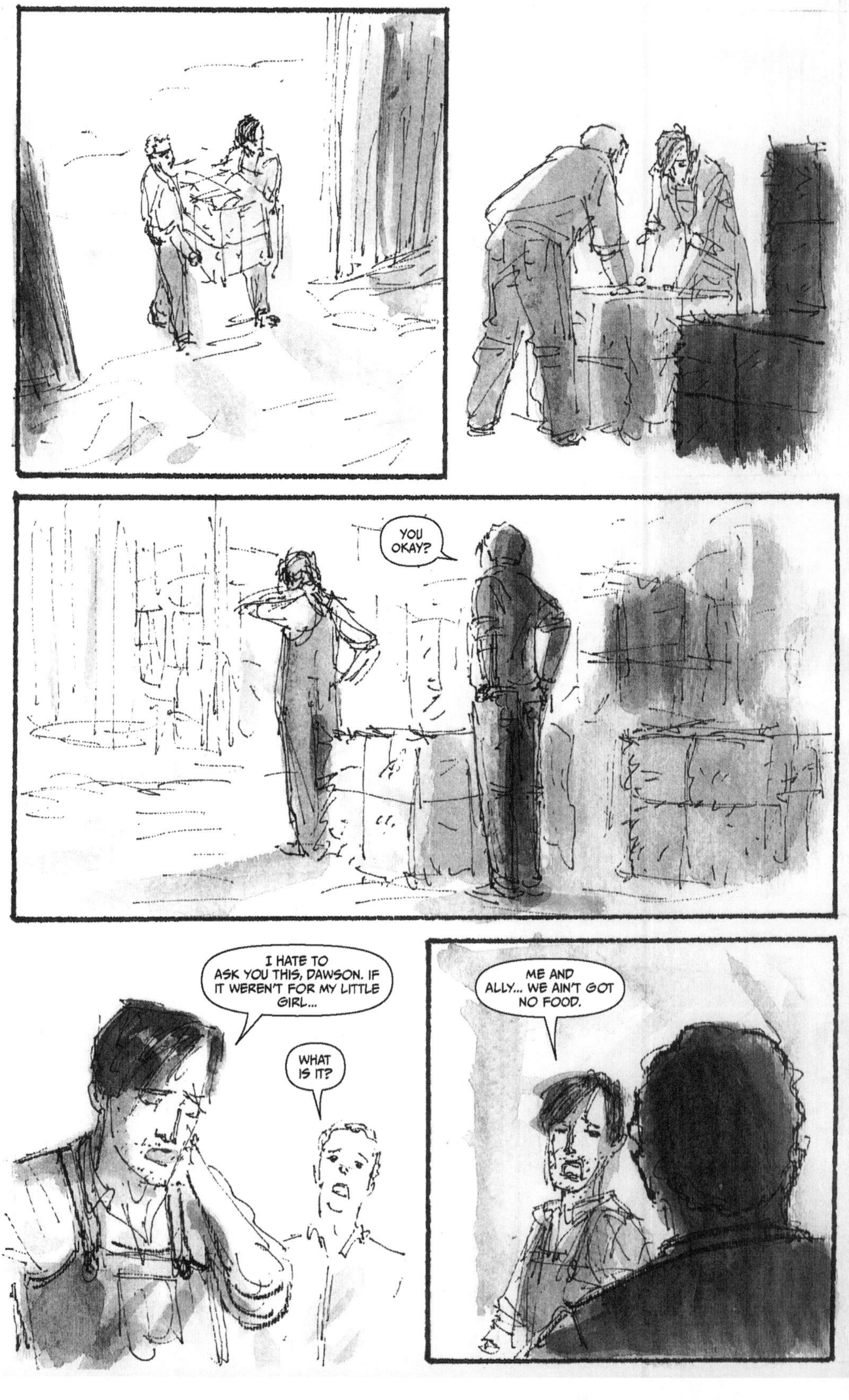
YOU OKAY?
I HATE TO ASK YOU THIS, DAWSON. IF IT WEREN'T FOR MY LITTLE GIRL...
WHAT IS IT?
ME AND ALLY... WE AIN'T GOT NO FOOD.

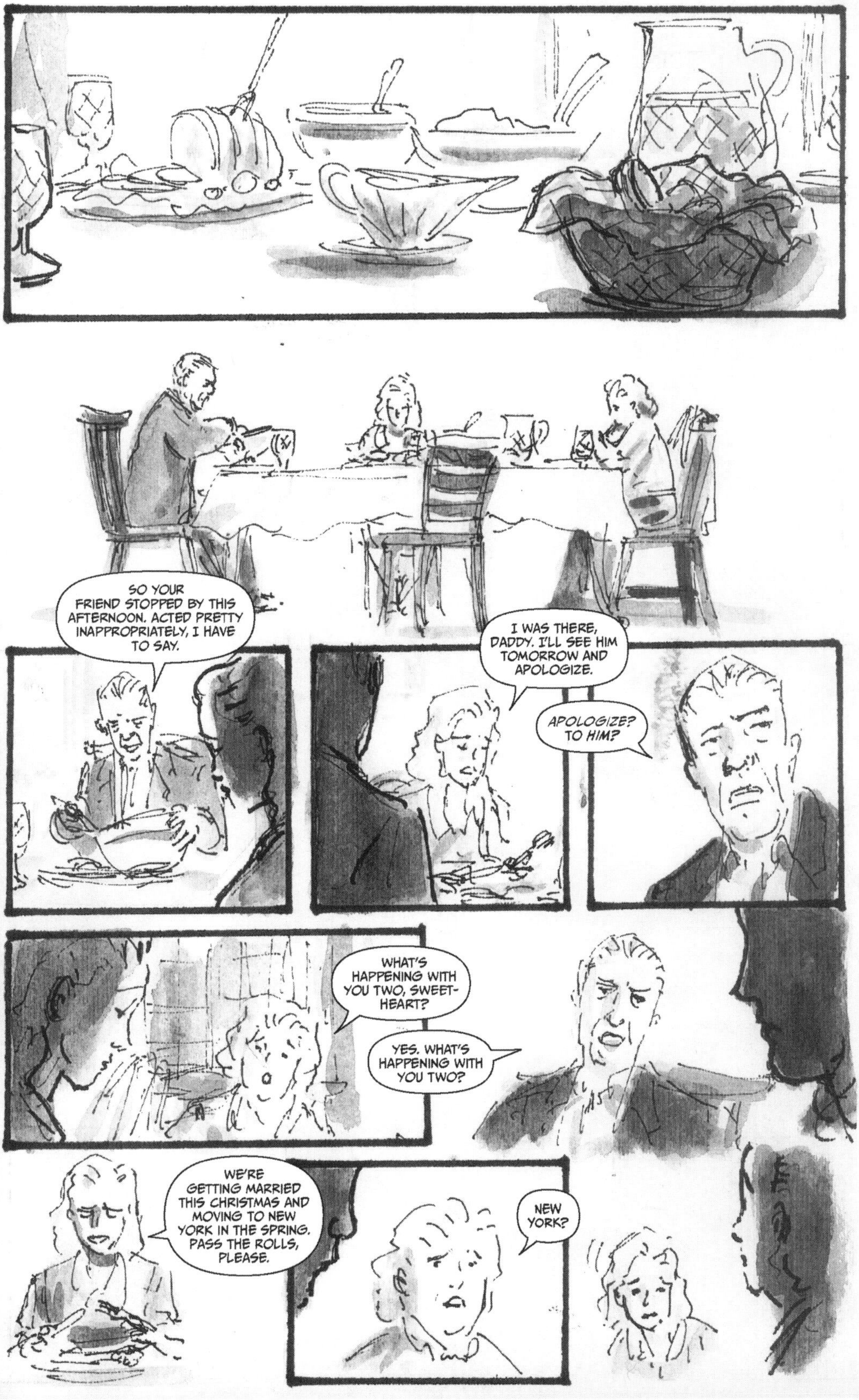
SO YOUR FRIEND STOPPED BY THIS AFTERNOON. ACTED PRETTY INAPPROPRIATELY, I HAVE TO SAY.
I WAS THERE, DADDY. I'LL SEE HIM TOMORROW AND APOLOGIZE.
APOLOGIZE? TO HIM?
WHAT'S HAPPENING WITH YOU TWO, SWEET-HEART?
YES. WHAT'S HAPPENING WITH YOU TWO?
WE'RE GETTING MARRIED THIS CHRISTMAS AND MOVING TO NEW YORK IN THE SPRING. PASS THE ROLLS, PLEASE.
NEW YORK?

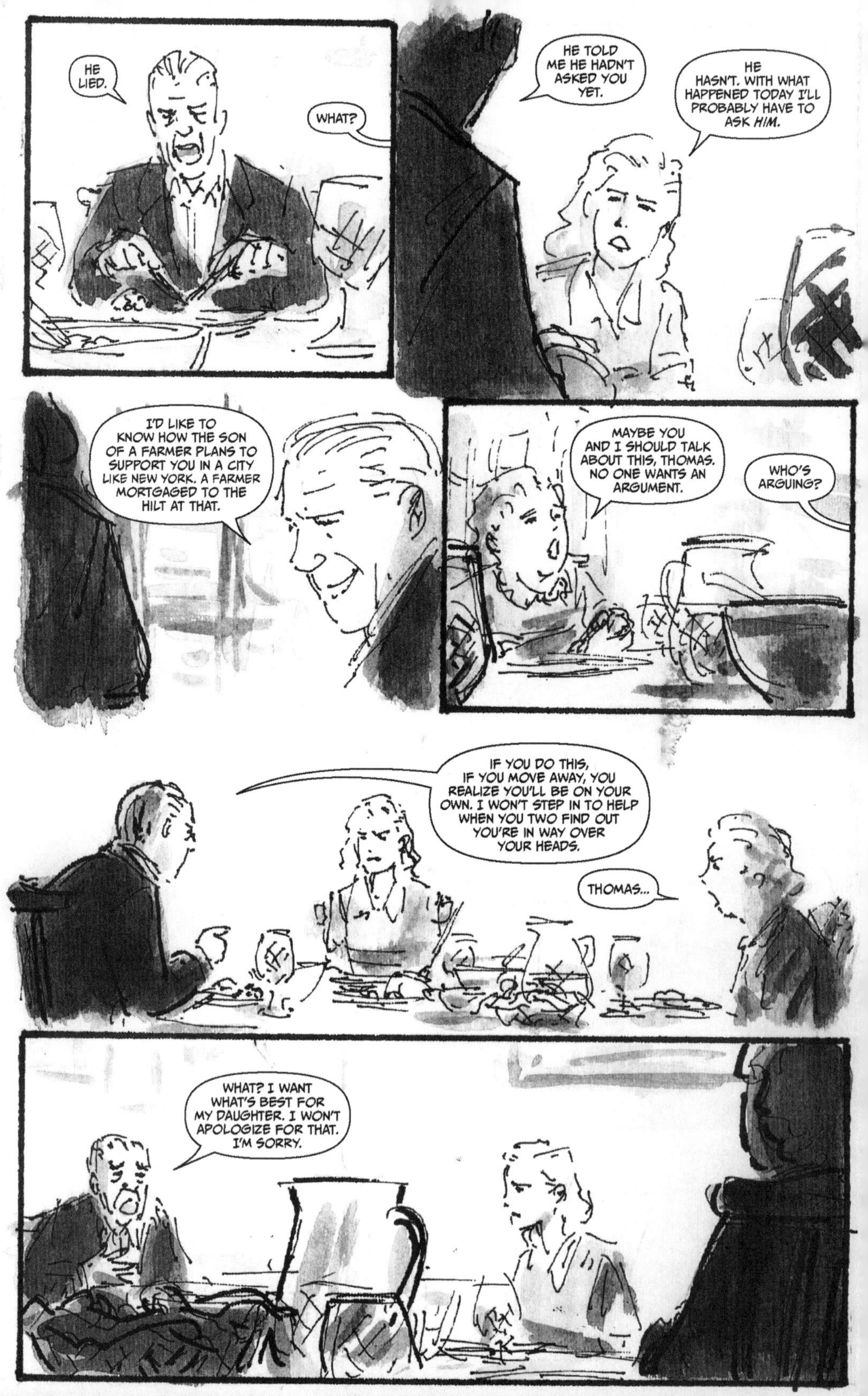
HE LIED.
WHAT?
HE TOLD ME HE HADN'T ASKED YOU YET.
HE HASN'T. WITH WHAT HAPPENED TODAY I'LL PROBABLY HAVE TO ASK *HIM*.
I'D LIKE TO KNOW HOW THE SON OF A FARMER PLANS TO SUPPORT YOU IN A CITY LIKE NEW YORK. A FARMER MORTGAGED TO THE HILT AT THAT.
MAYBE YOU AND I SHOULD TALK ABOUT THIS, THOMAS. NO ONE WANTS AN ARGUMENT.
WHO'S ARGUING?
IF YOU DO THIS, IF YOU MOVE AWAY, YOU REALIZE YOU'LL BE ON YOUR OWN. I WON'T STEP IN TO HELP WHEN YOU TWO FIND OUT YOU'RE IN WAY OVER YOUR HEADS.
THOMAS...
WHAT? I WANT WHAT'S BEST FOR MY DAUGHTER. I WON'T APOLOGIZE FOR THAT. I'M SORRY.

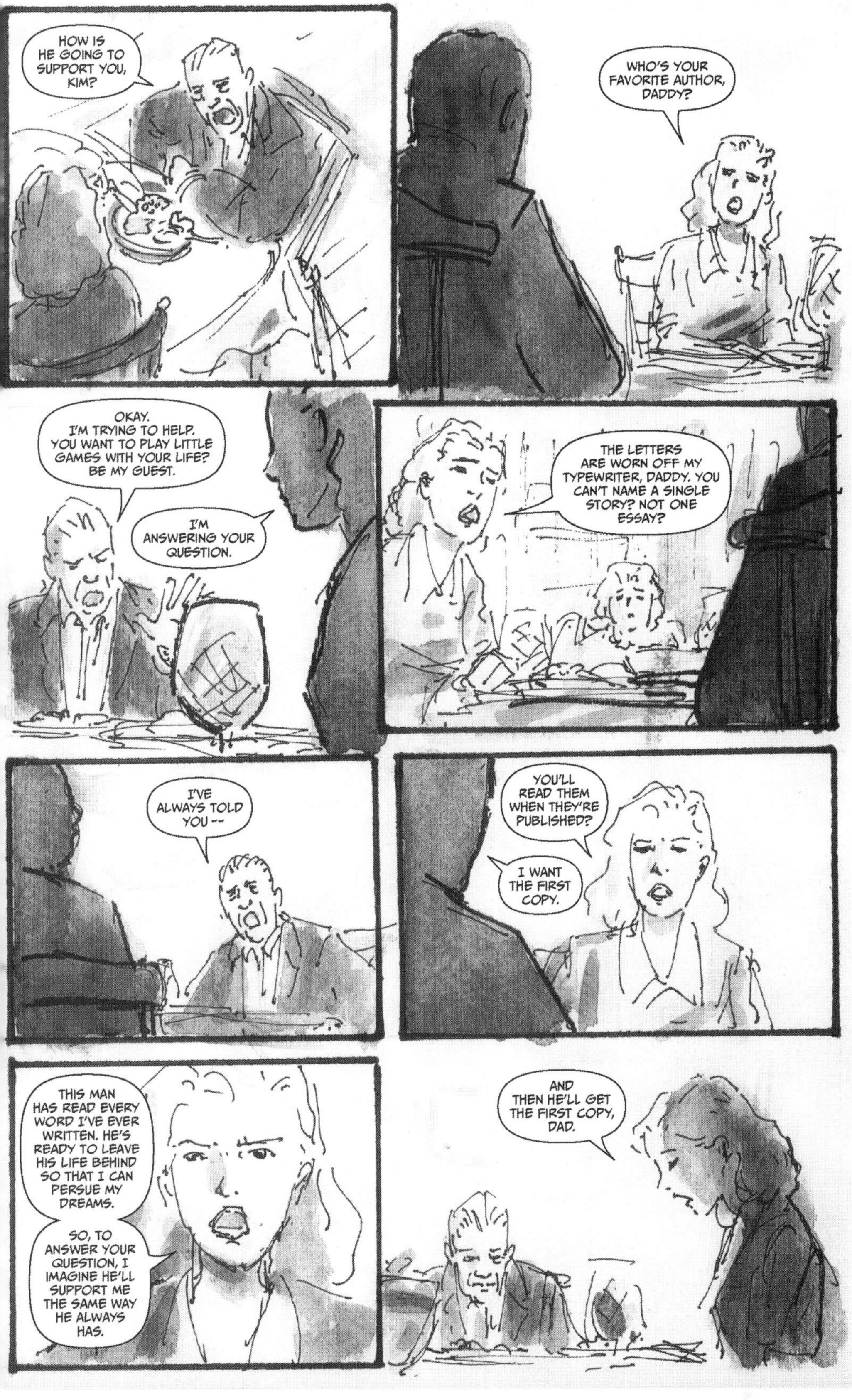
HOW IS HE GOING TO SUPPORT YOU, KIM?
WHO'S YOUR FAVORITE AUTHOR, DADDY?
OKAY. I'M TRYING TO HELP. YOU WANT TO PLAY LITTLE GAMES WITH YOUR LIFE? BE MY GUEST.
I'M ANSWERING YOUR QUESTION.
THE LETTERS ARE WORN OFF MY TYPEWRITER, DADDY. YOU CAN'T NAME A SINGLE STORY? NOT ONE ESSAY?
I'VE ALWAYS TOLD YOU --
YOU'LL READ THEM WHEN THEY'RE PUBLISHED?
I WANT THE FIRST COPY.
THIS MAN HAS READ EVERY WORD I'VE EVER WRITTEN. HE'S READY TO LEAVE HIS LIFE BEHIND SO THAT I CAN PERSUE MY DREAMS.
SO, TO ANSWER YOUR QUESTION, I IMAGINE HE'LL SUPPORT ME THE SAME WAY HE ALWAYS HAS.
AND THEN HE'LL GET THE FIRST COPY, DAD.

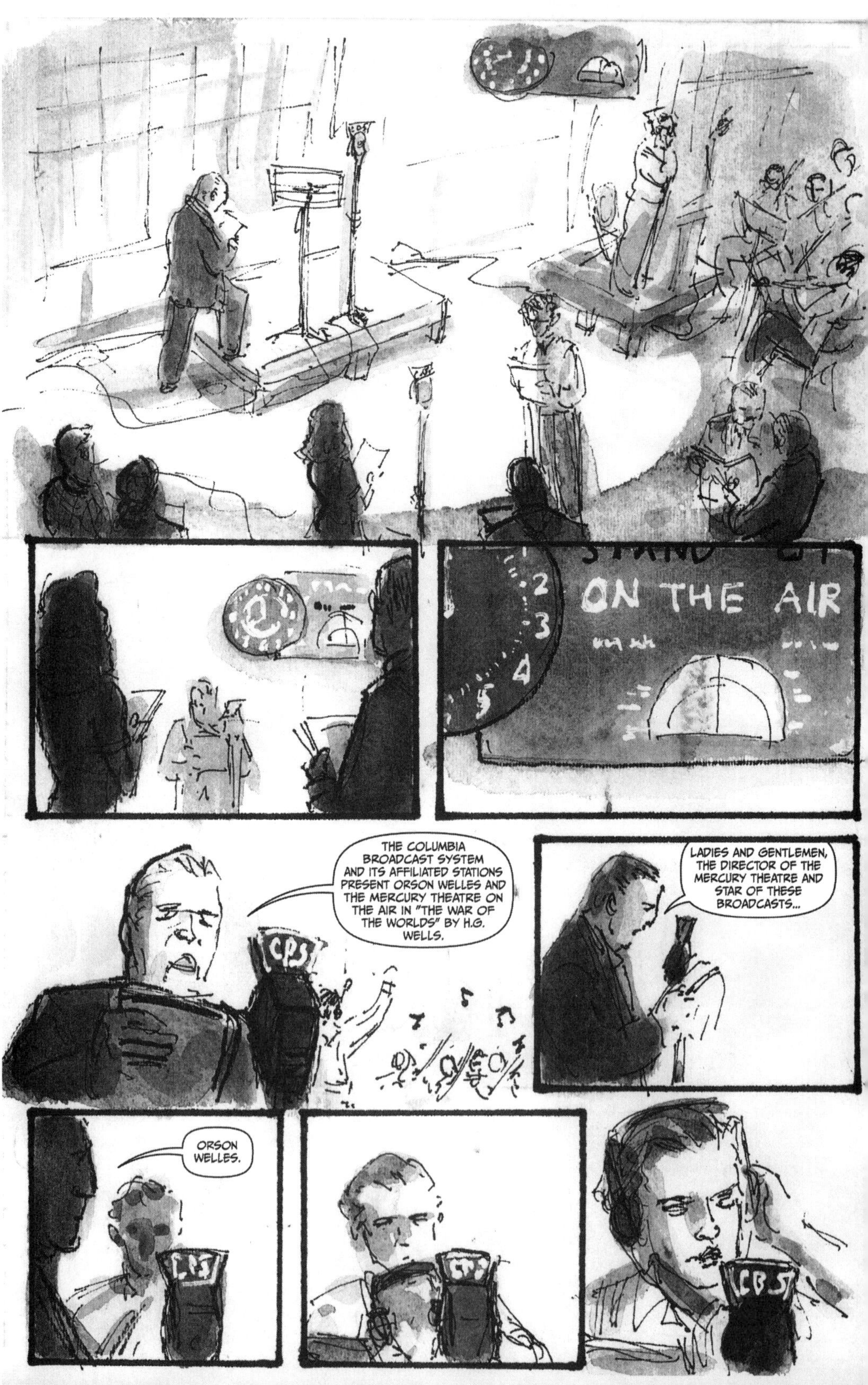
ON THE AIR
THE COLUMBIA BROADCAST SYSTEM AND ITS AFFILIATED STATIONS PRESENT ORSON WELLES AND THE MERCURY THEATRE ON THE AIR IN "THE WAR OF THE WORLDS" BY H.G. WELLS.
LADIES AND GENTLEMEN, THE DIRECTOR OF THE MERCURY THEATRE AND STAR OF THESE BROADCASTS...
ORSON WELLES.

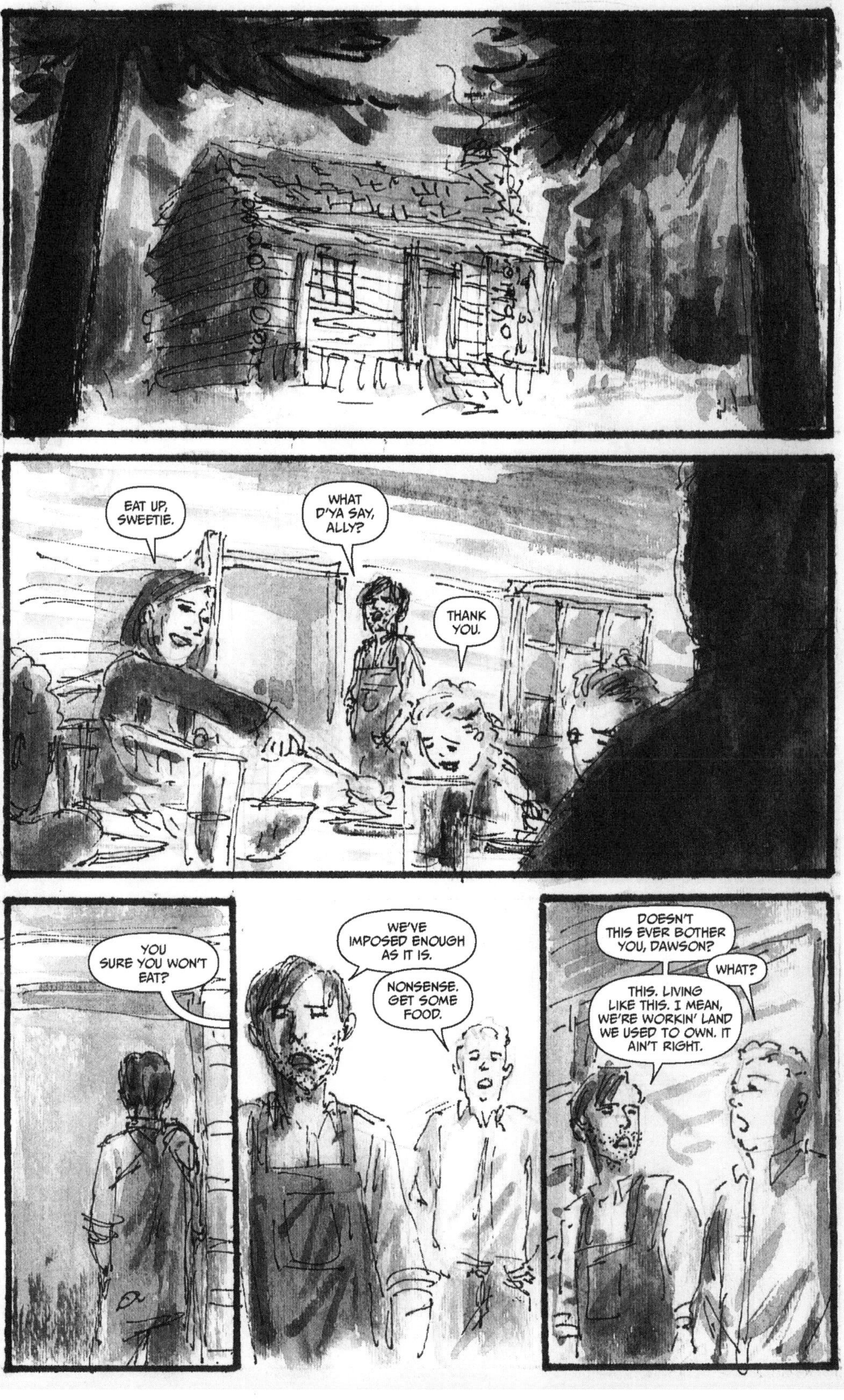
EAT UP, SWEETIE.
WHAT D'YA SAY, ALLY?
THANK YOU.
YOU SURE YOU WON'T EAT?
WE'VE IMPOSED ENOUGH AS IT IS.
NONSENSE. GET SOME FOOD.
DOESN'T THIS EVER BOTHER YOU, DAWSON?
WHAT?
THIS. LIVING LIKE THIS. I MEAN, WE'RE WORKIN' LAND WE USED TO OWN. IT AIN'T RIGHT.

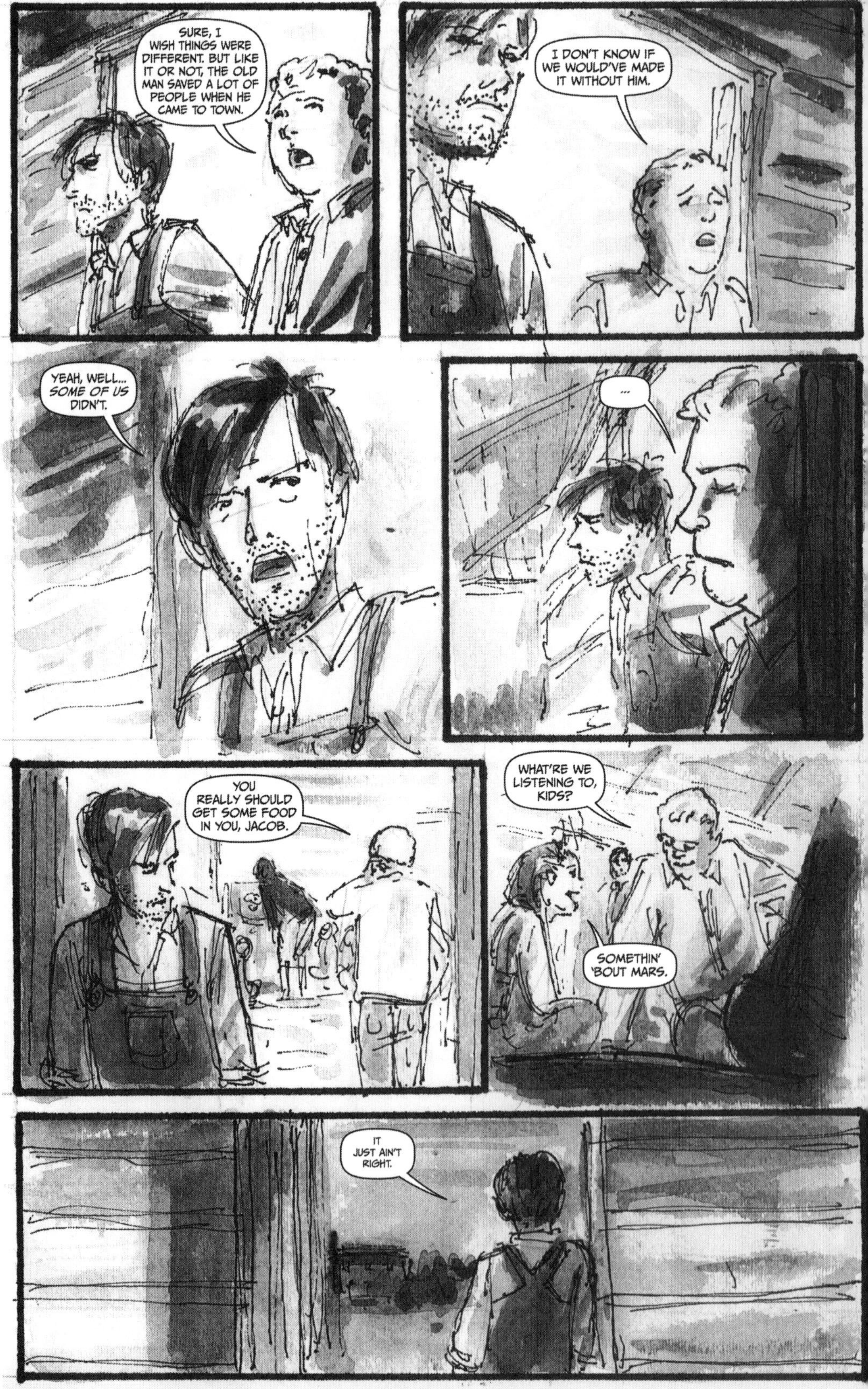
SURE, I WISH THINGS WERE DIFFERENT. BUT LIKE IT OR NOT, THE OLD MAN SAVED A LOT OF PEOPLE WHEN HE CAME TO TOWN.
I DON'T KNOW IF WE WOULD'VE MADE IT WITHOUT HIM.
YEAH, WELL... SOME OF US DIDN'T.
...
YOU REALLY SHOULD GET SOME FOOD IN YOU, JACOB.
WHAT'RE WE LISTENING TO, KIDS?
SOMETHIN' 'BOUT MARS.
IT JUST AIN'T RIGHT.

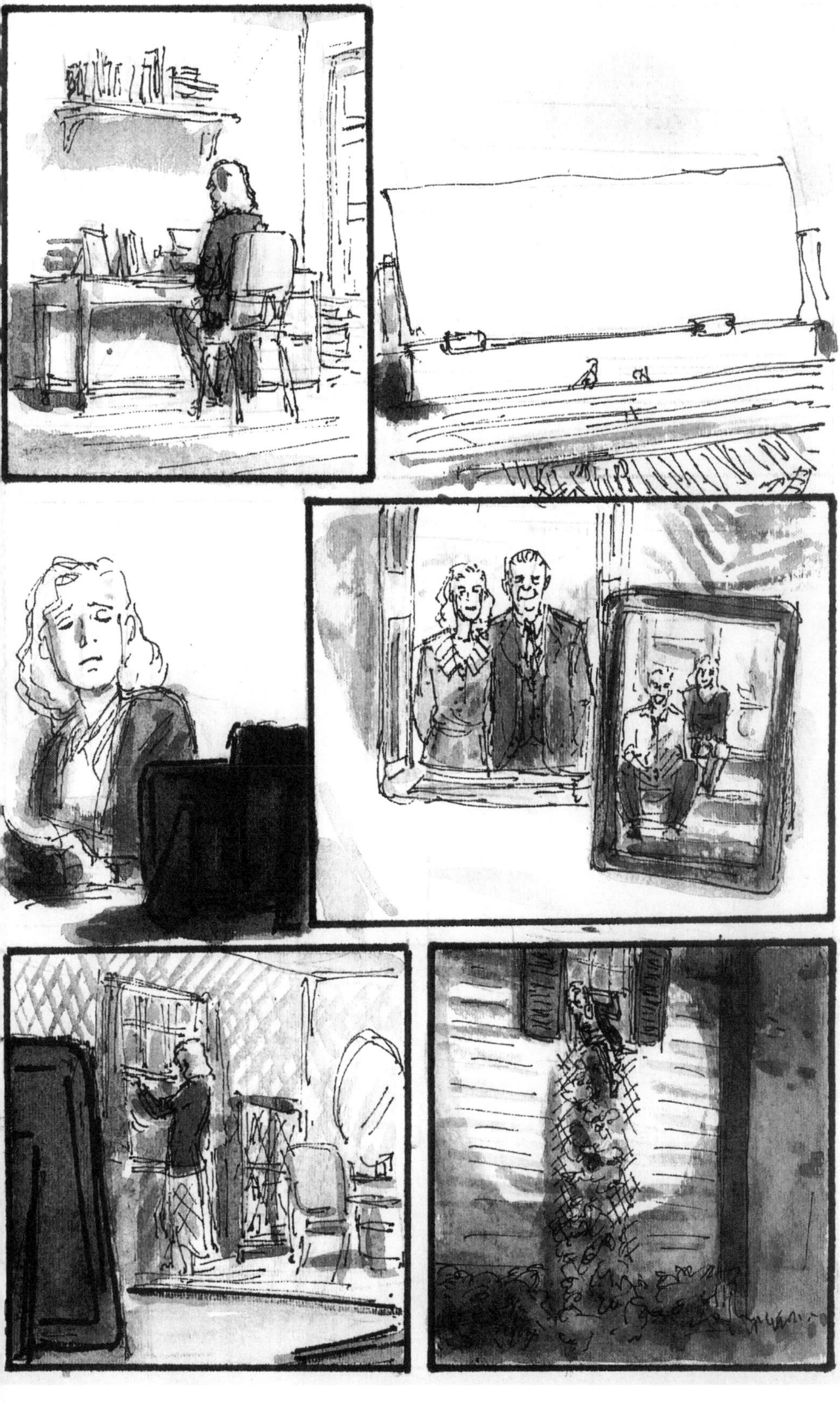

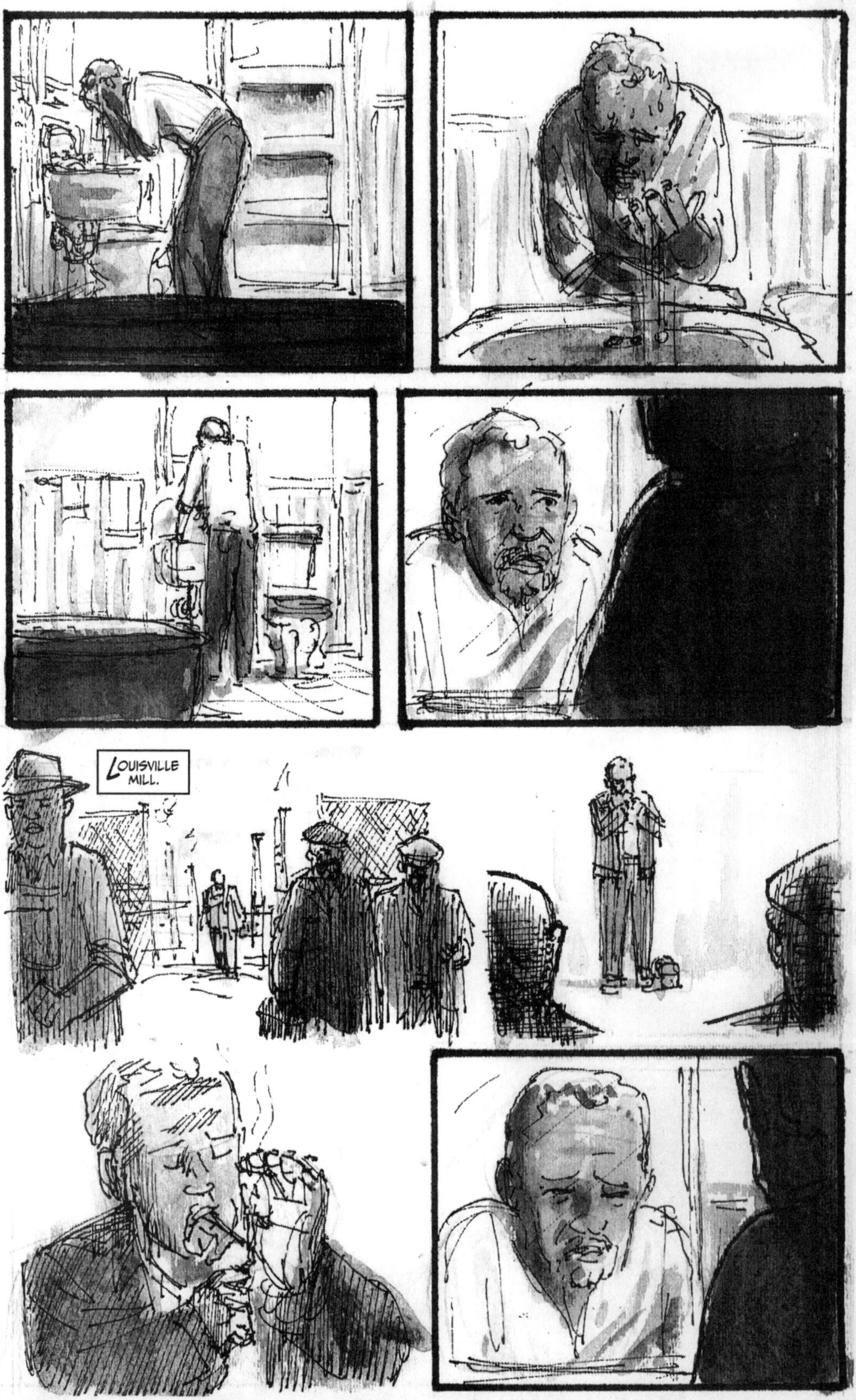
LOUISVILLE MILL.

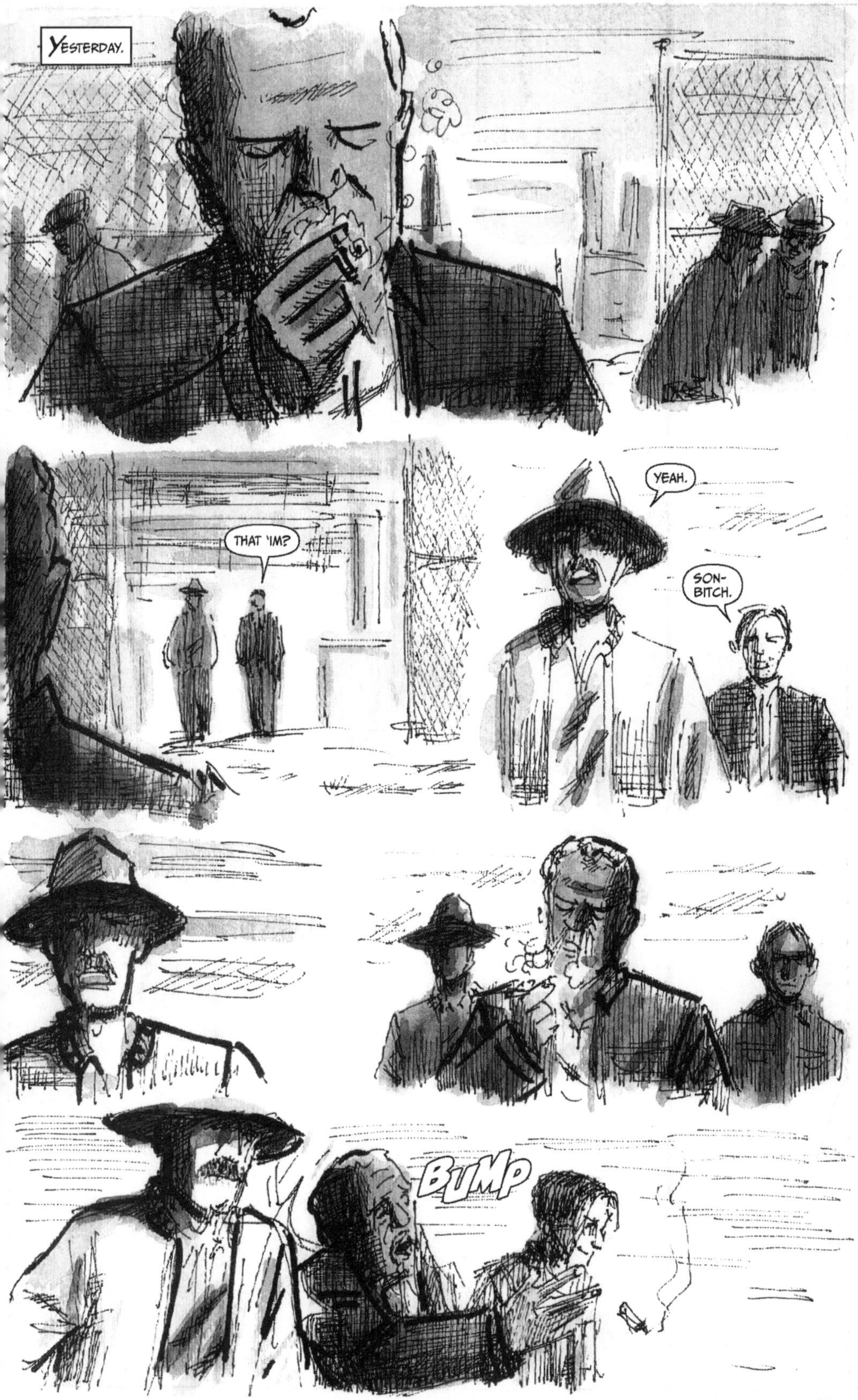
YESTERDAY.
THAT 'IM?
YEAH.
SON-BITCH.
BUMP

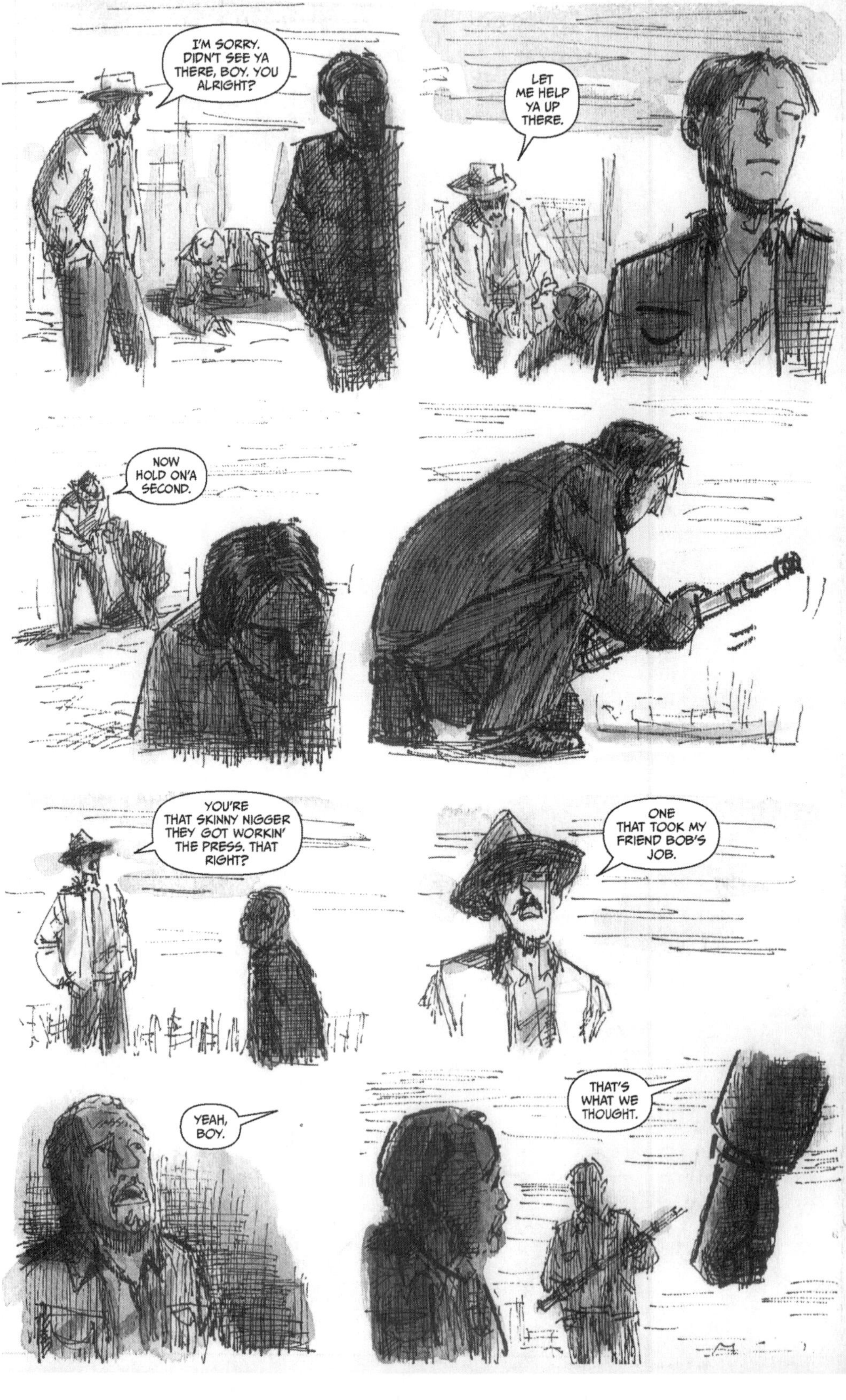
I'M SORRY. DIDN'T SEE YA THERE, BOY. YOU ALRIGHT?
LET ME HELP YA UP THERE.
NOW HOLD ON'A SECOND.
YOU'RE THAT SKINNY NIGGER THEY GOT WORKIN' THE PRESS. THAT RIGHT?
ONE THAT TOOK MY FRIEND BOB'S JOB.
YEAH, BOY.
THAT'S WHAT WE THOUGHT.

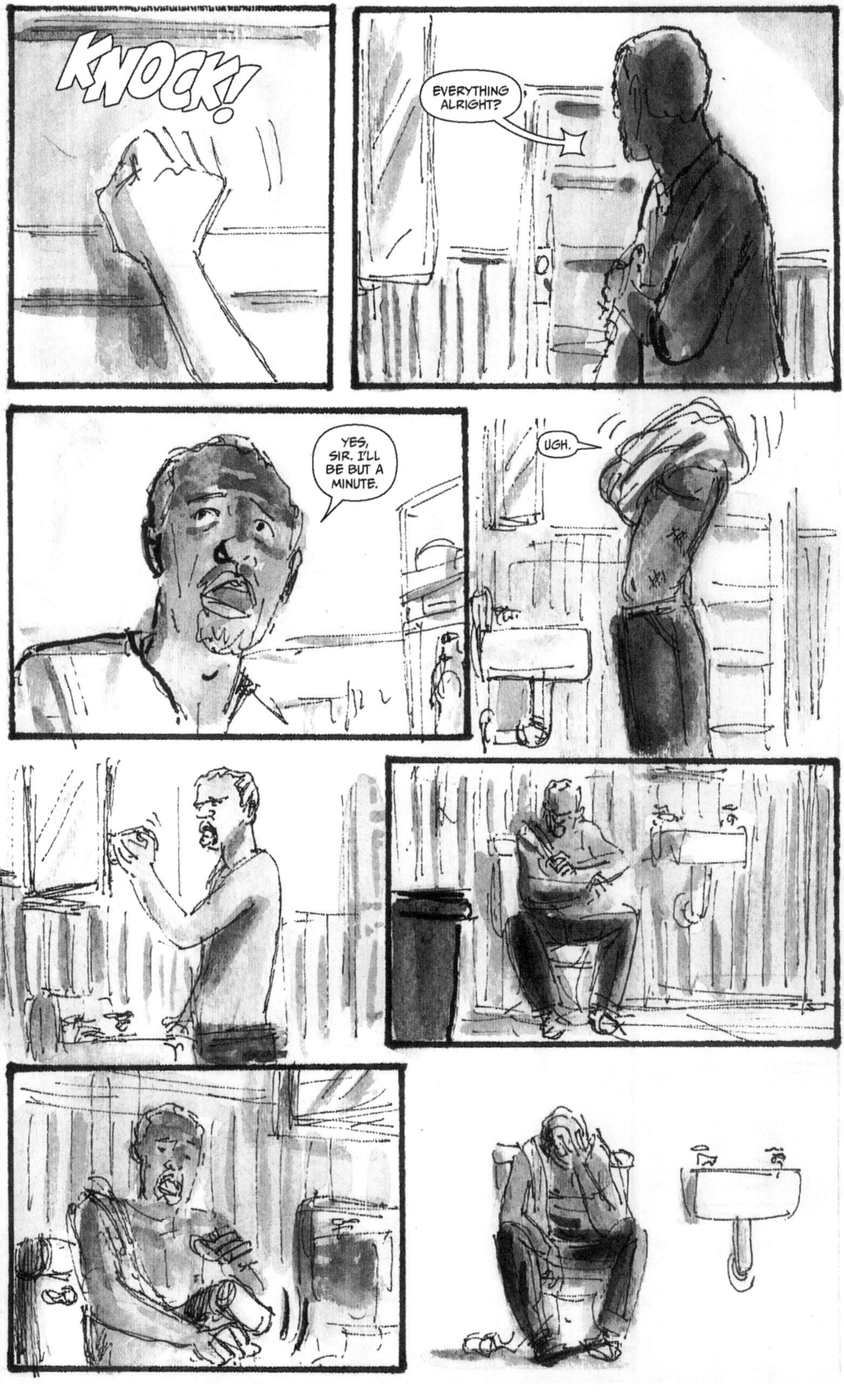
KNOCK!
EVERYTHING ALRIGHT?
YES, SIR. I'LL BE BUT A MINUTE.
UGH.

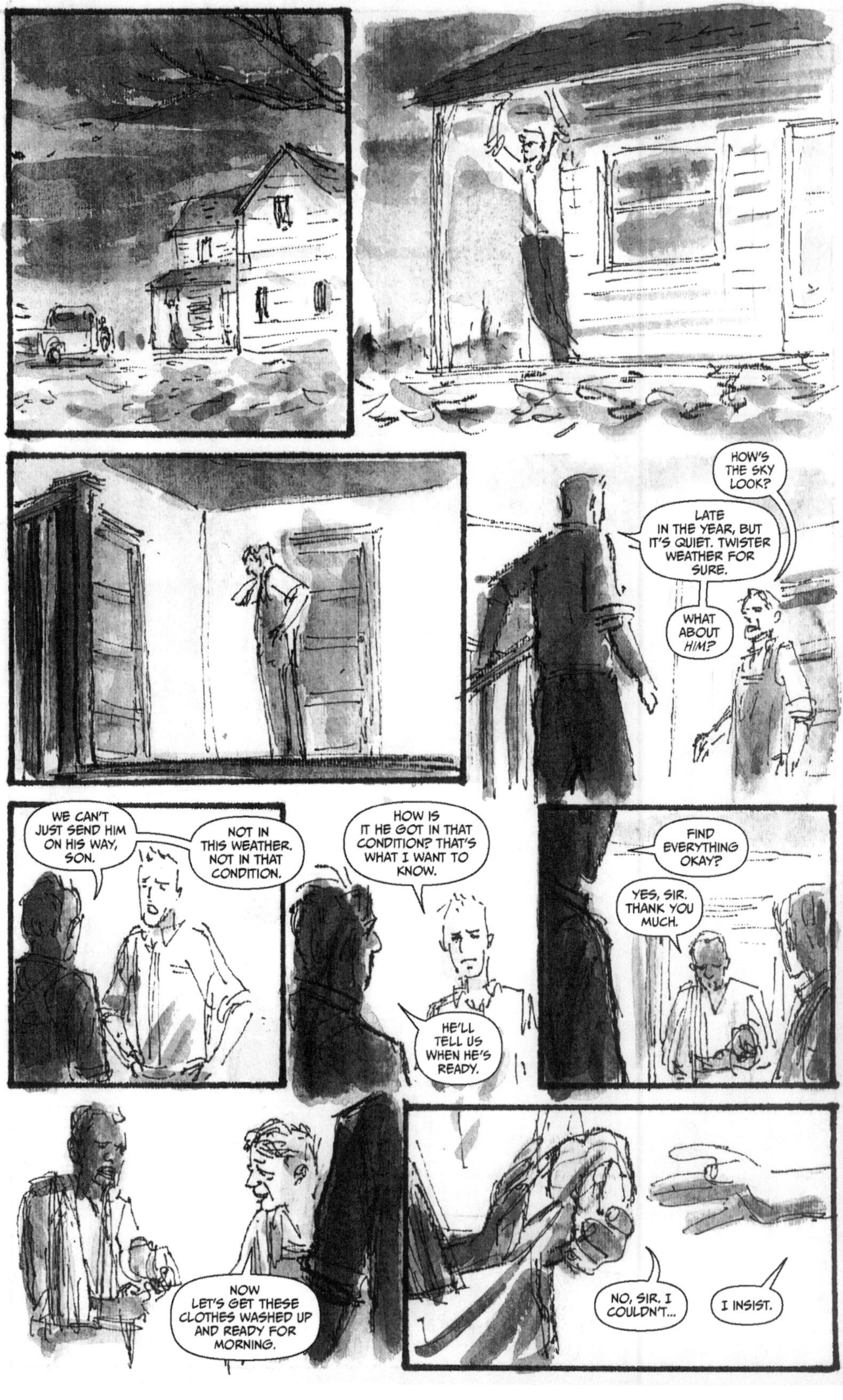
HOW'S THE SKY LOOK?
LATE IN THE YEAR, BUT IT'S QUIET. TWISTER WEATHER FOR SURE.
WHAT ABOUT *HIM?*
WE CAN'T JUST SEND HIM ON HIS WAY, SON.
NOT IN THIS WEATHER. NOT IN THAT CONDITION.
HOW IS IT HE GOT IN THAT CONDITION? THAT'S WHAT I WANT TO KNOW.
HE'LL TELL US WHEN HE'S READY.
FIND EVERYTHING OKAY?
YES, SIR. THANK YOU MUCH.
NOW LET'S GET THESE CLOTHES WASHED UP AND READY FOR MORNING.
NO, SIR. I COULDN'T...
I INSIST.

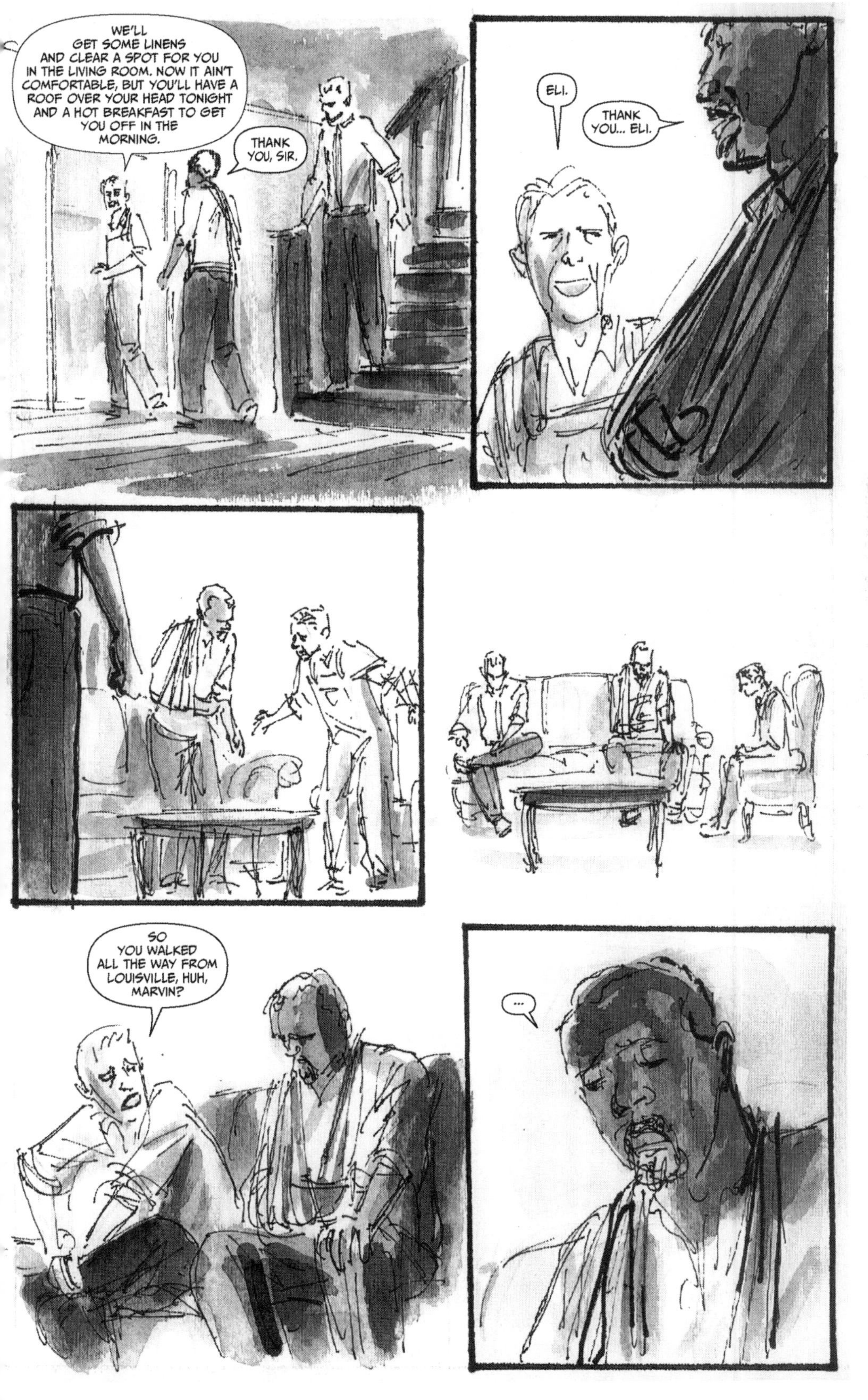
WE'LL GET SOME LINENS AND CLEAR A SPOT FOR YOU IN THE LIVING ROOM. NOW IT AIN'T COMFORTABLE, BUT YOU'LL HAVE A ROOF OVER YOUR HEAD TONIGHT AND A HOT BREAKFAST TO GET YOU OFF IN THE MORNING.
THANK YOU, SIR.
ELI.
THANK YOU... ELI.
SO YOU WALKED ALL THE WAY FROM LOUISVILLE, HUH, MARVIN?
...

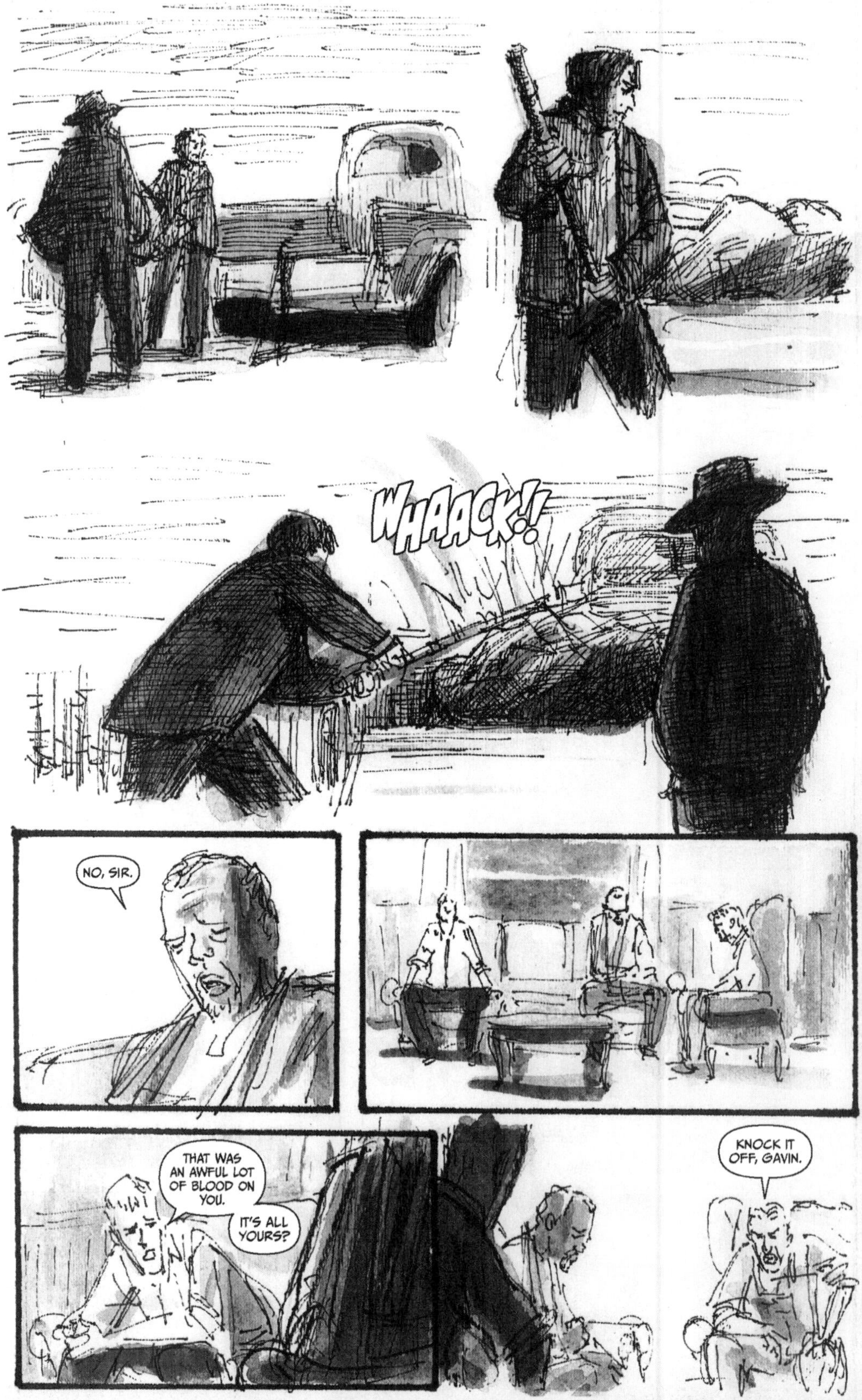
WHAACK!!
NO, SIR.
THAT WAS AN AWFUL LOT OF BLOOD ON YOU.
IT'S ALL YOURS?
KNOCK IT OFF, GAVIN.

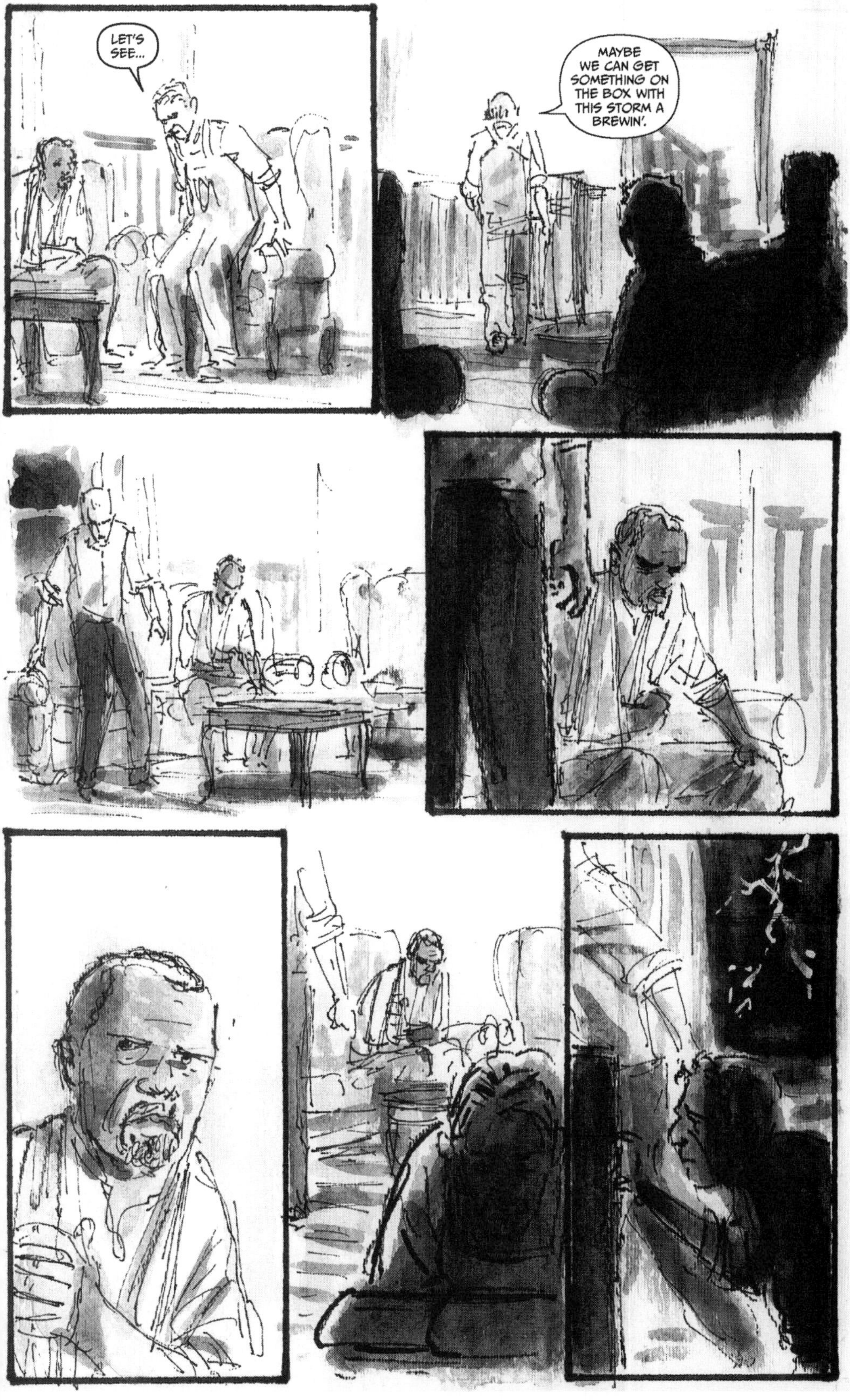
LET'S SEE...
MAYBE WE CAN GET SOMETHING ON THE BOX WITH THIS STORM A BREWIN'.

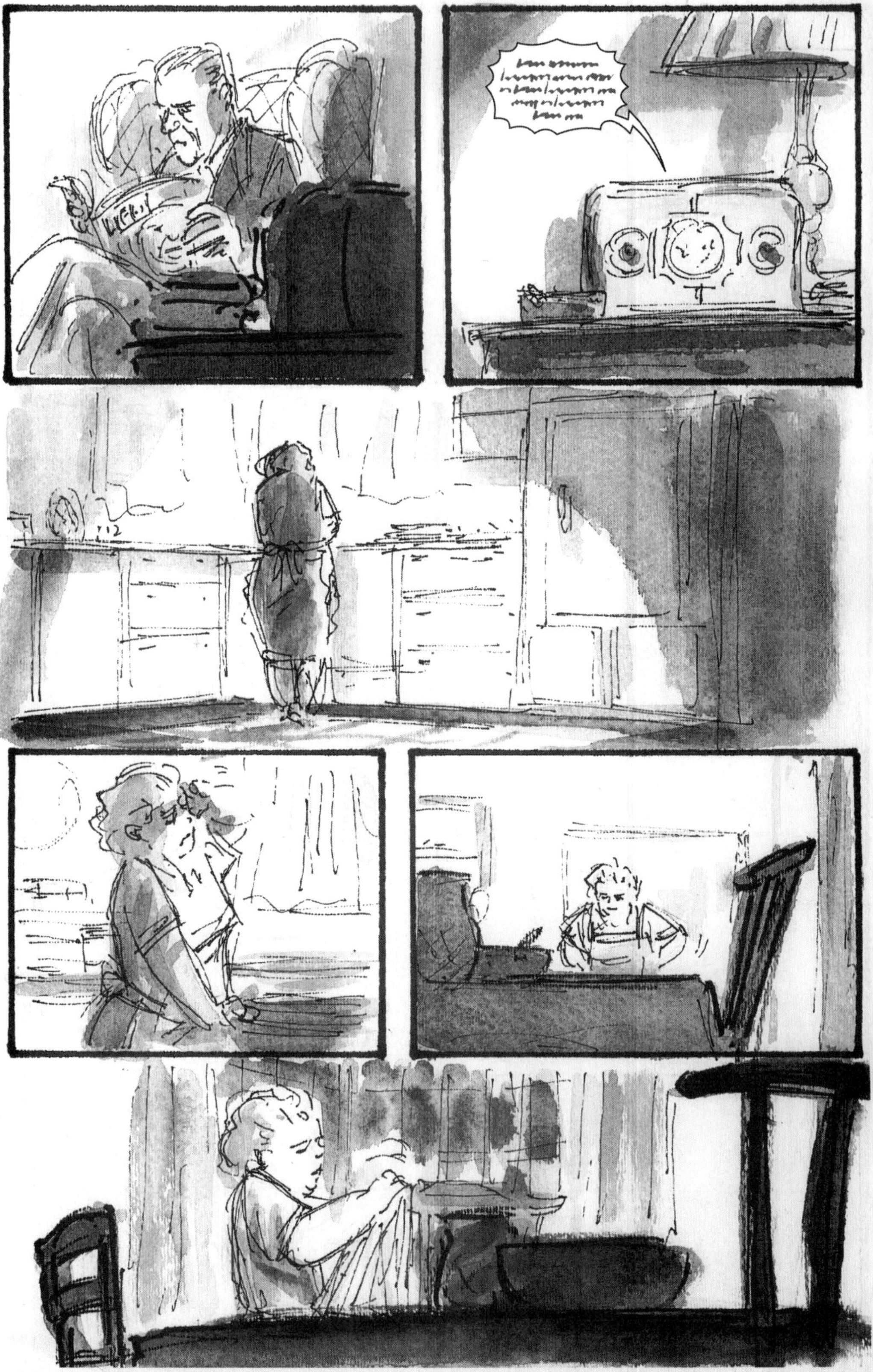

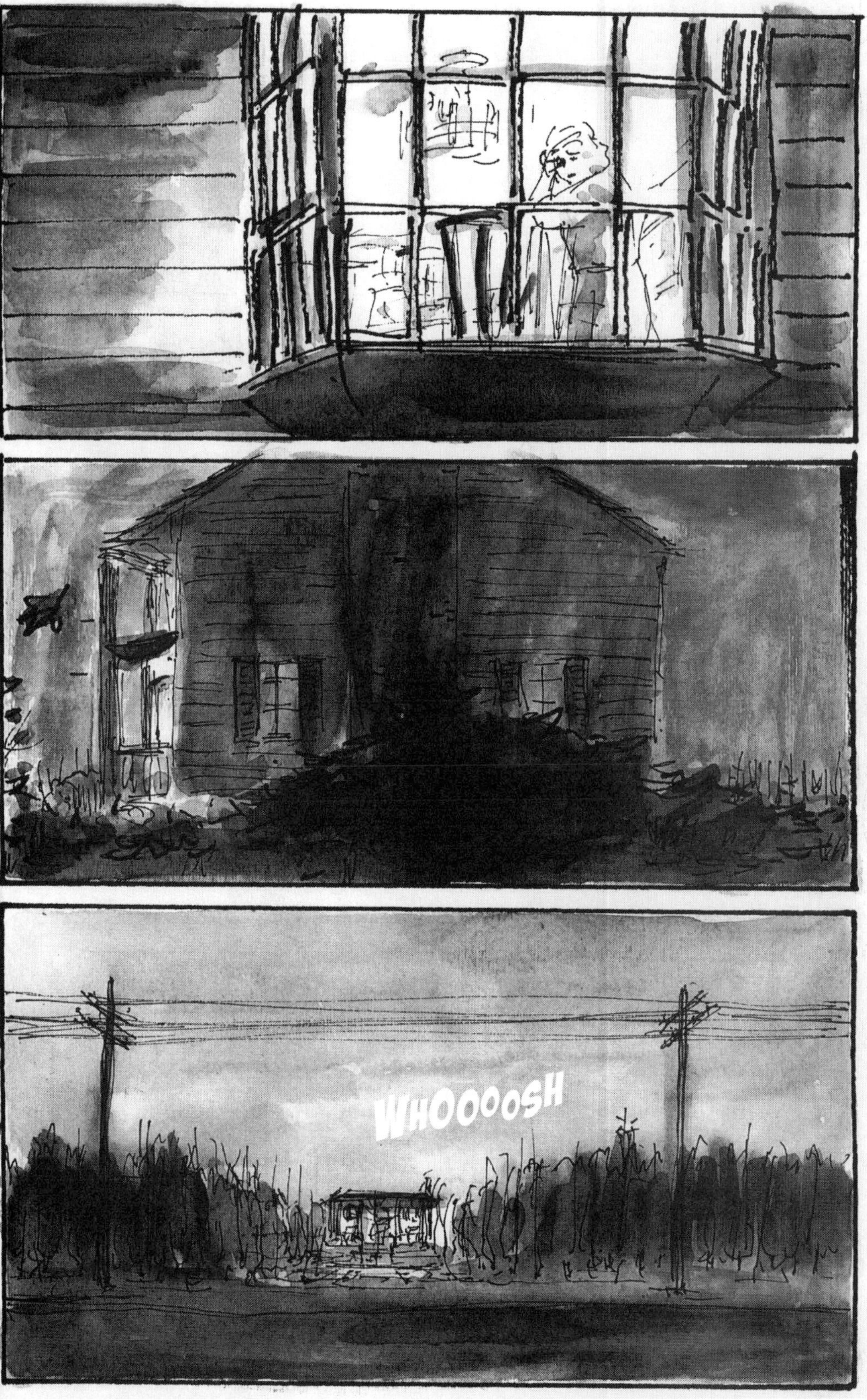
WHOOOOSH

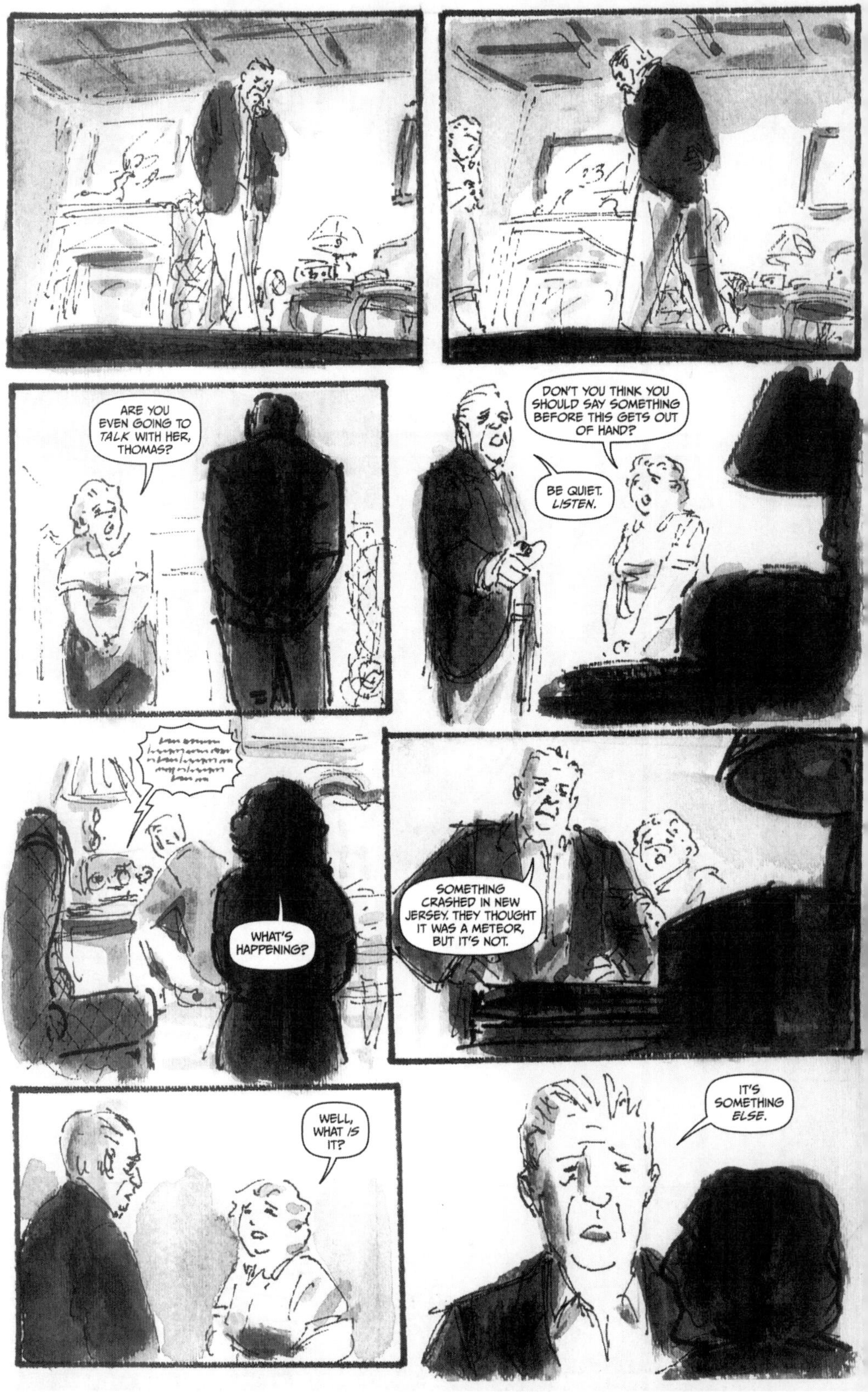
ARE YOU EVEN GOING TO TALK WITH HER, THOMAS?
DON'T YOU THINK YOU SHOULD SAY SOMETHING BEFORE THIS GETS OUT OF HAND?
BE QUIET. LISTEN.
WHAT'S HAPPENING?
SOMETHING CRASHED IN NEW JERSEY. THEY THOUGHT IT WAS A METEOR, BUT IT'S NOT.
WELL, WHAT IS IT?
IT'S SOMETHING ELSE.

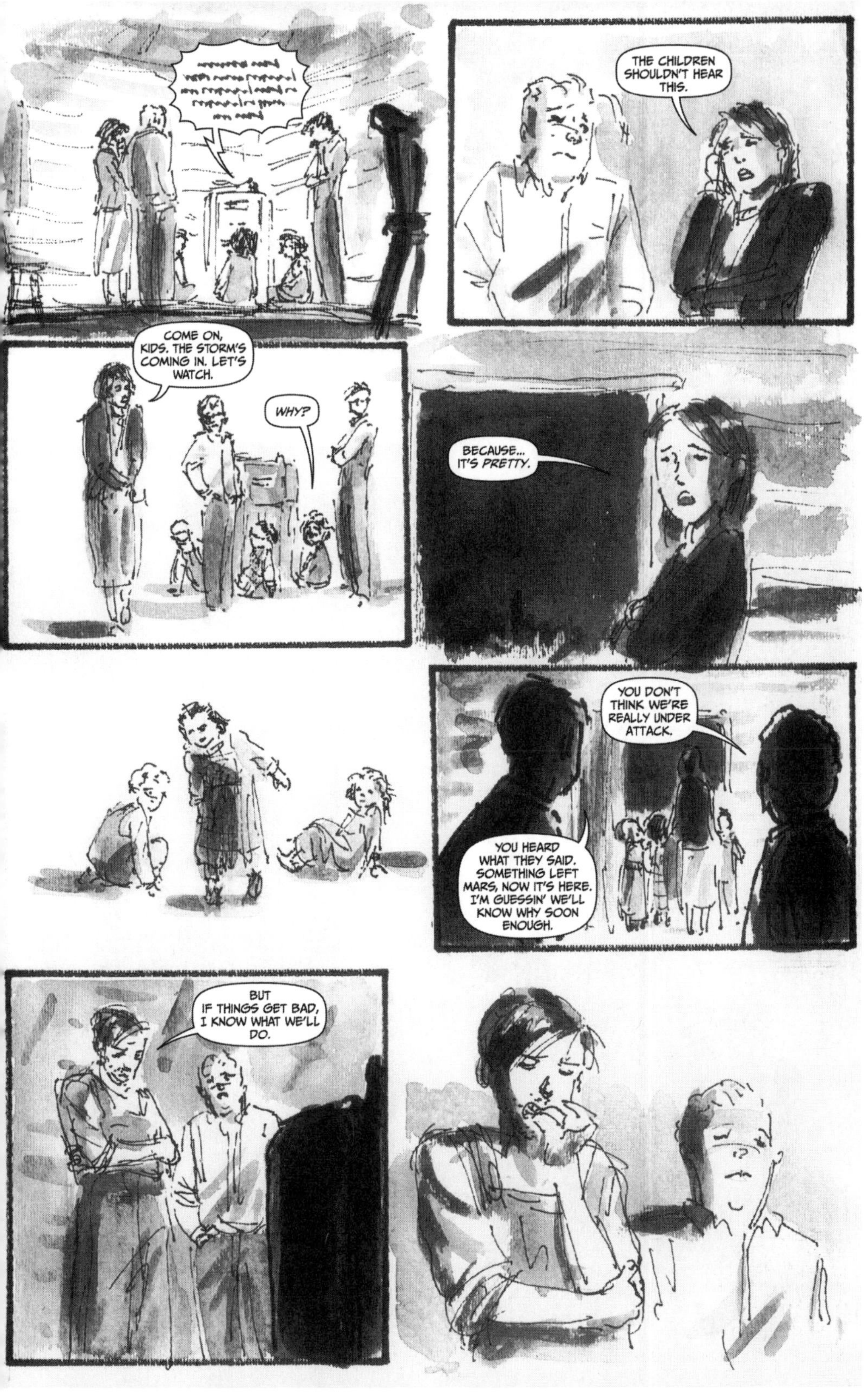
THE CHILDREN SHOULDN'T HEAR THIS.
COME ON, KIDS. THE STORM'S COMING IN. LET'S WATCH.
WHY?
BECAUSE... IT'S PRETTY.
YOU DON'T THINK WE'RE REALLY UNDER ATTACK.
YOU HEARD WHAT THEY SAID. SOMETHING LEFT MARS, NOW IT'S HERE. I'M GUESSIN' WE'LL KNOW WHY SOON ENOUGH.
BUT IF THINGS GET BAD, I KNOW WHAT WE'LL DO.

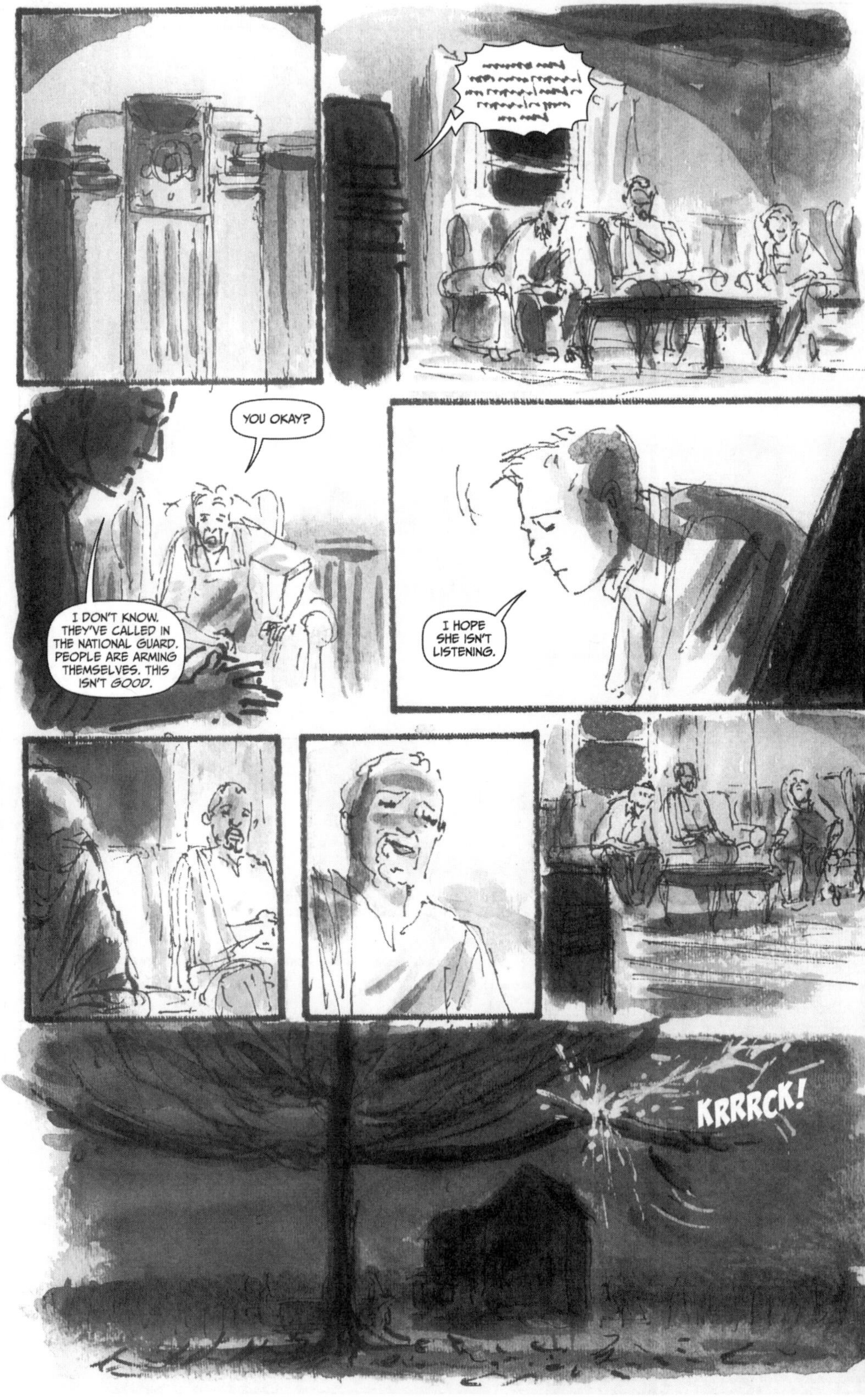
YOU OKAY?
I DON'T KNOW. THEY'VE CALLED IN THE NATIONAL GUARD. PEOPLE ARE ARMING THEMSELVES. THIS ISN'T *GOOD*.
I HOPE SHE ISN'T LISTENING.
KRRRCK!

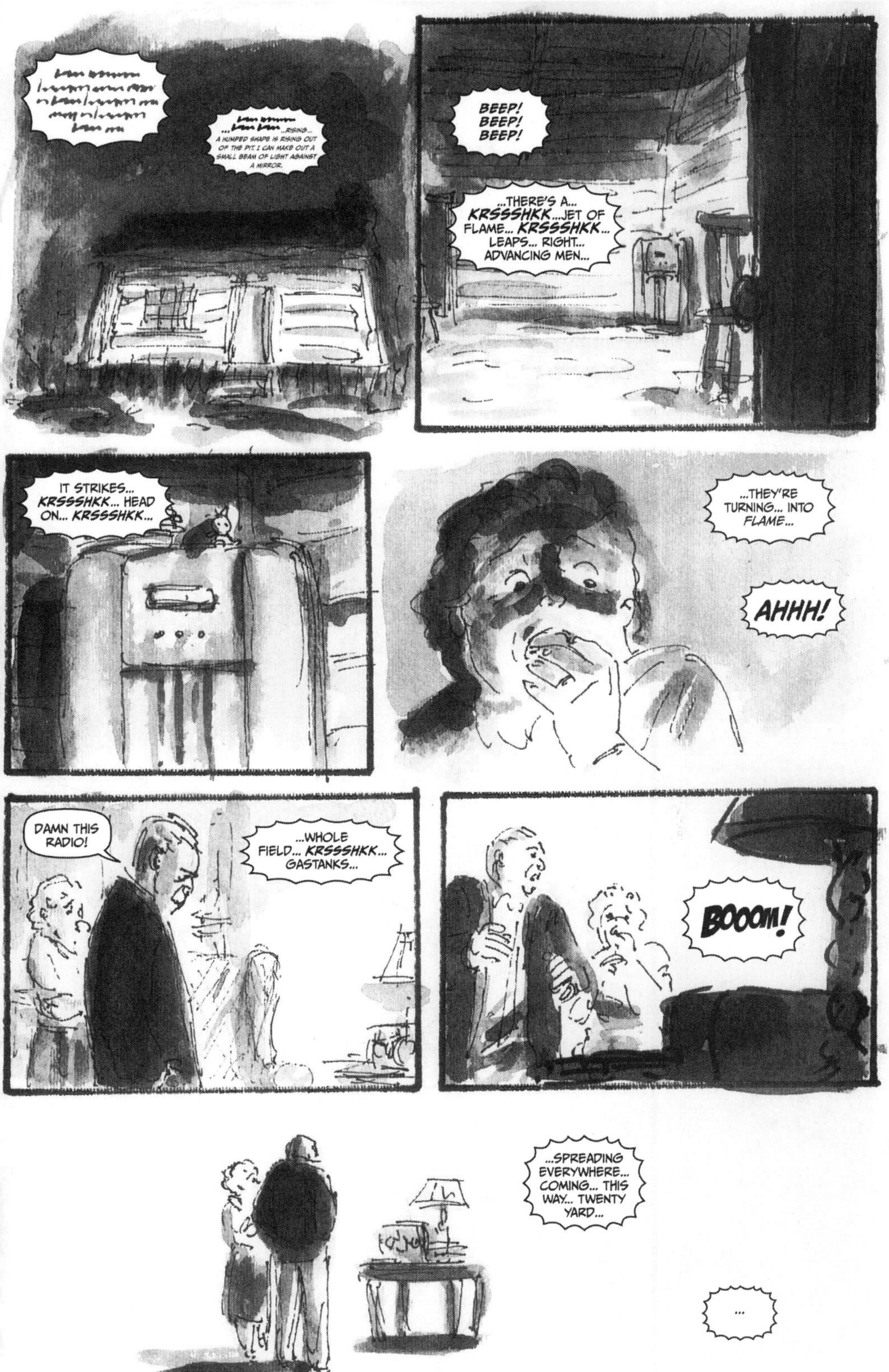
...RISING... A HUMPED SHAPE IS RISING OUT OF THE PIT. I CAN MAKE OUT A SMALL BEAM OF LIGHT AGAINST A MIRROR.
BEEP! BEEP! BEEP!
...THERE'S A... KRSSSHKK...JET OF FLAME... KRSSSHKK... LEAPS... RIGHT... ADVANCING MEN...
IT STRIKES... KRSSSHKK... HEAD ON... KRSSSHKK...
...THEY'RE TURNING... INTO FLAME...
AHHH!
DAMN THIS RADIO!
...WHOLE FIELD... KRSSSHKK... GASTANKS...
BOOOM!
...SPREADING EVERYWHERE... COMING... THIS WAY... TWENTY YARD...
...

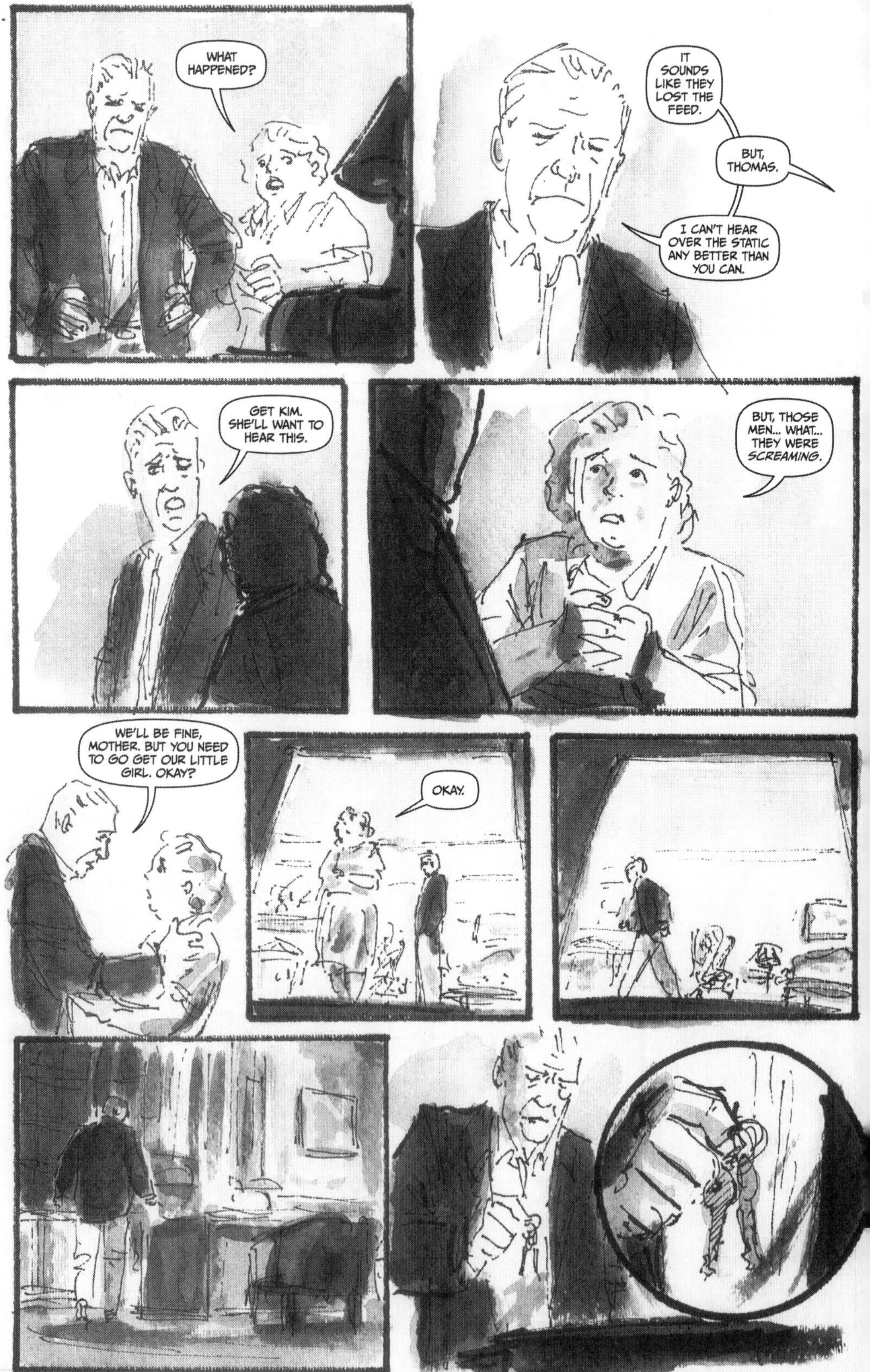
WHAT HAPPENED?
IT SOUNDS LIKE THEY LOST THE FEED.
BUT, THOMAS.
I CAN'T HEAR OVER THE STATIC ANY BETTER THAN YOU CAN.
GET KIM. SHE'LL WANT TO HEAR THIS.
BUT, THOSE MEN... WHAT... THEY WERE *SCREAMING*.
WE'LL BE FINE, MOTHER. BUT YOU NEED TO GO GET OUR LITTLE GIRL. OKAY?
OKAY.

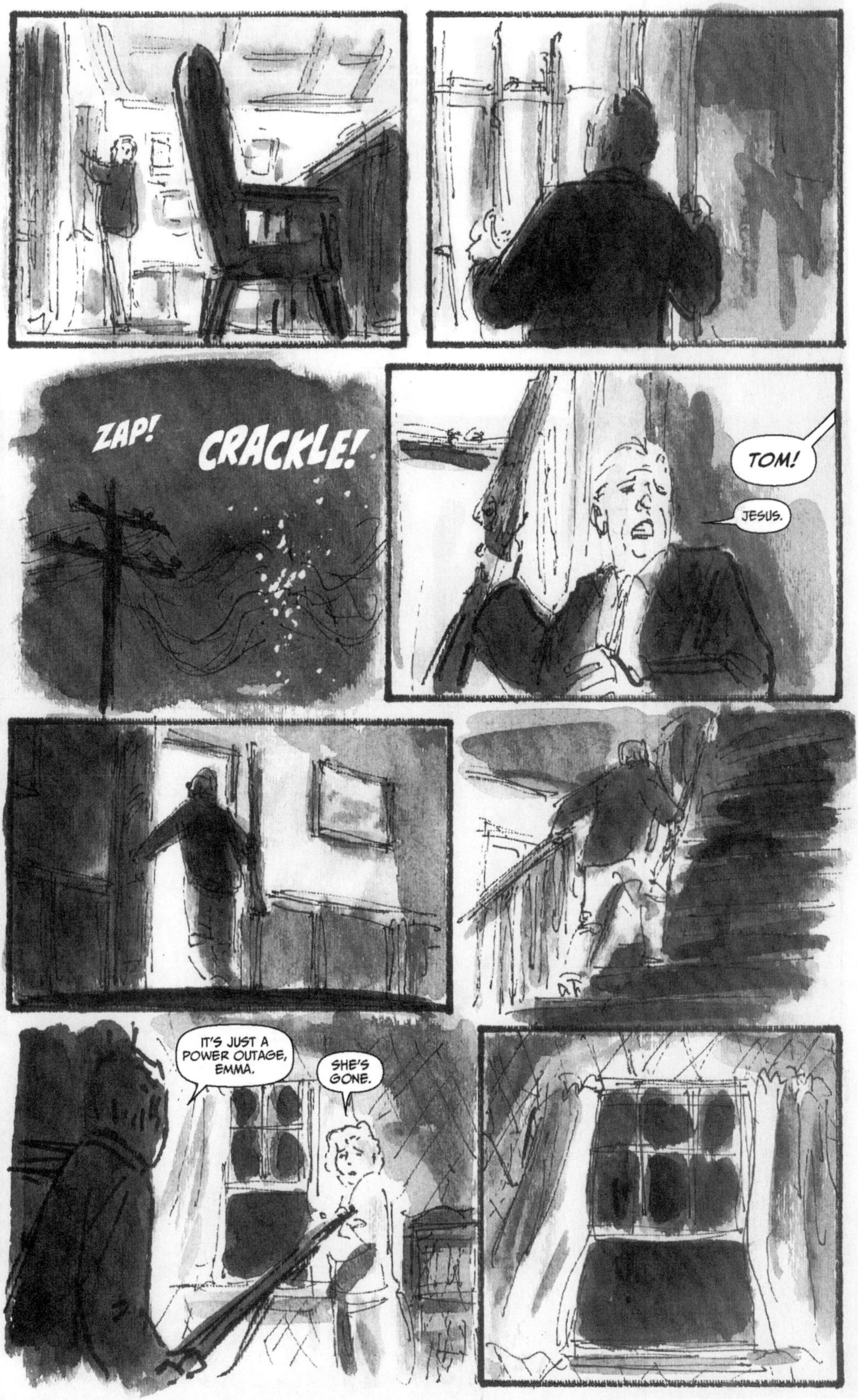
ZAP!
CRACKLE!
TOM!
JESUS.
IT'S JUST A POWER OUTAGE, EMMA.
SHE'S GONE.

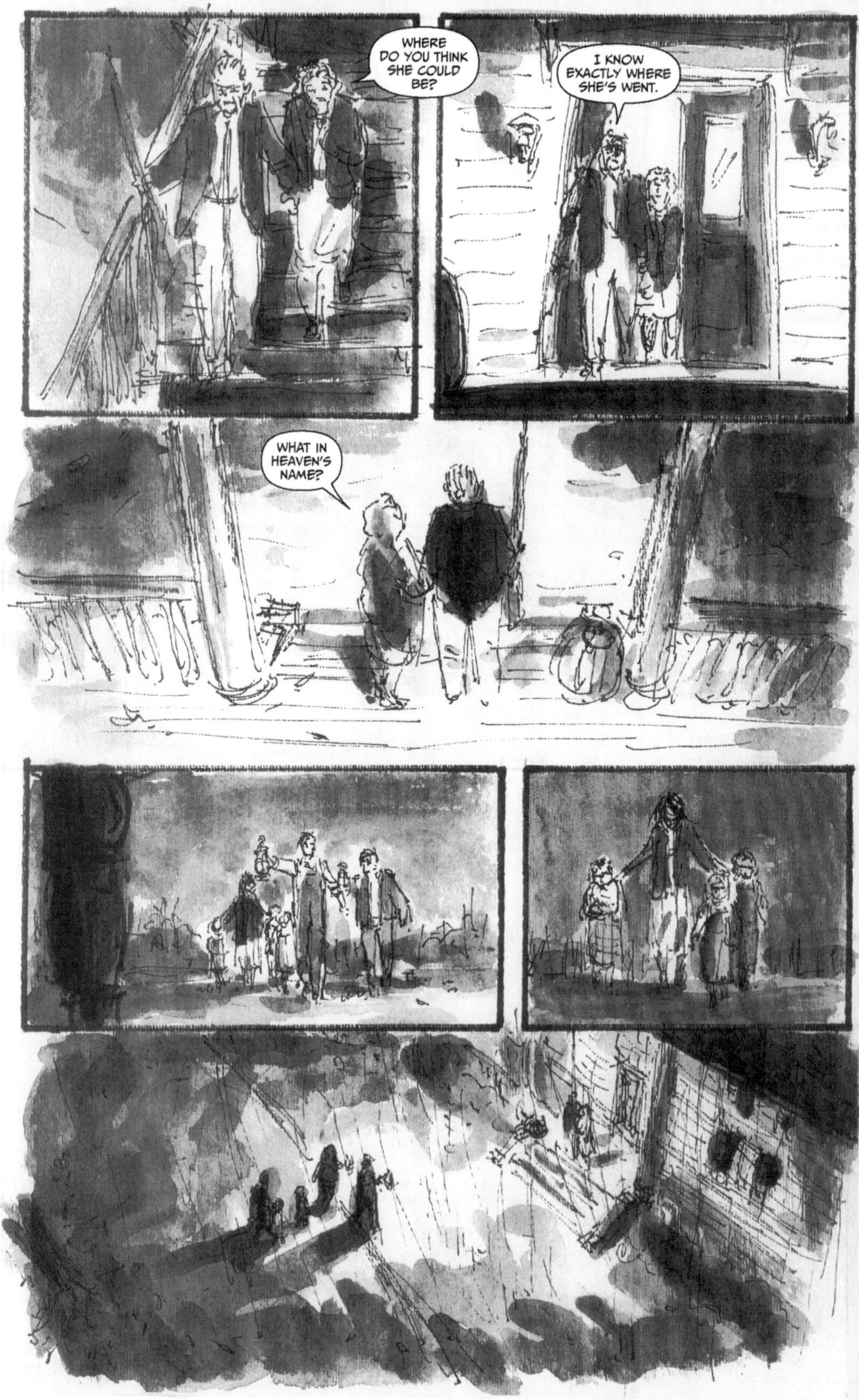
WHERE DO YOU THINK SHE COULD BE?
I KNOW EXACTLY WHERE SHE'S WENT.
WHAT IN HEAVEN'S NAME?

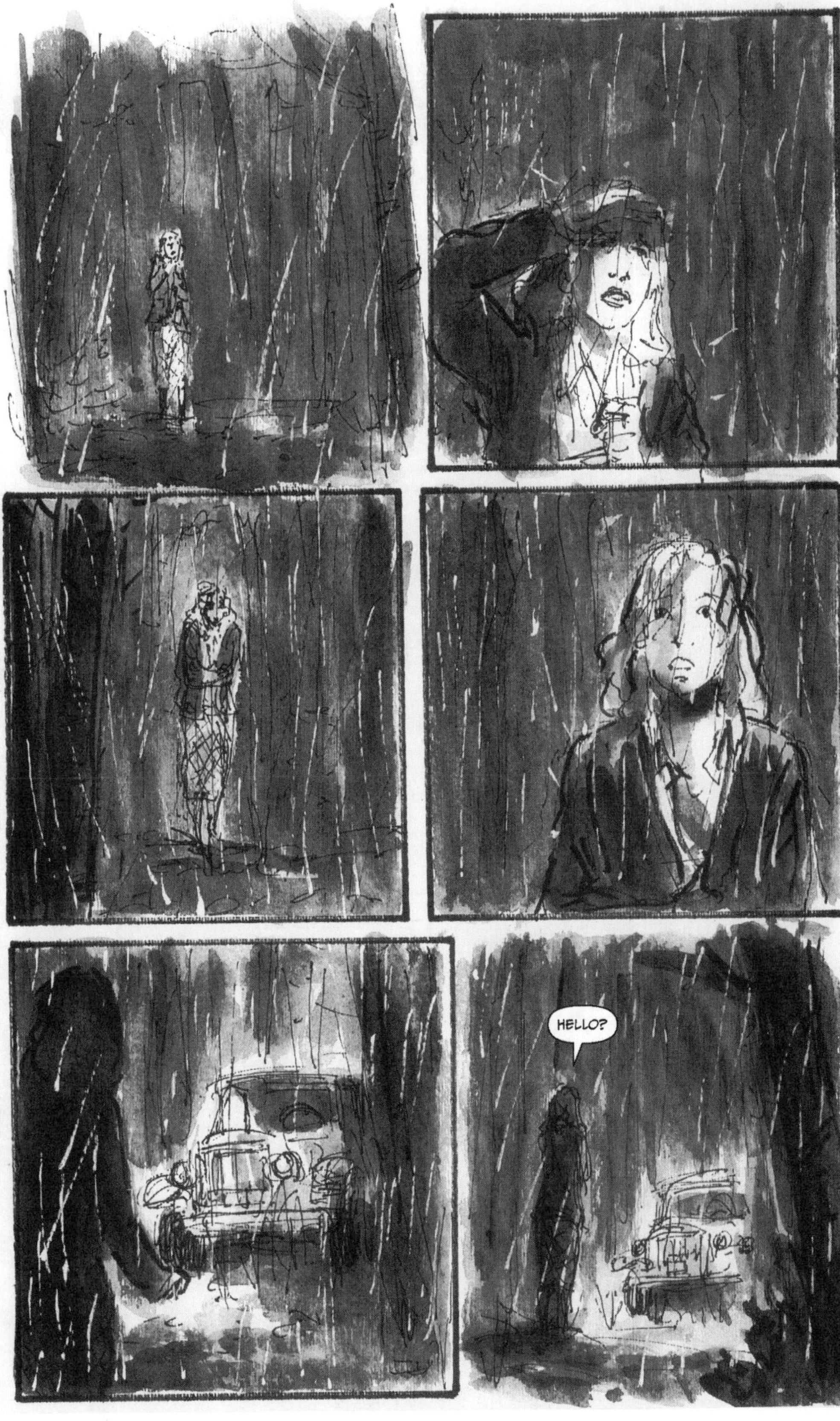
HELLO?

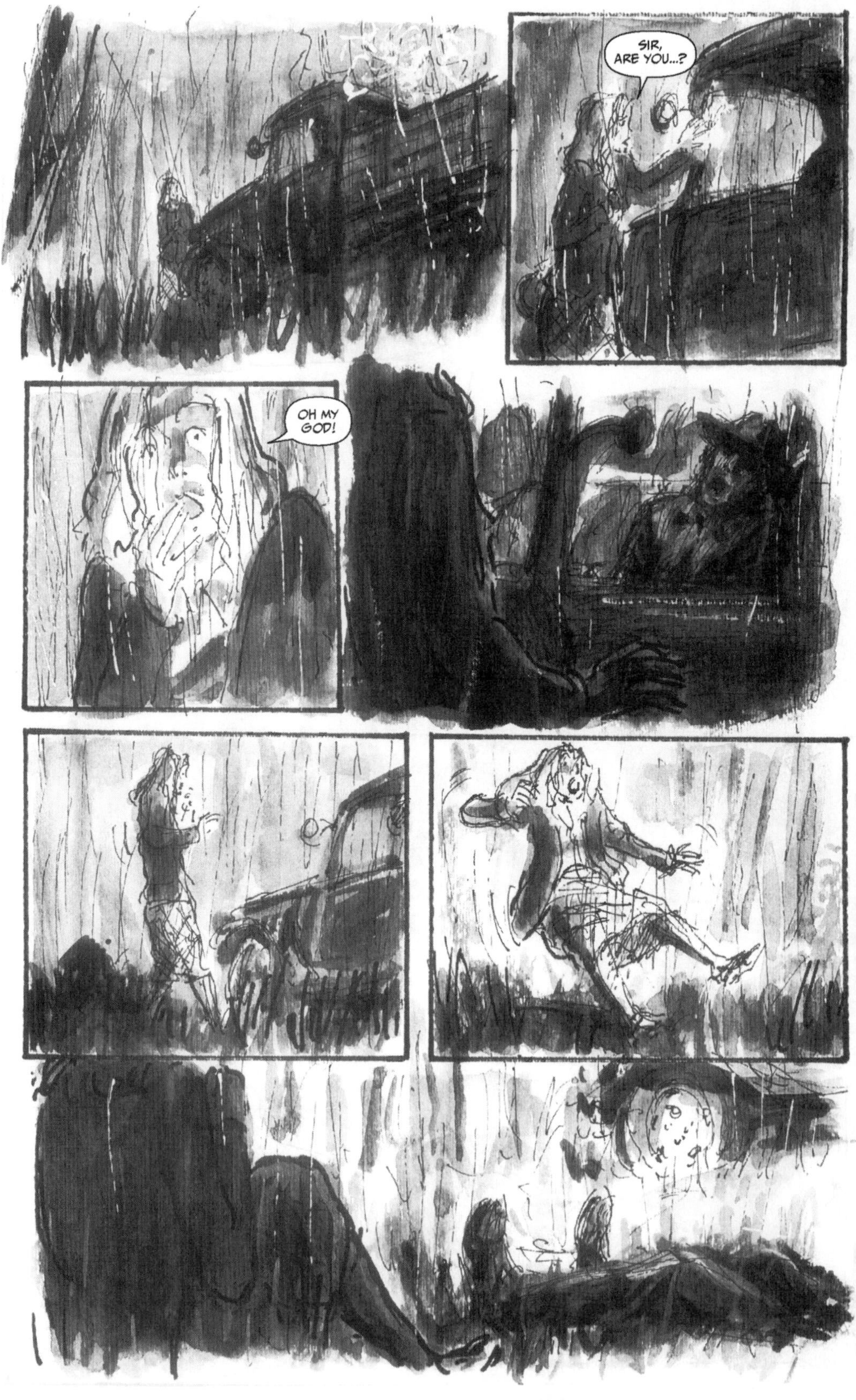
SIR, ARE YOU...?
OH MY GOD!

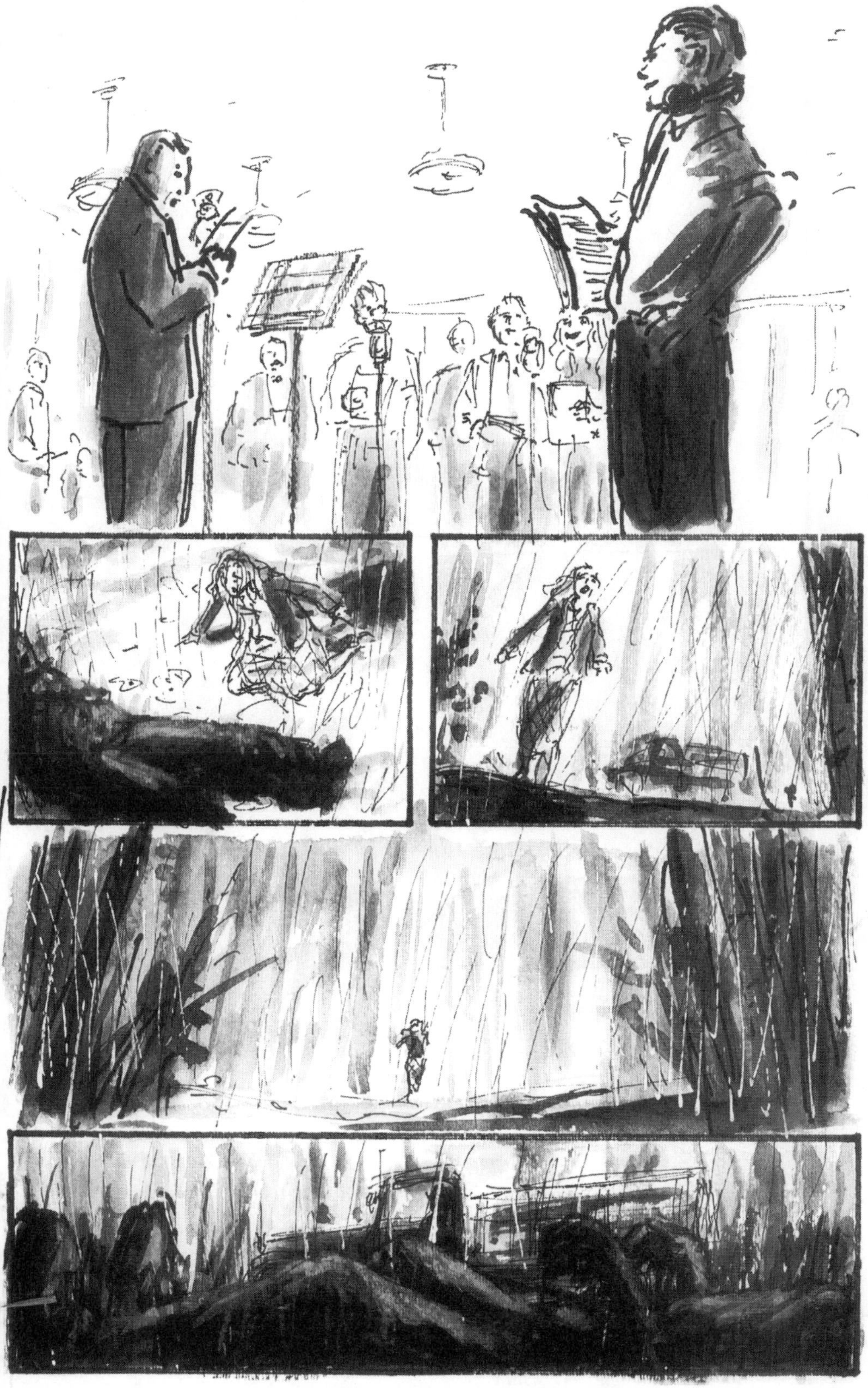

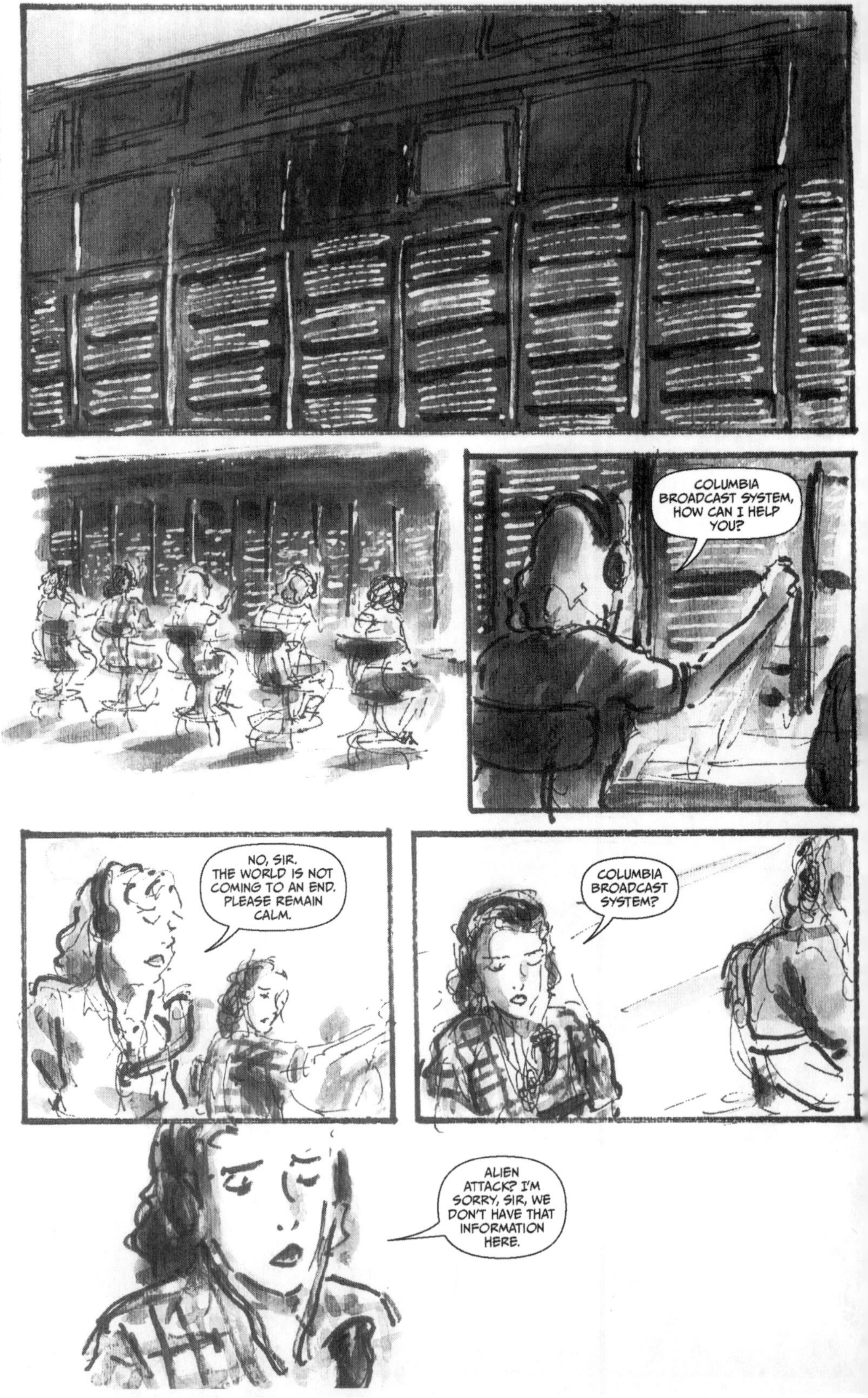
COLUMBIA BROADCAST SYSTEM, HOW CAN I HELP YOU?
NO, SIR. THE WORLD IS NOT COMING TO AN END. PLEASE REMAIN CALM.
COLUMBIA BROADCAST SYSTEM?
ALIEN ATTACK? I'M SORRY, SIR, WE DON'T HAVE THAT INFORMATION HERE.

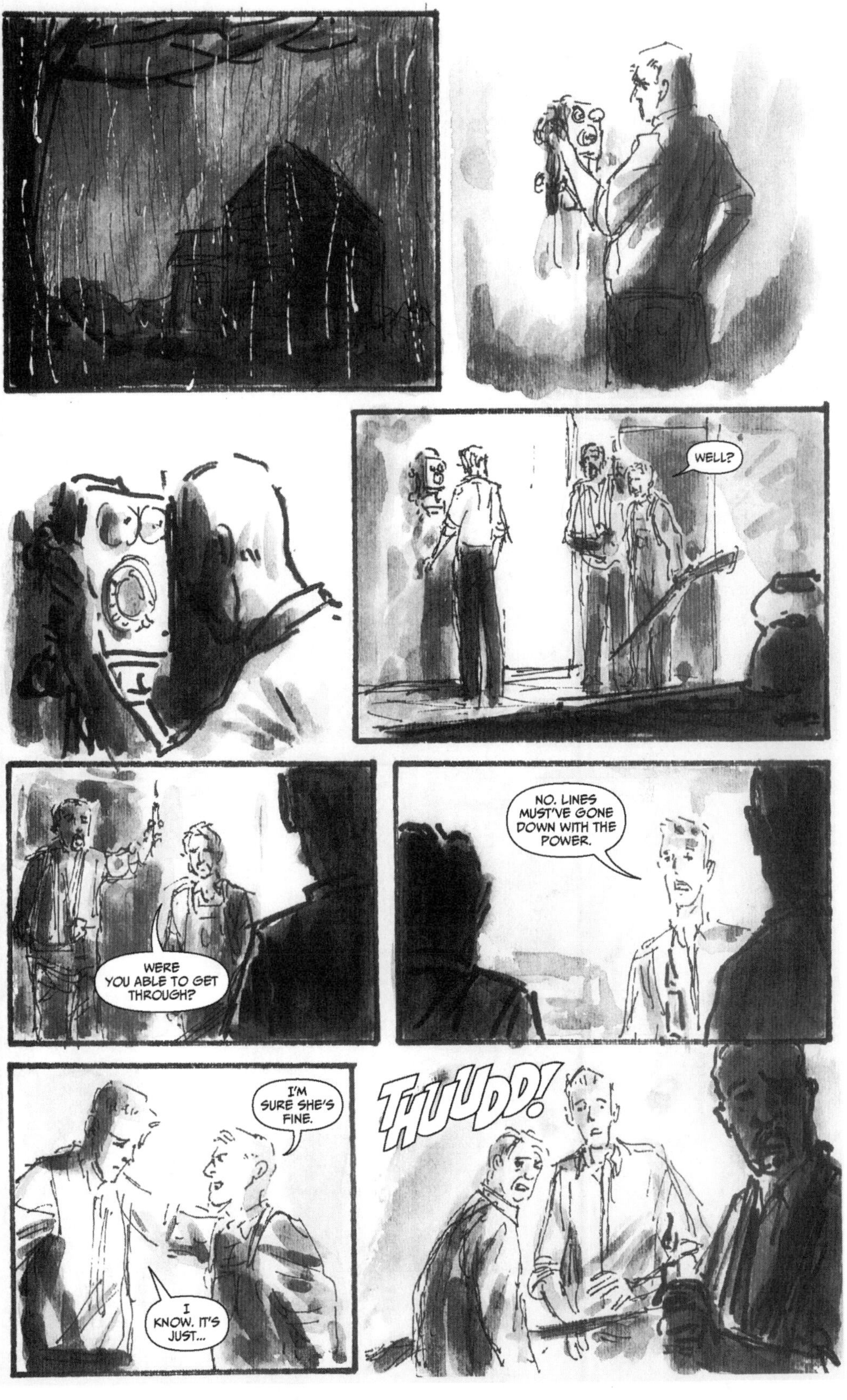
WELL?
WERE YOU ABLE TO GET THROUGH?
NO. LINES MUST'VE GONE DOWN WITH THE POWER.
I'M SURE SHE'S FINE.
I KNOW. IT'S JUST...
THUUDD!

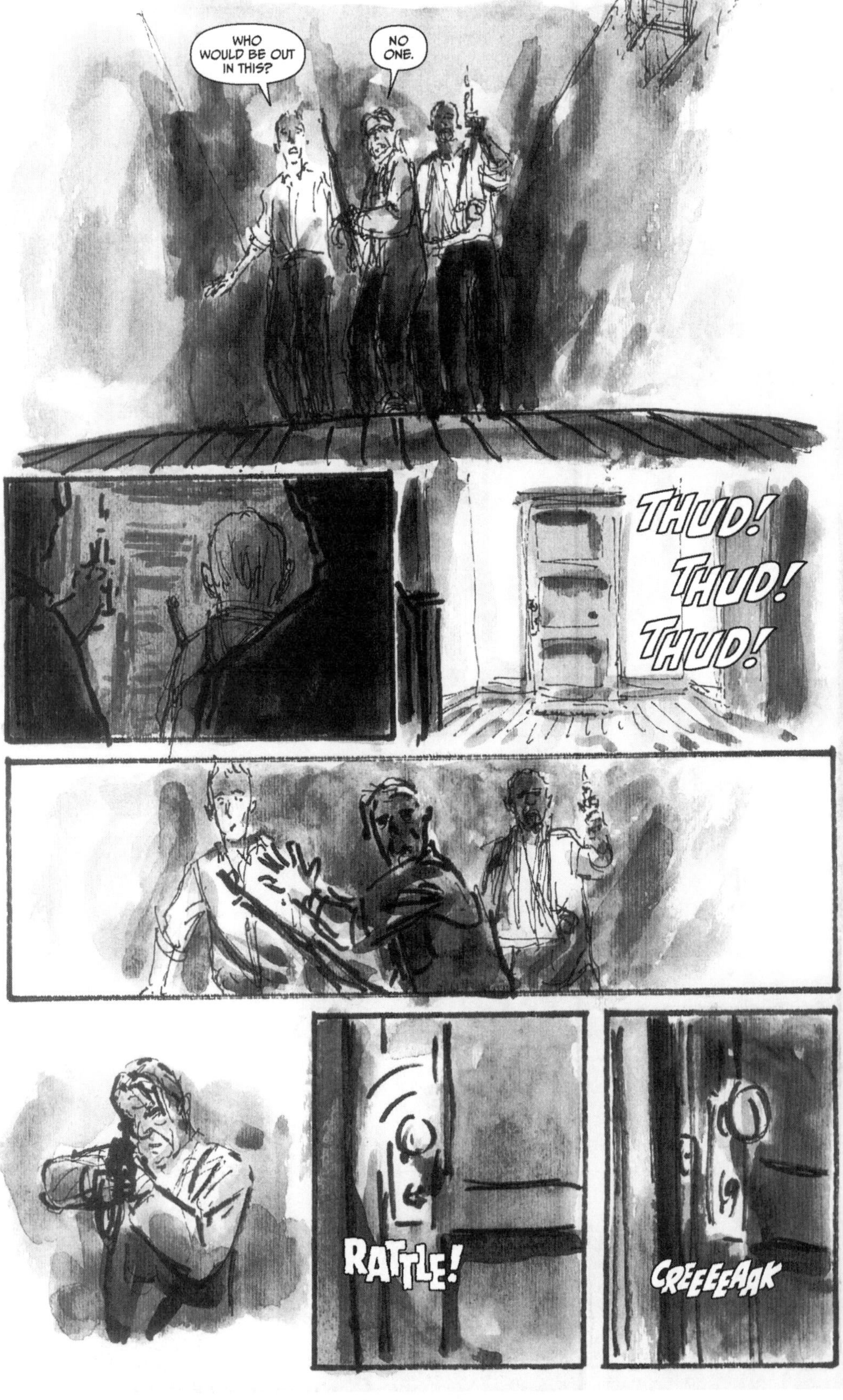
WHO WOULD BE OUT IN THIS?
NO ONE.
THUD! THUD! THUD!
RATTLE!
CREEEEAAK

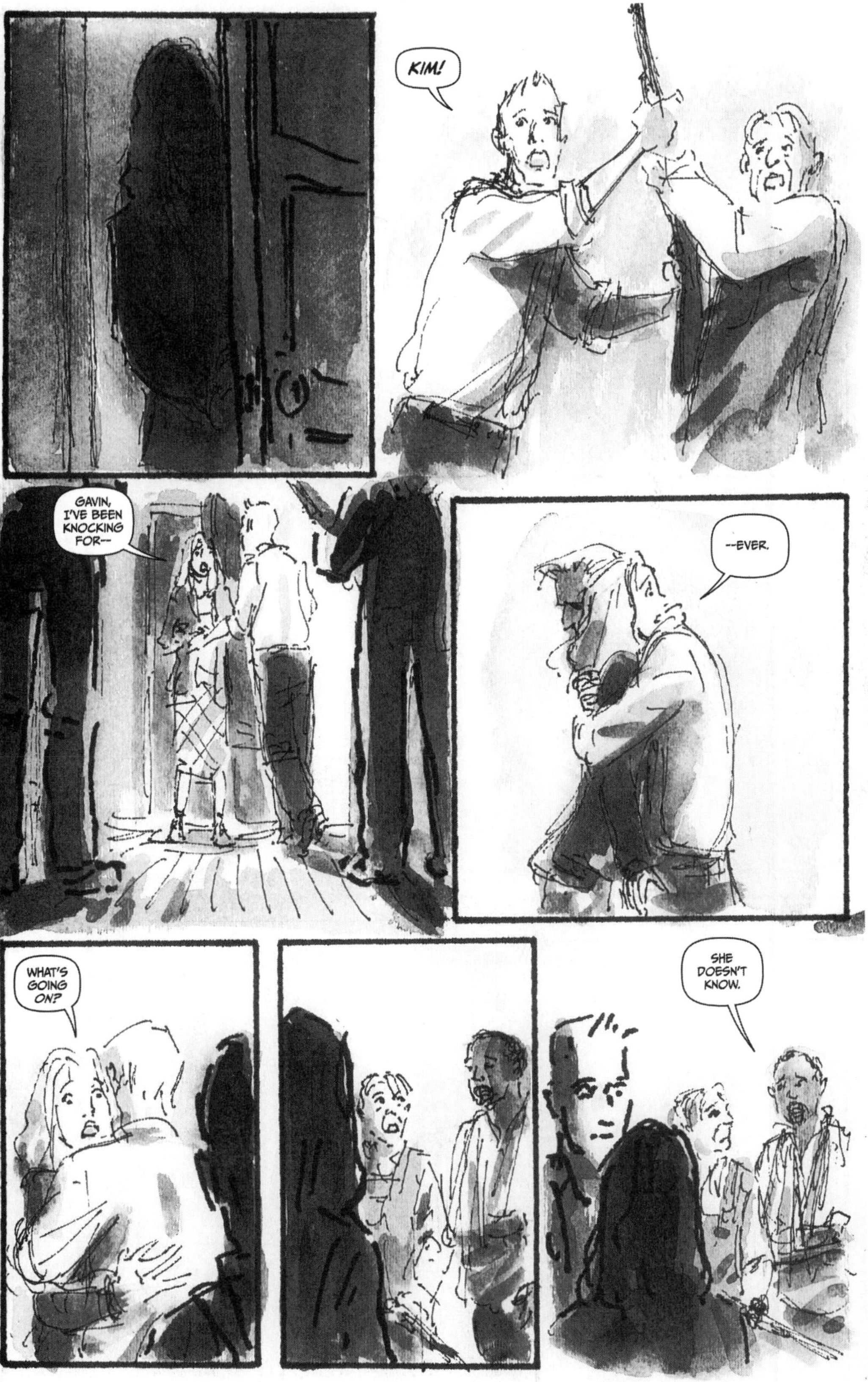
KIM!
GAVIN, I'VE BEEN KNOCKING FOR--
--EVER.
WHAT'S GOING ON?
SHE DOESN'T KNOW.

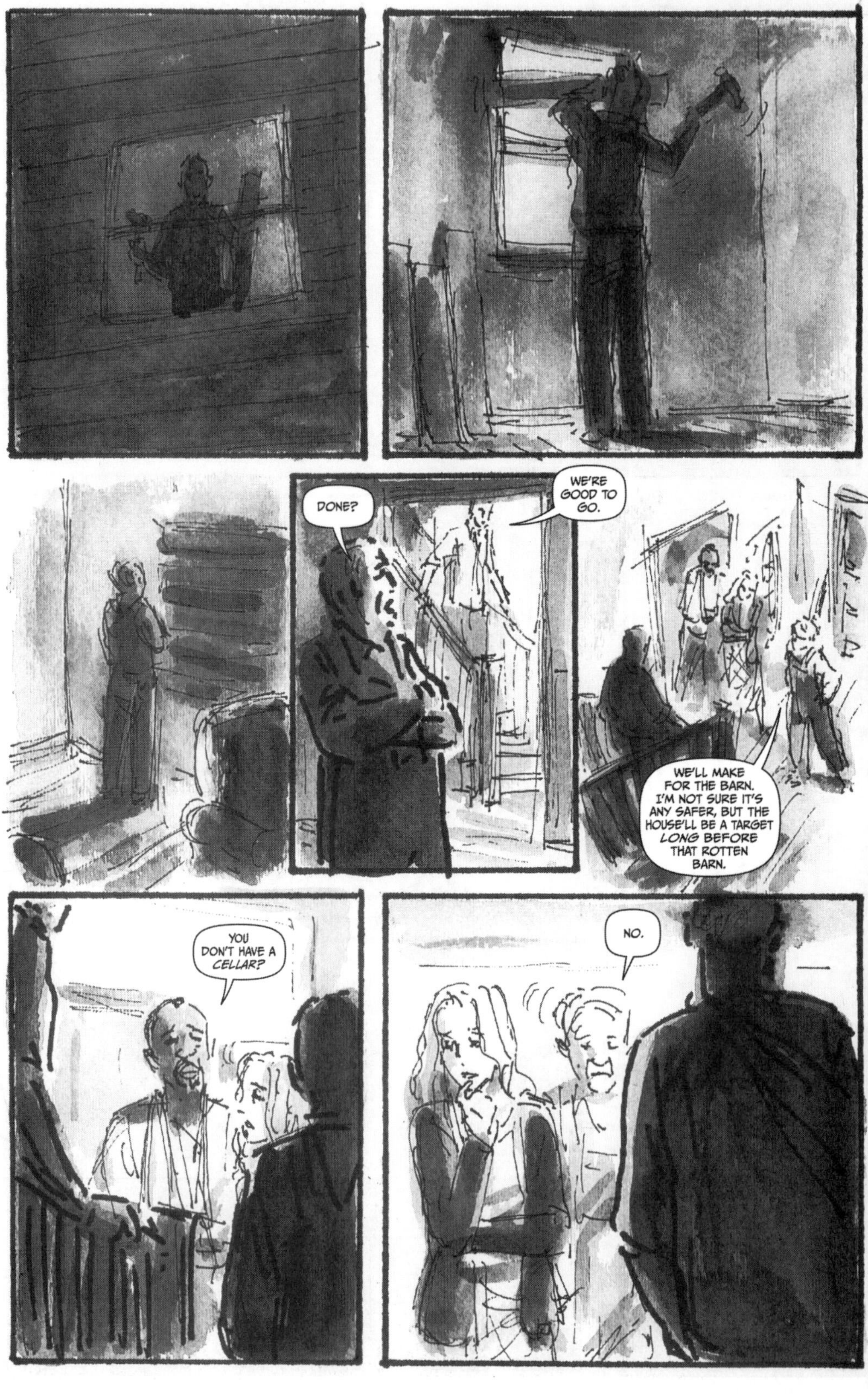
DONE?
WE'RE GOOD TO GO.
WE'LL MAKE FOR THE BARN. I'M NOT SURE IT'S ANY SAFER, BUT THE HOUSE'LL BE A TARGET *LONG* BEFORE THAT ROTTEN BARN.
YOU DON'T HAVE A *CELLAR*?
NO.

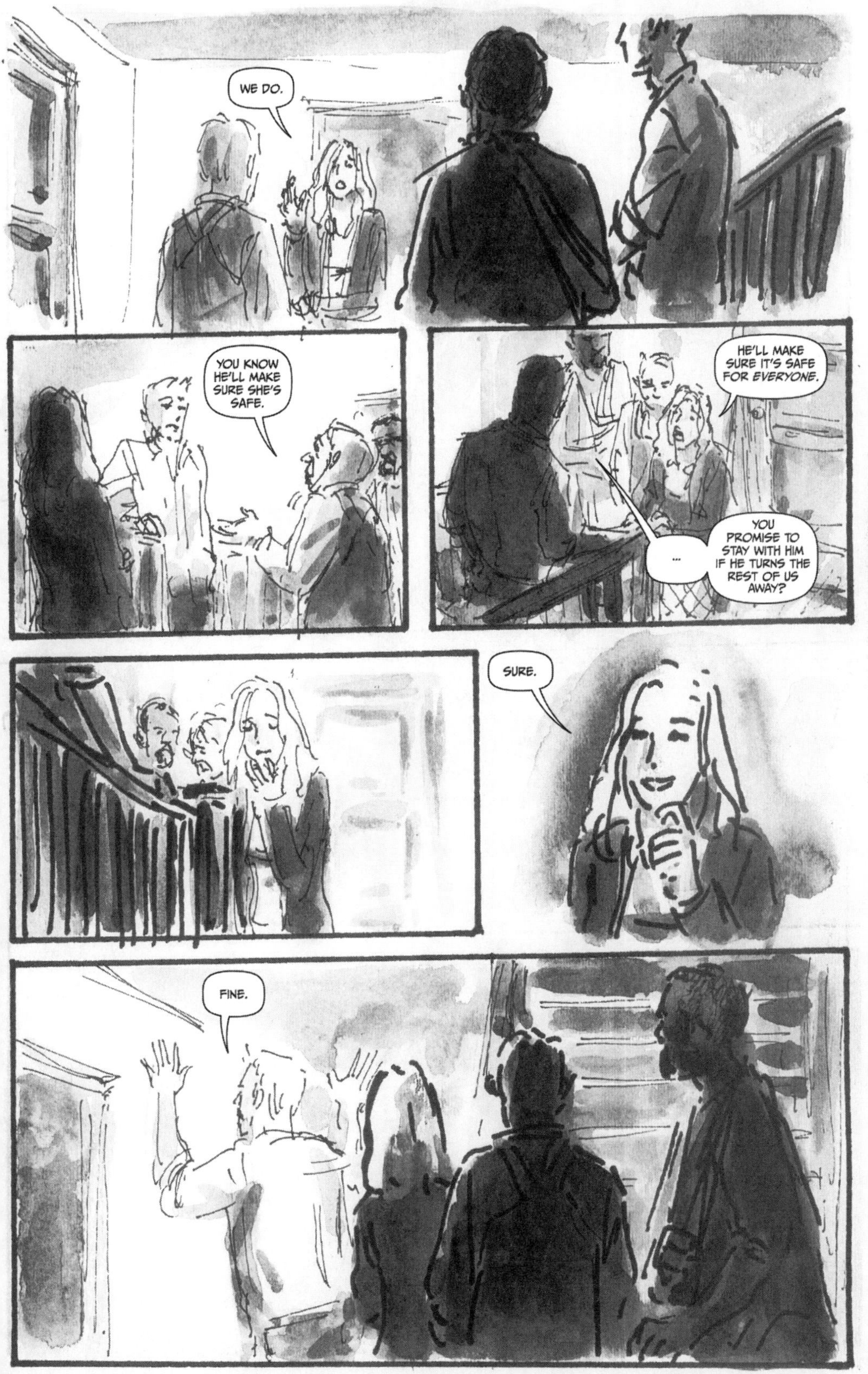
WE DO.
YOU KNOW HE'LL MAKE SURE SHE'S SAFE.
HE'LL MAKE SURE IT'S SAFE FOR *EVERYONE*.
YOU PROMISE TO STAY WITH HIM IF HE TURNS THE REST OF US AWAY?
...
SURE.
FINE.

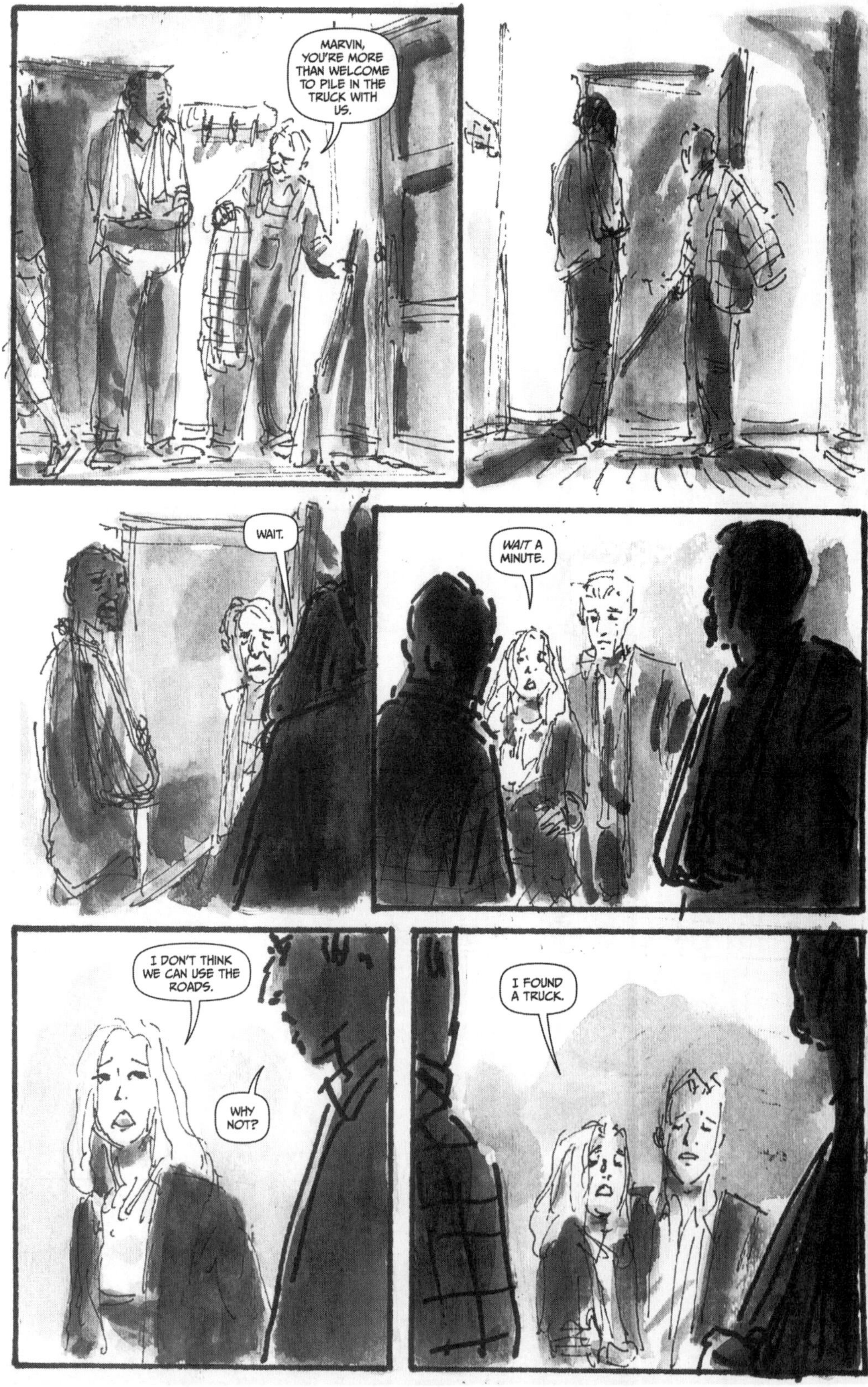

MARVIN, YOU'RE MORE THAN WELCOME TO PILE IN THE TRUCK WITH US.
WAIT.
WAIT A MINUTE.
I DON'T THINK WE CAN USE THE ROADS.
WHY NOT?
I FOUND A TRUCK.

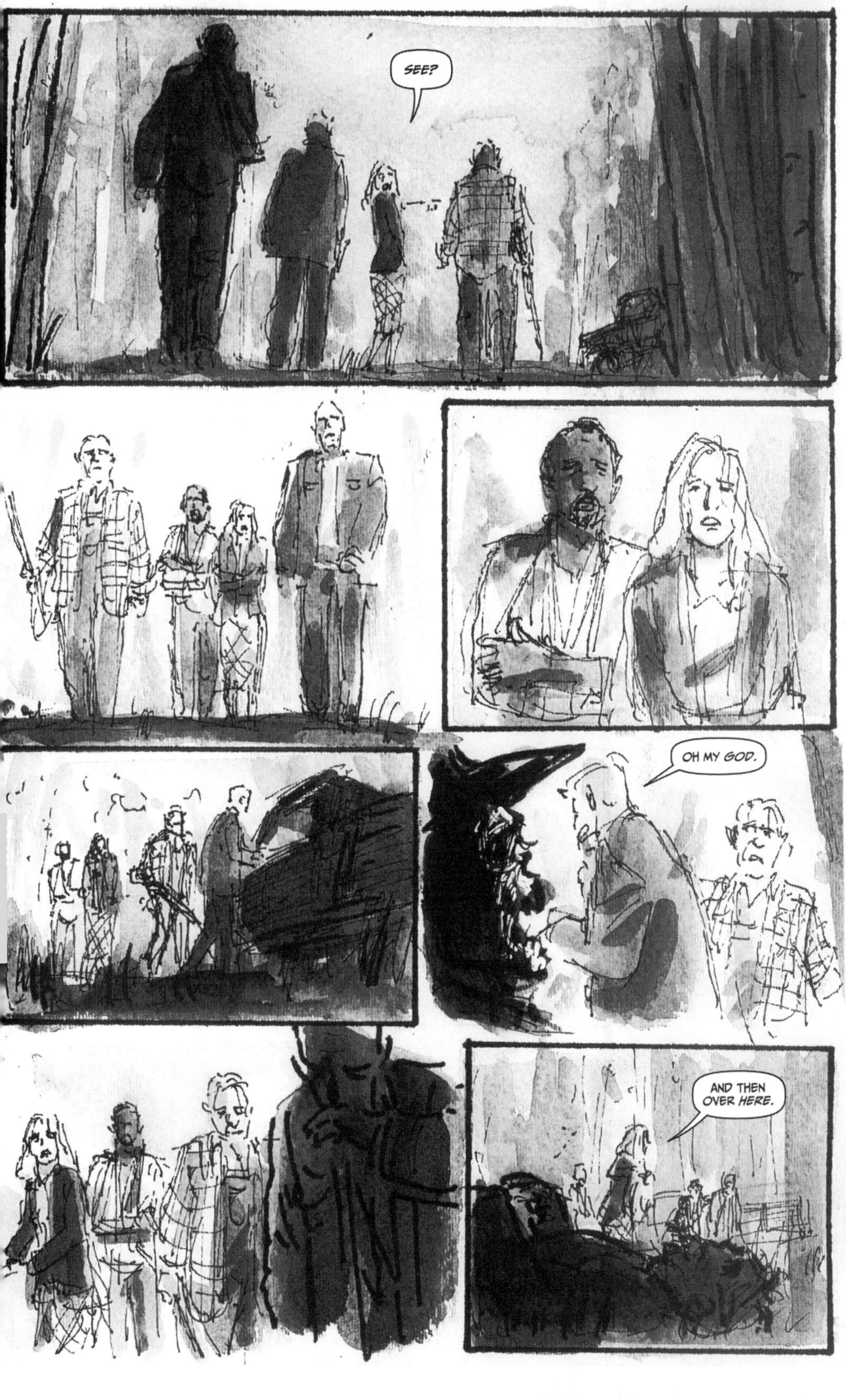
SEE?
OH MY GOD.
AND THEN OVER HERE.

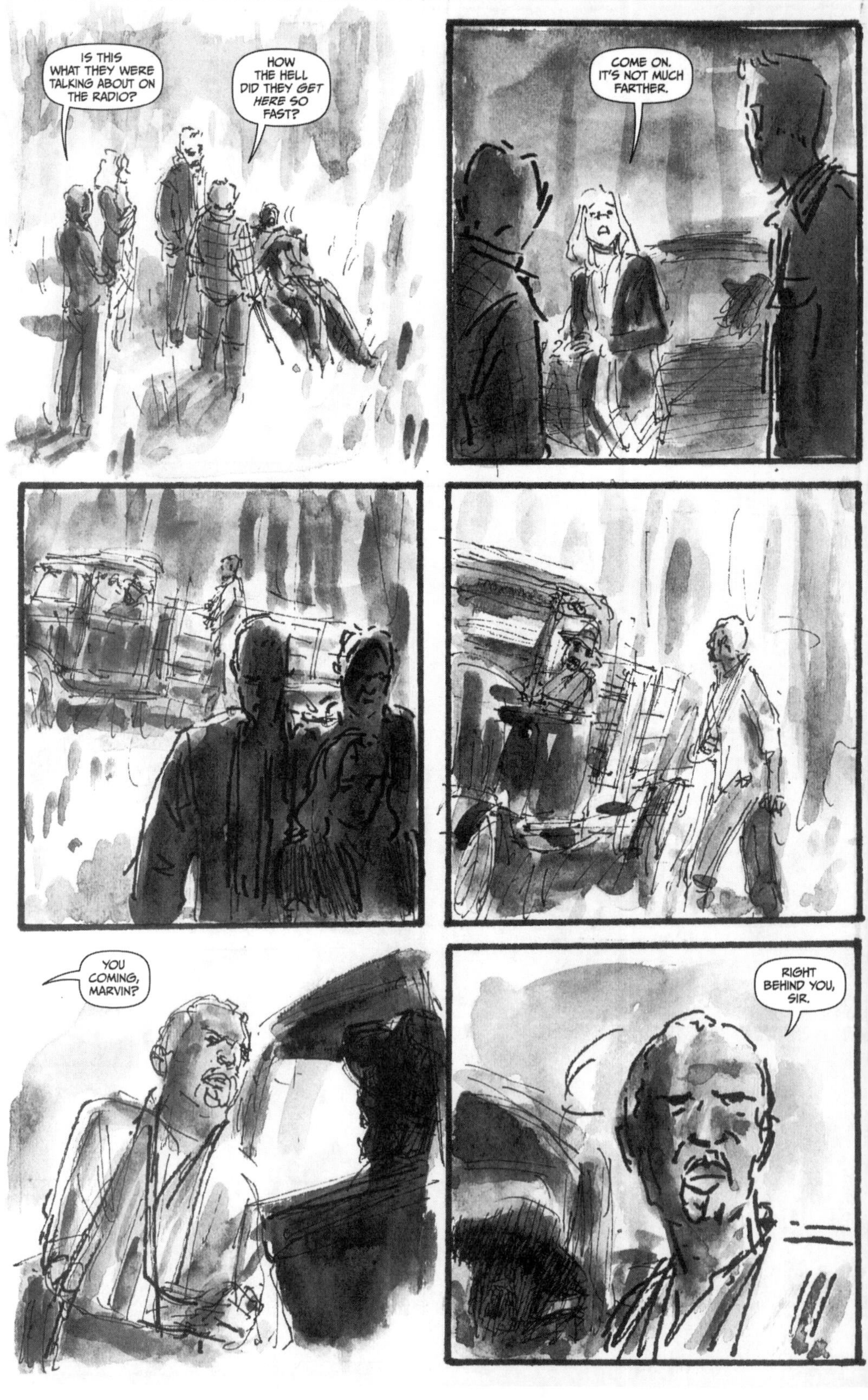
IS THIS WHAT THEY WERE TALKING ABOUT ON THE RADIO?
HOW THE HELL DID THEY *GET HERE* SO FAST?
COME ON. IT'S NOT MUCH FARTHER.
YOU COMING, MARVIN?
RIGHT BEHIND YOU, SIR.

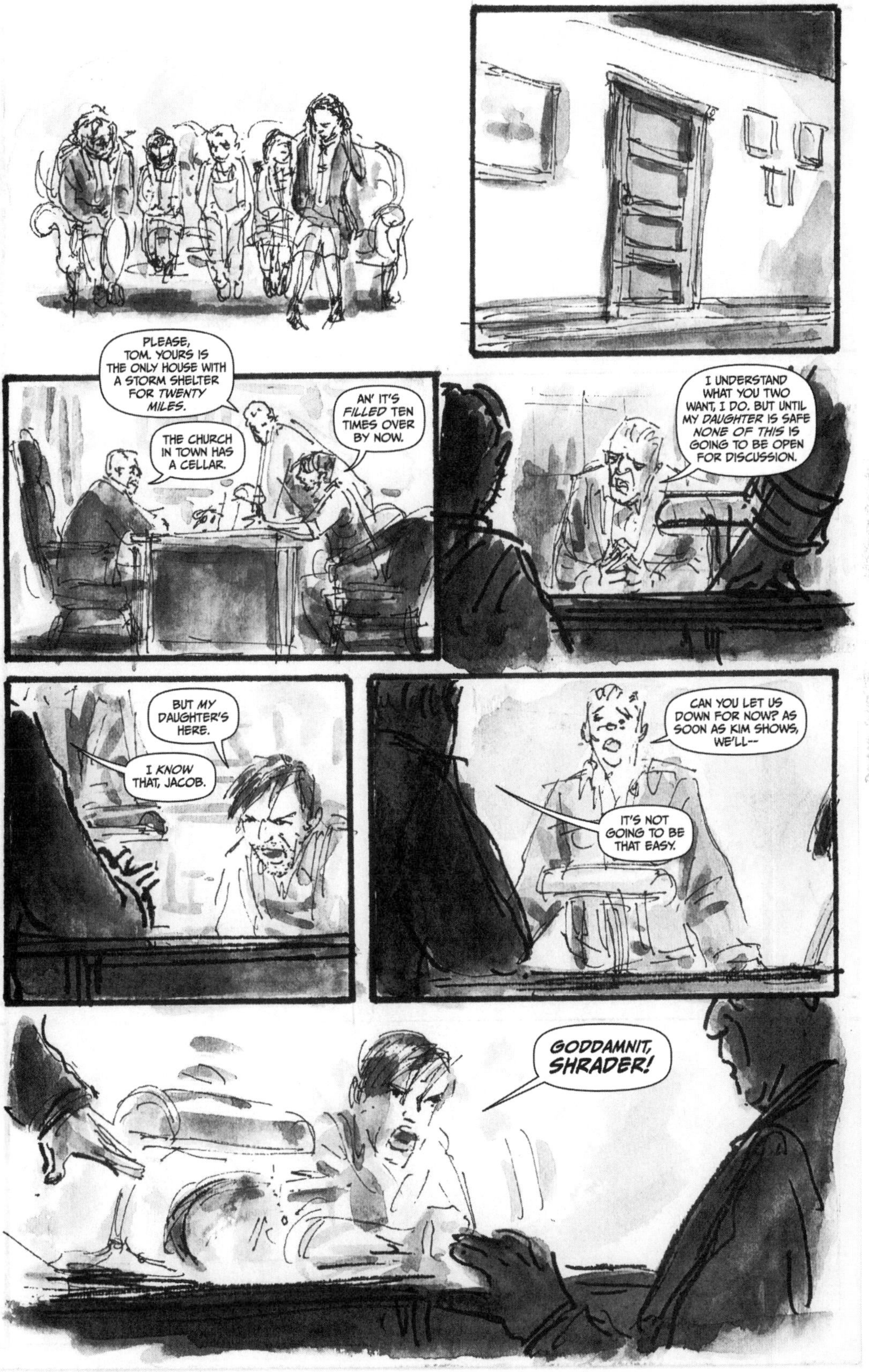
PLEASE, TOM. YOURS IS THE ONLY HOUSE WITH A STORM SHELTER FOR TWENTY MILES.
THE CHURCH IN TOWN HAS A CELLAR.
AN' IT'S FILLED TEN TIMES OVER BY NOW.
I UNDERSTAND WHAT YOU TWO WANT, I DO. BUT UNTIL MY DAUGHTER IS SAFE NONE OF THIS IS GOING TO BE OPEN FOR DISCUSSION.
BUT MY DAUGHTER'S HERE.
I KNOW THAT, JACOB.
CAN YOU LET US DOWN FOR NOW? AS SOON AS KIM SHOWS, WE'LL--
IT'S NOT GOING TO BE THAT EASY.
GODDAMNIT, SHRADER!

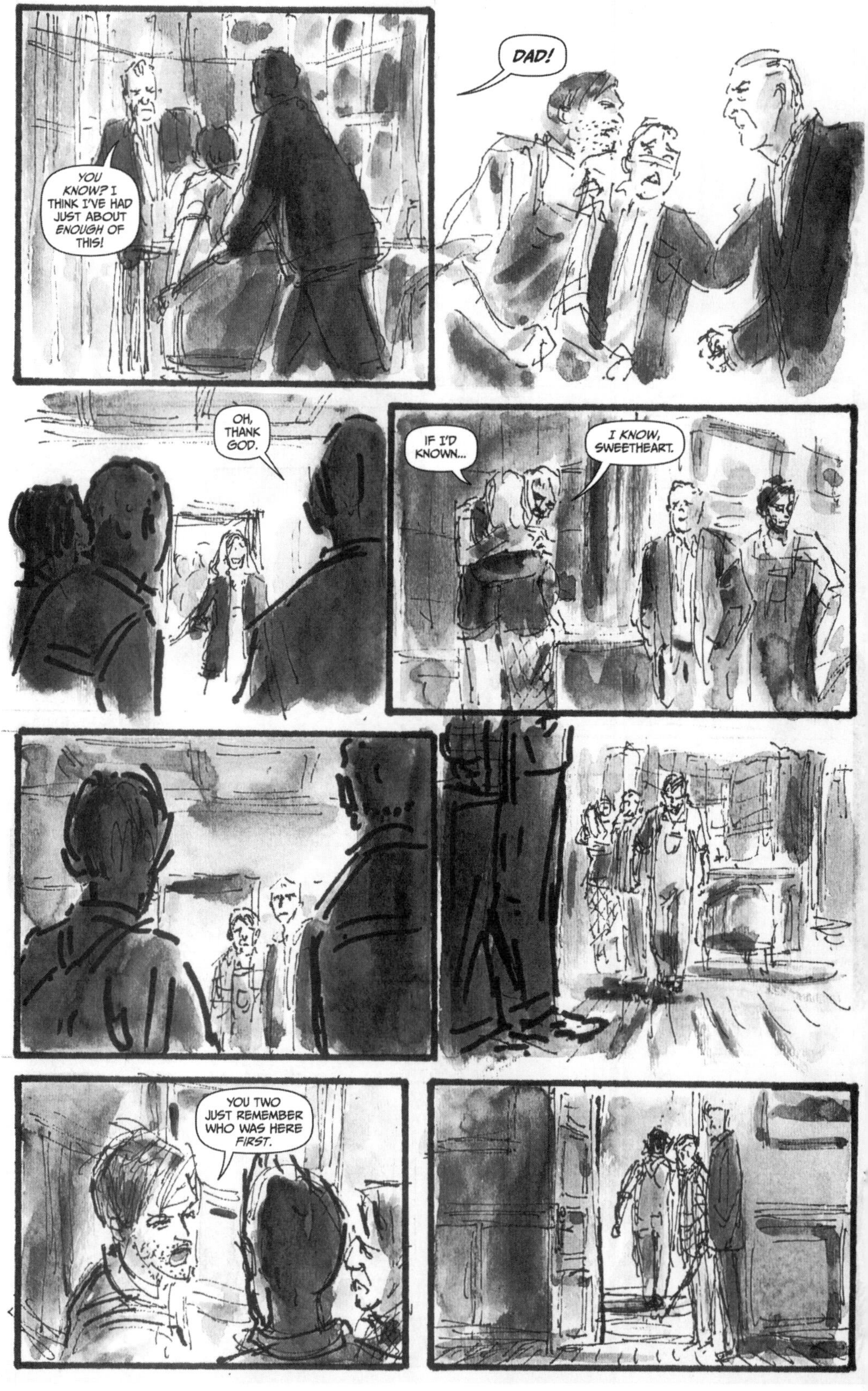
YOU KNOW? I THINK I'VE HAD JUST ABOUT ENOUGH OF THIS!
DAD!
OH, THANK GOD.
IF I'D KNOWN...
I KNOW, SWEETHEART.
YOU TWO JUST REMEMBER WHO WAS HERE FIRST.

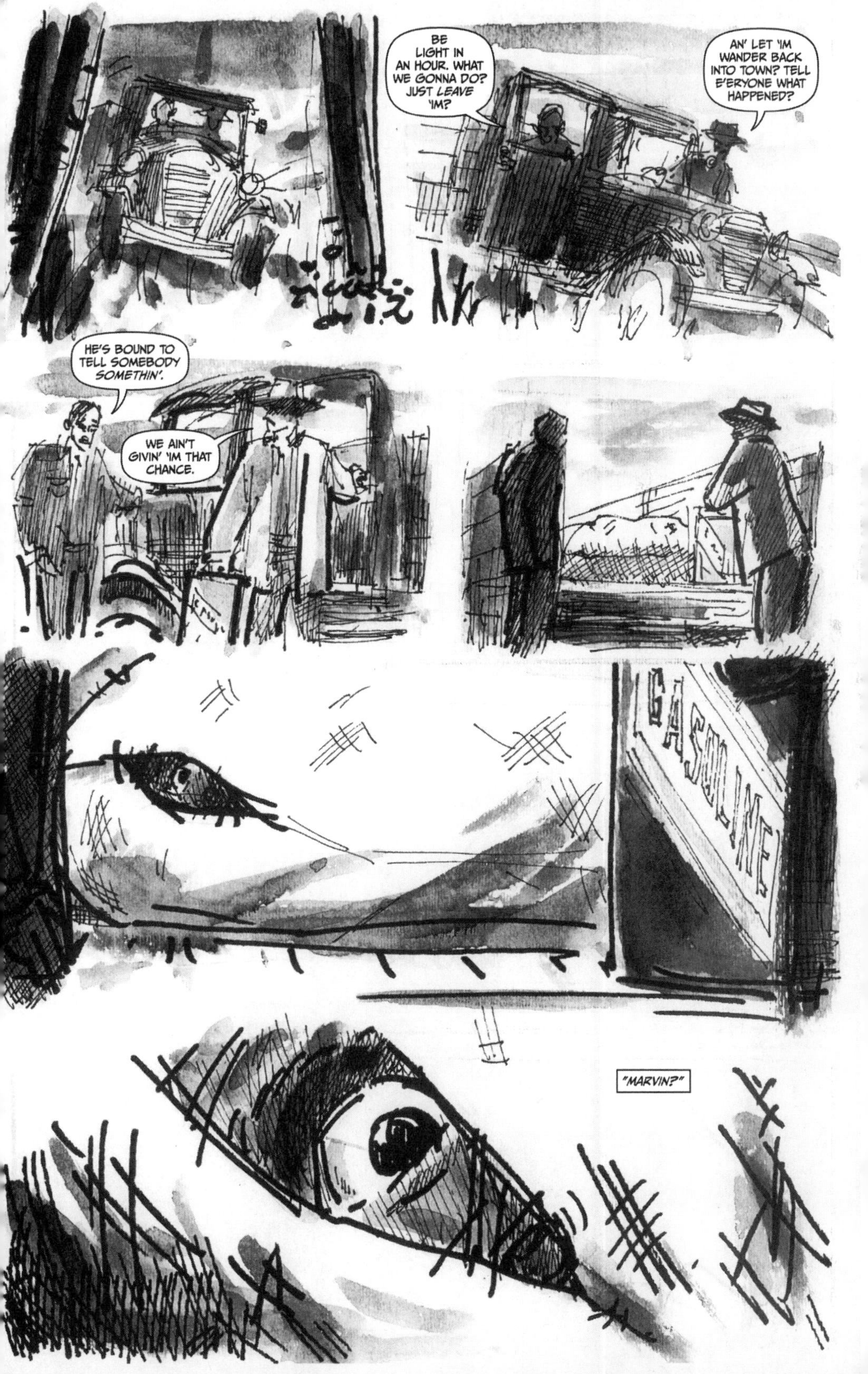
BE LIGHT IN AN HOUR. WHAT WE GONNA DO? JUST *LEAVE* 'IM?
AN' LET 'IM WANDER BACK INTO TOWN? TELL E'ERYONE WHAT HAPPENED?
HE'S BOUND TO TELL SOMEBODY *SOMETHIN'*.
WE AIN'T GIVIN' 'IM THAT CHANCE.
GASOLINE
"MARVIN?"

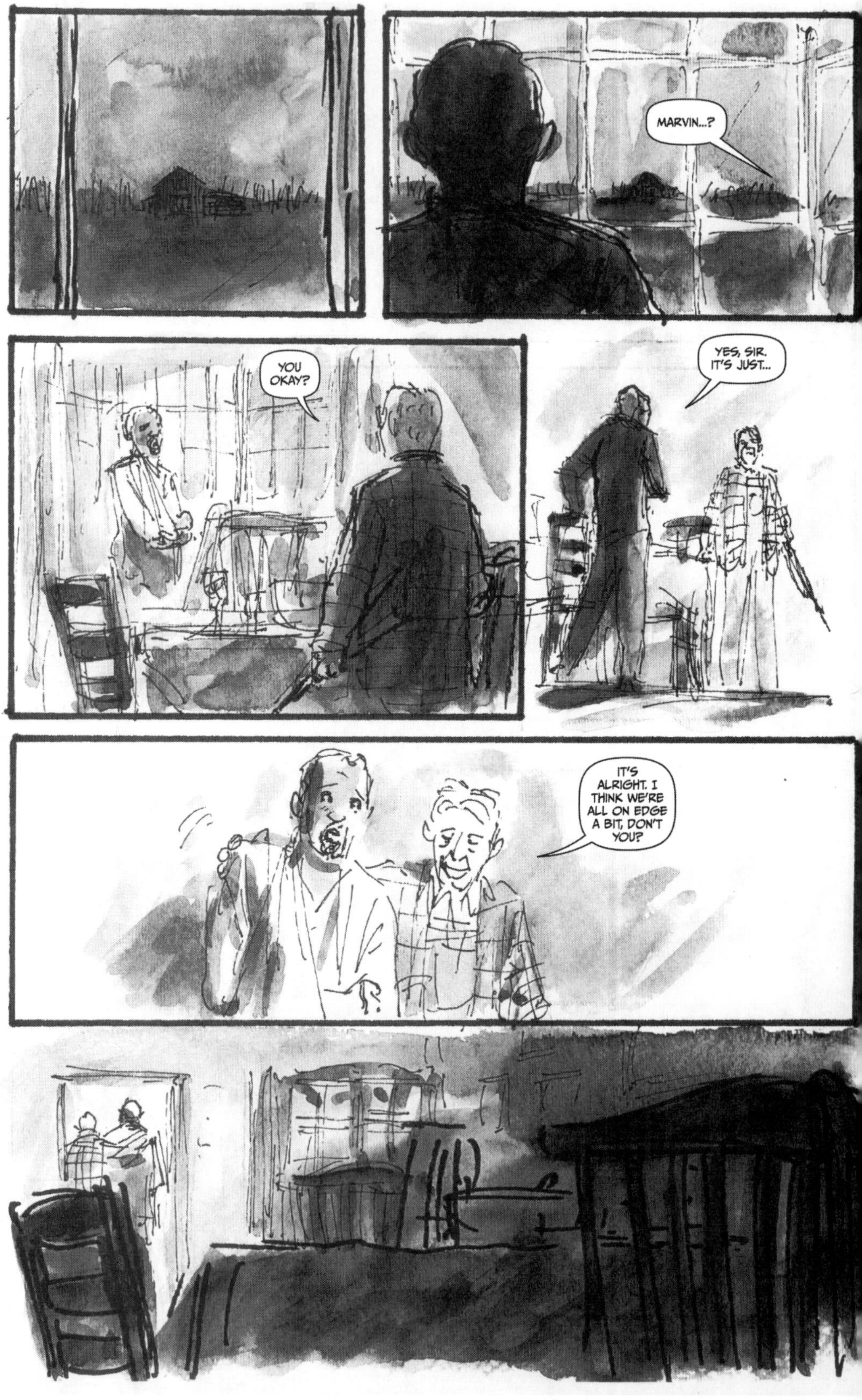

MARVIN...?
YOU OKAY?
YES, SIR. IT'S JUST...
IT'S ALRIGHT. I THINK WE'RE ALL ON EDGE A BIT, DON'T YOU?

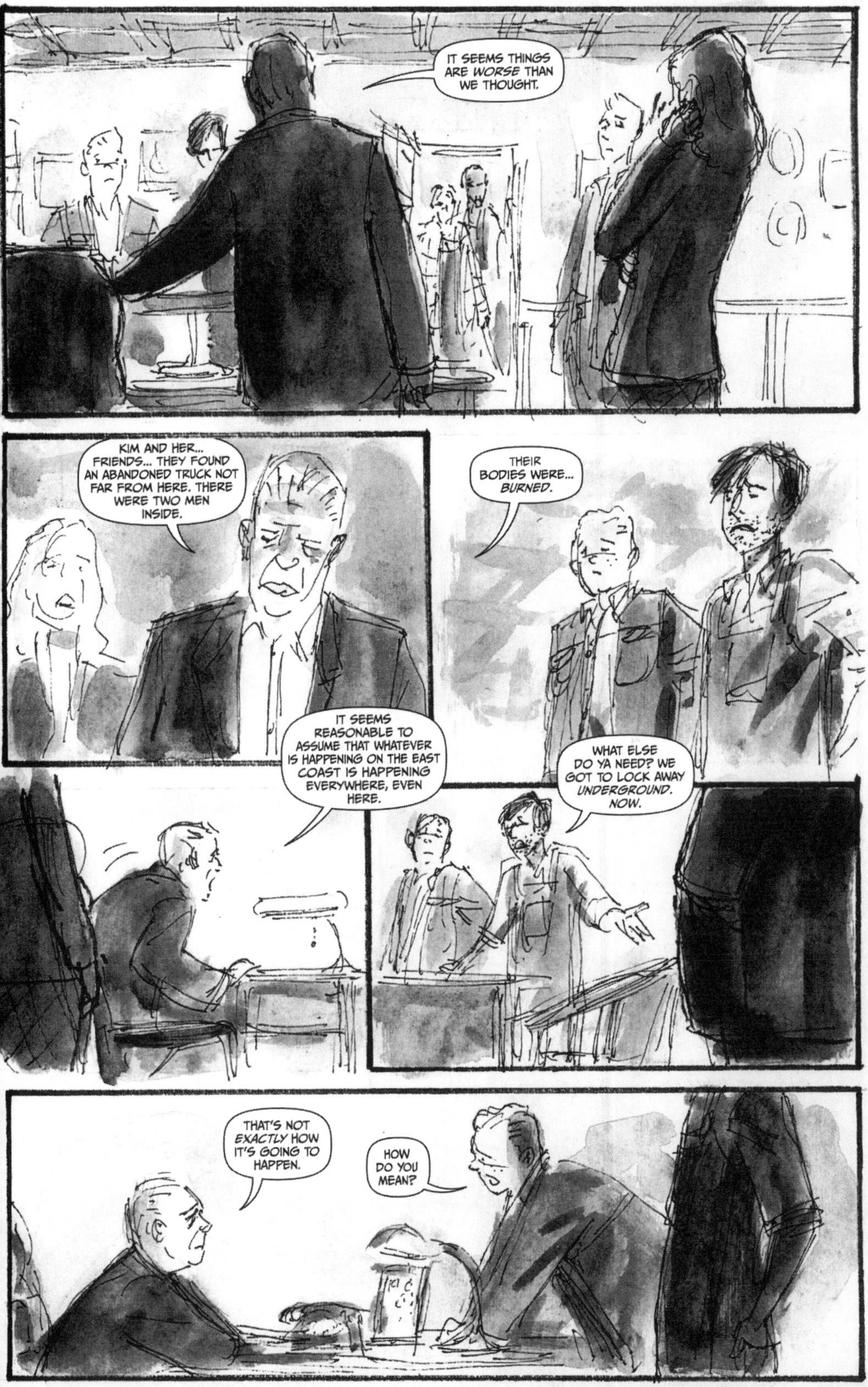
IT SEEMS THINGS ARE *WORSE* THAN WE THOUGHT.
KIM AND HER... FRIENDS... THEY FOUND AN ABANDONED TRUCK NOT FAR FROM HERE. THERE WERE TWO MEN INSIDE.
THEIR BODIES WERE... *BURNED*.
IT SEEMS REASONABLE TO ASSUME THAT WHATEVER IS HAPPENING ON THE EAST COAST IS HAPPENING EVERYWHERE, EVEN HERE.
WHAT ELSE DO YA NEED? WE GOT TO LOCK AWAY *UNDERGROUND*. *NOW*.
THAT'S NOT *EXACTLY* HOW IT'S GOING TO HAPPEN.
HOW DO YOU MEAN?

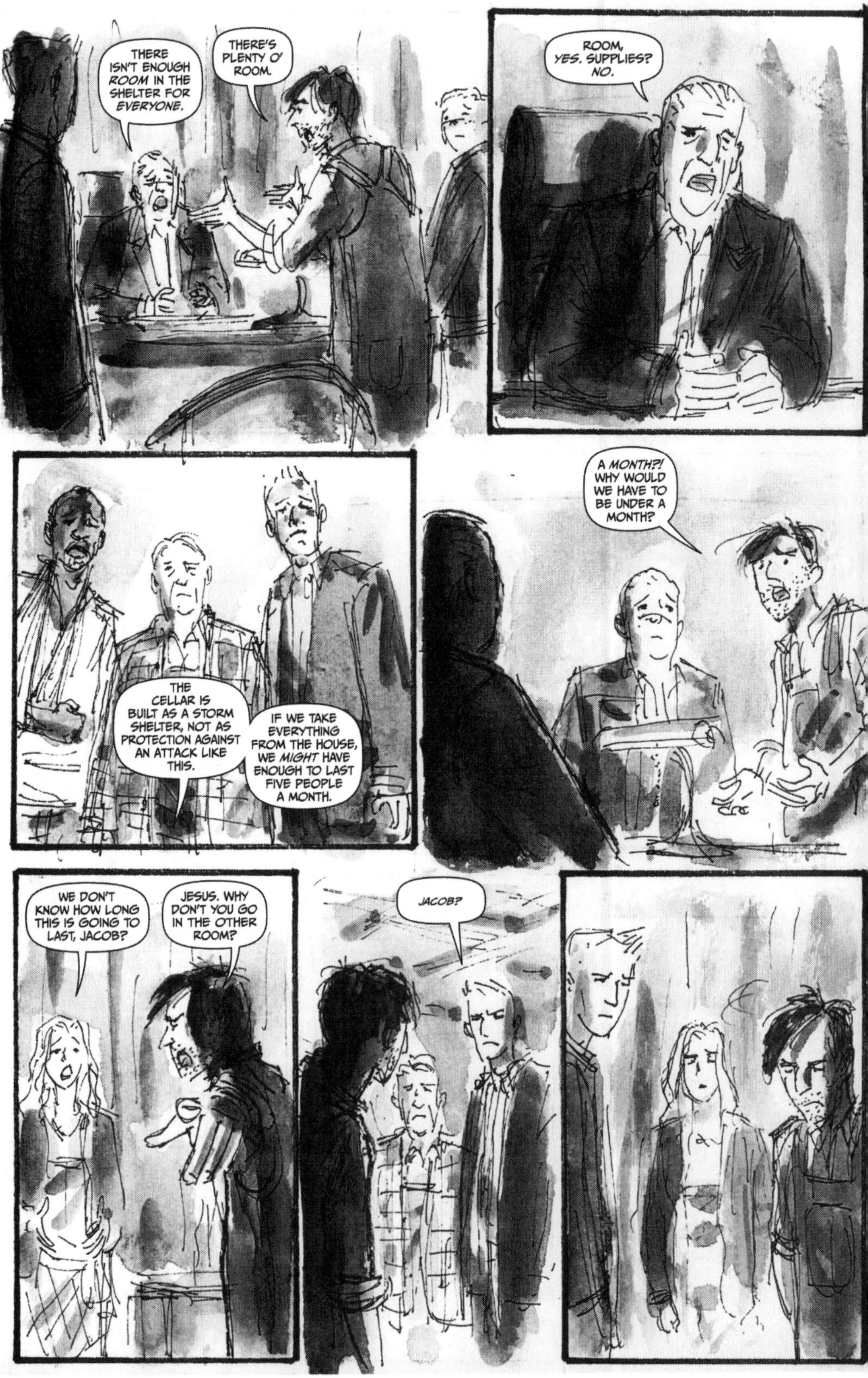
THERE ISN'T ENOUGH *ROOM* IN THE SHELTER FOR *EVERYONE*.
THERE'S PLENTY O' ROOM.
ROOM, *YES*. SUPPLIES? *NO*.
THE CELLAR IS BUILT AS A STORM SHELTER, NOT AS PROTECTION AGAINST AN ATTACK LIKE THIS.
IF WE TAKE EVERYTHING FROM THE HOUSE, WE *MIGHT* HAVE ENOUGH TO LAST FIVE PEOPLE A MONTH.
A *MONTH?!* WHY WOULD WE HAVE TO BE UNDER A MONTH?
WE DON'T KNOW HOW LONG THIS IS GOING TO LAST, JACOB?
JESUS. WHY DON'T YOU GO IN THE OTHER ROOM?
JACOB?

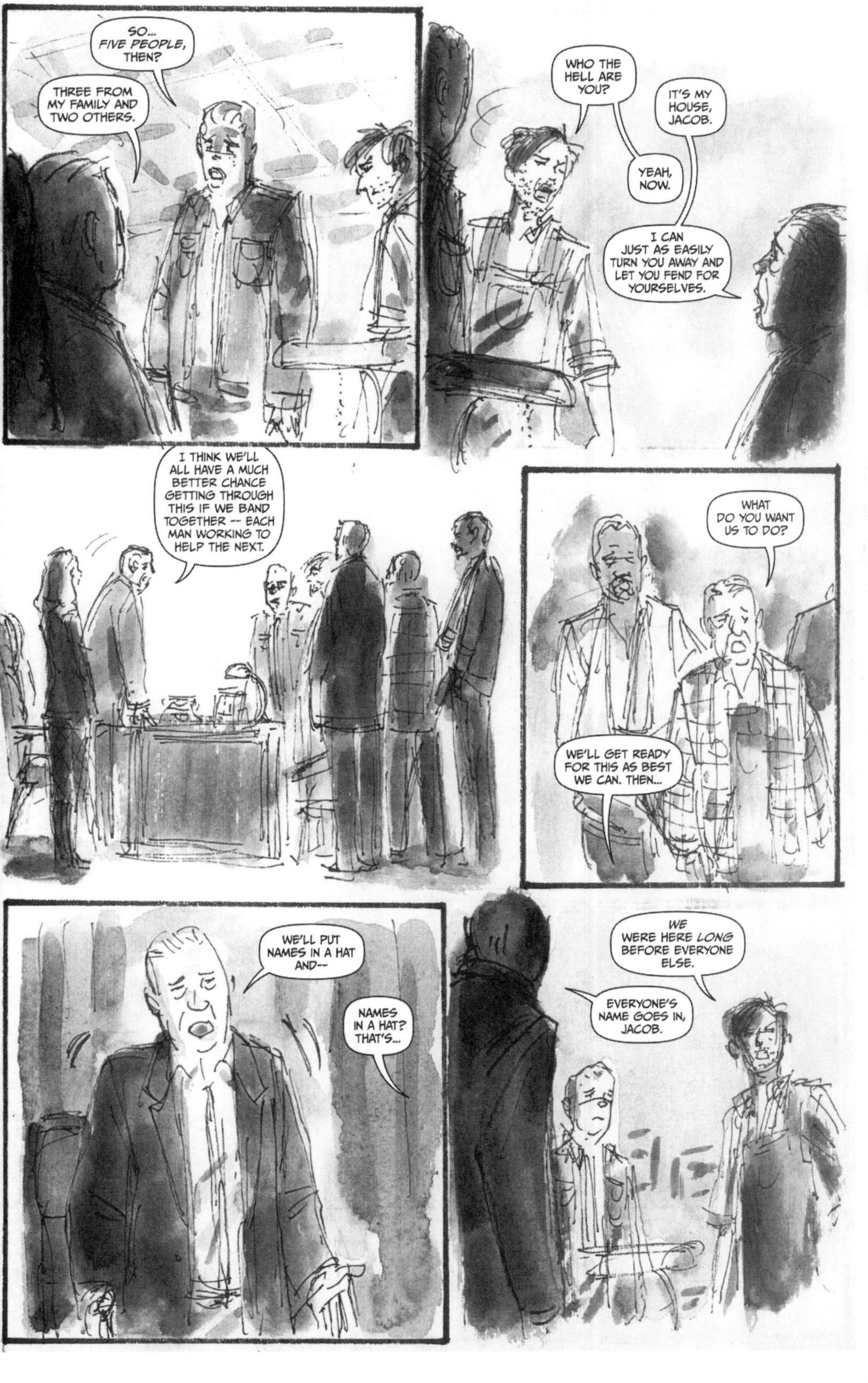
SO... FIVE PEOPLE, THEN?
THREE FROM MY FAMILY AND TWO OTHERS.
WHO THE HELL ARE YOU?
IT'S MY HOUSE, JACOB.
YEAH, NOW.
I CAN JUST AS EASILY TURN YOU AWAY AND LET YOU FEND FOR YOURSELVES.
I THINK WE'LL ALL HAVE A MUCH BETTER CHANCE GETTING THROUGH THIS IF WE BAND TOGETHER -- EACH MAN WORKING TO HELP THE NEXT.
WHAT DO YOU WANT US TO DO?
WE'LL GET READY FOR THIS AS BEST WE CAN. THEN...
WE'LL PUT NAMES IN A HAT AND--
NAMES IN A HAT? THAT'S...
WE WERE HERE LONG BEFORE EVERYONE ELSE.
EVERYONE'S NAME GOES IN, JACOB.

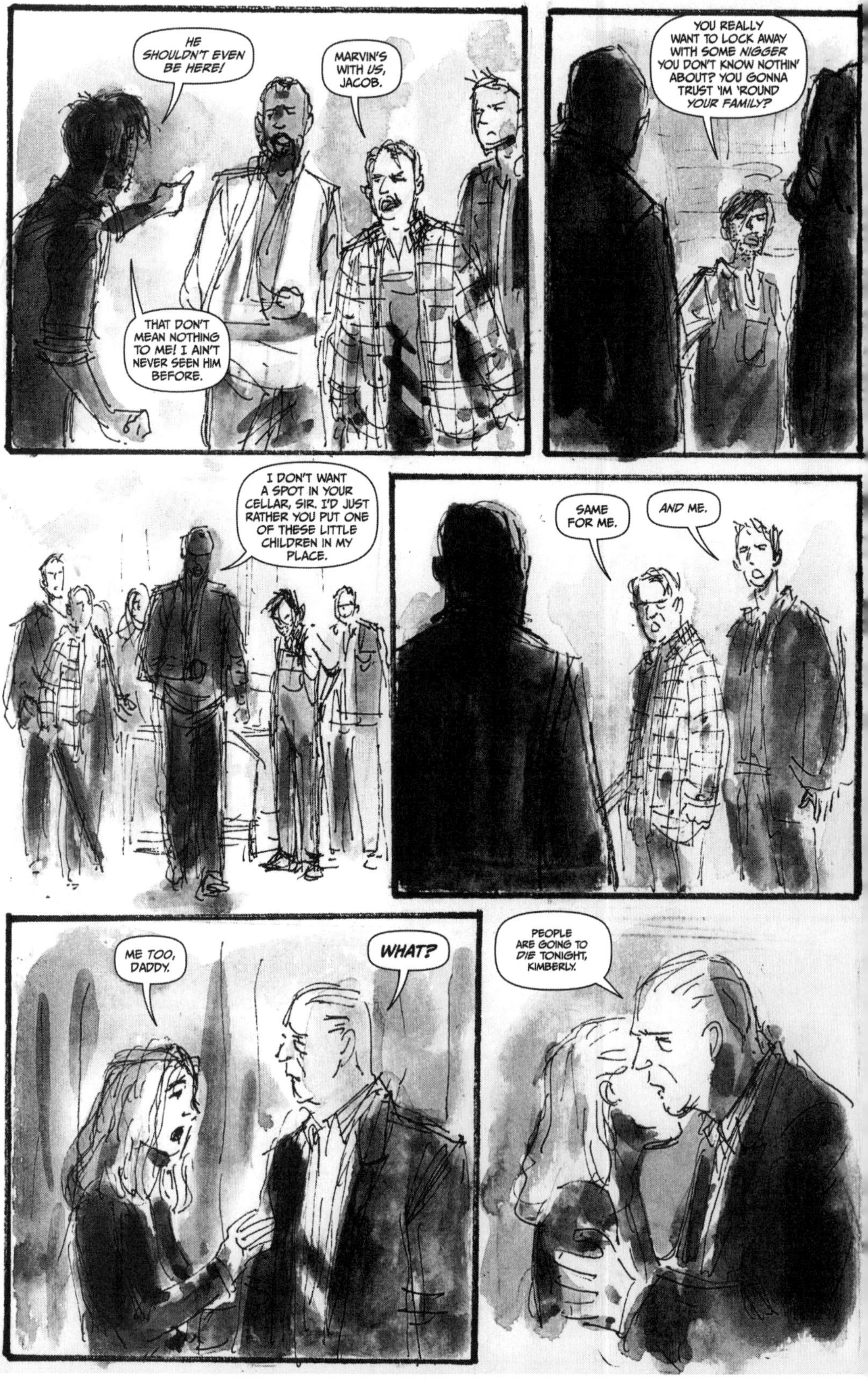
HE SHOULDN'T EVEN BE HERE!
MARVIN'S WITH US, JACOB.
THAT DON'T MEAN NOTHING TO ME! I AIN'T NEVER SEEN HIM BEFORE.
YOU REALLY WANT TO LOCK AWAY WITH SOME NIGGER YOU DON'T KNOW NOTHIN' ABOUT? YOU GONNA TRUST 'IM 'ROUND YOUR FAMILY?
I DON'T WANT A SPOT IN YOUR CELLAR, SIR. I'D JUST RATHER YOU PUT ONE OF THESE LITTLE CHILDREN IN MY PLACE.
SAME FOR ME.
AND ME.
ME TOO, DADDY.
WHAT?
PEOPLE ARE GOING TO DIE TONIGHT, KIMBERLY.

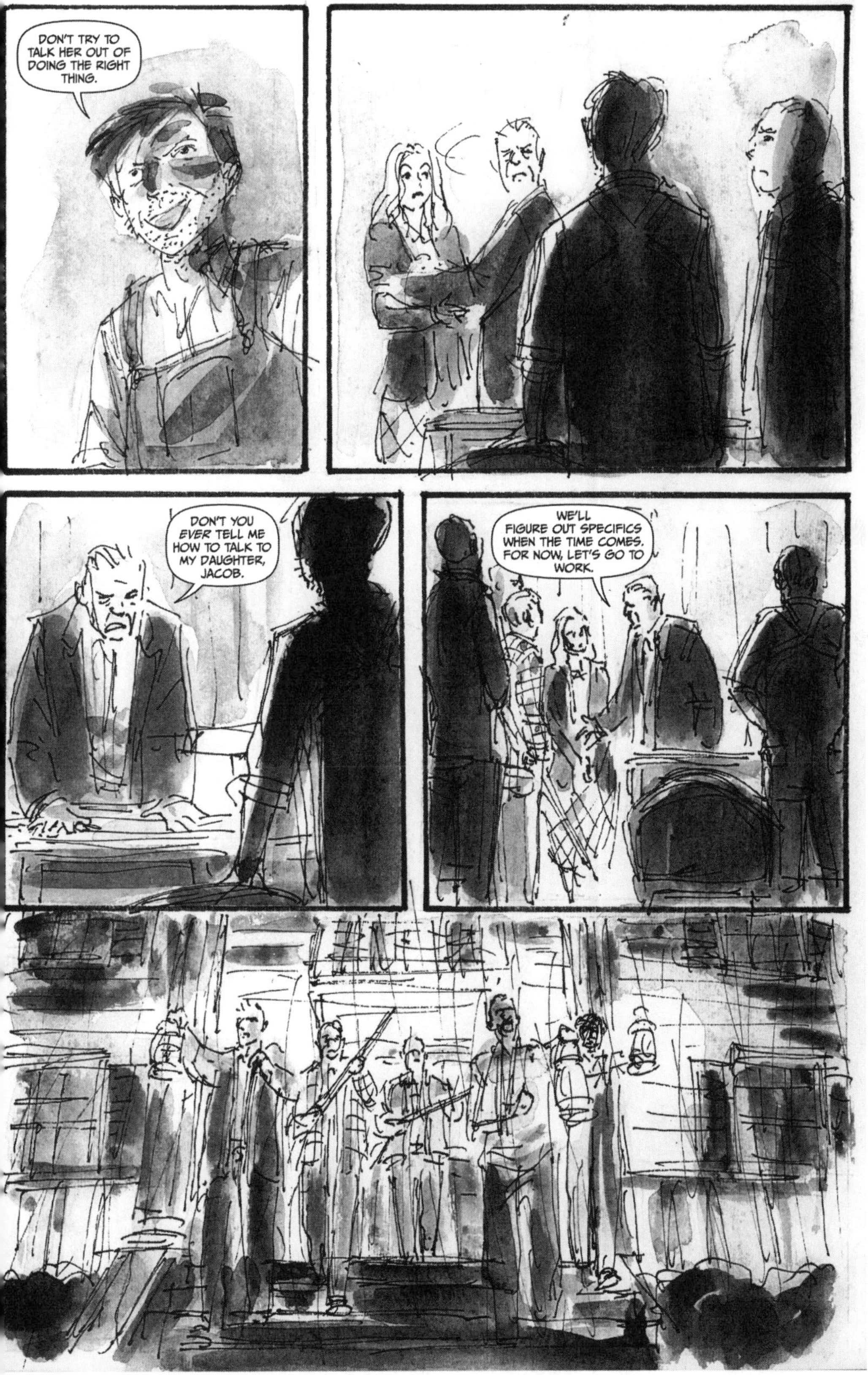
DON'T TRY TO TALK HER OUT OF DOING THE RIGHT THING.
DON'T YOU *EVER* TELL ME HOW TO TALK TO MY DAUGHTER, JACOB.
WE'LL FIGURE OUT SPECIFICS WHEN THE TIME COMES. FOR NOW, LET'S GO TO WORK.

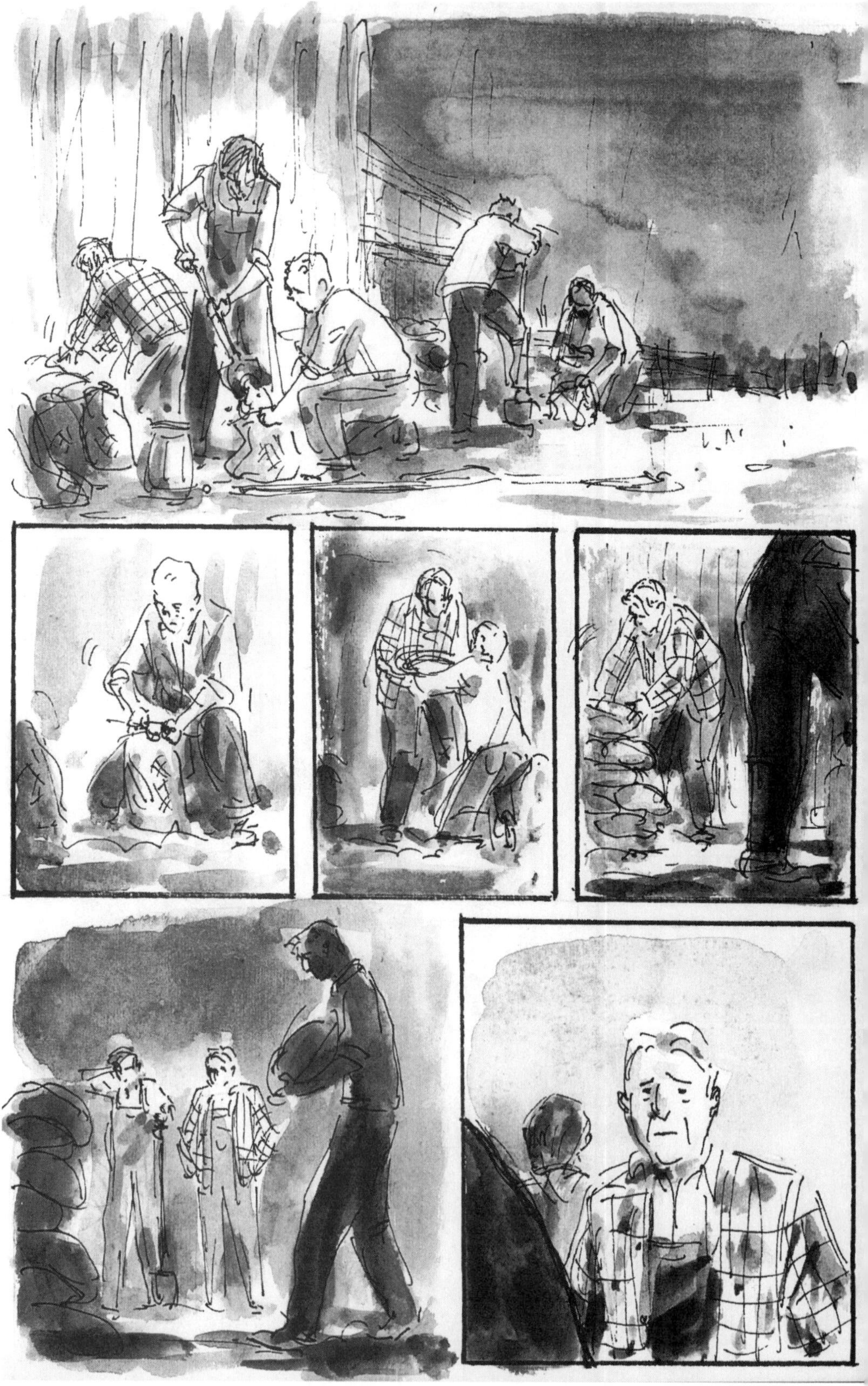

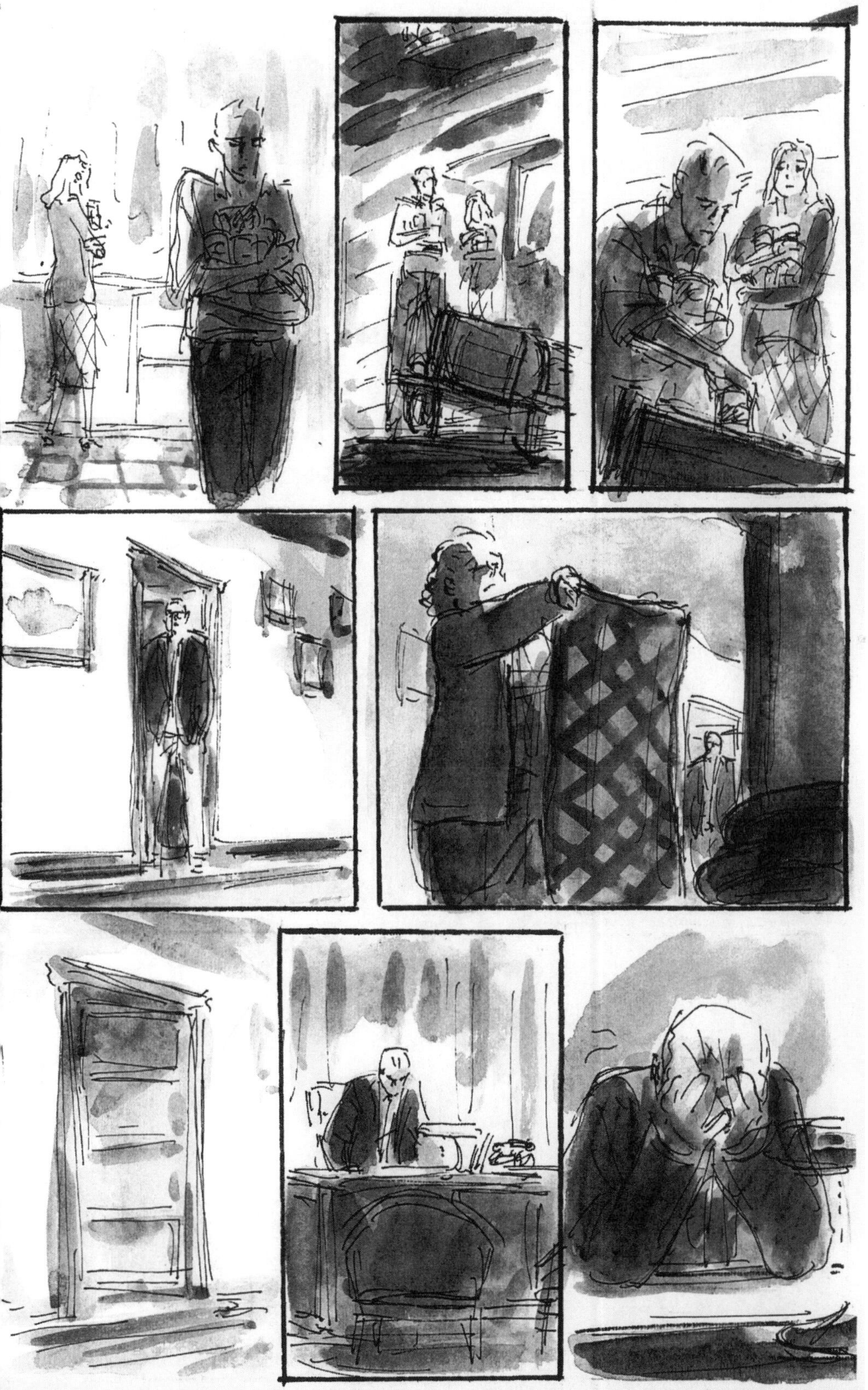

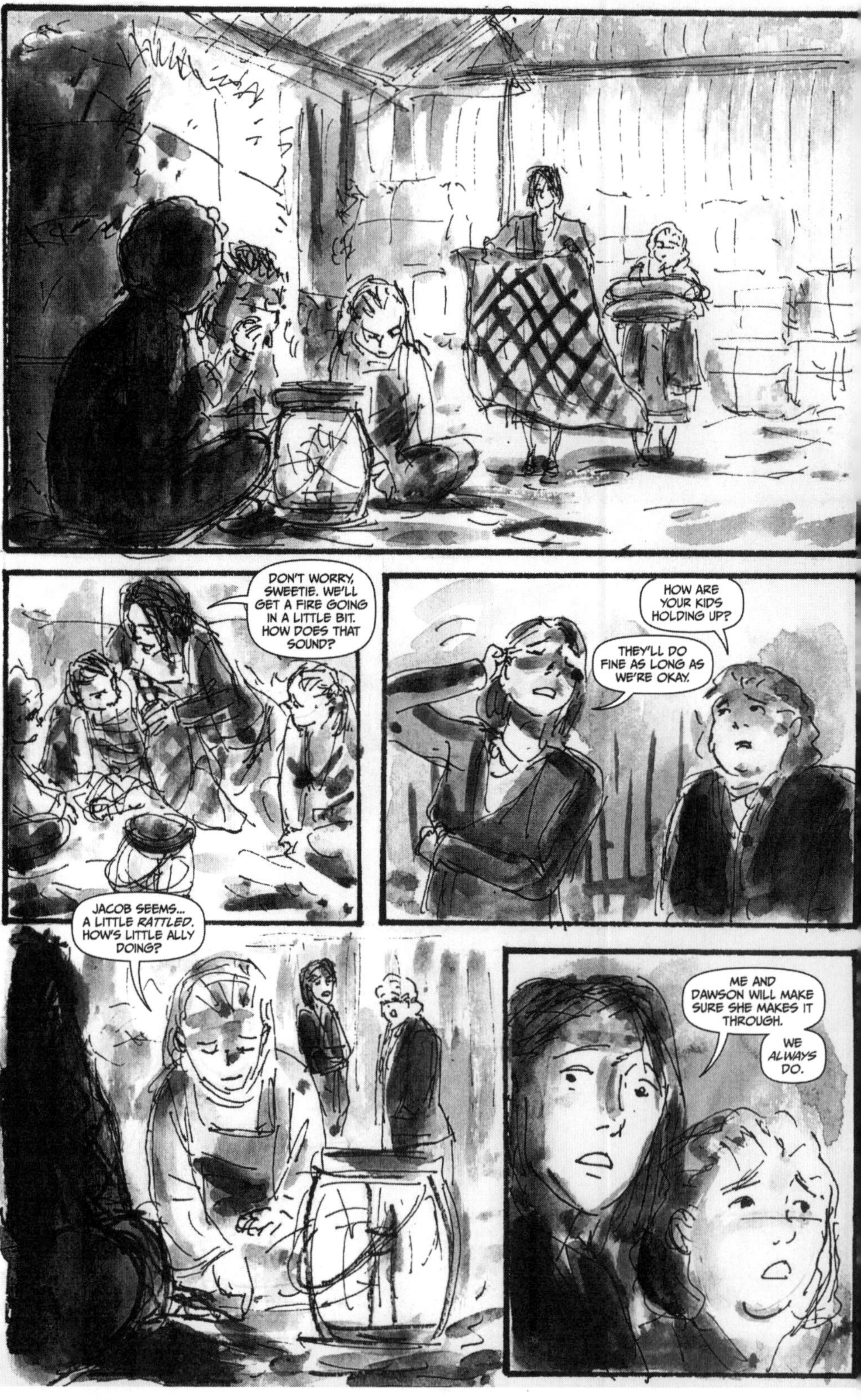
DON'T WORRY, SWEETIE. WE'LL GET A FIRE GOING IN A LITTLE BIT. HOW DOES THAT SOUND?
HOW ARE YOUR KIDS HOLDING UP?
THEY'LL DO FINE AS LONG AS WE'RE OKAY.
JACOB SEEMS... A LITTLE *RATTLED*. HOW'S LITTLE ALLY DOING?
ME AND DAWSON WILL MAKE SURE SHE MAKES IT THROUGH.
WE *ALWAYS* DO.

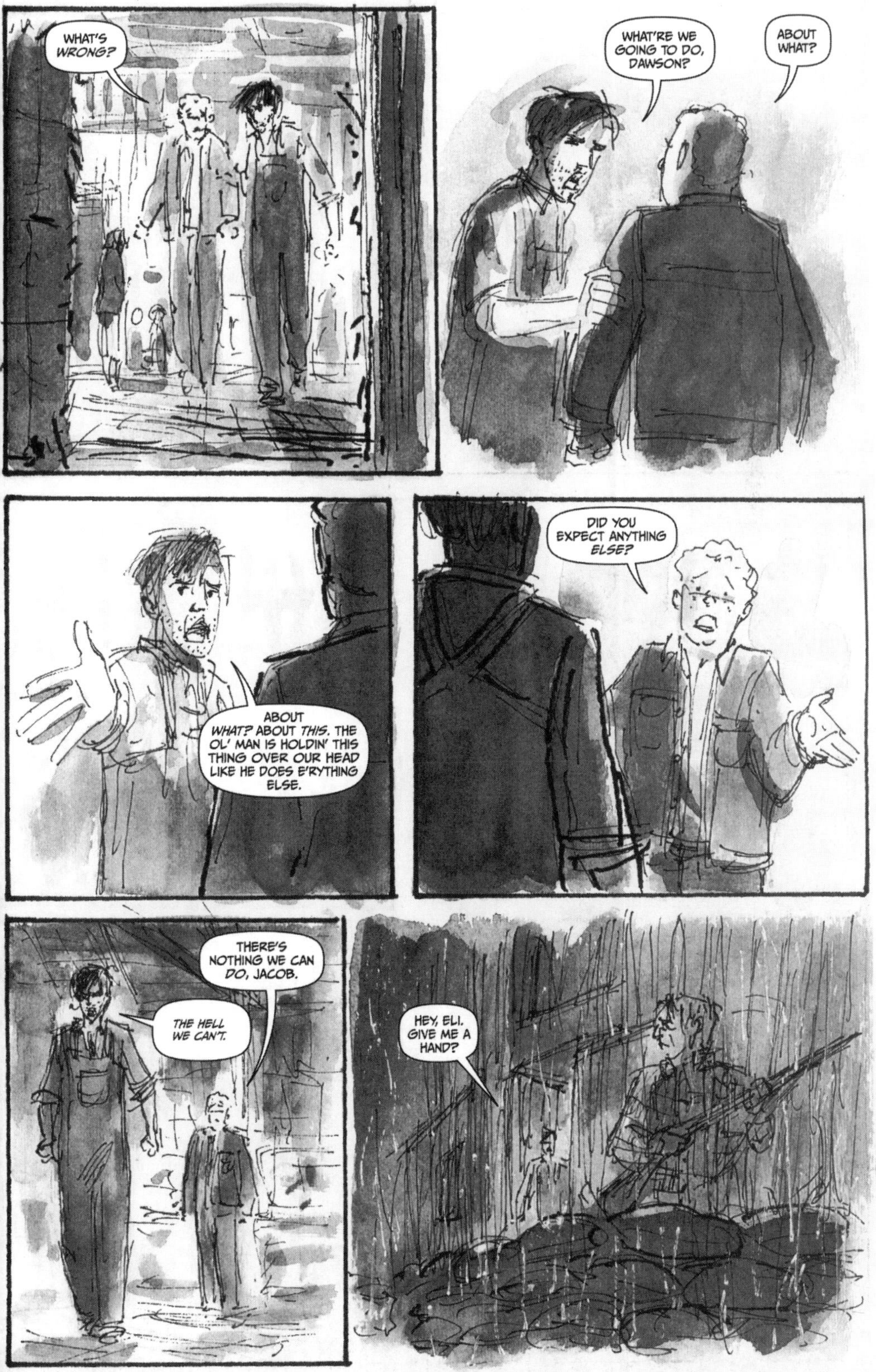
WHAT'S WRONG?
WHAT'RE WE GOING TO DO, DAWSON?
ABOUT WHAT?
ABOUT WHAT? ABOUT THIS. THE OL' MAN IS HOLDIN' THIS THING OVER OUR HEAD LIKE HE DOES E'RYTHING ELSE.
DID YOU EXPECT ANYTHING ELSE?
THERE'S NOTHING WE CAN DO, JACOB.
THE HELL WE CAN'T.
HEY, ELI. GIVE ME A HAND?

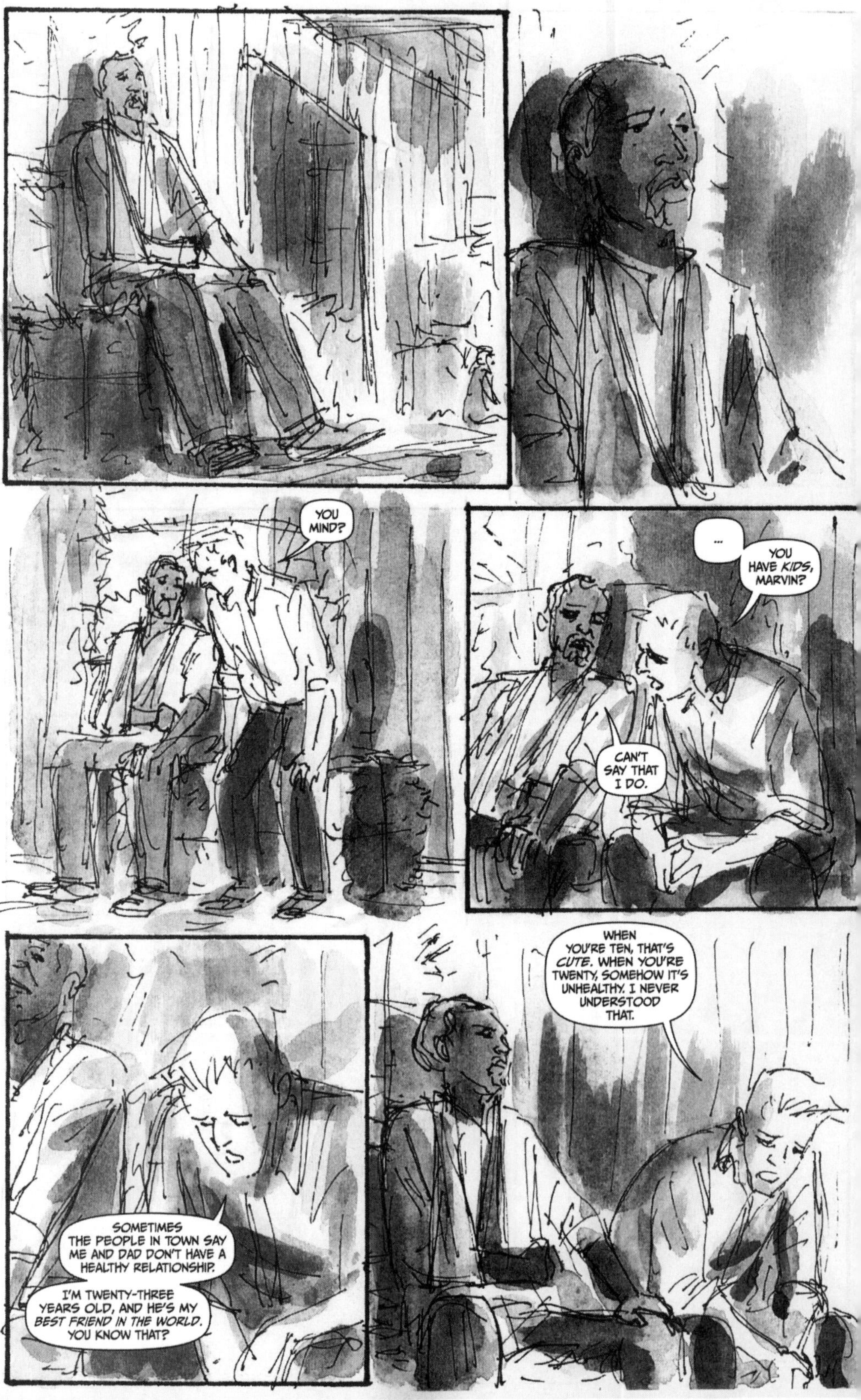
YOU MIND?
...
YOU HAVE *KIDS*, MARVIN?
CAN'T SAY THAT I DO.
SOMETIMES THE PEOPLE IN TOWN SAY ME AND DAD DON'T HAVE A HEALTHY RELATIONSHIP.
I'M TWENTY-THREE YEARS OLD, AND HE'S MY *BEST FRIEND IN THE WORLD.* YOU KNOW THAT?
WHEN YOU'RE TEN, THAT'S *CUTE*. WHEN YOU'RE TWENTY, SOMEHOW IT'S UNHEALTHY. I NEVER UNDERSTOOD THAT.

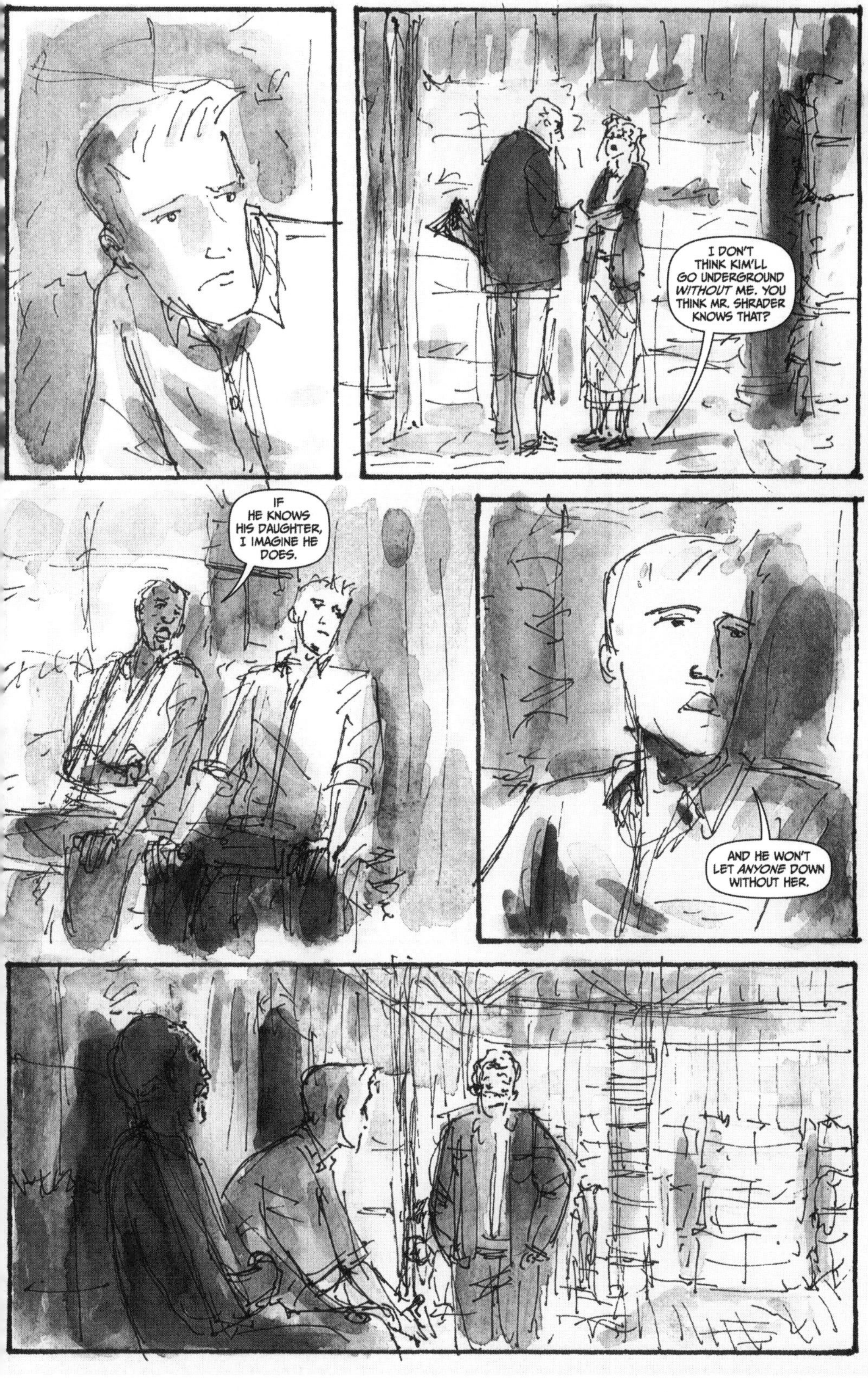
I DON'T THINK KIM'LL GO UNDERGROUND *WITHOUT* ME. YOU THINK MR. SHRADER KNOWS THAT?
IF HE KNOWS HIS DAUGHTER, I IMAGINE HE DOES.
AND HE WON'T LET *ANYONE* DOWN WITHOUT HER.

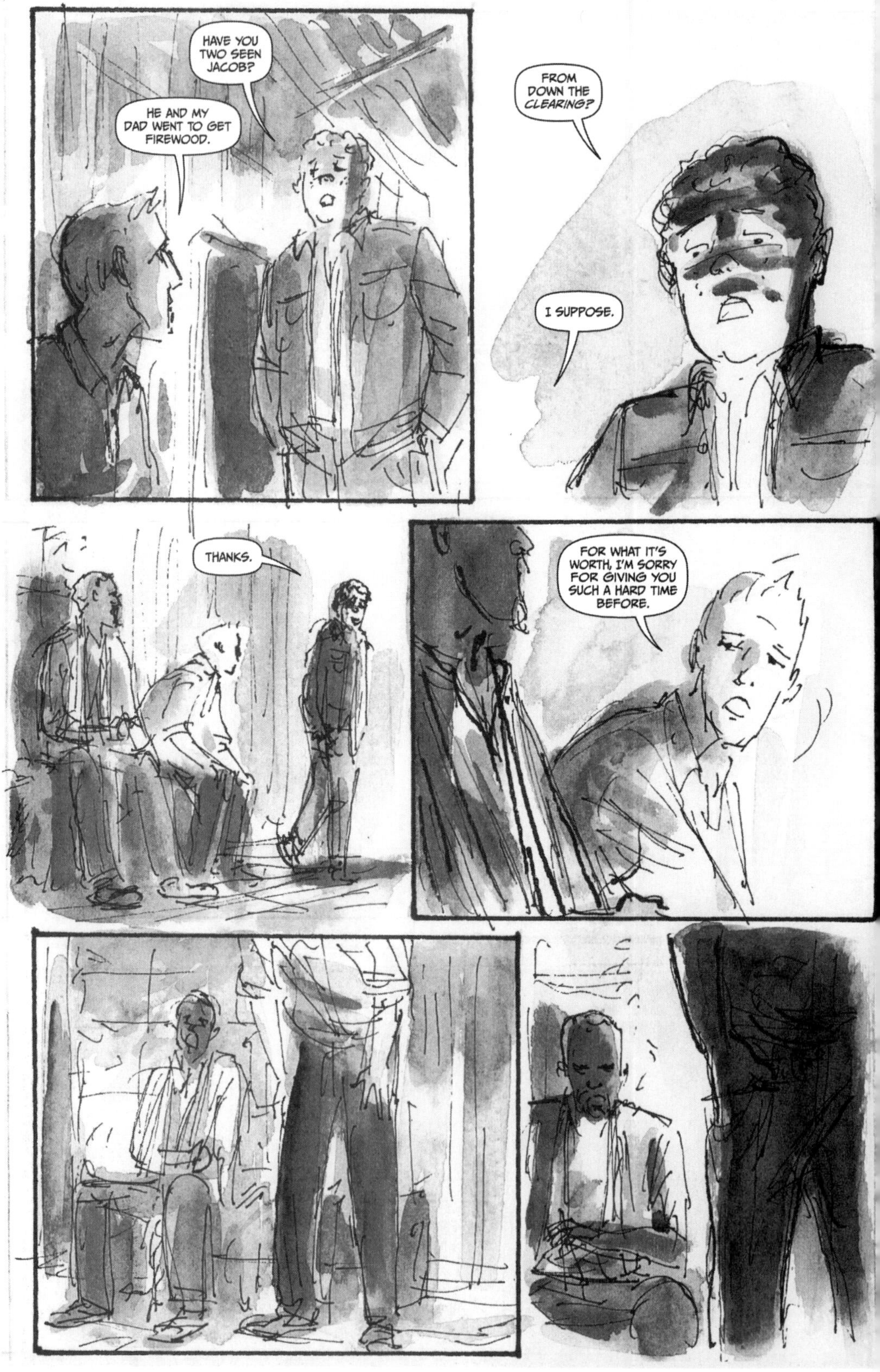
HAVE YOU TWO SEEN JACOB?
HE AND MY DAD WENT TO GET FIREWOOD.
FROM DOWN THE *CLEARING?*
I SUPPOSE.
THANKS.
FOR WHAT IT'S WORTH, I'M SORRY FOR GIVING YOU SUCH A HARD TIME BEFORE.

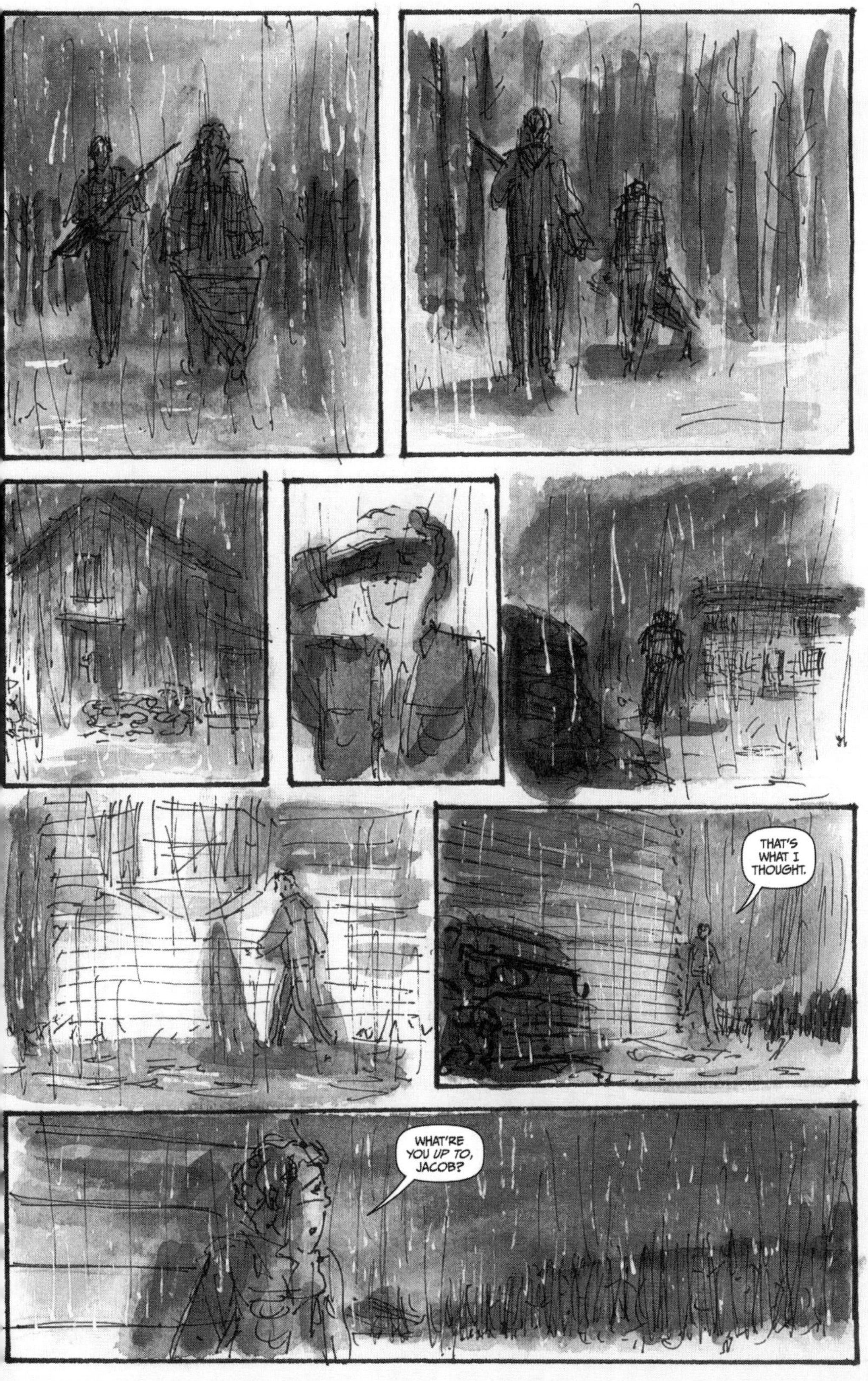
THAT'S WHAT I THOUGHT.
WHAT'RE YOU UP TO, JACOB?

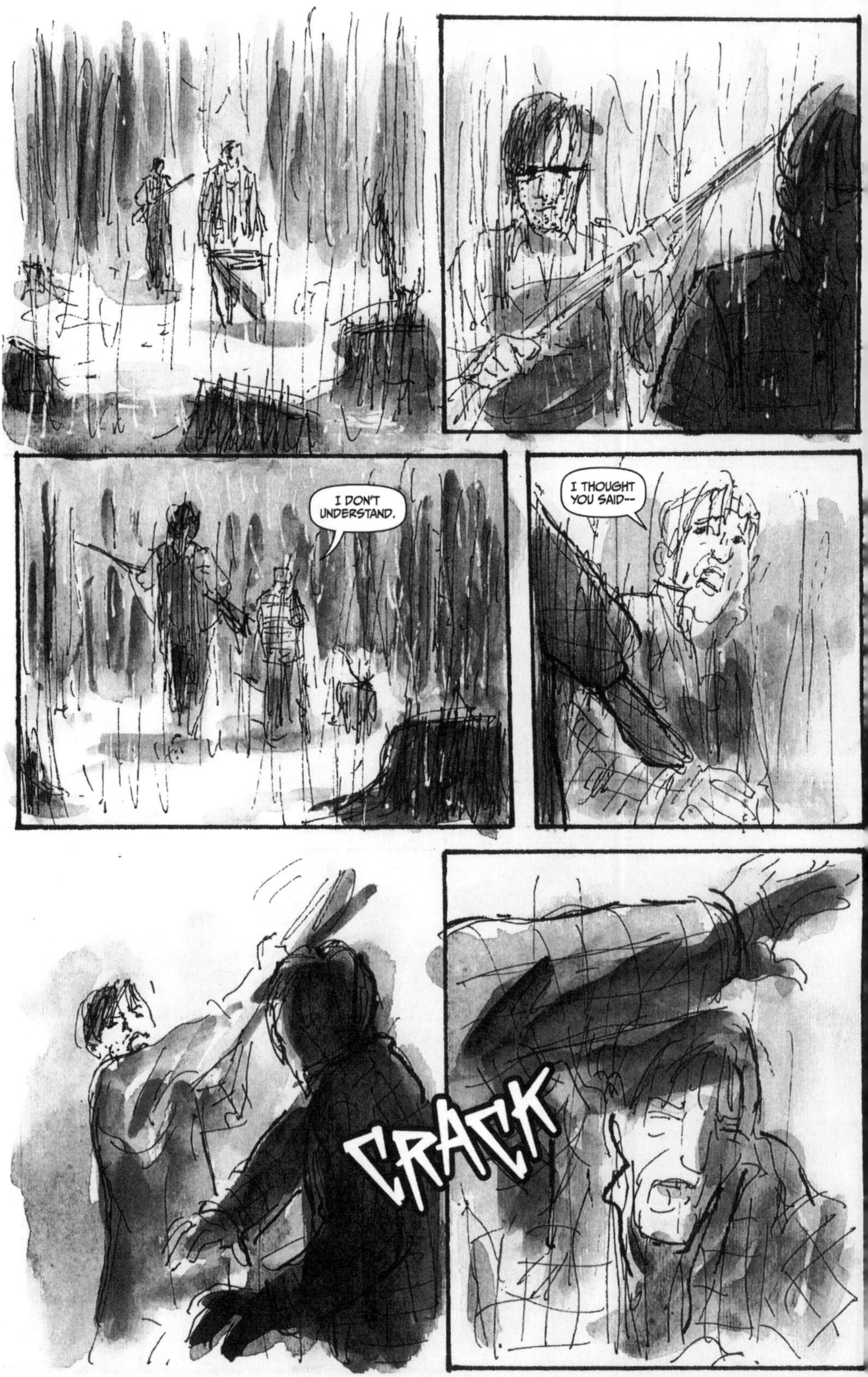
I DON'T UNDERSTAND.
I THOUGHT YOU SAID--
CRACK

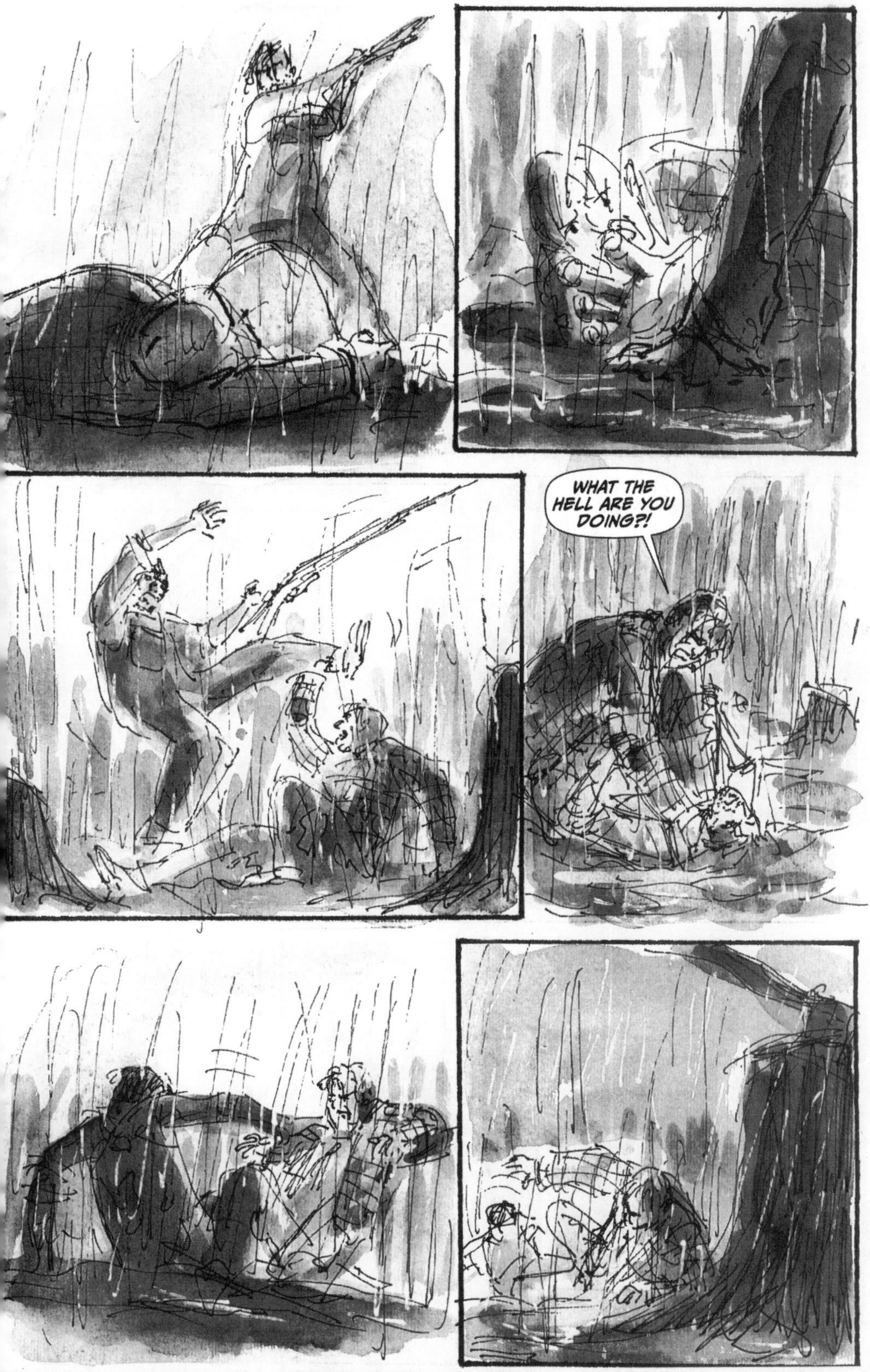
WHAT THE HELL ARE YOU DOING?!

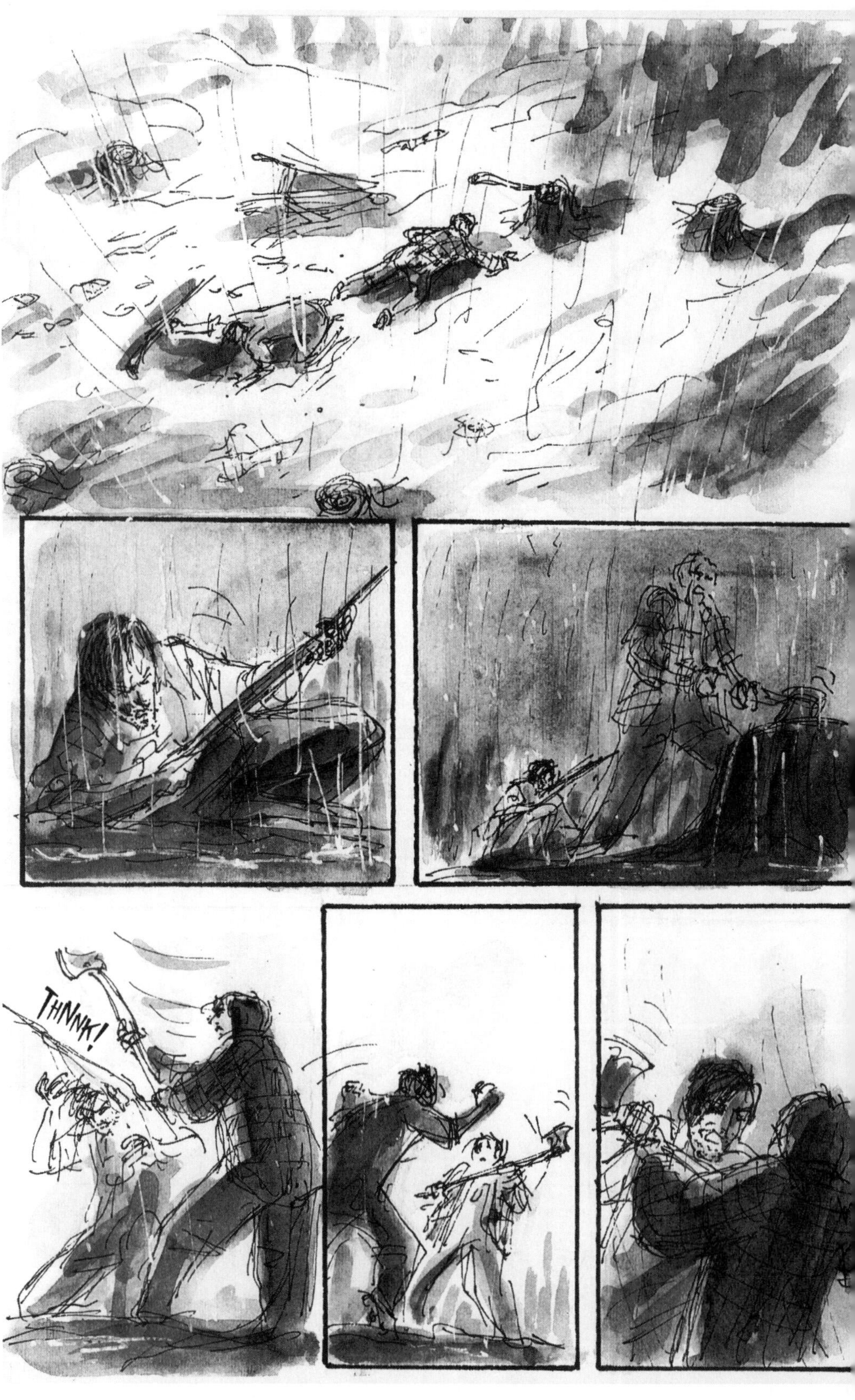
THNNK!

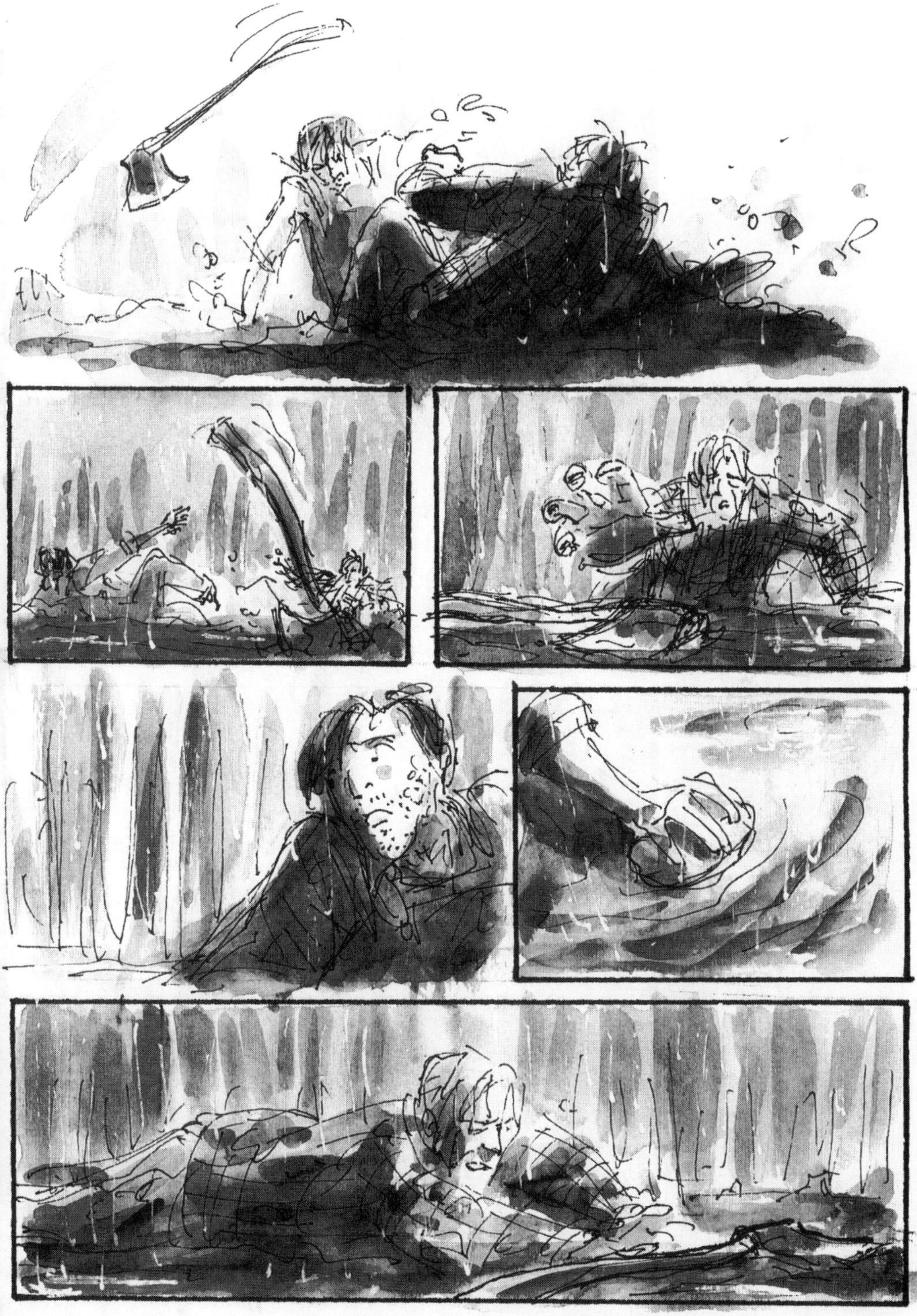

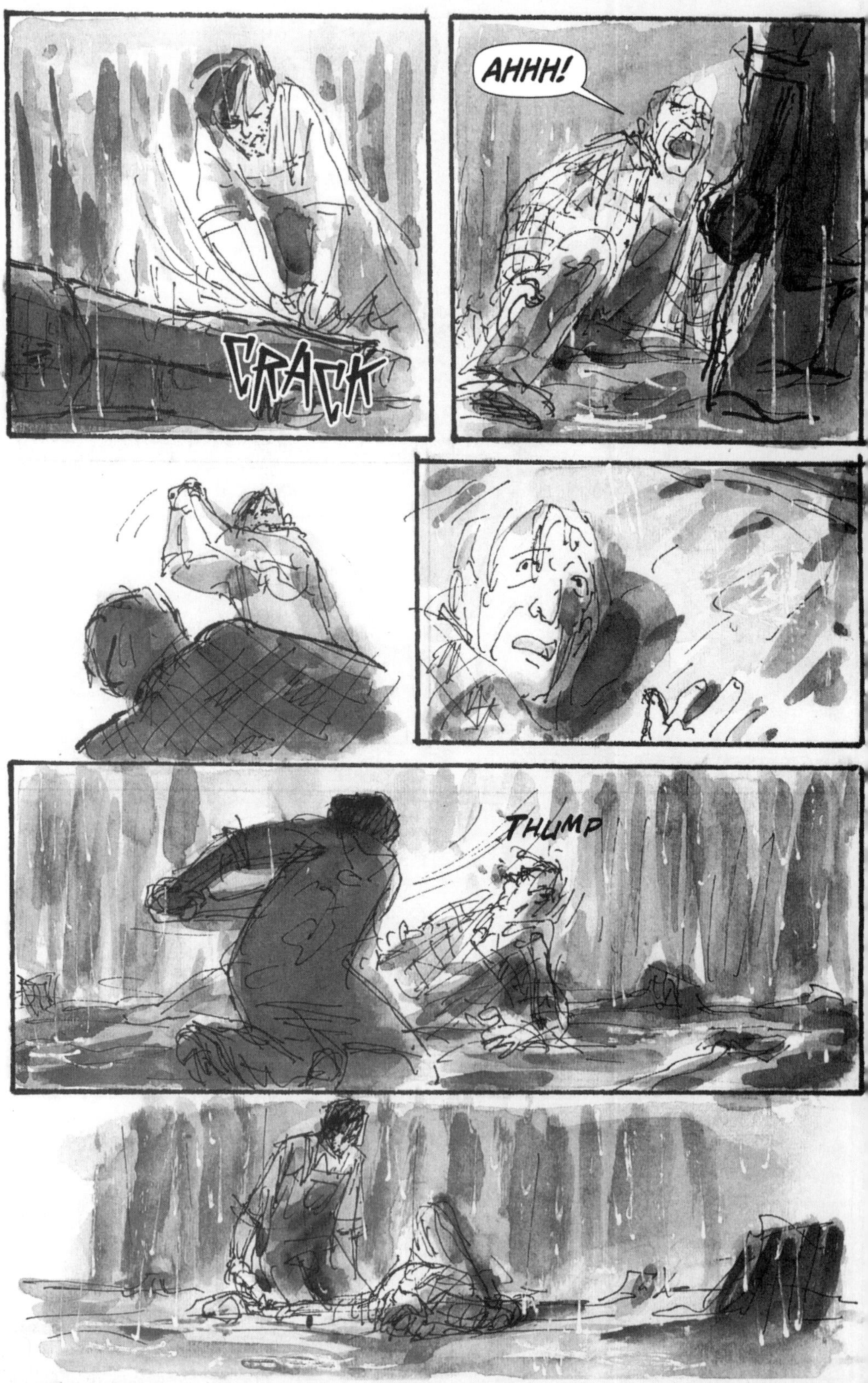
CRACK
AHHH!
THUMP

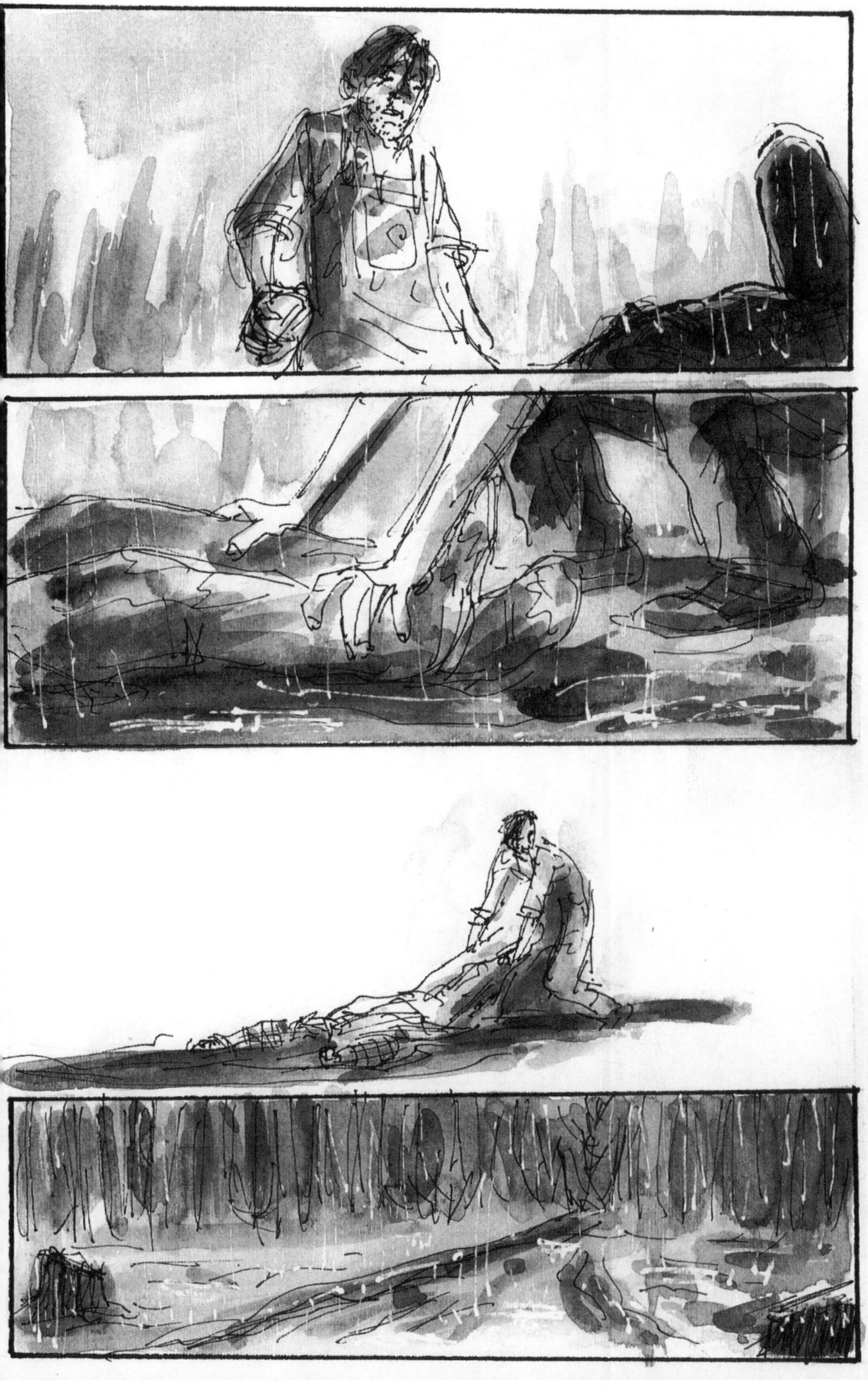

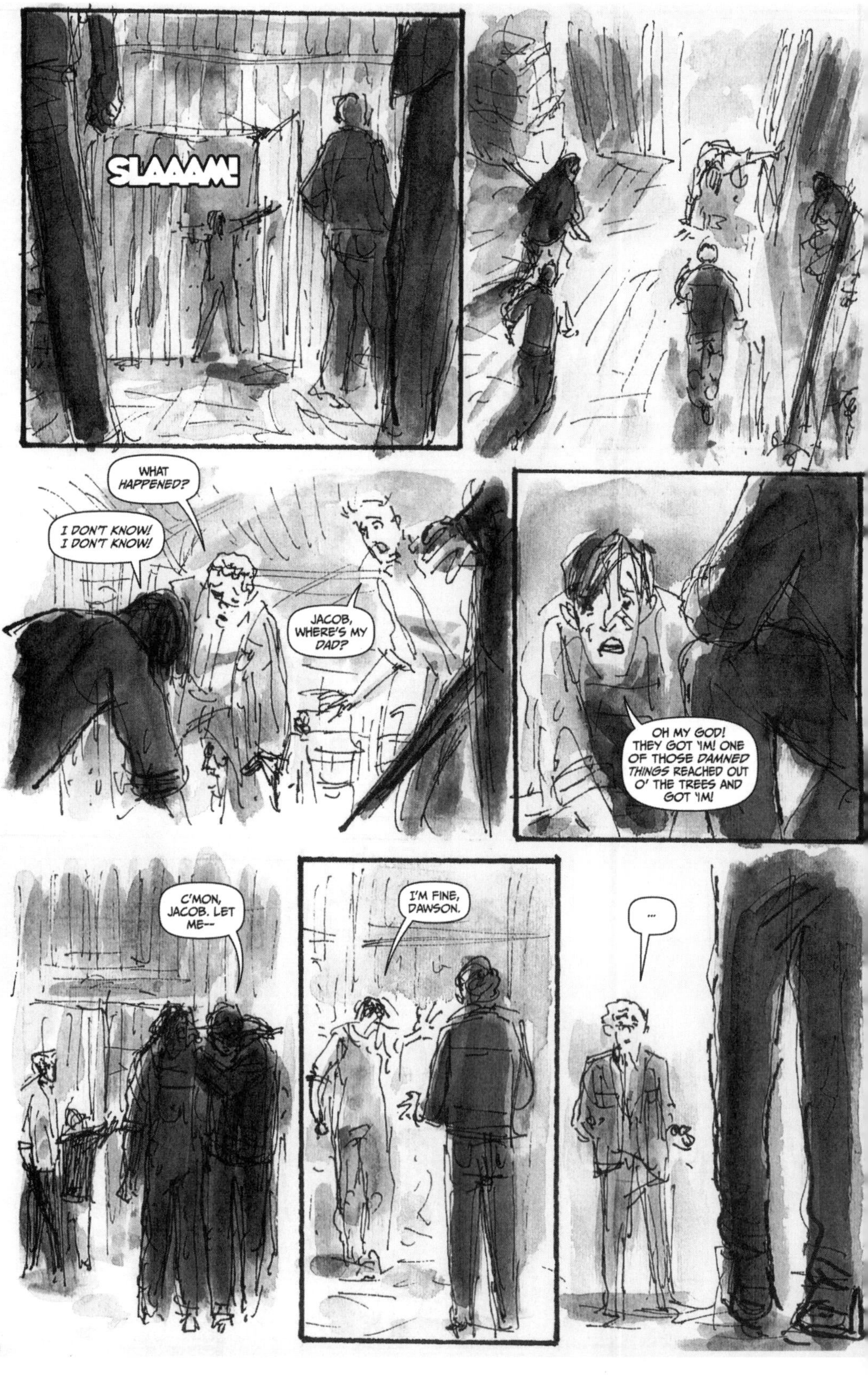
SLAAAM!
WHAT *HAPPENED?*
I DON'T KNOW! I DON'T KNOW!
JACOB, WHERE'S MY *DAD?*
OH MY GOD! THEY GOT 'IM! ONE OF THOSE *DAMNED THINGS* REACHED OUT O' THE TREES AND GOT 'IM!
C'MON, JACOB. LET ME--
I'M FINE, DAWSON.
...

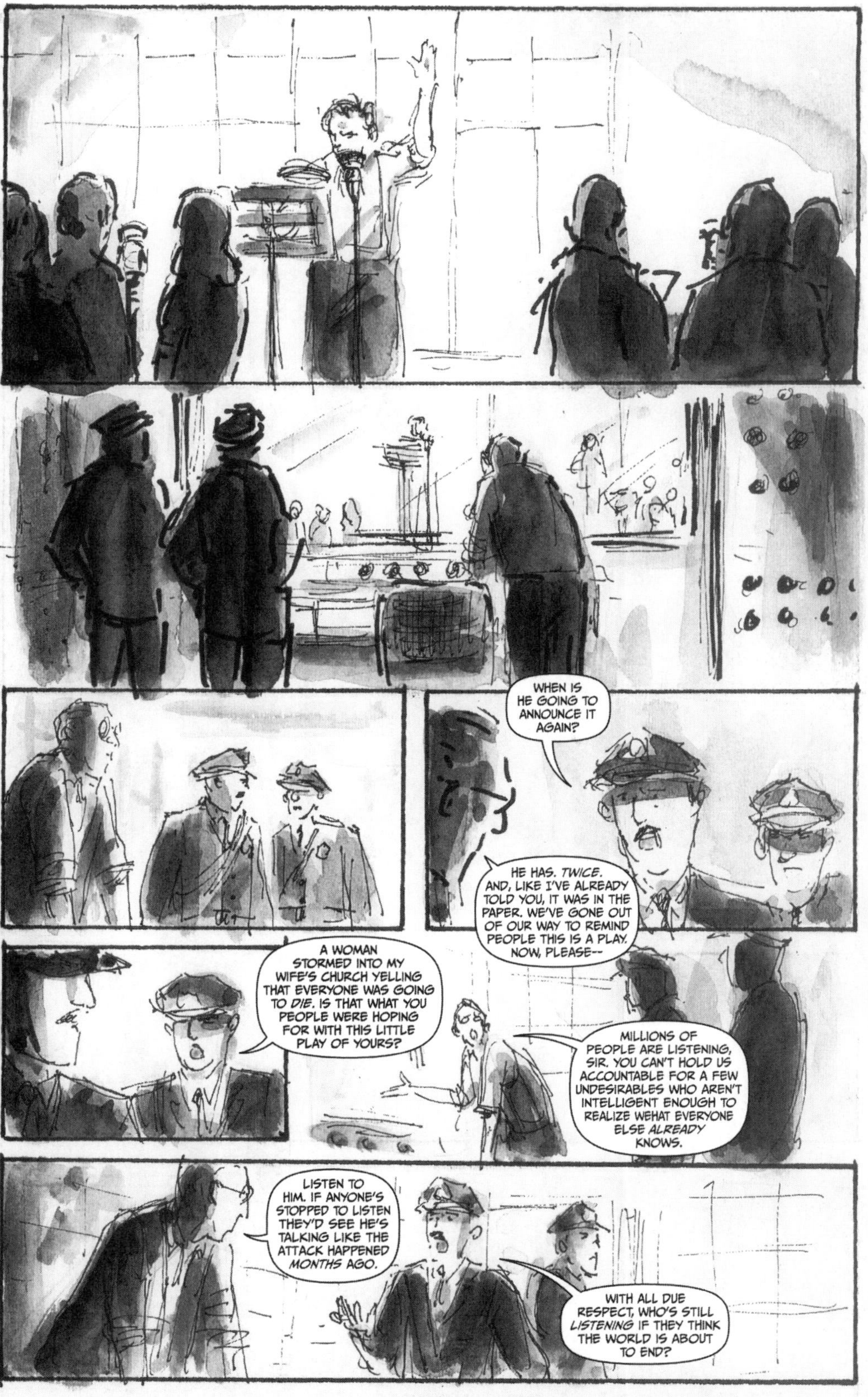
WHEN IS HE GOING TO ANNOUNCE IT AGAIN?
HE HAS. *TWICE*. AND, LIKE I'VE ALREADY TOLD YOU, IT WAS IN THE PAPER. WE'VE GONE OUT OF OUR WAY TO REMIND PEOPLE THIS IS A PLAY. NOW, PLEASE--
A WOMAN STORMED INTO MY WIFE'S CHURCH YELLING THAT EVERYONE WAS GOING TO *DIE*. IS THAT WHAT YOU PEOPLE WERE HOPING FOR WITH THIS LITTLE PLAY OF YOURS?
MILLIONS OF PEOPLE ARE LISTENING, SIR. YOU CAN'T HOLD US ACCOUNTABLE FOR A FEW UNDESIRABLES WHO AREN'T INTELLIGENT ENOUGH TO REALIZE WEHAT EVERYONE ELSE *ALREADY* KNOWS.
LISTEN TO HIM. IF ANYONE'S STOPPED TO LISTEN THEY'D SEE HE'S TALKING LIKE THE ATTACK HAPPENED *MONTHS* AGO.
WITH ALL DUE RESPECT, WHO'S STILL *LISTENING* IF THEY THINK THE WORLD IS ABOUT TO END?

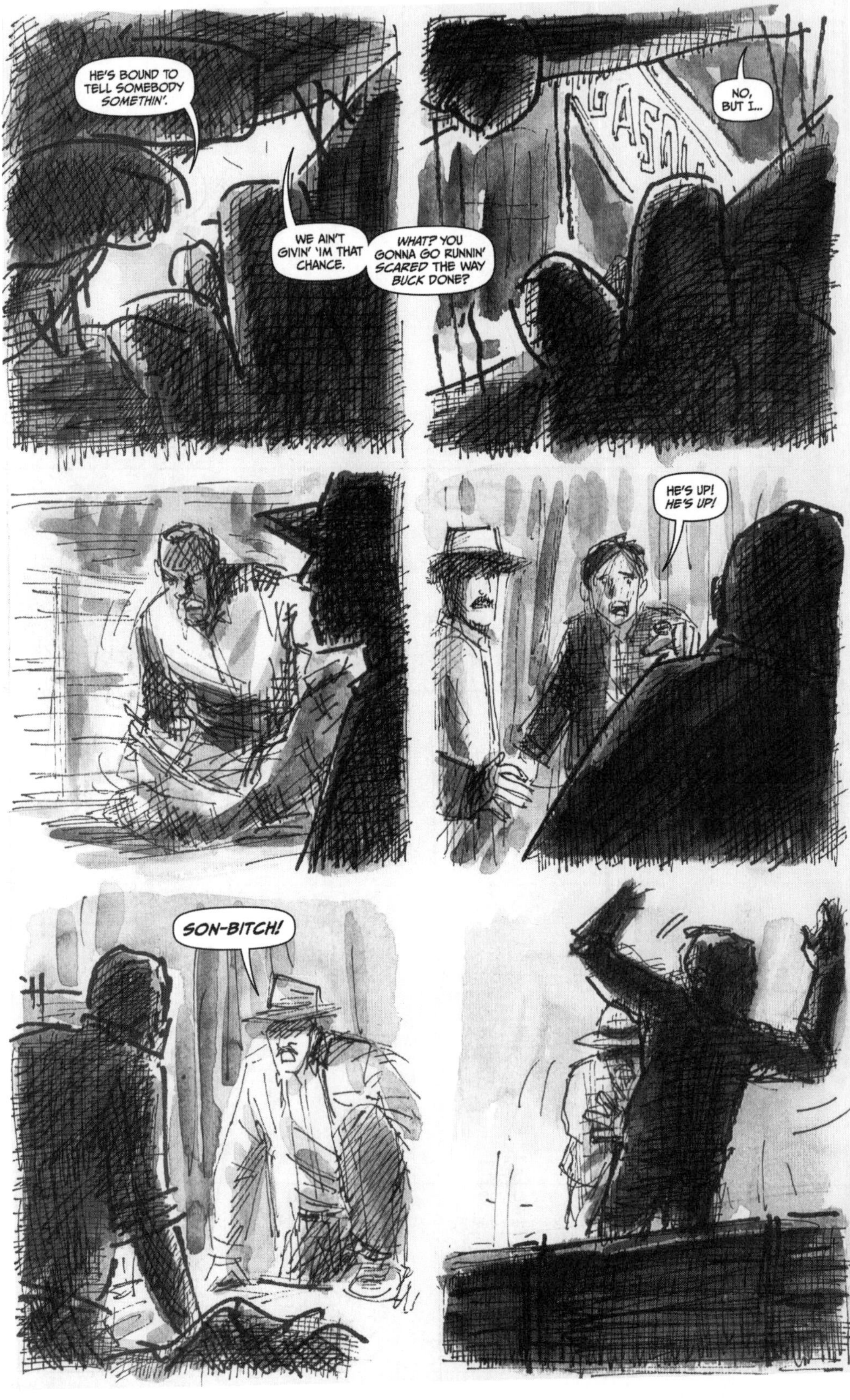
HE'S BOUND TO TELL SOMEBODY *SOMETHIN'*.
WE AIN'T GIVIN' 'IM THAT CHANCE.
WHAT? YOU GONNA GO RUNNIN' *SCARED* THE WAY *BUCK* DONE?
NO, BUT I...
GASOL
HE'S UP! *HE'S UP!*
SON-BITCH!

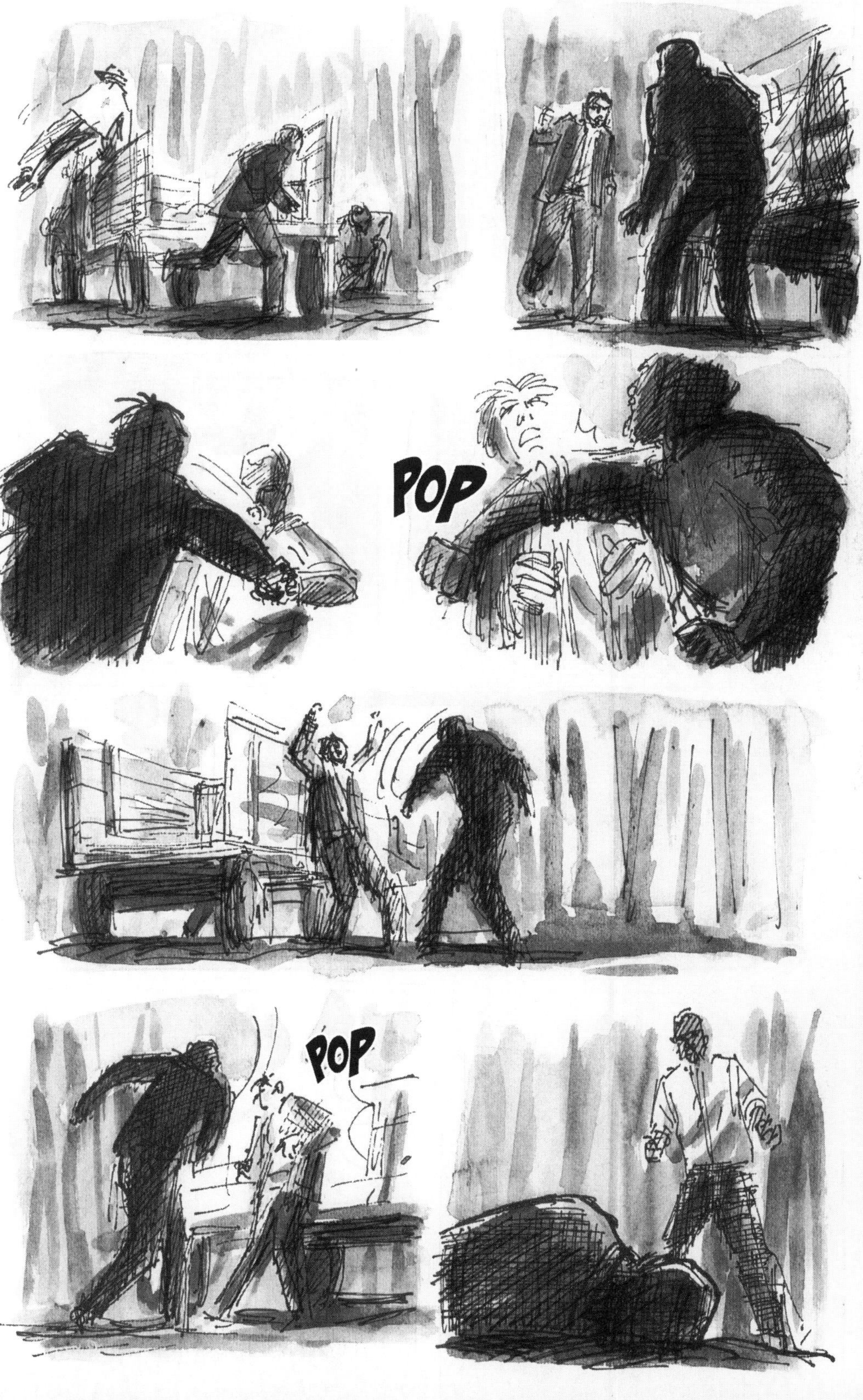
POP
POP

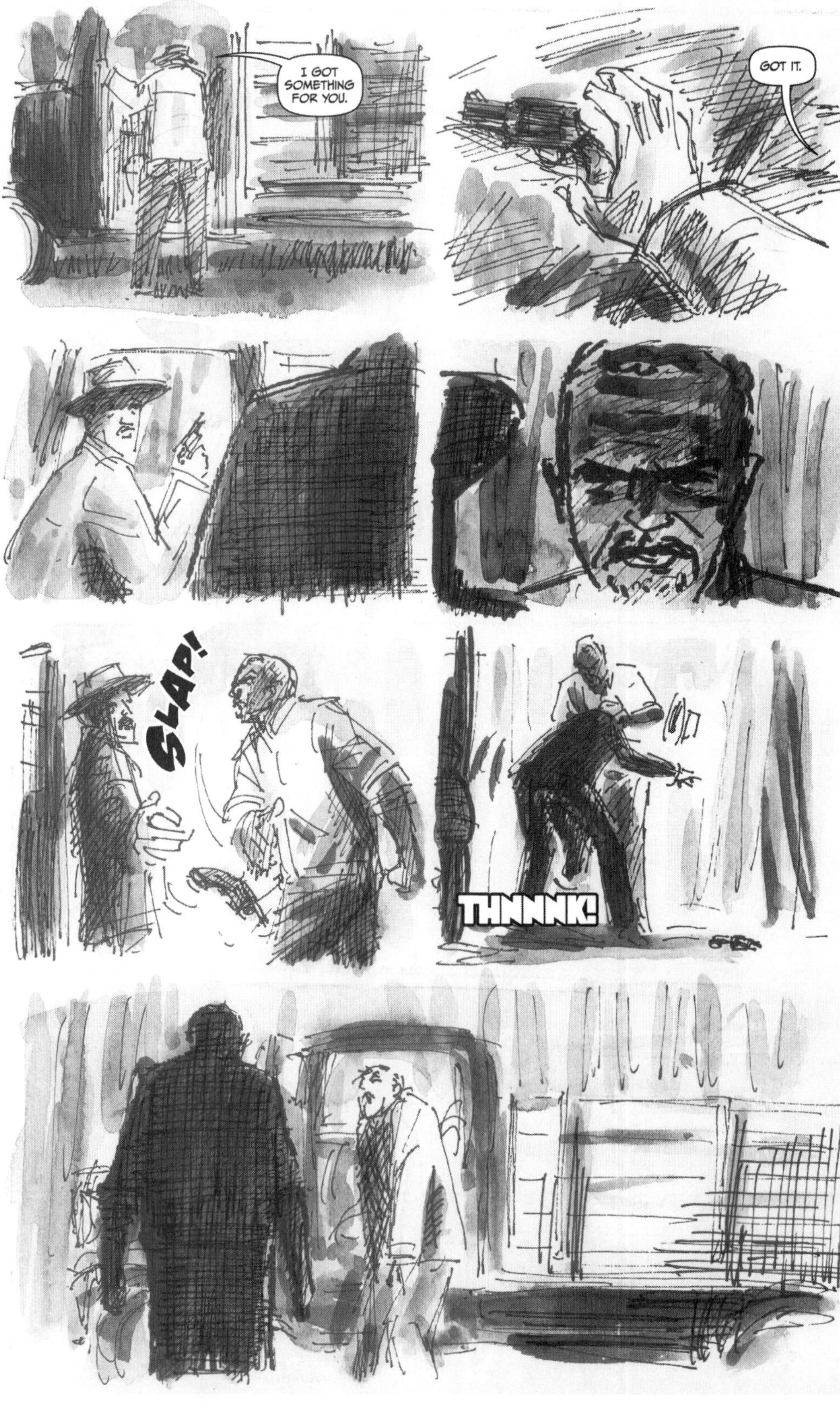
I GOT SOMETHING FOR YOU.
GOT IT.
SLAP!
THNNNK!

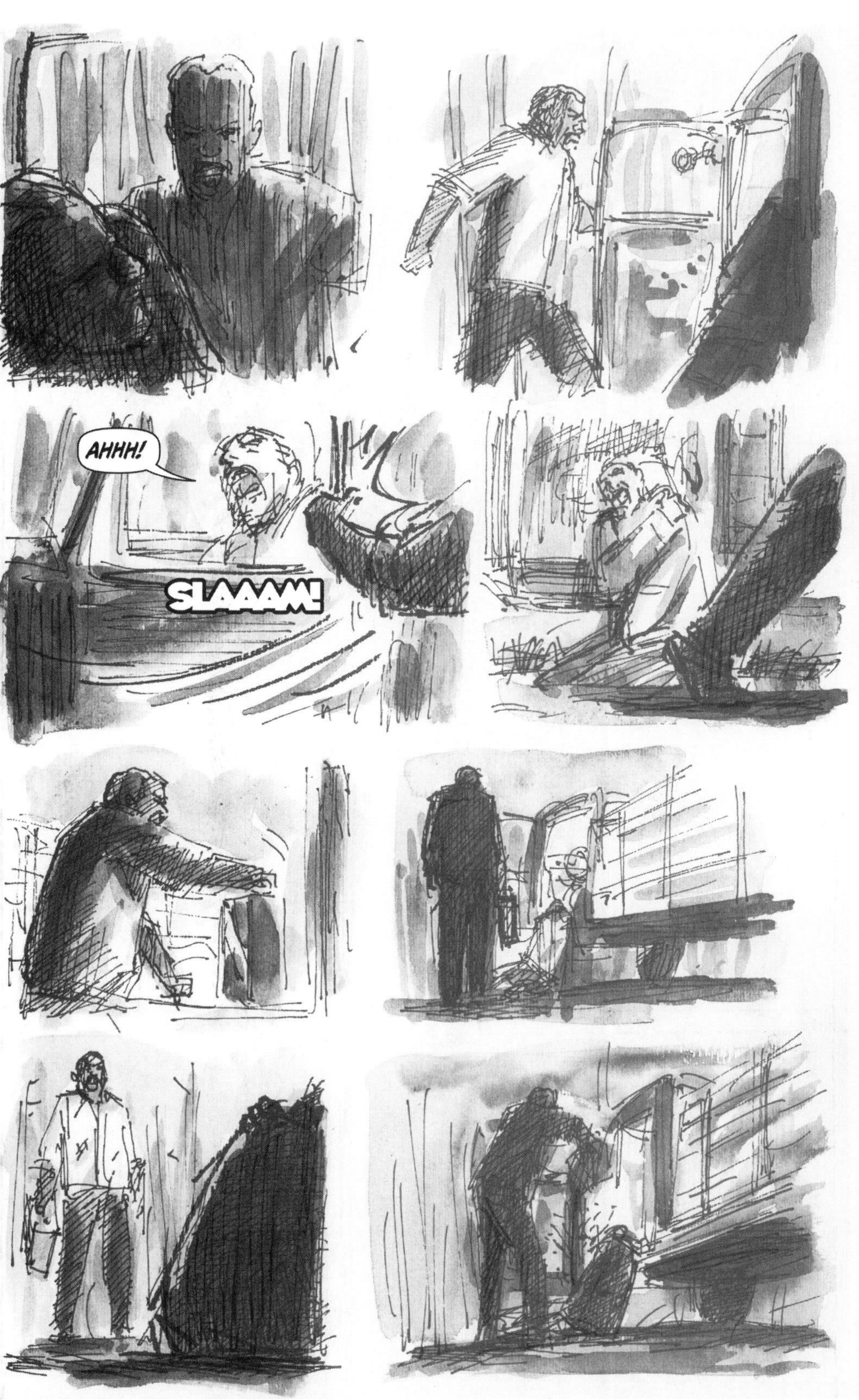
AHHH!
SLAAAAM!

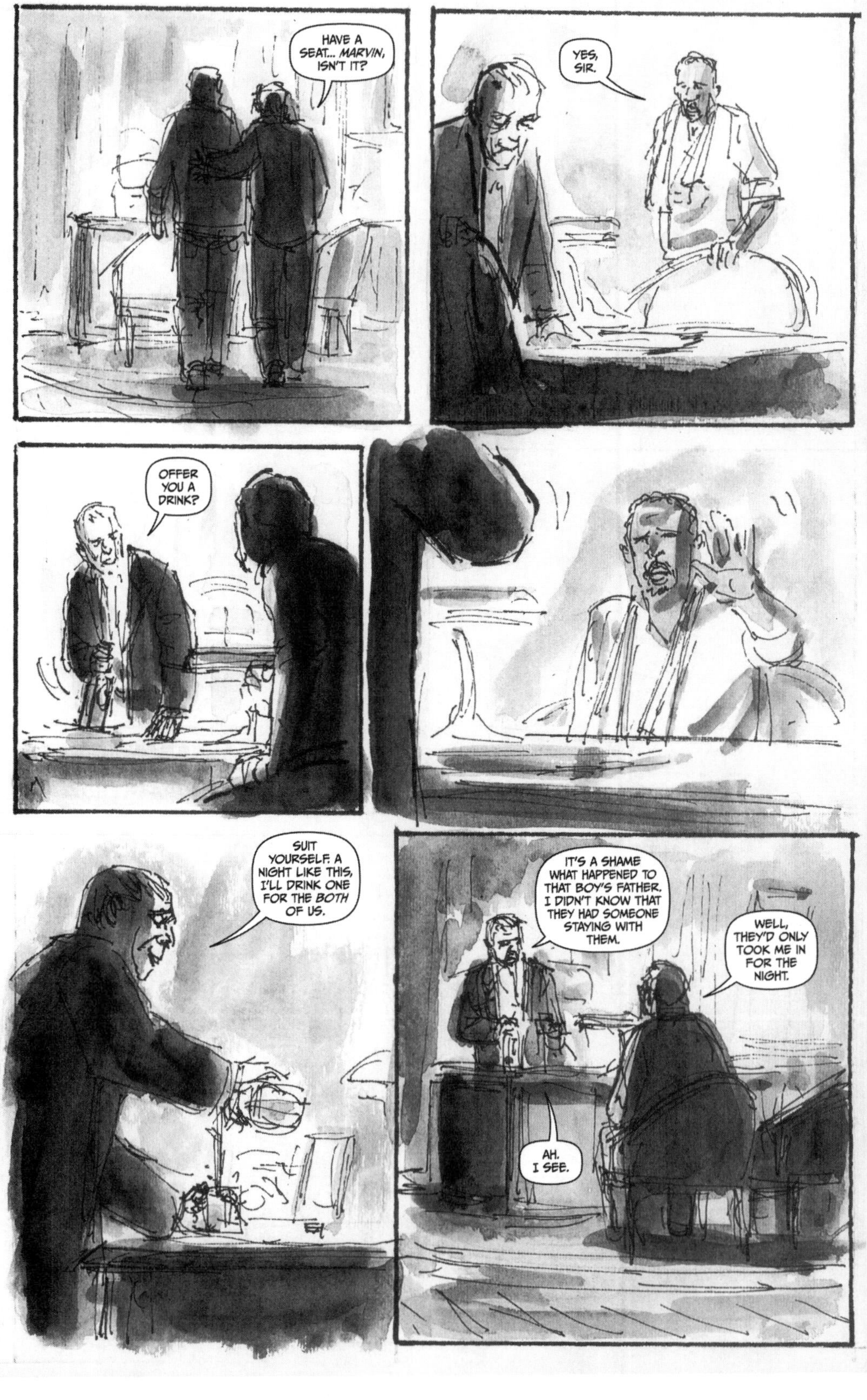

HAVE A SEAT... MARVIN, ISN'T IT?
YES, SIR.
OFFER YOU A DRINK?
SUIT YOURSELF. A NIGHT LIKE THIS, I'LL DRINK ONE FOR THE BOTH OF US.
IT'S A SHAME WHAT HAPPENED TO THAT BOY'S FATHER. I DIDN'T KNOW THAT THEY HAD SOMEONE STAYING WITH THEM.
WELL, THEY'D ONLY TOOK ME IN FOR THE NIGHT.
AH. I SEE.

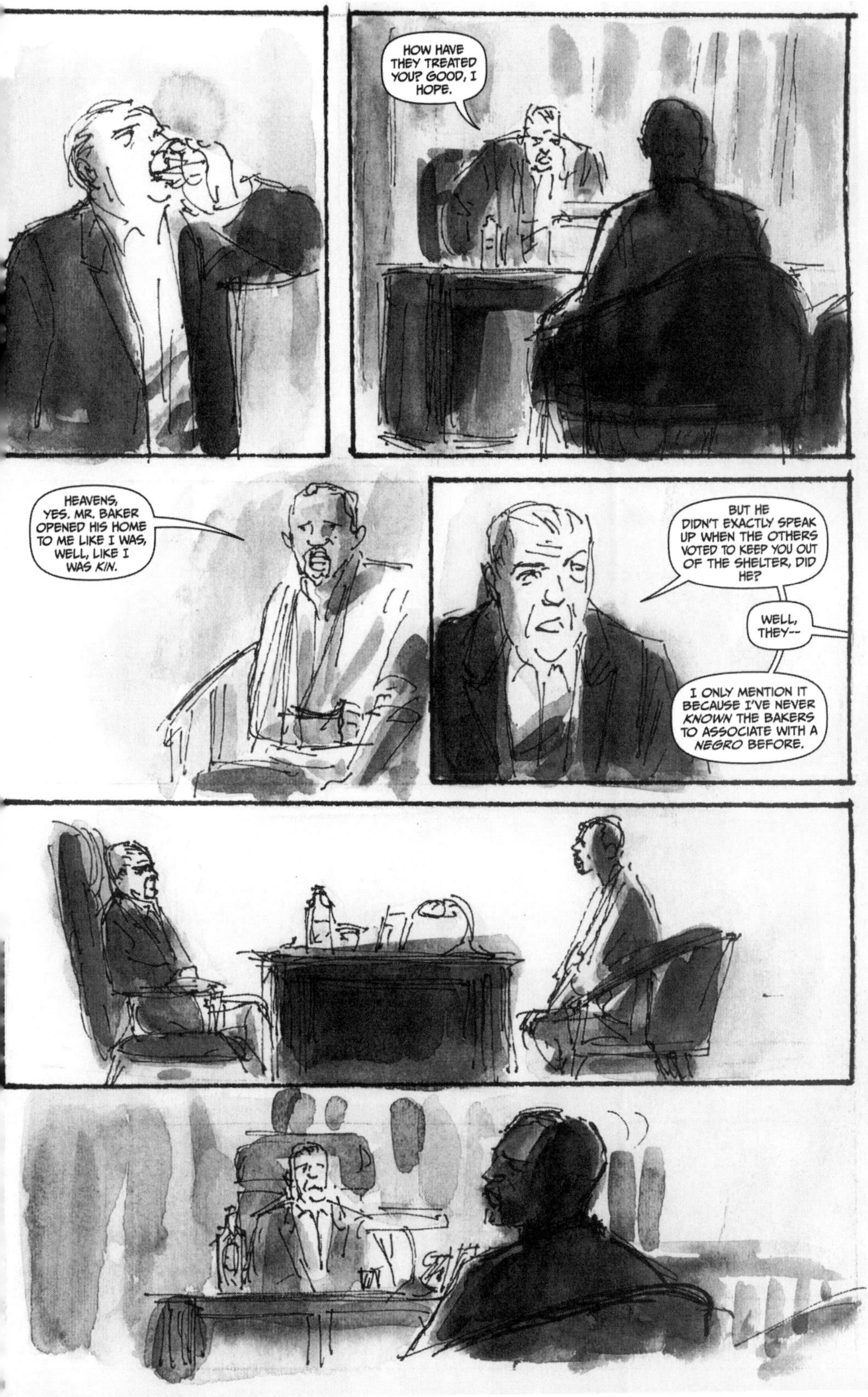
HOW HAVE THEY TREATED YOU? GOOD, I HOPE.
HEAVENS, YES. MR. BAKER OPENED HIS HOME TO ME LIKE I WAS, WELL, LIKE I WAS *KIN*.
BUT HE DIDN'T EXACTLY SPEAK UP WHEN THE OTHERS VOTED TO KEEP YOU OUT OF THE SHELTER, DID HE?
WELL, THEY--
I ONLY MENTION IT BECAUSE I'VE NEVER *KNOWN* THE BAKERS TO ASSOCIATE WITH A *NEGRO* BEFORE.

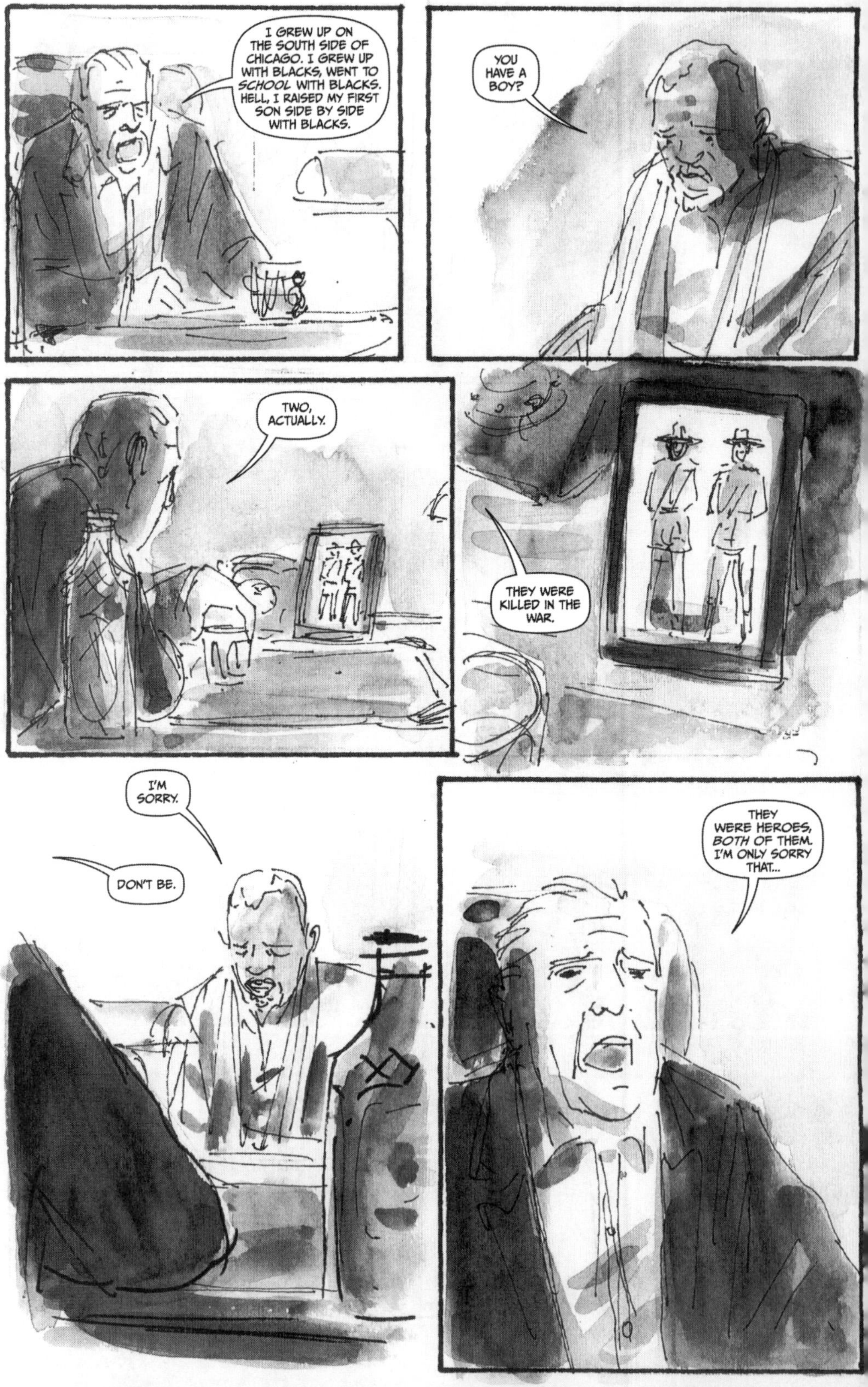
I GREW UP ON THE SOUTH SIDE OF CHICAGO. I GREW UP WITH BLACKS, WENT TO *SCHOOL* WITH BLACKS. HELL, I RAISED MY FIRST SON SIDE BY SIDE WITH BLACKS.
YOU HAVE A BOY?
TWO, ACTUALLY.
THEY WERE KILLED IN THE WAR.
I'M SORRY.
DON'T BE.
THEY WERE HEROES, *BOTH* OF THEM. I'M ONLY SORRY THAT...

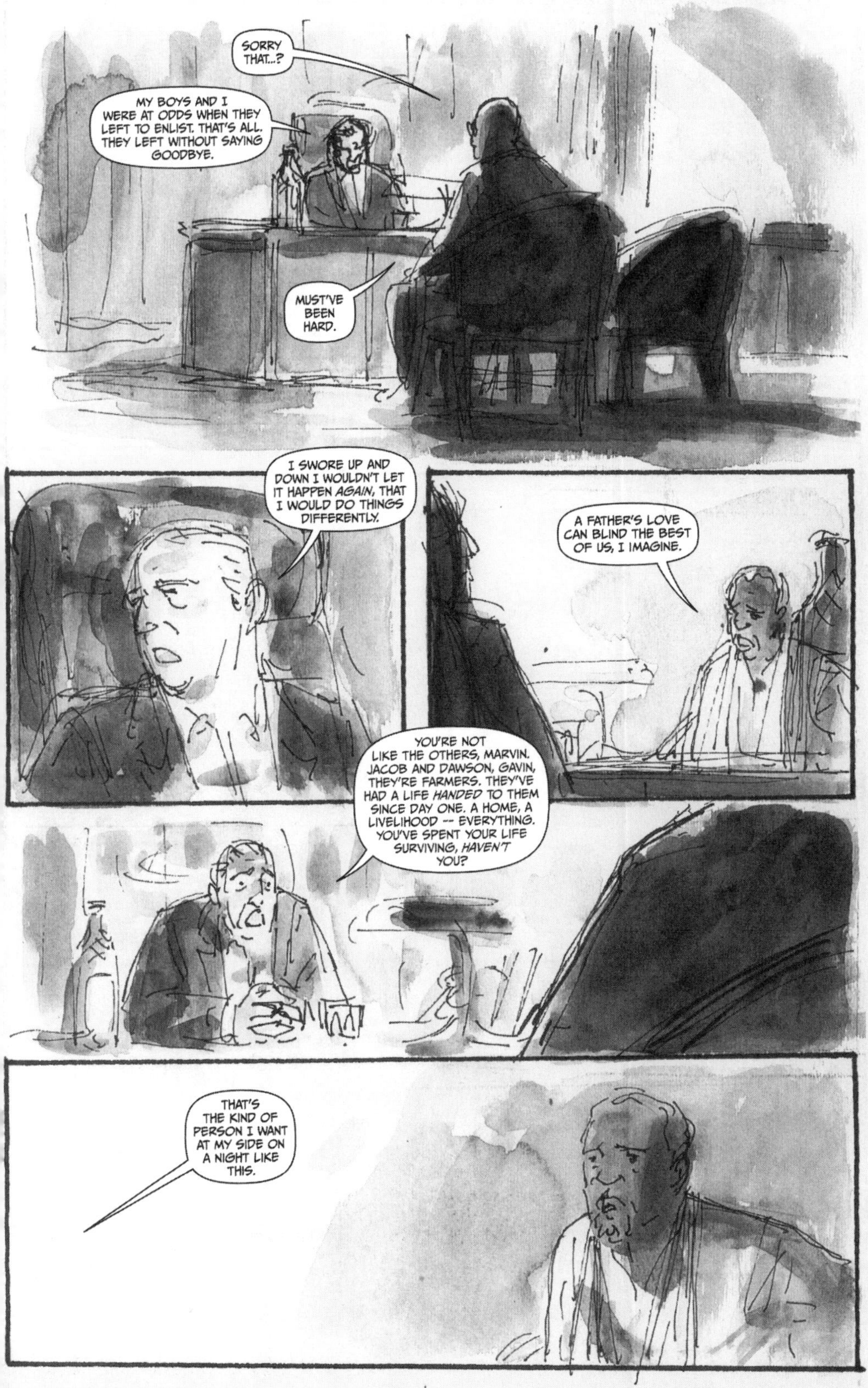
SORRY THAT...?
MY BOYS AND I WERE AT ODDS WHEN THEY LEFT TO ENLIST. THAT'S ALL. THEY LEFT WITHOUT SAYING GOODBYE.
MUST'VE BEEN HARD.
I SWORE UP AND DOWN I WOULDN'T LET IT HAPPEN *AGAIN*, THAT I WOULD DO THINGS DIFFERENTLY.
A FATHER'S LOVE CAN BLIND THE BEST OF US, I IMAGINE.
YOU'RE NOT LIKE THE OTHERS, MARVIN. JACOB AND DAWSON, GAVIN, THEY'RE FARMERS. THEY'VE HAD A LIFE *HANDED* TO THEM SINCE DAY ONE. A HOME, A LIVELIHOOD -- EVERYTHING. YOU'VE SPENT YOUR LIFE SURVIVING, *HAVEN'T* YOU?
THAT'S THE KIND OF PERSON I WANT AT MY SIDE ON A NIGHT LIKE THIS.

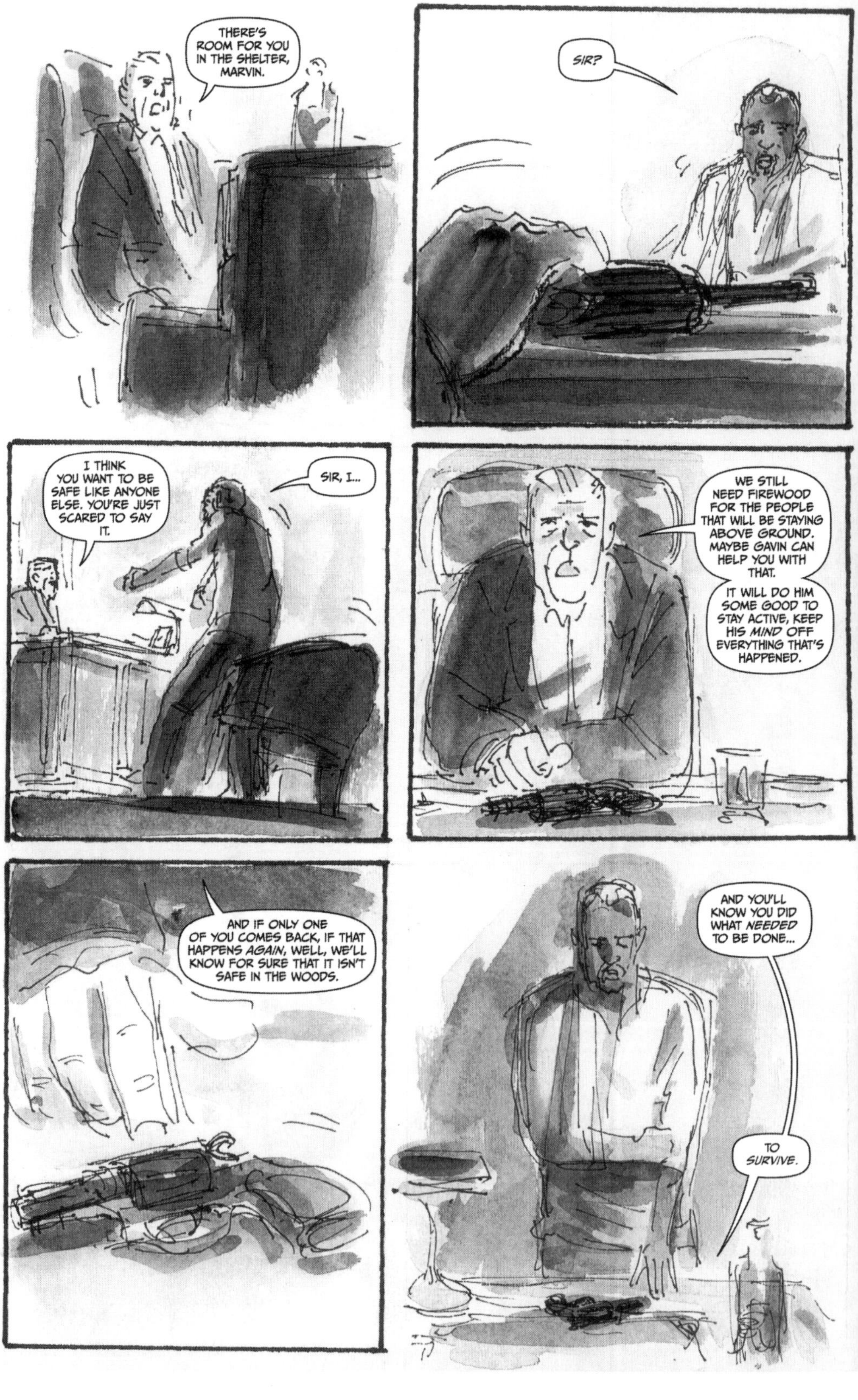
THERE'S ROOM FOR YOU IN THE SHELTER, MARVIN.
SIR?
I THINK YOU WANT TO BE SAFE LIKE ANYONE ELSE. YOU'RE JUST SCARED TO SAY IT.
SIR, I...
WE STILL NEED FIREWOOD FOR THE PEOPLE THAT WILL BE STAYING ABOVE GROUND. MAYBE GAVIN CAN HELP YOU WITH THAT.
IT WILL DO HIM SOME GOOD TO STAY ACTIVE, KEEP HIS *MIND* OFF EVERYTHING THAT'S HAPPENED.
AND IF ONLY ONE OF YOU COMES BACK, IF THAT HAPPENS *AGAIN*, WELL, WE'LL KNOW FOR SURE THAT IT ISN'T SAFE IN THE WOODS.
AND YOU'LL KNOW YOU DID WHAT *NEEDED* TO BE DONE...
TO *SURVIVE*.

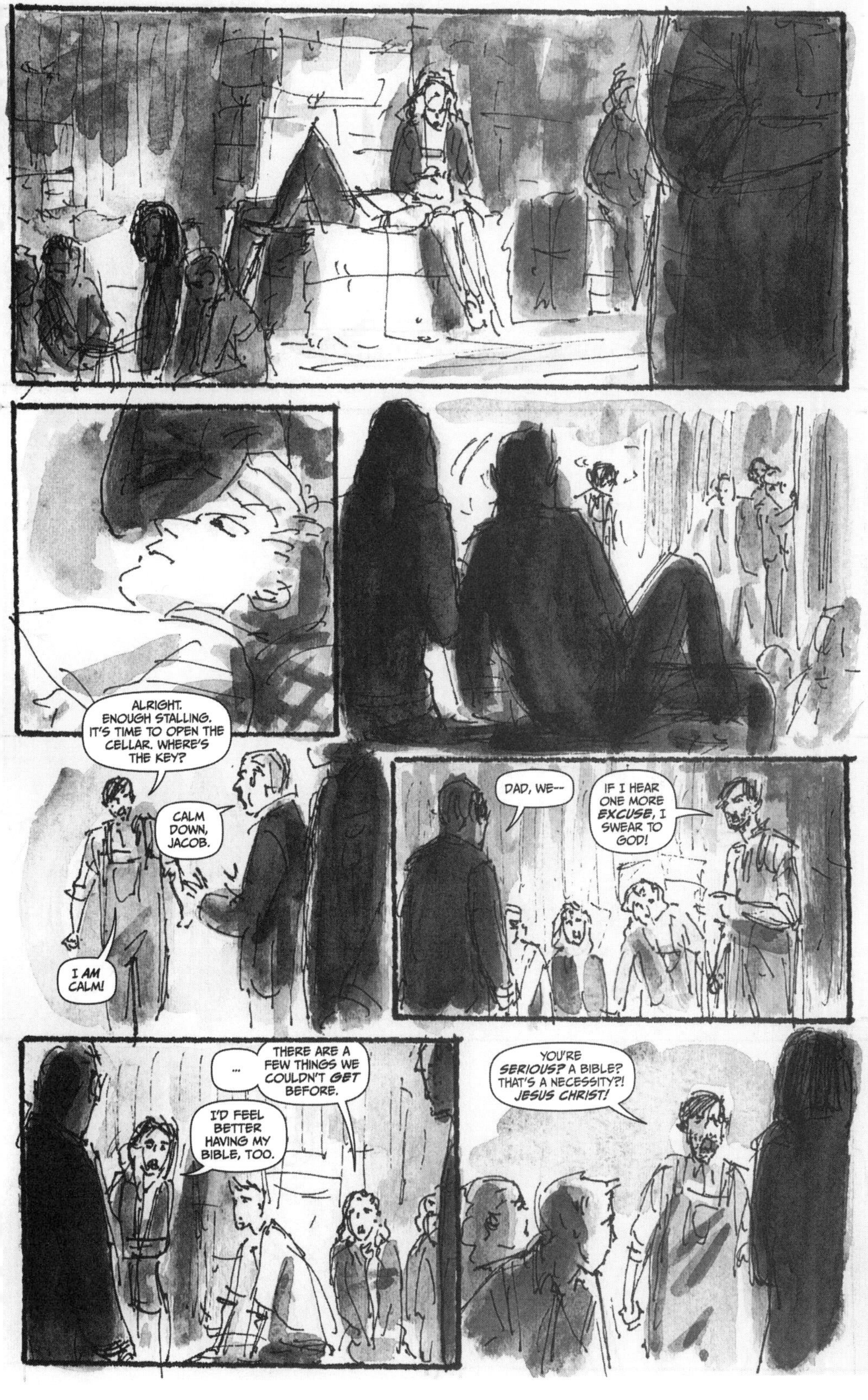
ALRIGHT. ENOUGH STALLING. IT'S TIME TO OPEN THE CELLAR. WHERE'S THE KEY?
CALM DOWN, JACOB.
I *AM* CALM!
DAD, WE--
IF I HEAR ONE MORE *EXCUSE*, I SWEAR TO GOD!
...
THERE ARE A FEW THINGS WE COULDN'T *GET* BEFORE.
I'D FEEL BETTER HAVING MY BIBLE, TOO.
YOU'RE *SERIOUS?* A BIBLE? THAT'S A NECESSITY?! *JESUS CHRIST!*

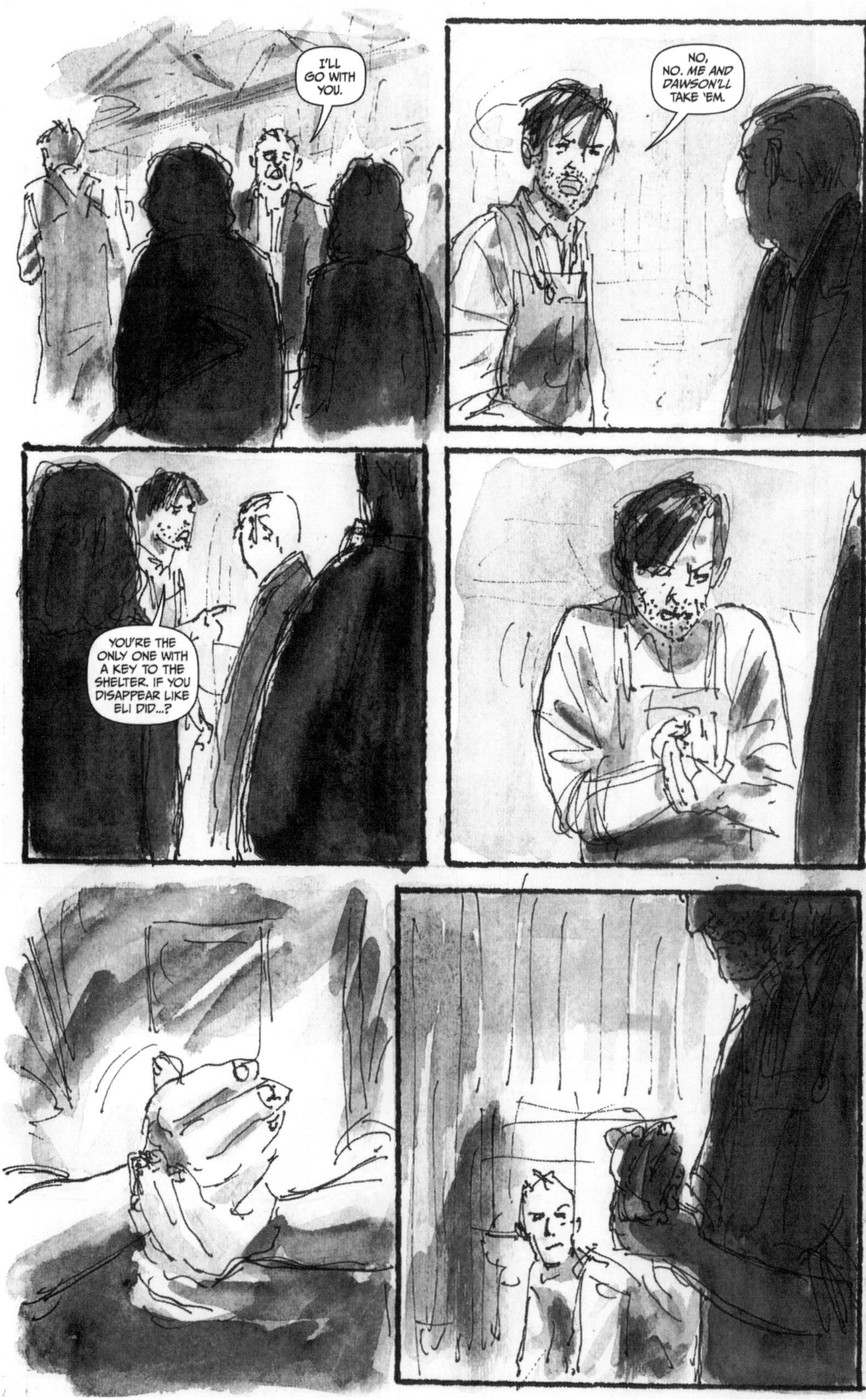
I'LL GO WITH YOU.
NO, NO. ME AND DAWSON'LL TAKE 'EM.
YOU'RE THE ONLY ONE WITH A KEY TO THE SHELTER. IF YOU DISAPPEAR LIKE ELI DID...?

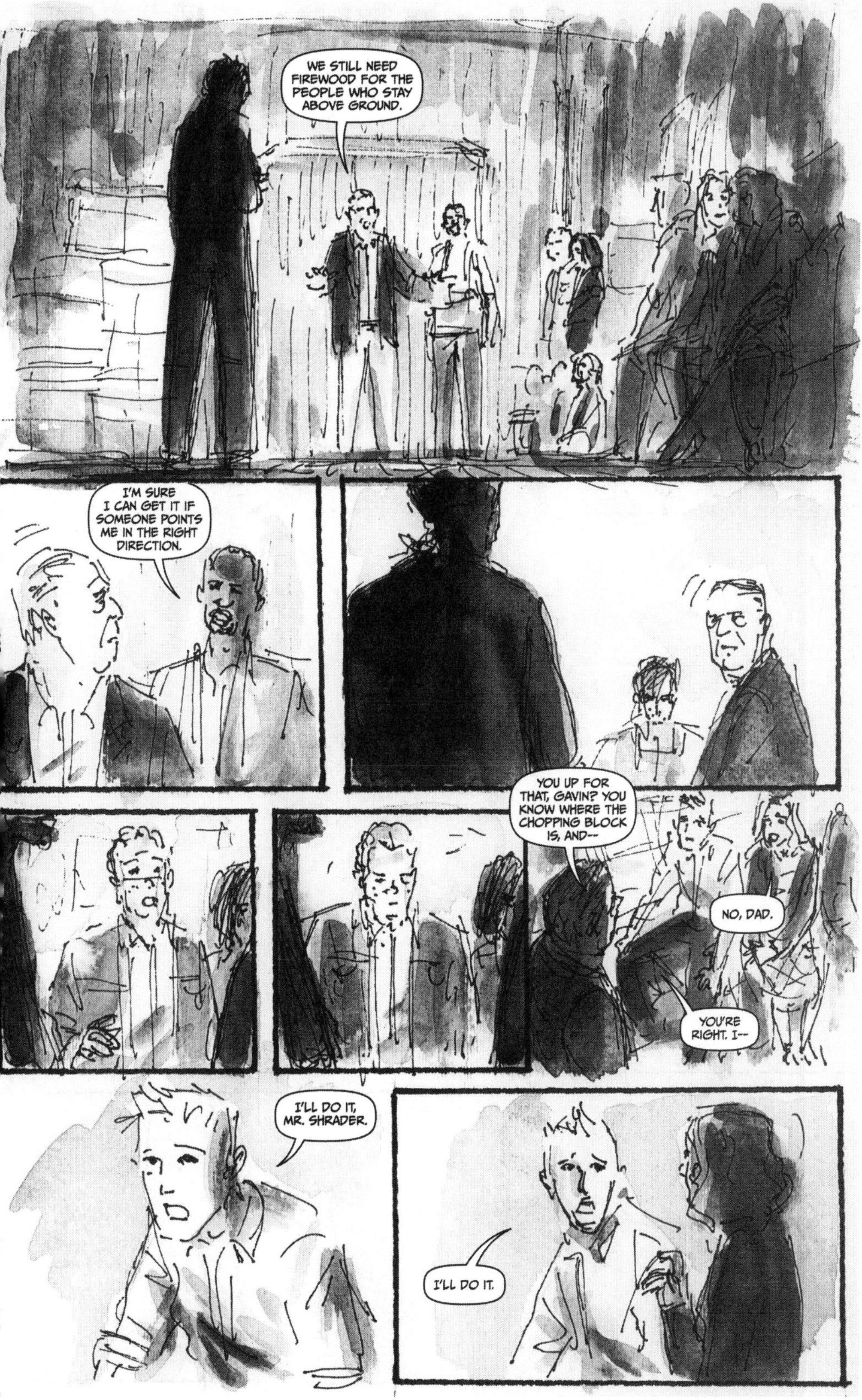
WE STILL NEED FIREWOOD FOR THE PEOPLE WHO STAY ABOVE GROUND.
I'M SURE I CAN GET IT IF SOMEONE POINTS ME IN THE RIGHT DIRECTION.
YOU UP FOR THAT, GAVIN? YOU KNOW WHERE THE CHOPPING BLOCK IS, AND--
NO, DAD.
YOU'RE RIGHT. I--
I'LL DO IT, MR. SHRADER.
I'LL DO IT.

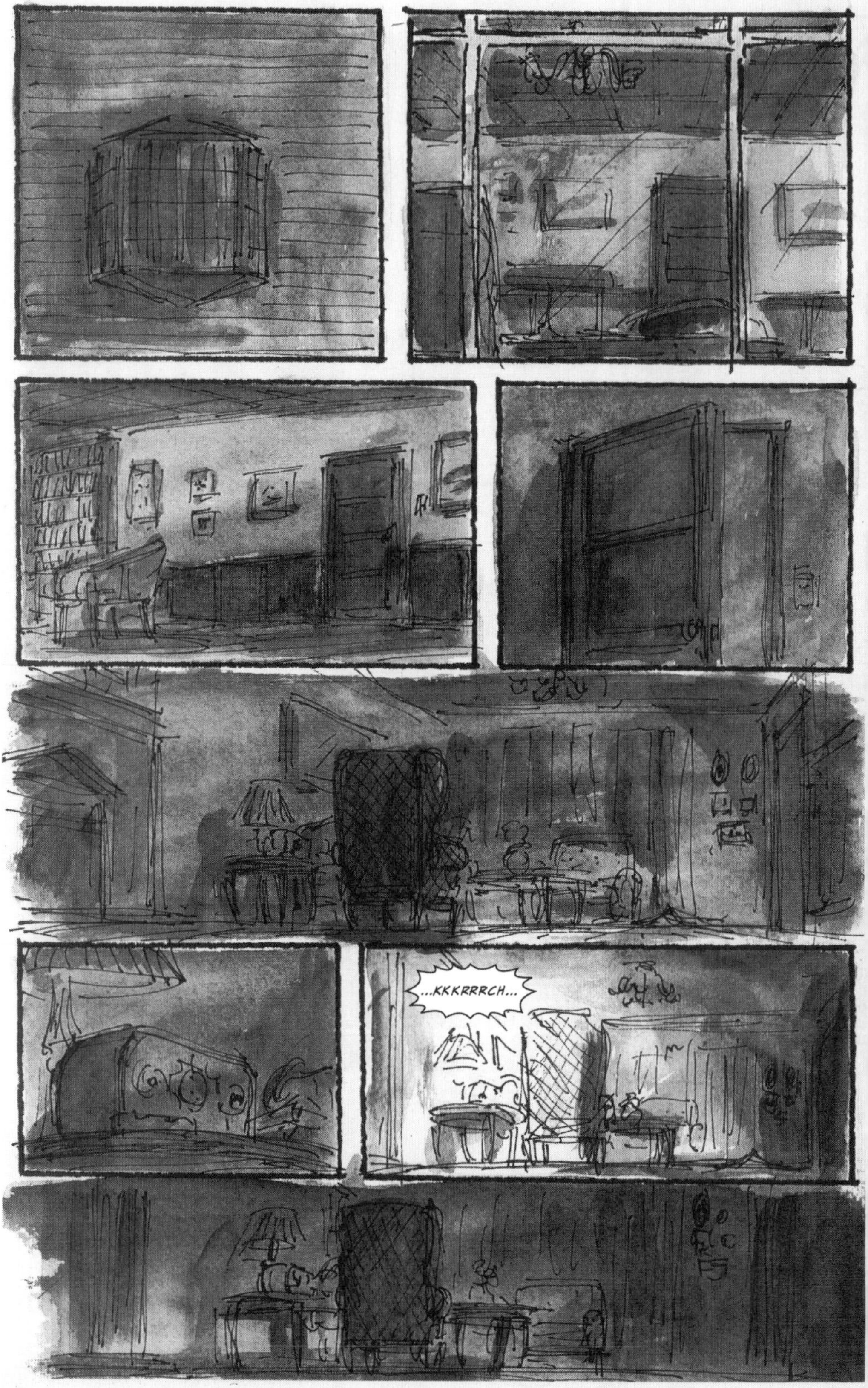
...KKKRRRCH...

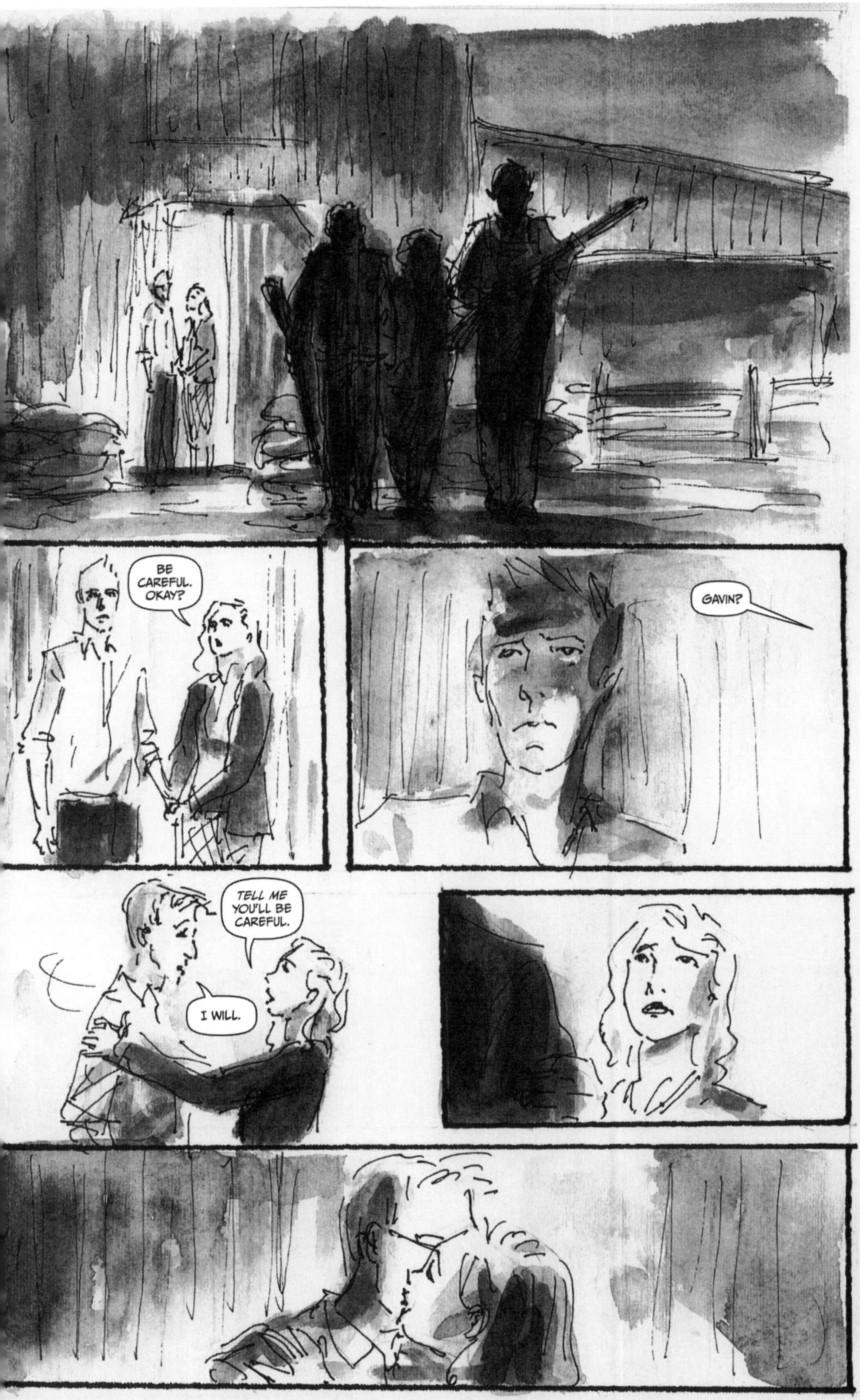
BE CAREFUL. OKAY?
GAVIN?
TELL ME YOU'LL BE CAREFUL.
I WILL.

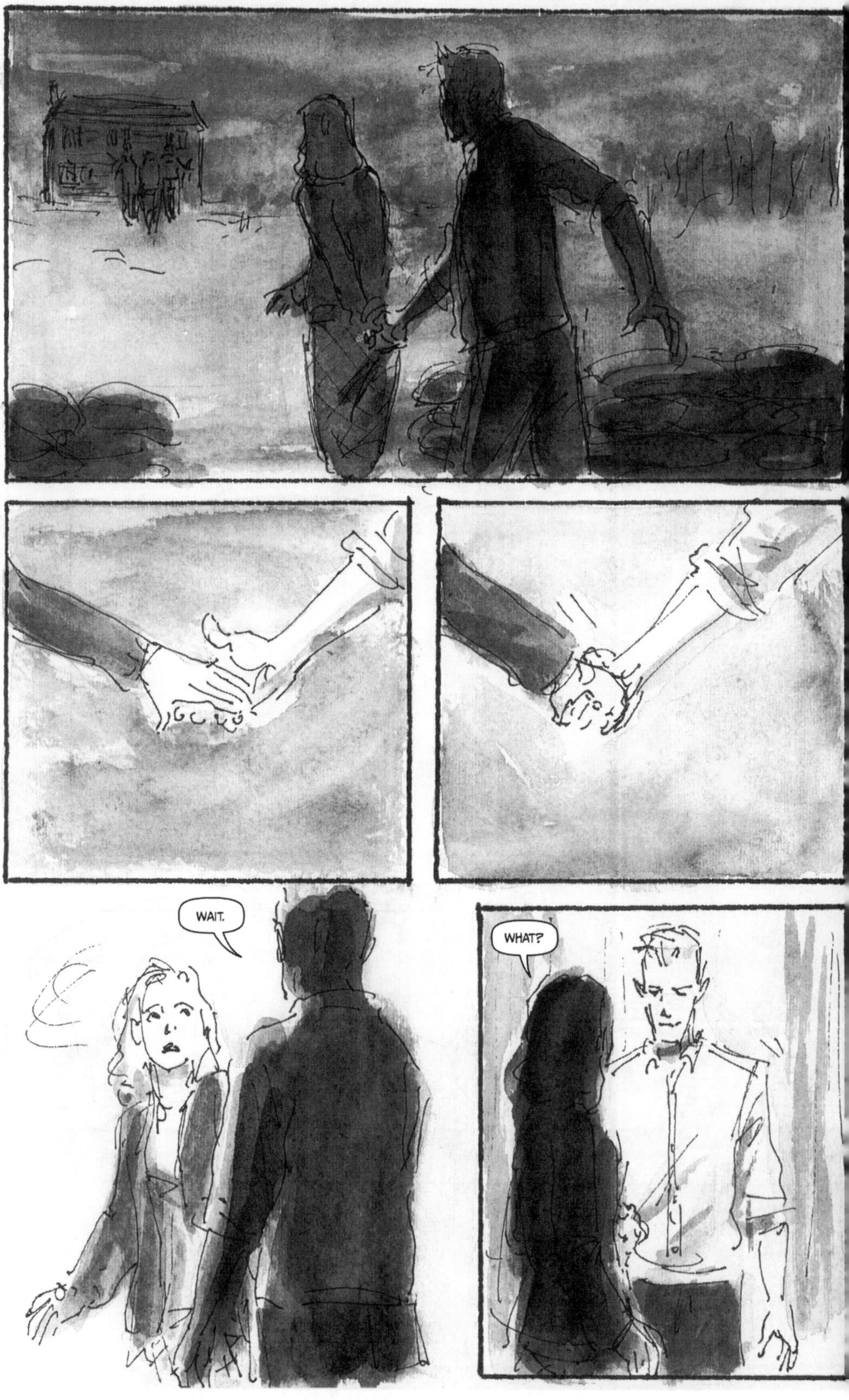
WAIT.
WHAT?

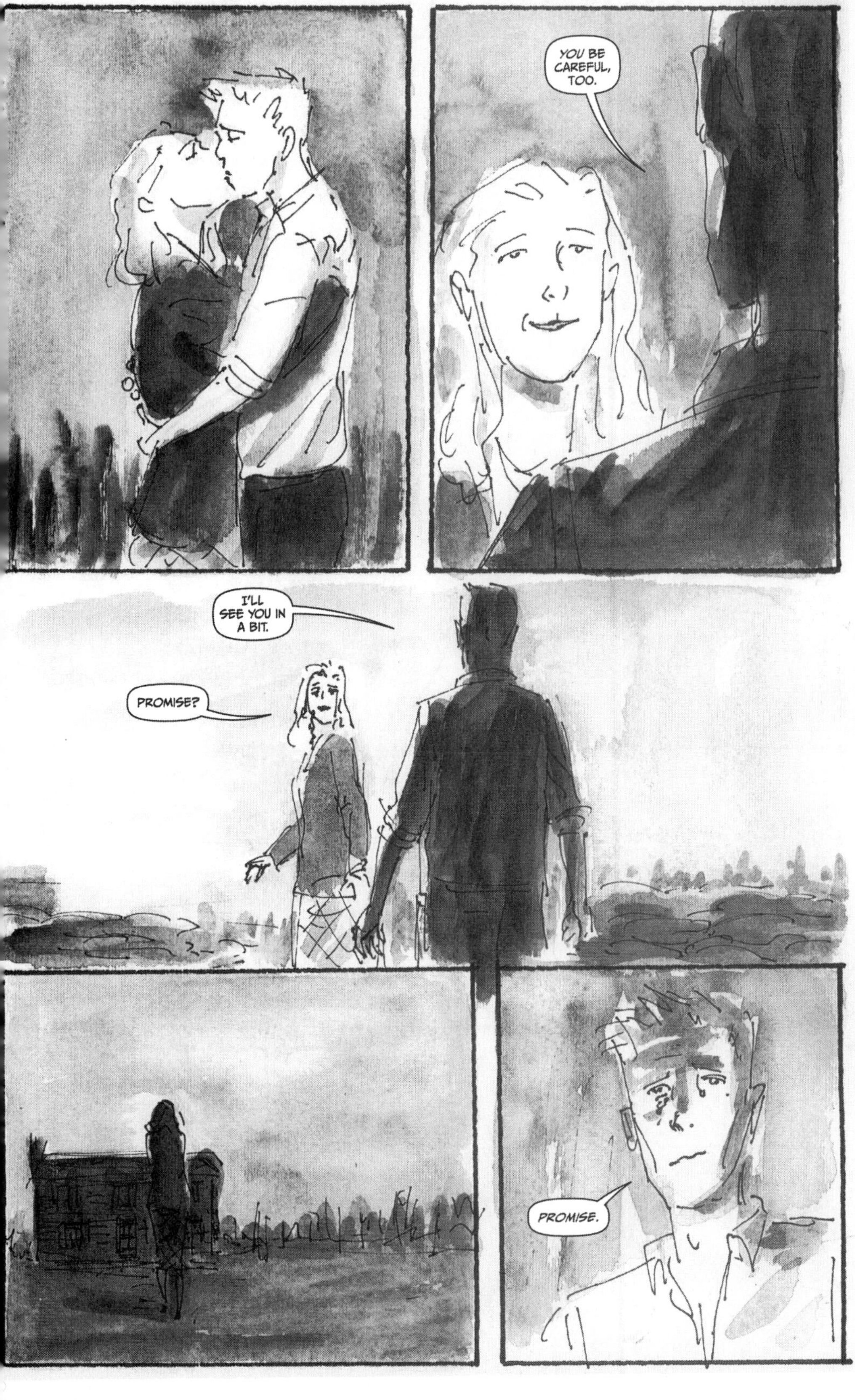
YOU BE CAREFUL, TOO.
I'LL SEE YOU IN A BIT.
PROMISE?
PROMISE.

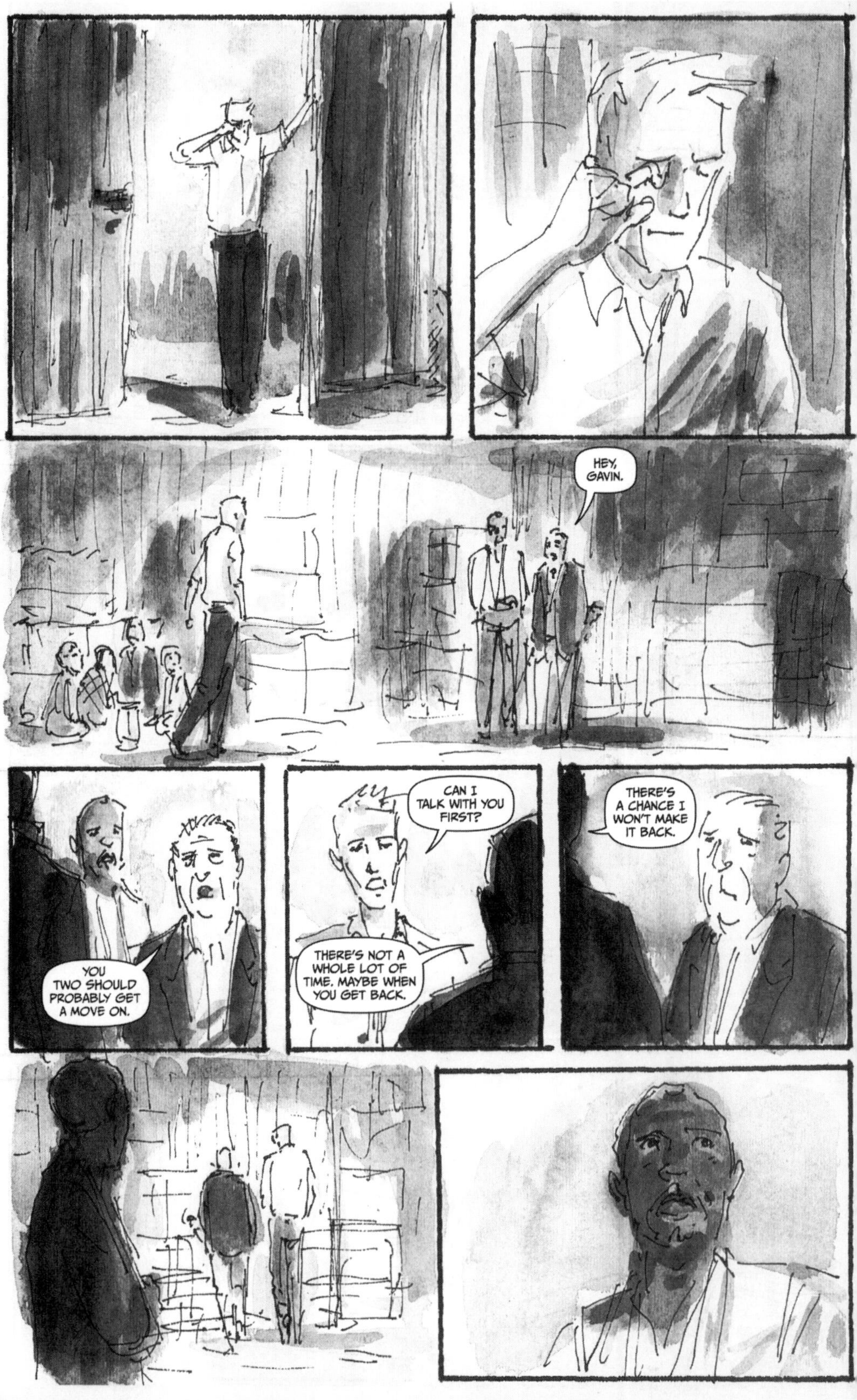
HEY, GAVIN.
YOU TWO SHOULD PROBABLY GET A MOVE ON.
CAN I TALK WITH YOU FIRST?
THERE'S NOT A WHOLE LOT OF TIME. MAYBE WHEN YOU GET BACK.
THERE'S A CHANCE I WON'T MAKE IT BACK.

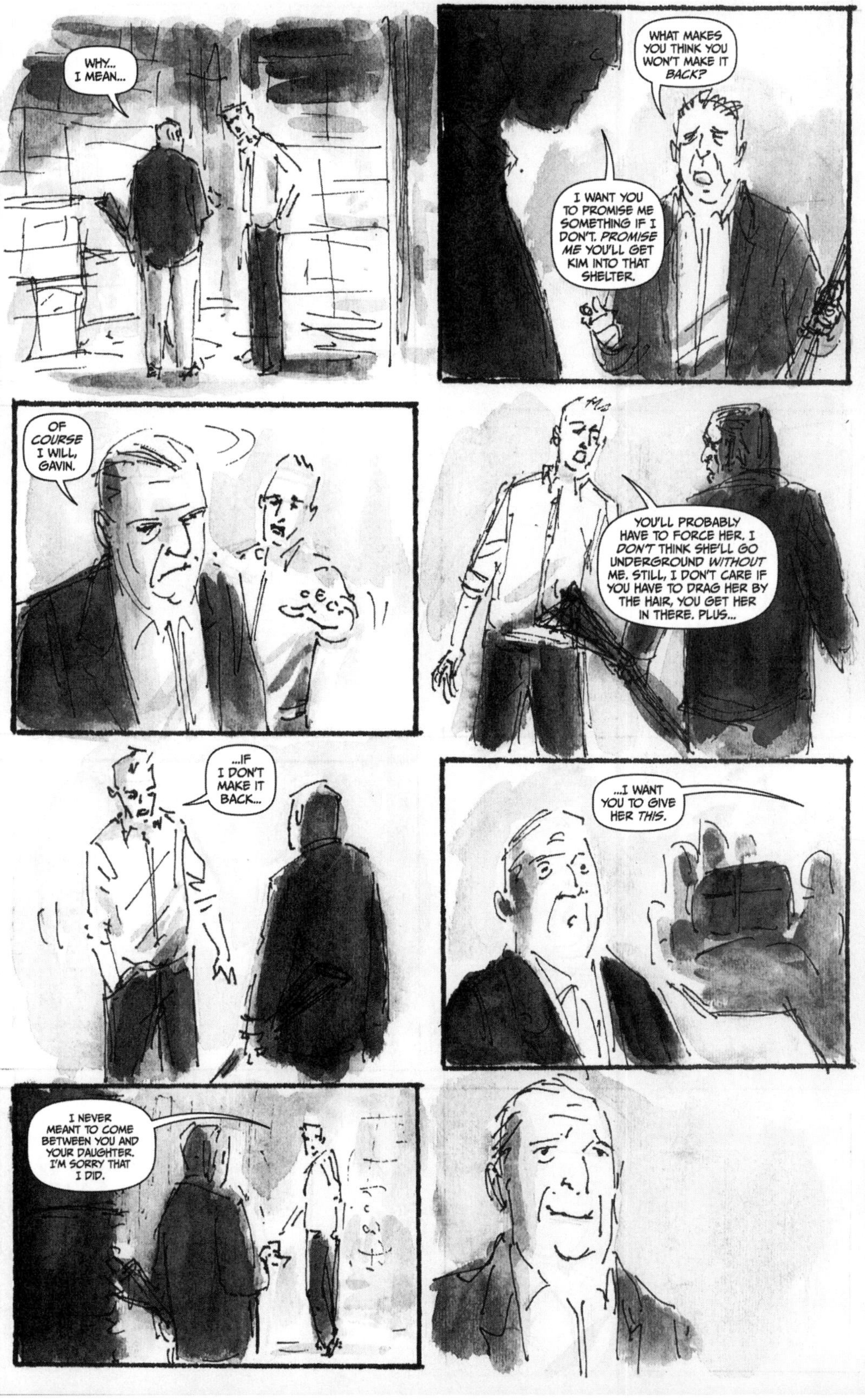
WHY... I MEAN...
WHAT MAKES YOU THINK YOU WON'T MAKE IT *BACK?*
I WANT YOU TO PROMISE ME SOMETHING IF I DON'T. *PROMISE ME* YOU'LL GET KIM INTO THAT SHELTER.
OF *COURSE* I WILL, GAVIN.
YOU'LL PROBABLY HAVE TO FORCE HER. I *DON'T* THINK SHE'LL GO UNDERGROUND *WITHOUT* ME. STILL, I DON'T CARE IF YOU HAVE TO DRAG HER BY THE HAIR, YOU GET HER IN THERE. PLUS...
...IF I DON'T MAKE IT BACK...
...I WANT YOU TO GIVE HER *THIS.*
I NEVER MEANT TO COME BETWEEN YOU AND YOUR DAUGHTER. I'M SORRY THAT I DID.

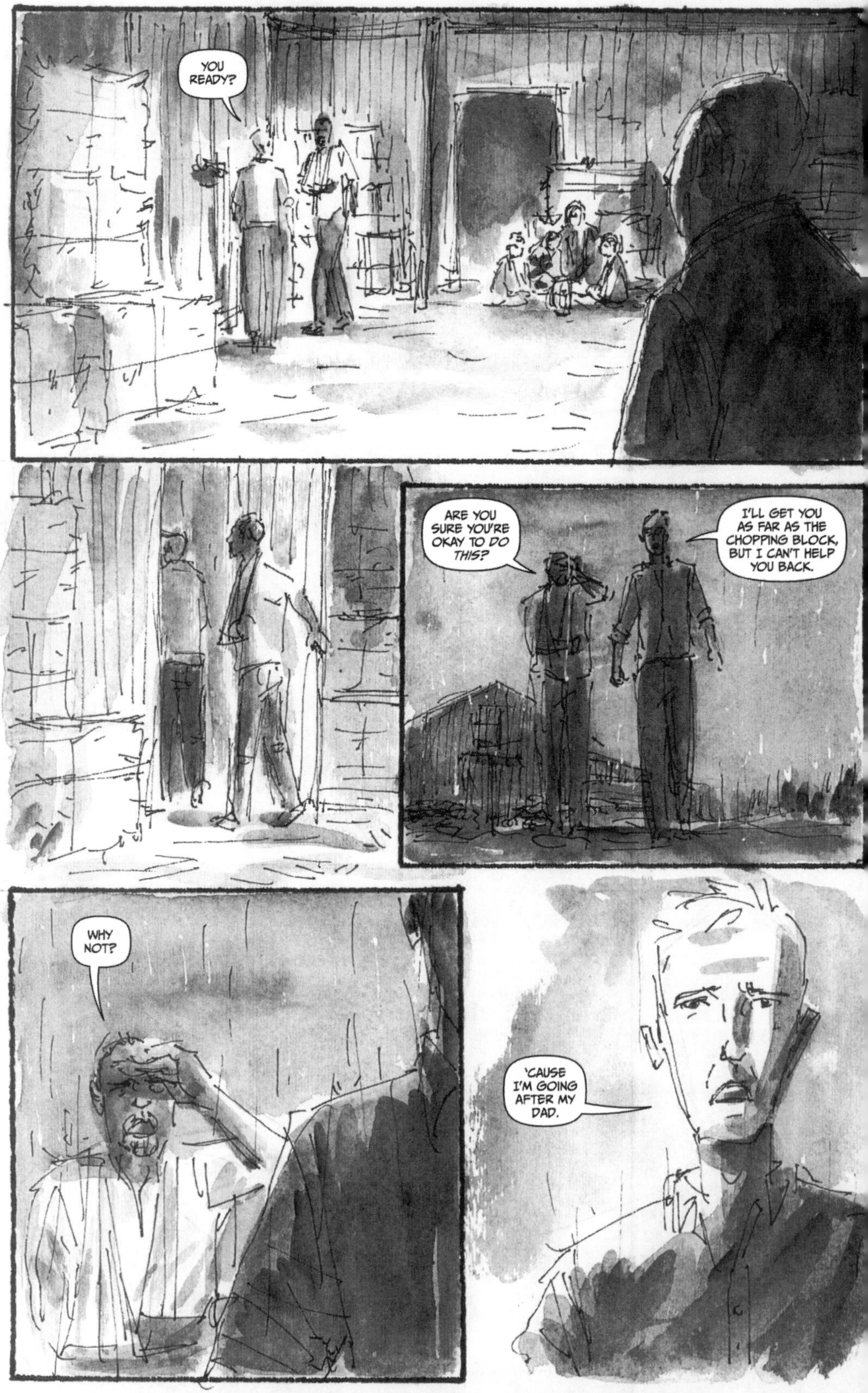
YOU READY?
ARE YOU SURE YOU'RE OKAY TO DO *THIS?*
I'LL GET YOU AS FAR AS THE CHOPPING BLOCK, BUT I CAN'T HELP YOU BACK.
WHY NOT?
'CAUSE I'M GOING AFTER MY DAD.

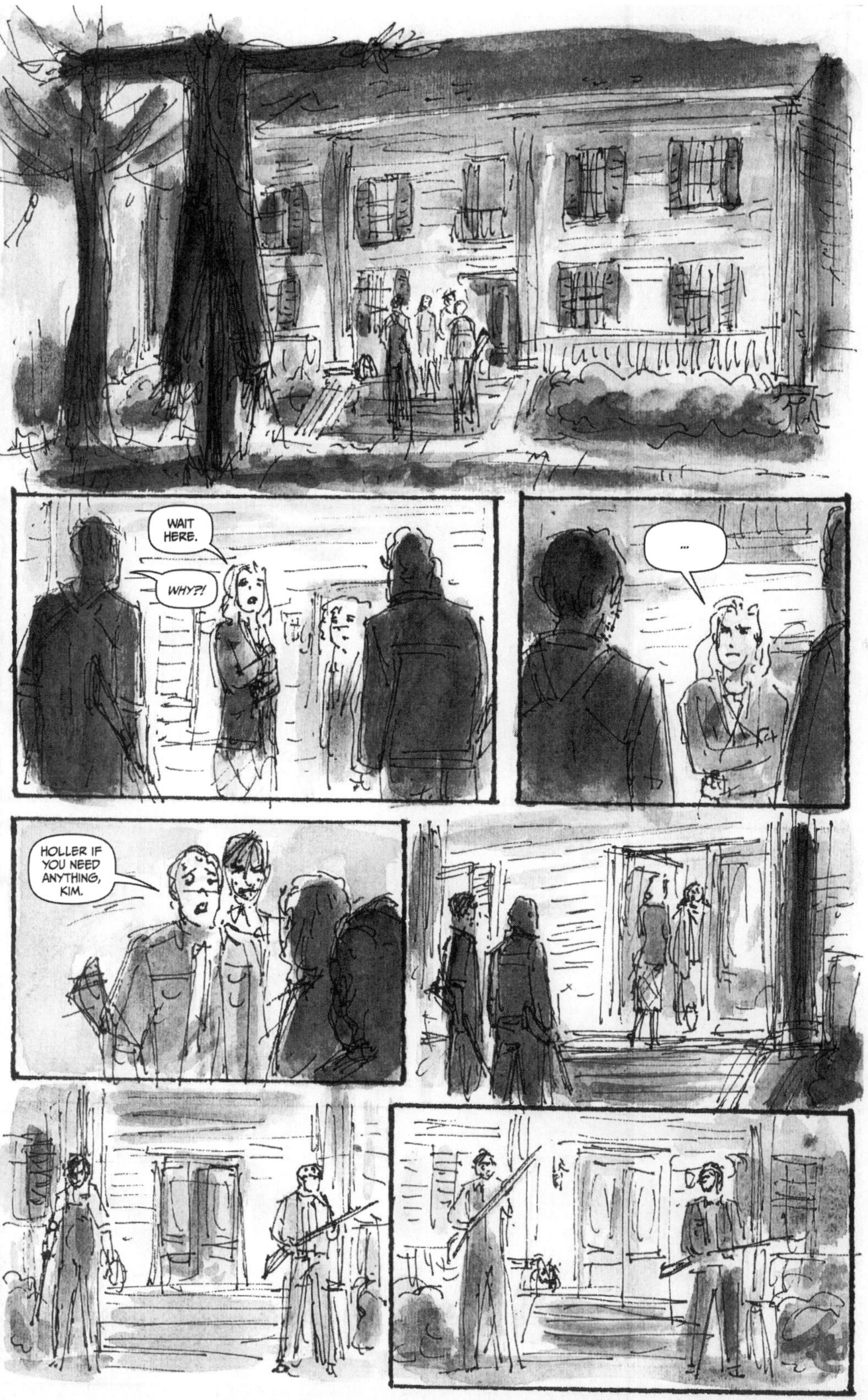
WAIT HERE.
WHY?!
...
HOLLER IF YOU NEED ANYTHING, KIM.

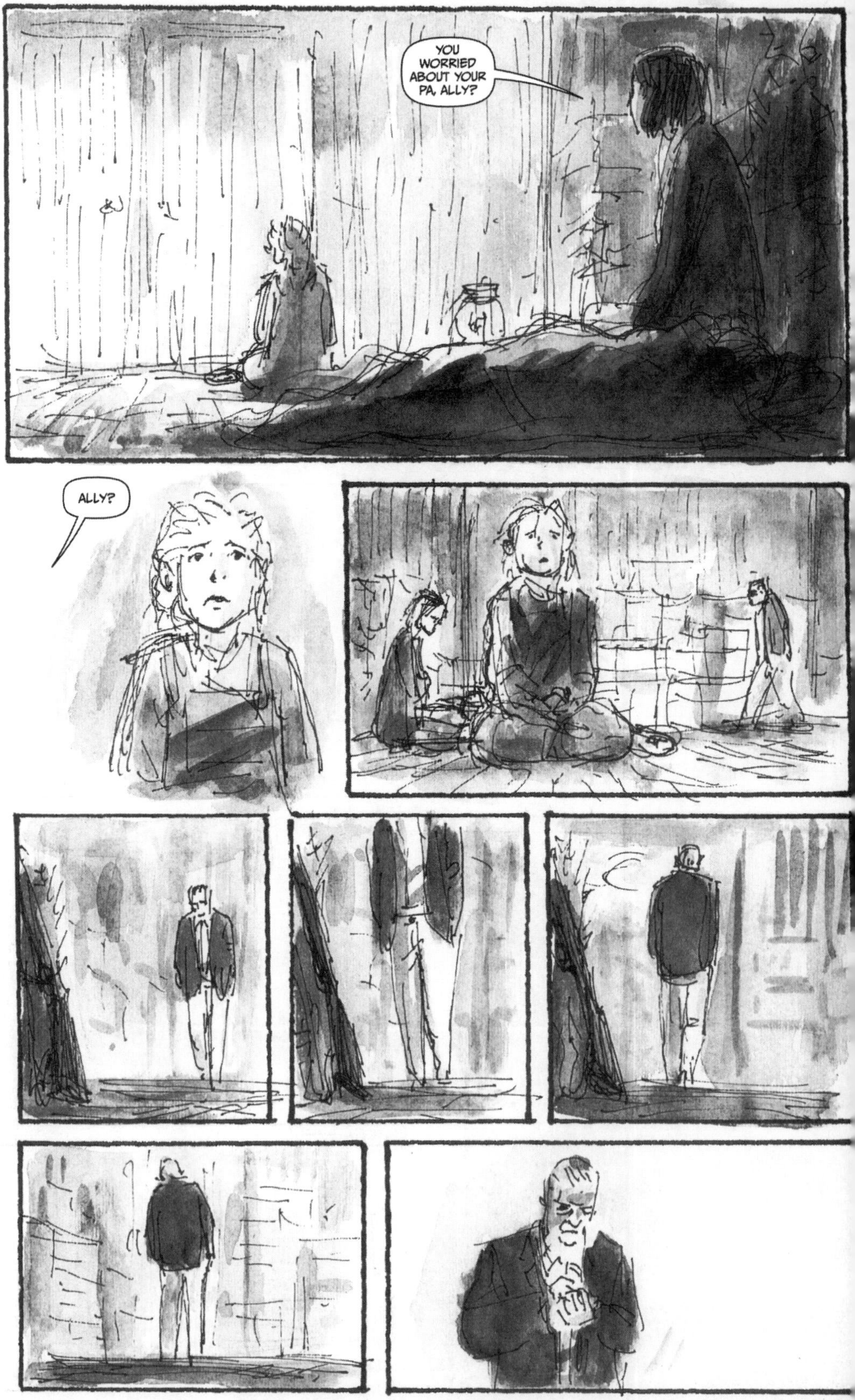
YOU WORRIED ABOUT YOUR PA, ALLY?
ALLY?

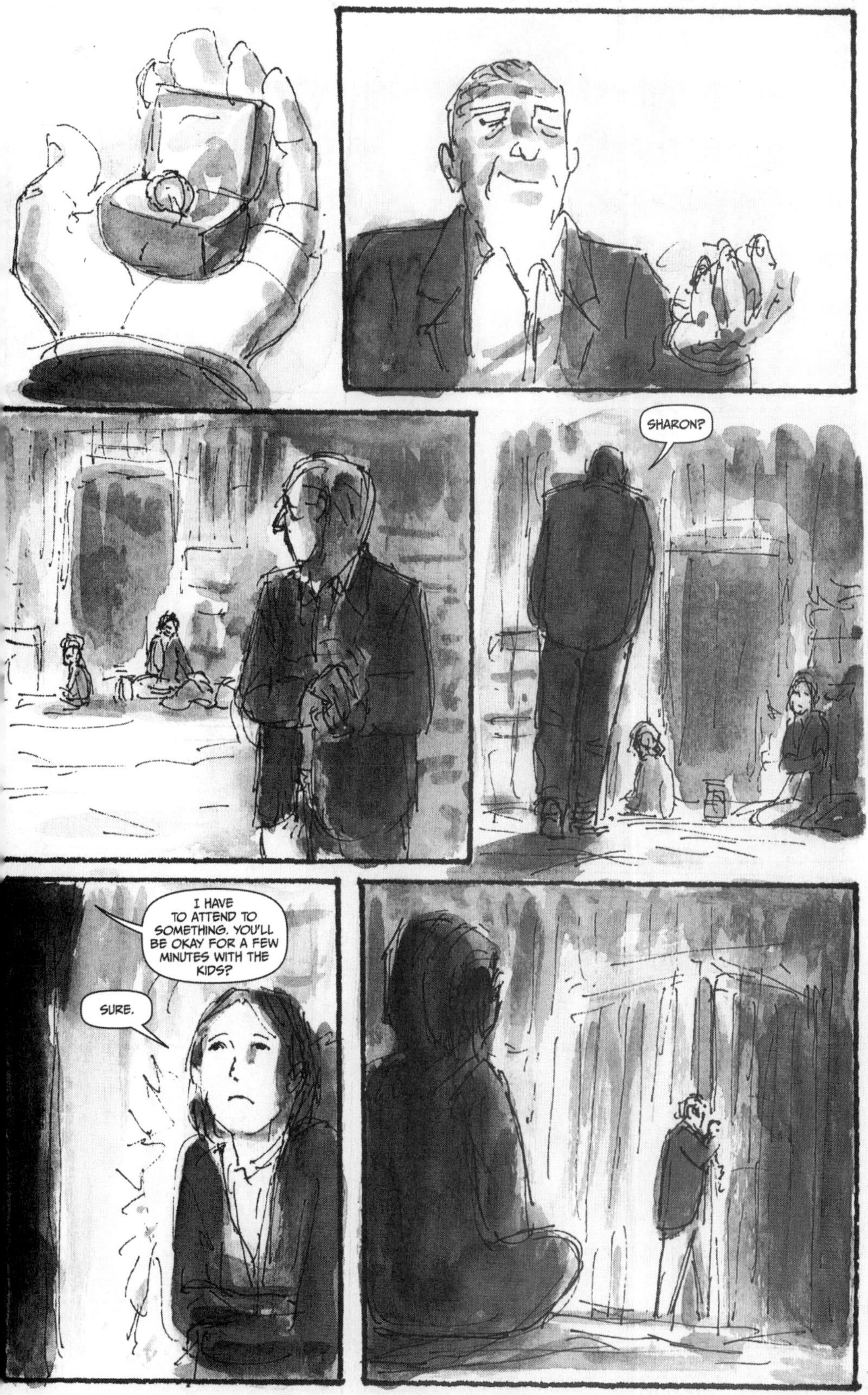
SHARON?
I HAVE TO ATTEND TO SOMETHING. YOU'LL BE OKAY FOR A FEW MINUTES WITH THE KIDS?
SURE.

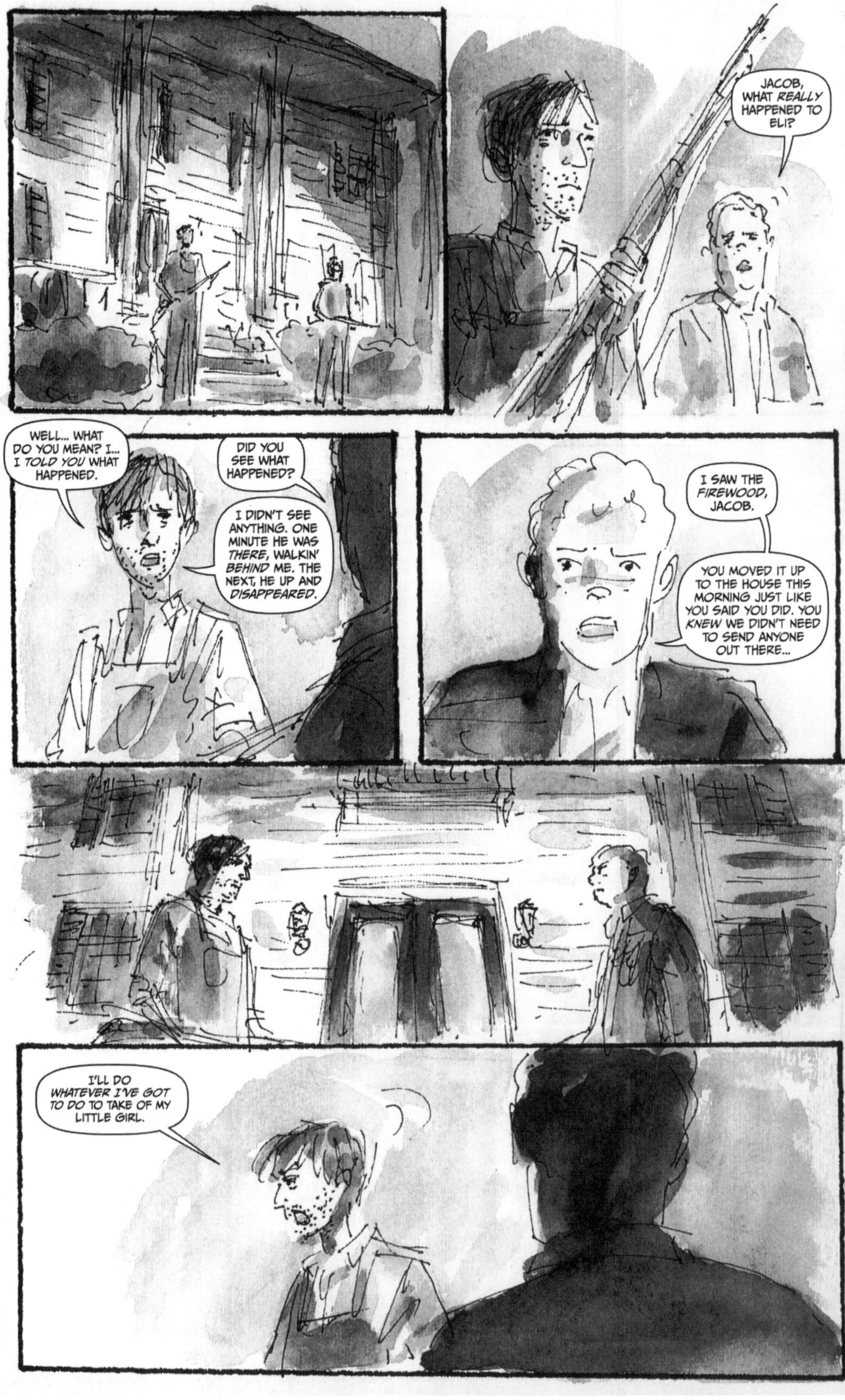
JACOB, WHAT *REALLY* HAPPENED TO ELI?
WELL... WHAT DO YOU MEAN? I... I *TOLD YOU* WHAT HAPPENED.
DID YOU SEE WHAT HAPPENED?
I DIDN'T SEE ANYTHING. ONE MINUTE HE WAS *THERE*, WALKIN' *BEHIND* ME. THE NEXT, HE UP AND *DISAPPEARED*.
I SAW THE *FIREWOOD*, JACOB.
YOU MOVED IT UP TO THE HOUSE THIS MORNING JUST LIKE YOU SAID YOU DID. YOU *KNEW* WE DIDN'T NEED TO SEND ANYONE OUT THERE...
I'LL DO *WHATEVER I'VE GOT TO DO* TO TAKE OF MY LITTLE GIRL.

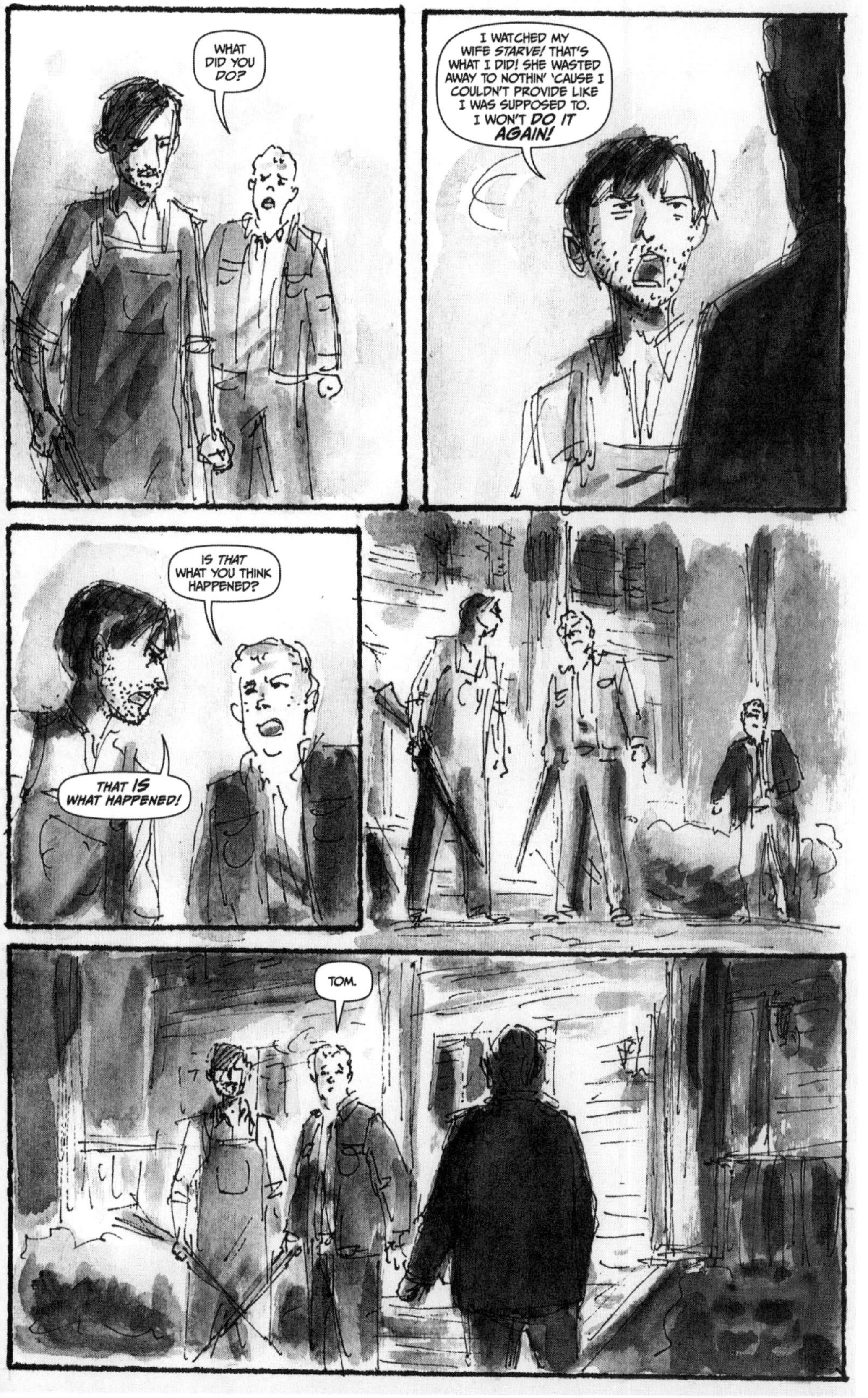
WHAT DID YOU DO?
I WATCHED MY WIFE STARVE! THAT'S WHAT I DID! SHE WASTED AWAY TO NOTHIN' 'CAUSE I COULDN'T PROVIDE LIKE I WAS SUPPOSED TO. I WON'T DO IT AGAIN!
IS THAT WHAT YOU THINK HAPPENED?
THAT IS WHAT HAPPENED!
TOM.

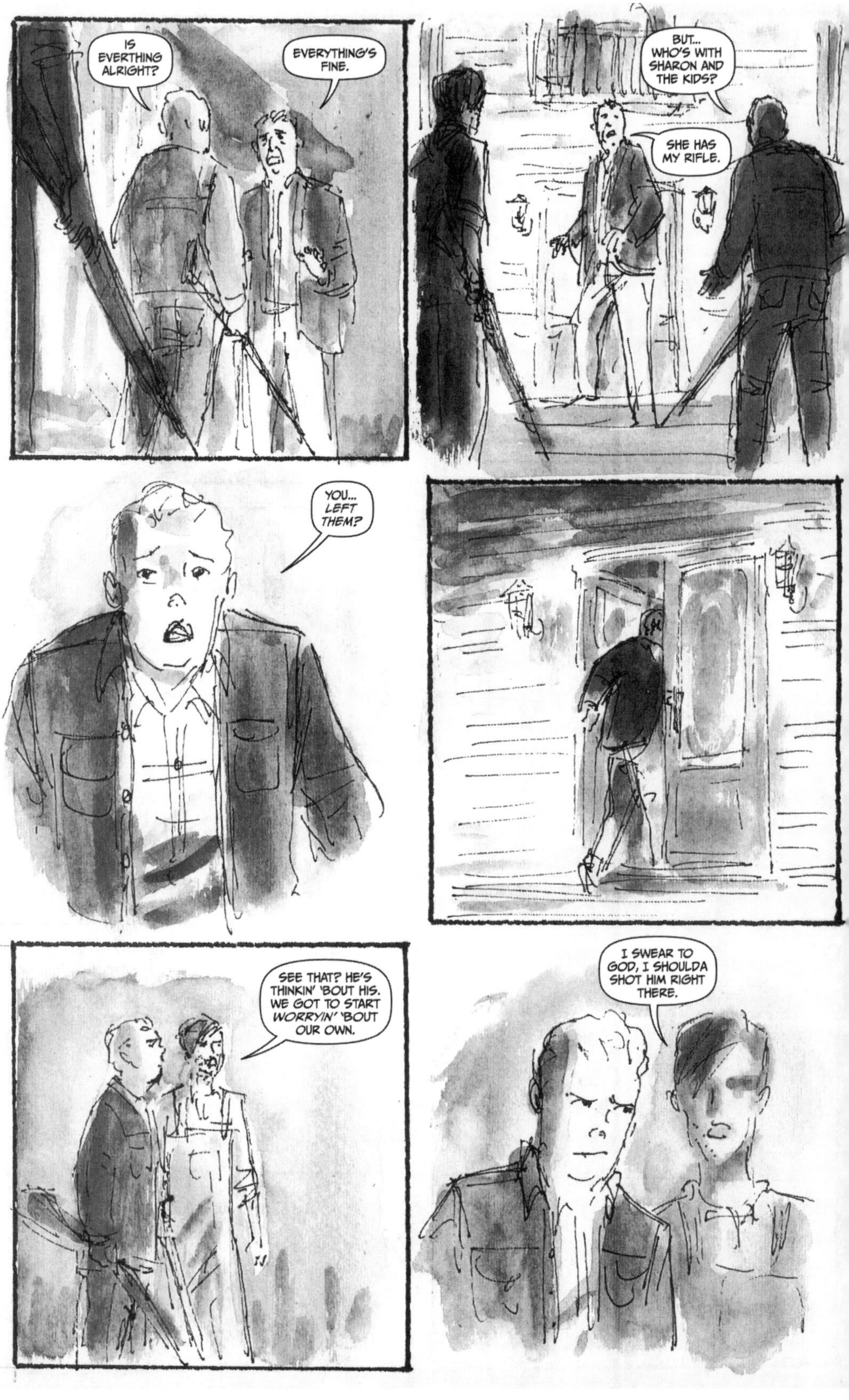
IS EVERTHING ALRIGHT?
EVERYTHING'S FINE.
BUT... WHO'S WITH SHARON AND THE KIDS?
SHE HAS MY RIFLE.
YOU... *LEFT* THEM?
SEE THAT? HE'S THINKIN' 'BOUT HIS. WE GOT TO START *WORRYIN'* 'BOUT OUR OWN.
I SWEAR TO GOD, I SHOULDA SHOT HIM RIGHT THERE.

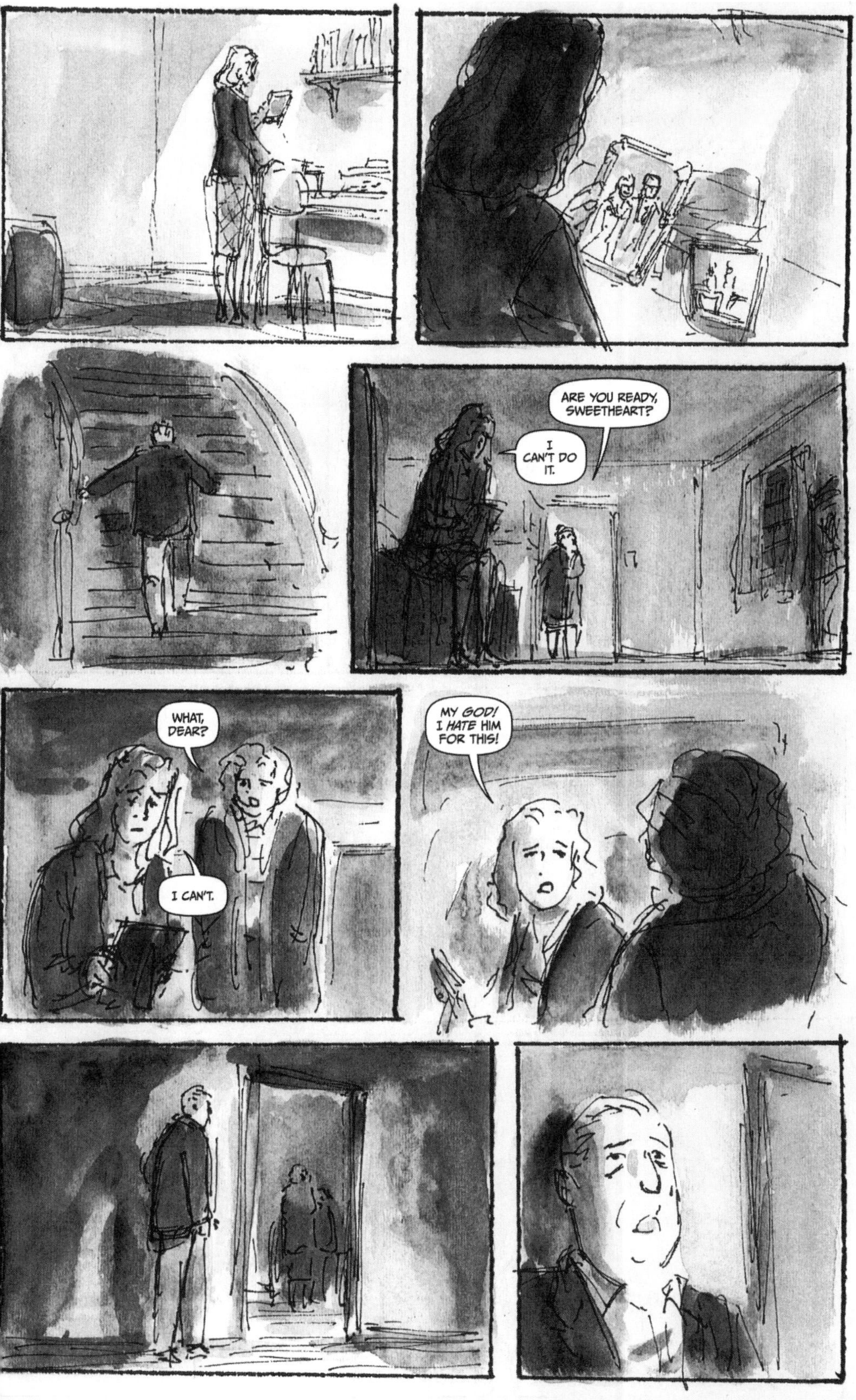
ARE YOU READY, SWEETHEART?
I CAN'T DO IT.
WHAT, DEAR?
I CAN'T.
MY *GOD!* I *HATE* HIM FOR THIS!

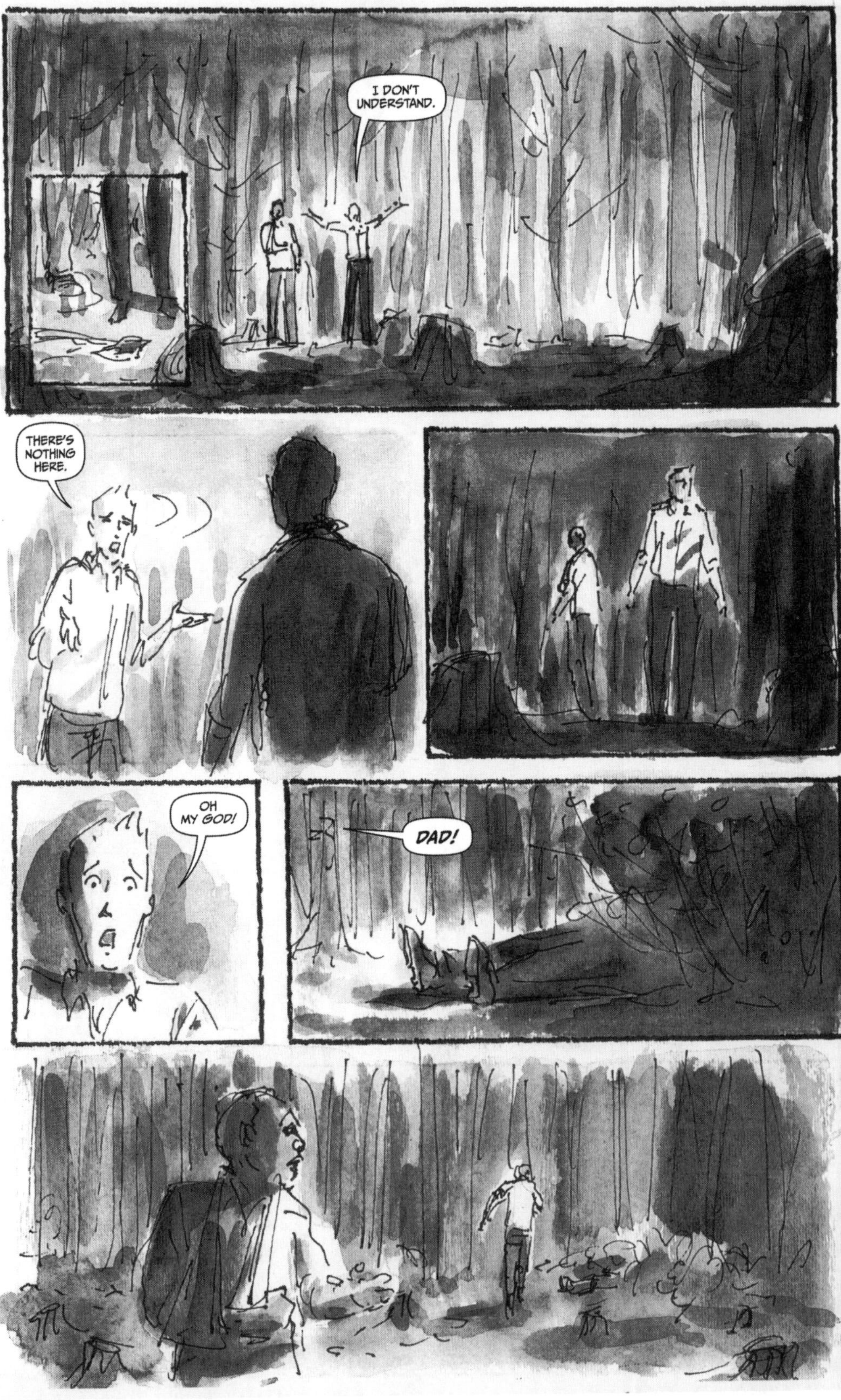
I DON'T UNDERSTAND.
THERE'S NOTHING HERE.
OH MY GOD!
DAD!

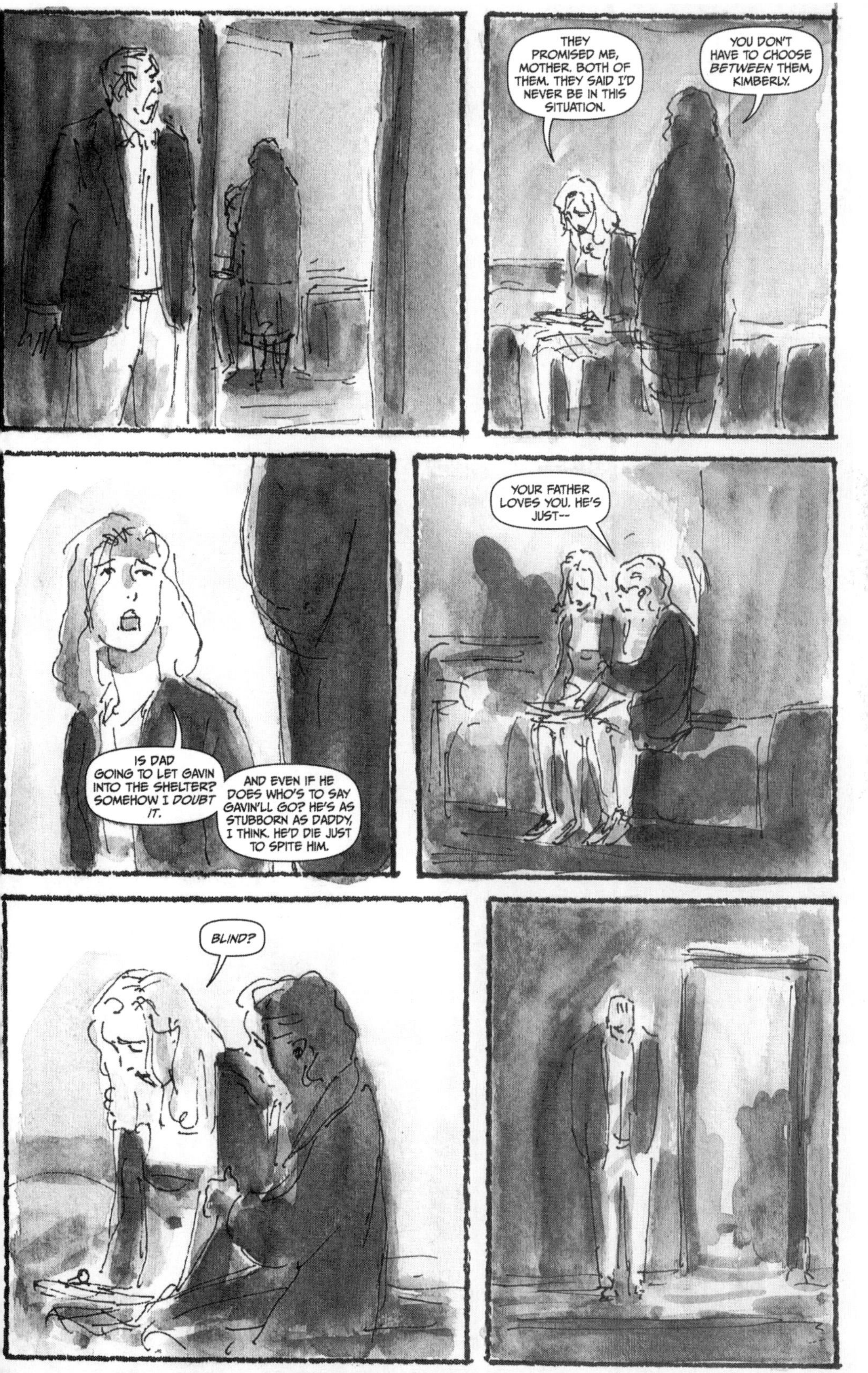
THEY PROMISED ME, MOTHER. BOTH OF THEM. THEY SAID I'D NEVER BE IN THIS SITUATION.
YOU DON'T HAVE TO CHOOSE *BETWEEN* THEM, KIMBERLY.
IS DAD GOING TO LET GAVIN INTO THE SHELTER? SOMEHOW I *DOUBT IT.*
AND EVEN IF HE DOES WHO'S TO SAY GAVIN'LL GO? HE'S AS STUBBORN AS DADDY, I THINK. HE'D DIE JUST TO SPITE HIM.
YOUR FATHER LOVES YOU. HE'S JUST--
BLIND?

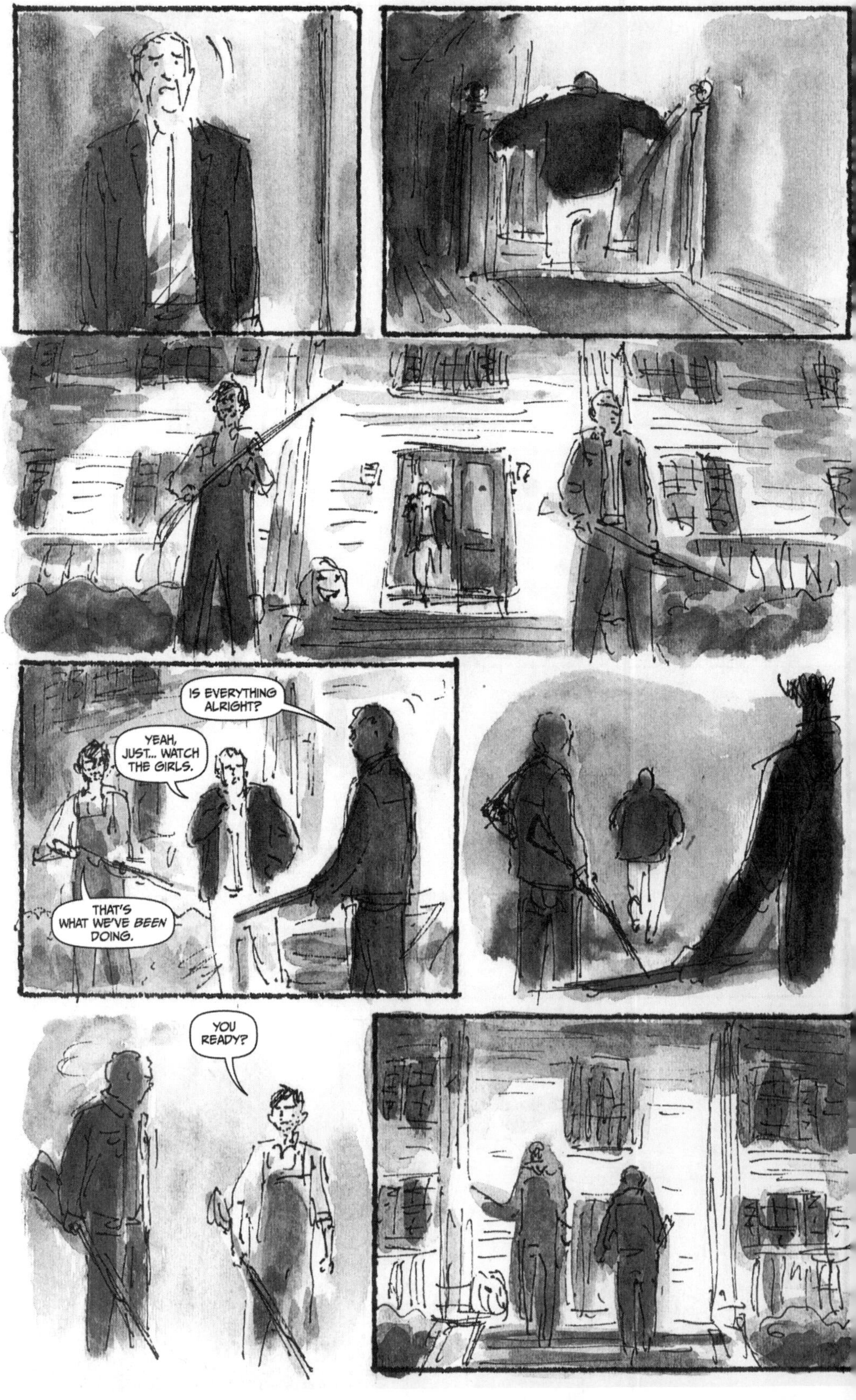
IS EVERYTHING ALRIGHT?
YEAH, JUST... WATCH THE GIRLS.
THAT'S WHAT WE'VE *BEEN* DOING.
YOU READY?

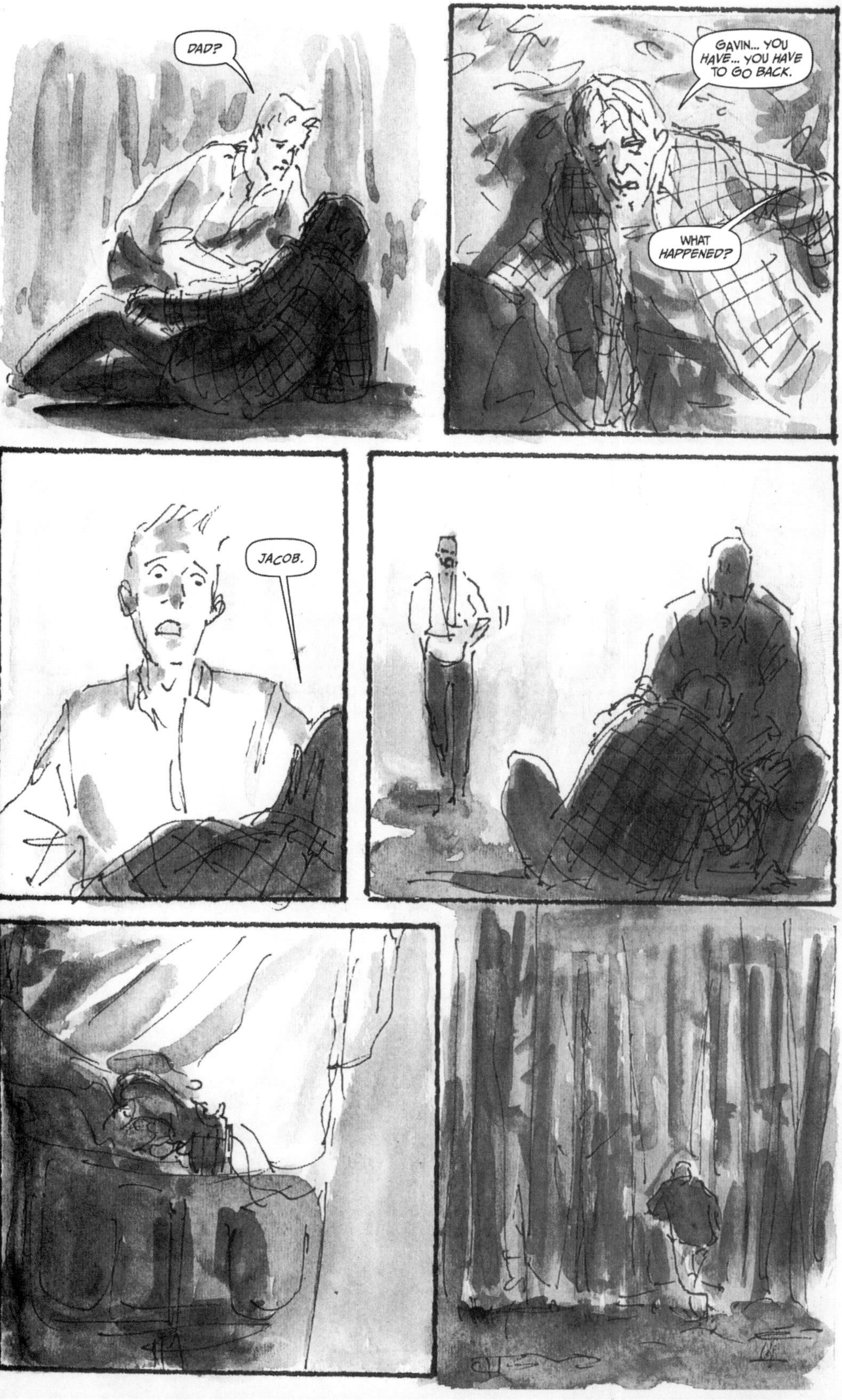
DAD?
GAVIN... YOU HAVE... YOU HAVE TO GO BACK.
WHAT HAPPENED?
JACOB.

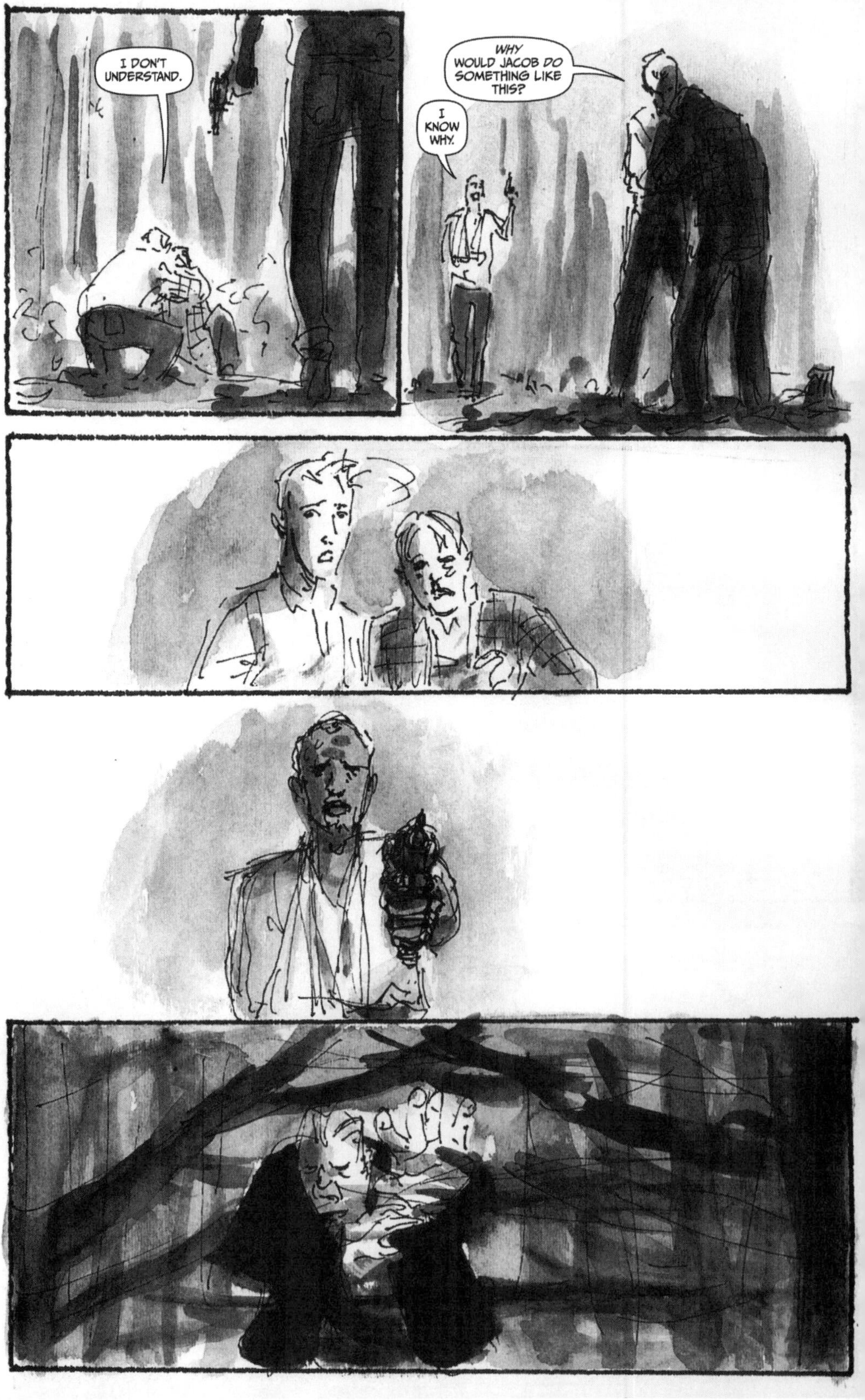
I DON'T UNDERSTAND.
WHY WOULD JACOB DO SOMETHING LIKE THIS?
I KNOW WHY.

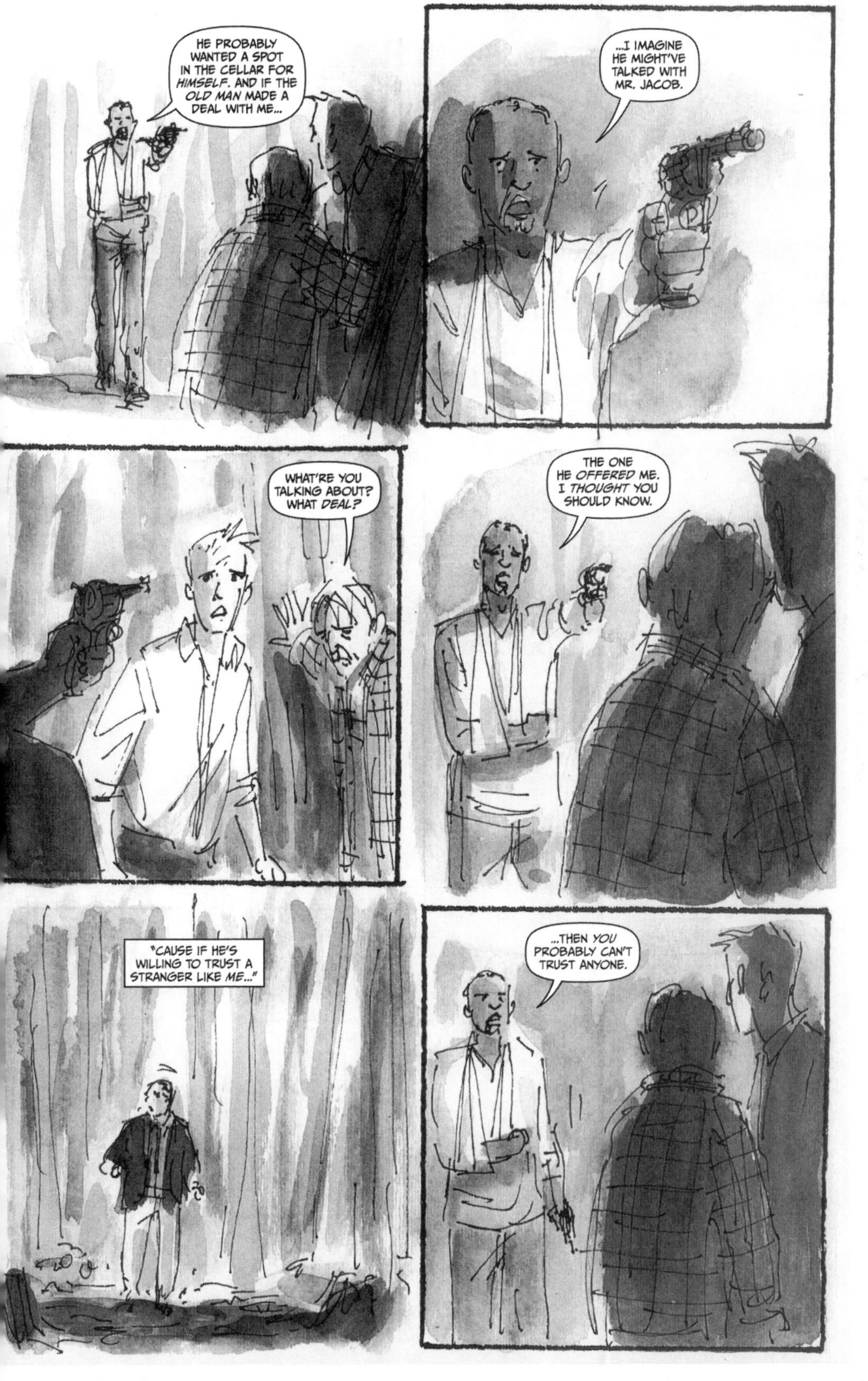
HE PROBABLY WANTED A SPOT IN THE CELLAR FOR HIMSELF. AND IF THE OLD MAN MADE A DEAL WITH ME...
...I IMAGINE HE MIGHT'VE TALKED WITH MR. JACOB.
WHAT'RE YOU TALKING ABOUT? WHAT DEAL?
THE ONE HE OFFERED ME. I THOUGHT YOU SHOULD KNOW.
"CAUSE IF HE'S WILLING TO TRUST A STRANGER LIKE ME..."
...THEN YOU PROBABLY CAN'T TRUST ANYONE.

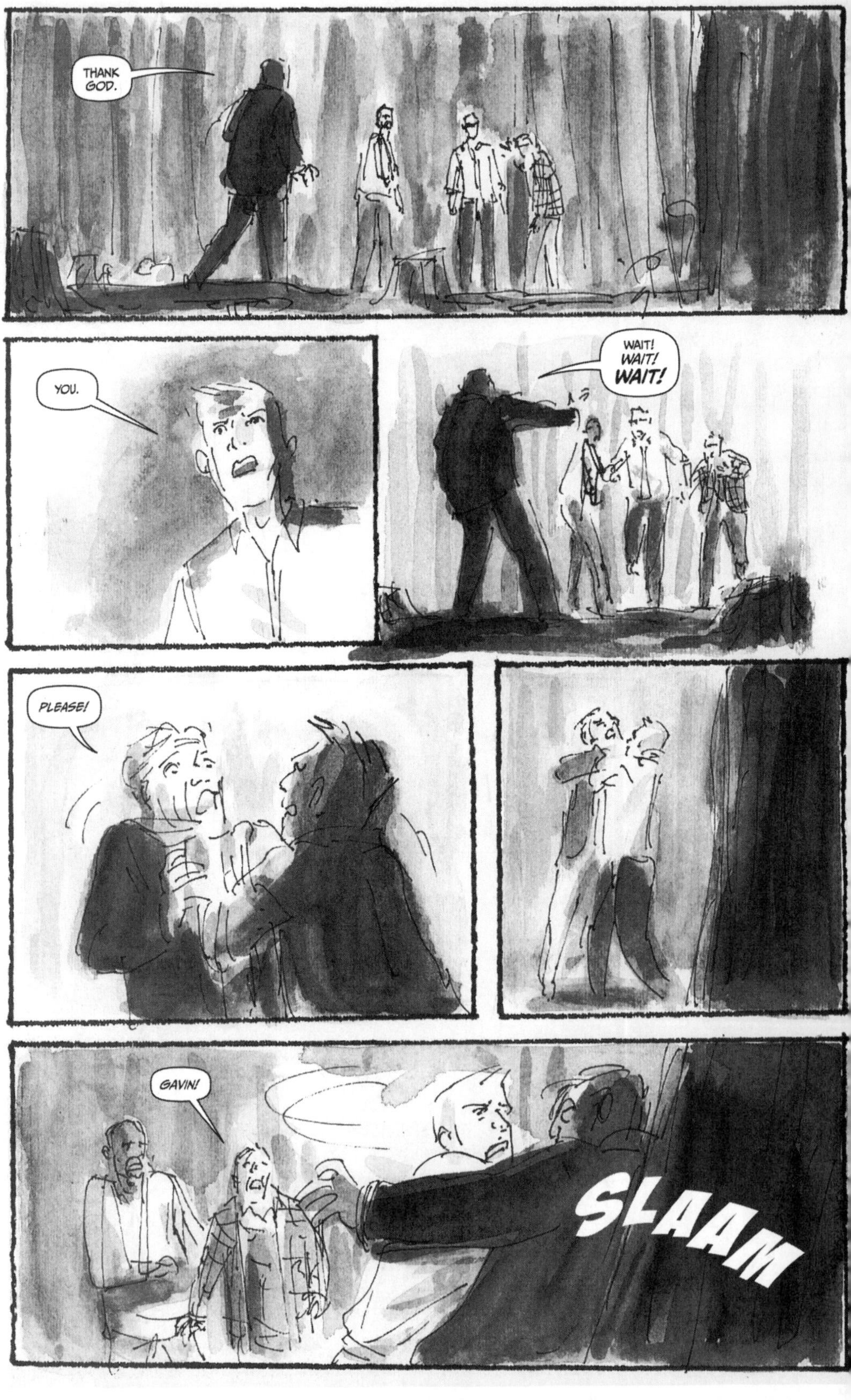
THANK GOD.
YOU.
WAIT! WAIT! WAIT!
PLEASE!
GAVIN!
SLAAM

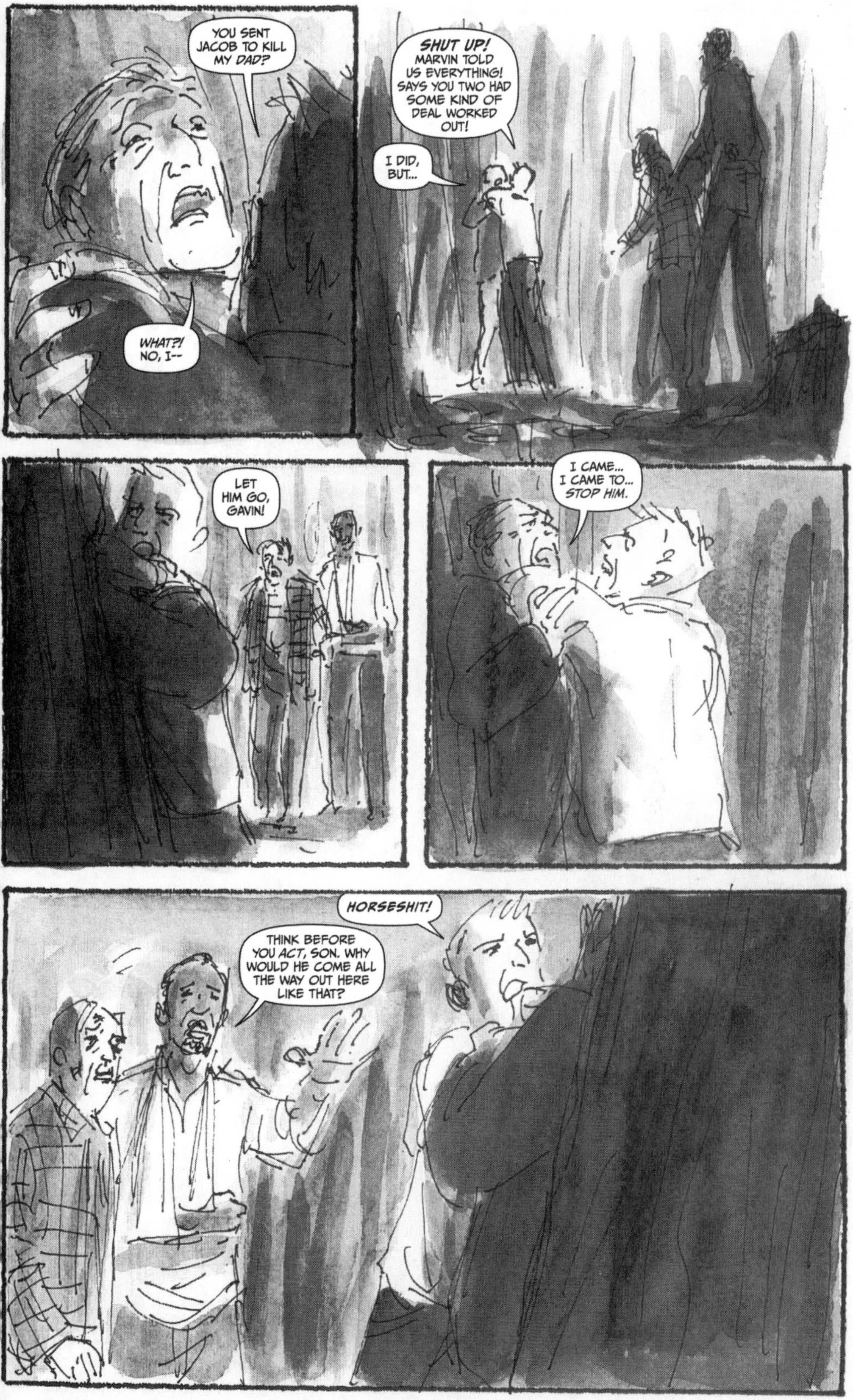
YOU SENT JACOB TO KILL MY *DAD?*
WHAT?! NO, I--
SHUT UP! MARVIN TOLD US EVERYTHING! SAYS YOU TWO HAD SOME KIND OF DEAL WORKED OUT!
I DID, BUT...
LET HIM GO, GAVIN!
I CAME... I CAME TO... *STOP HIM.*
HORSESHIT!
THINK BEFORE YOU *ACT*, SON. WHY WOULD HE COME ALL THE WAY OUT HERE LIKE THAT?

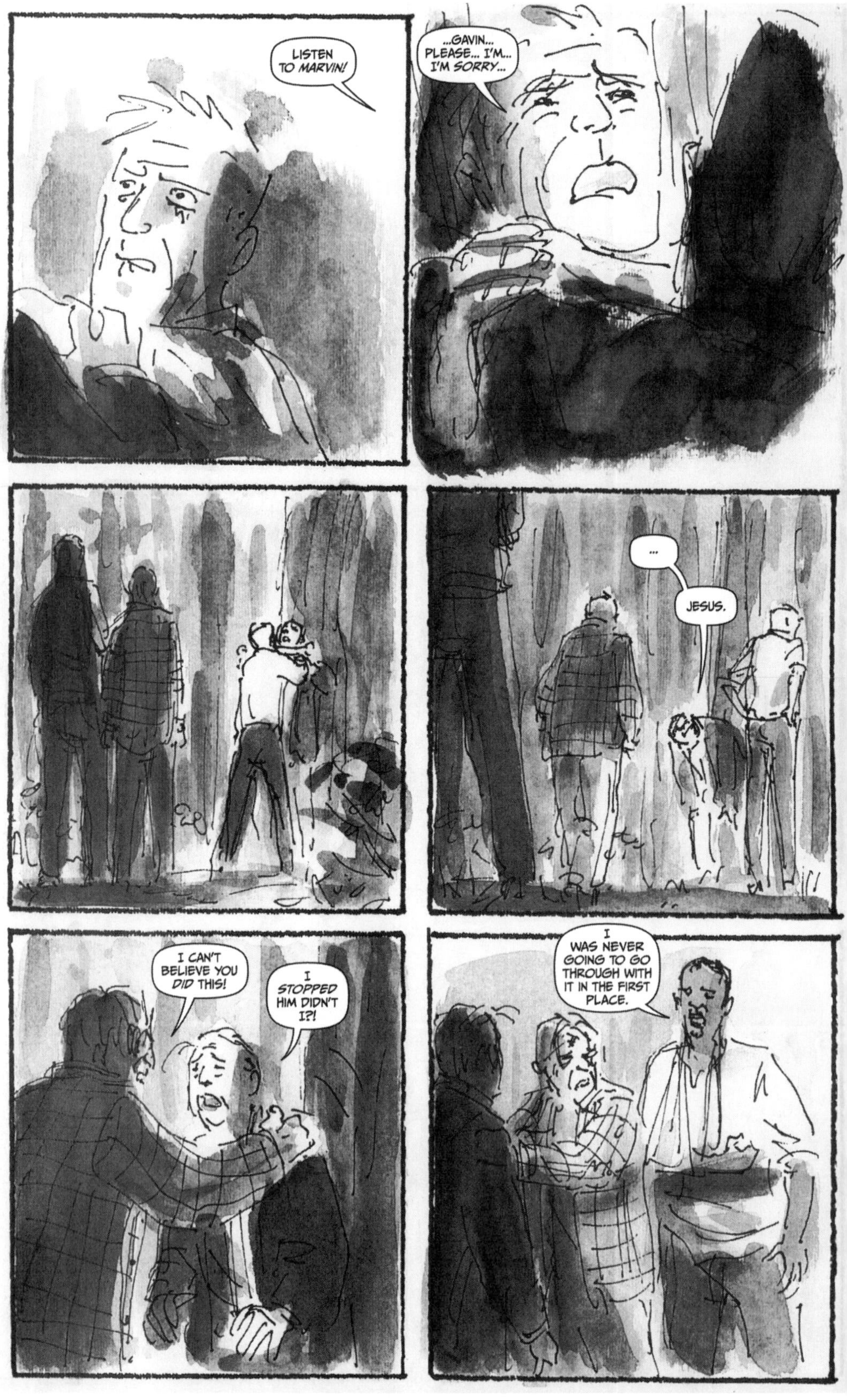
LISTEN TO MARVIN!
...GAVIN... PLEASE... I'M... I'M SORRY...
...
JESUS.
I CAN'T BELIEVE YOU DID THIS!
I STOPPED HIM DIDN'T I?!
I WAS NEVER GOING TO GO THROUGH WITH IT IN THE FIRST PLACE.

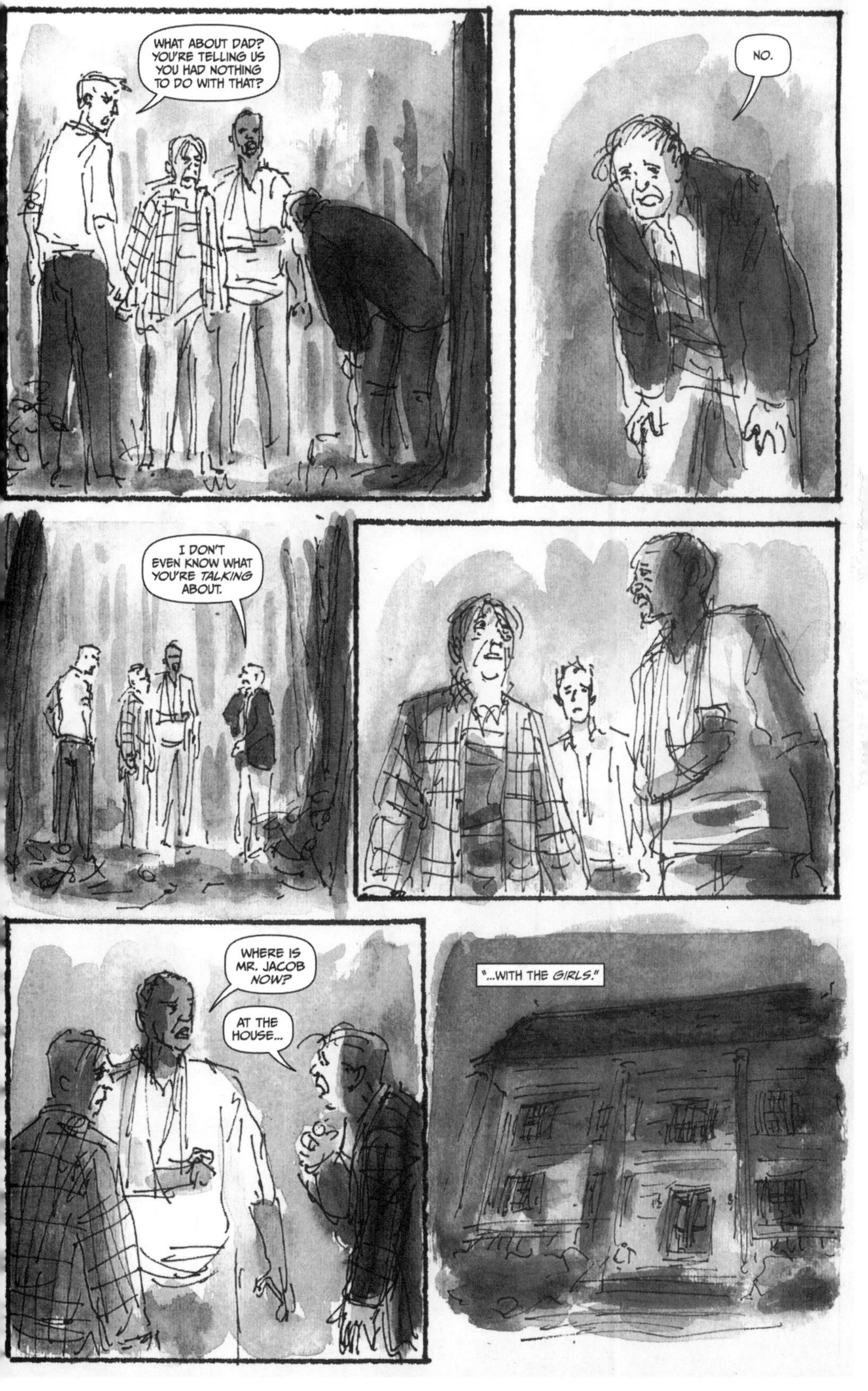
WHAT ABOUT DAD? YOU'RE TELLING US YOU HAD NOTHING TO DO WITH THAT?
NO.
I DON'T EVEN KNOW WHAT YOU'RE *TALKING* ABOUT.
WHERE IS MR. JACOB *NOW?*
AT THE HOUSE...
"...WITH THE *GIRLS.*"

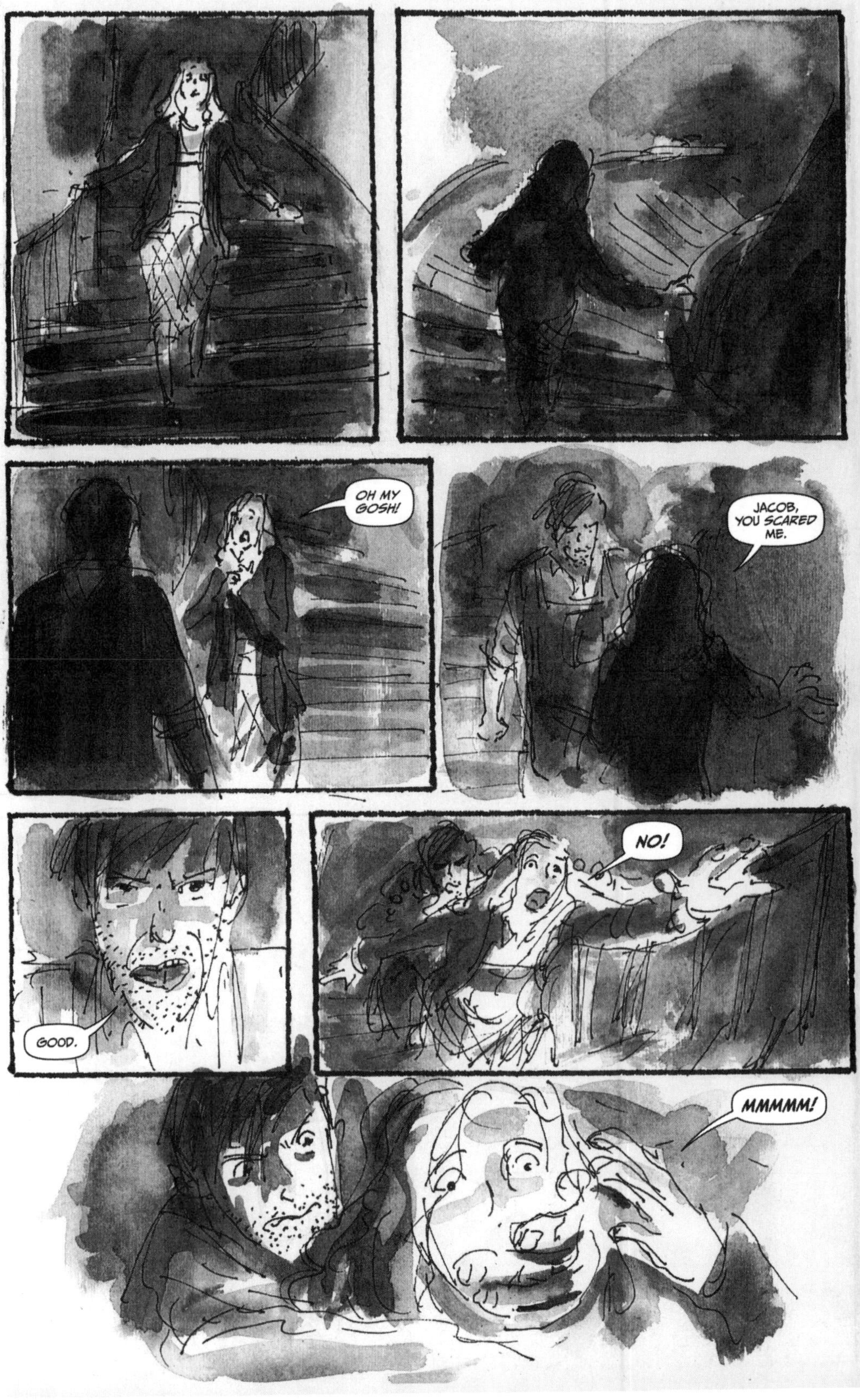
OH MY GOSH!
JACOB, YOU SCARED ME.
GOOD.
NO!
MMMMM!

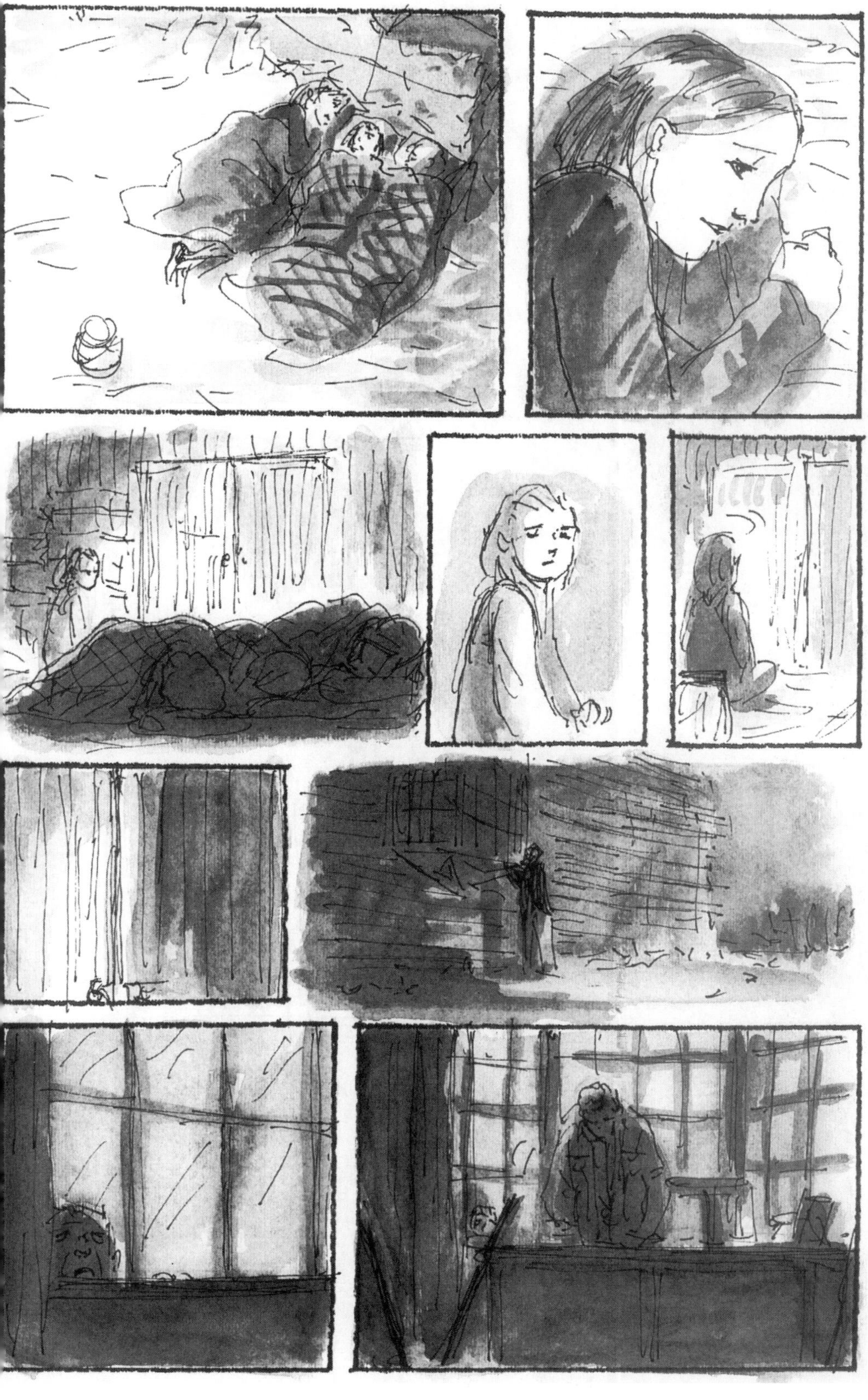

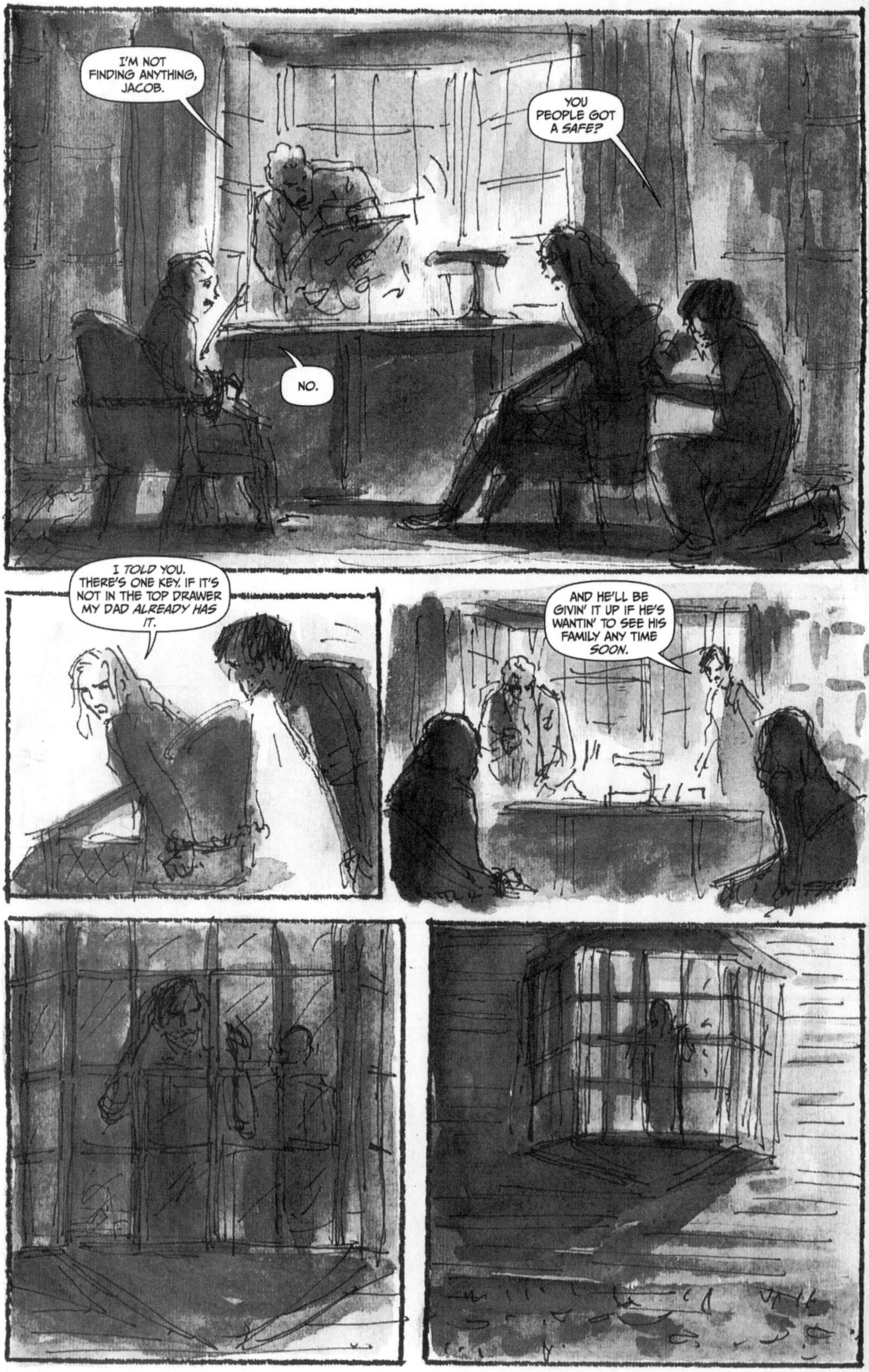
I'M NOT FINDING ANYTHING, JACOB.
YOU PEOPLE GOT A SAFE?
NO.
I TOLD YOU. THERE'S ONE KEY. IF IT'S NOT IN THE TOP DRAWER MY DAD ALREADY HAS IT.
AND HE'LL BE GIVIN' IT UP IF HE'S WANTIN' TO SEE HIS FAMILY ANY TIME SOON.

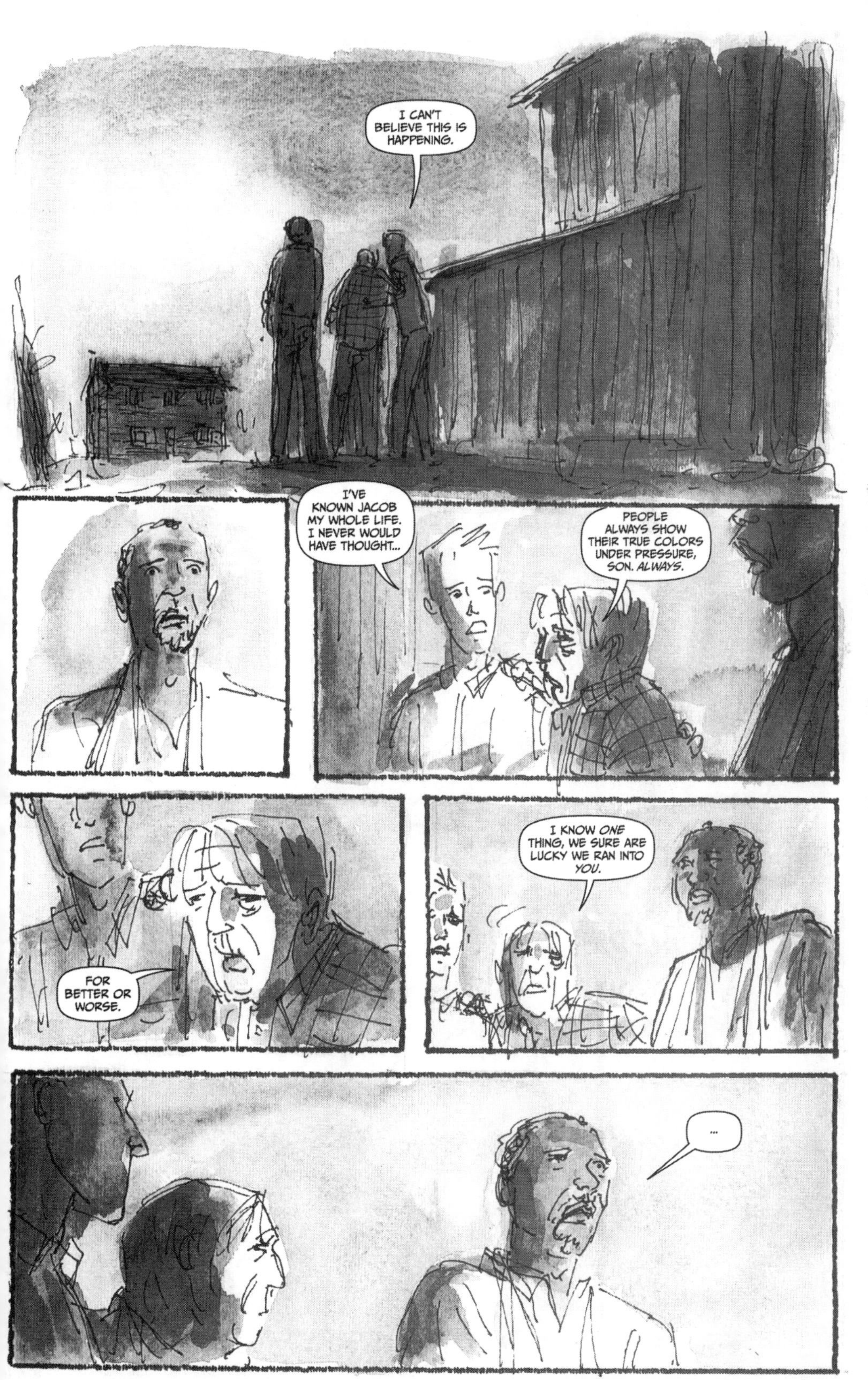
I CAN'T BELIEVE THIS IS HAPPENING.
I'VE KNOWN JACOB MY WHOLE LIFE. I NEVER WOULD HAVE THOUGHT...
PEOPLE ALWAYS SHOW THEIR TRUE COLORS UNDER PRESSURE, SON. ALWAYS.
FOR BETTER OR WORSE.
I KNOW ONE THING, WE SURE ARE LUCKY WE RAN INTO YOU.
...

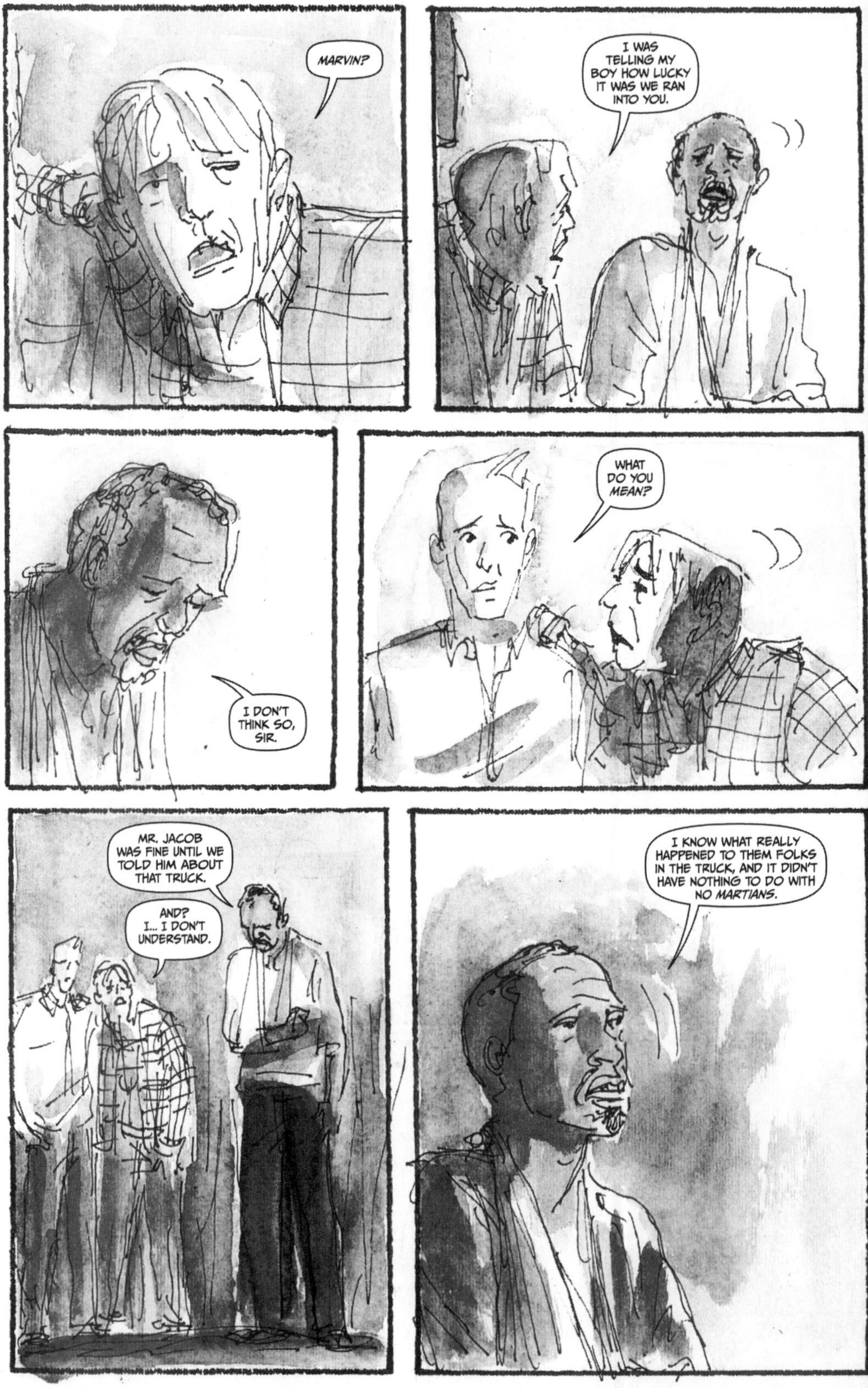
MARVIN?
I WAS TELLING MY BOY HOW LUCKY IT WAS WE RAN INTO YOU.
I DON'T THINK SO, SIR.
WHAT DO YOU MEAN?
MR. JACOB WAS FINE UNTIL WE TOLD HIM ABOUT THAT TRUCK.
AND? I... I DON'T UNDERSTAND.
I KNOW WHAT REALLY HAPPENED TO THEM FOLKS IN THE TRUCK, AND IT DIDN'T HAVE NOTHING TO DO WITH NO MARTIANS.

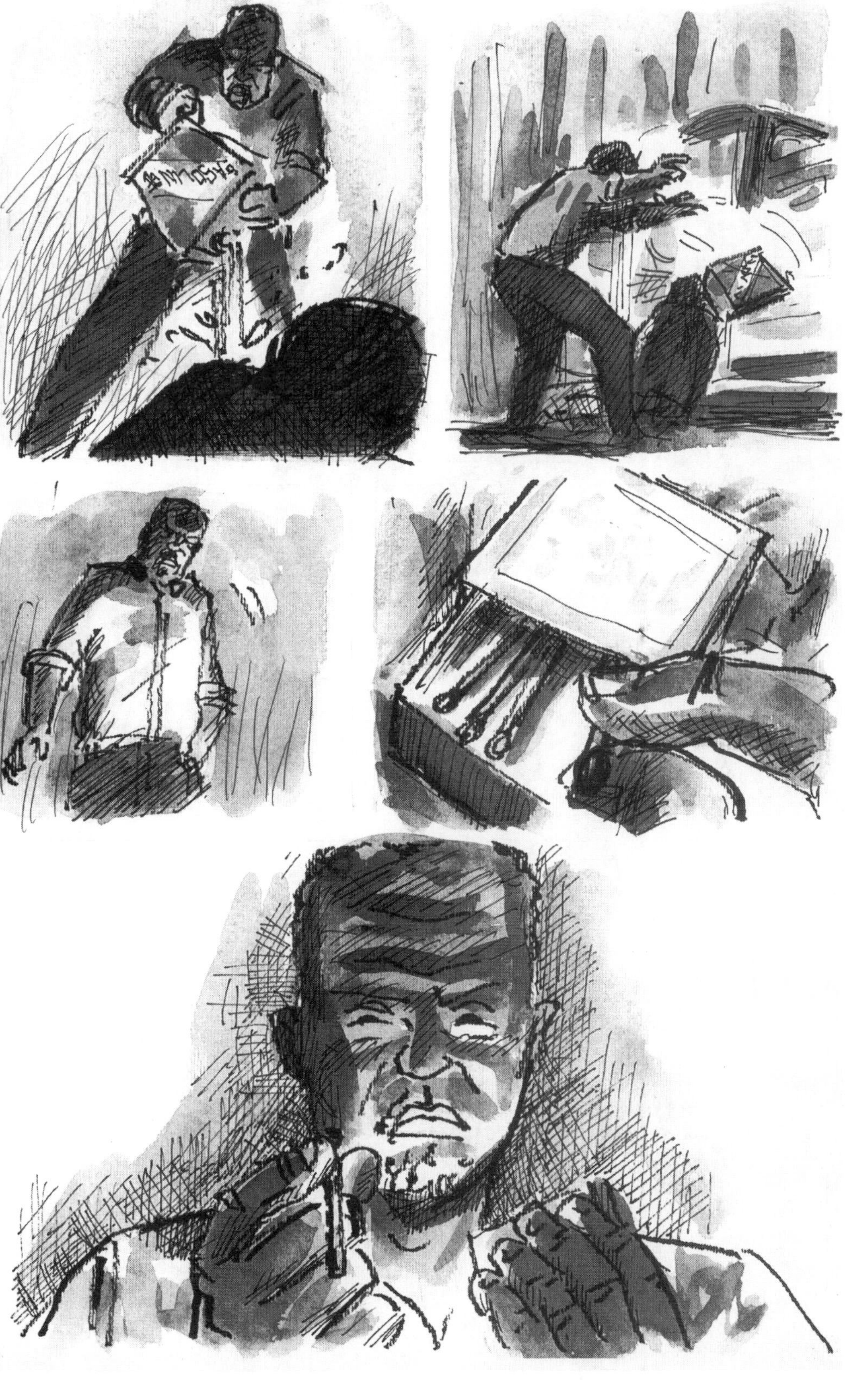

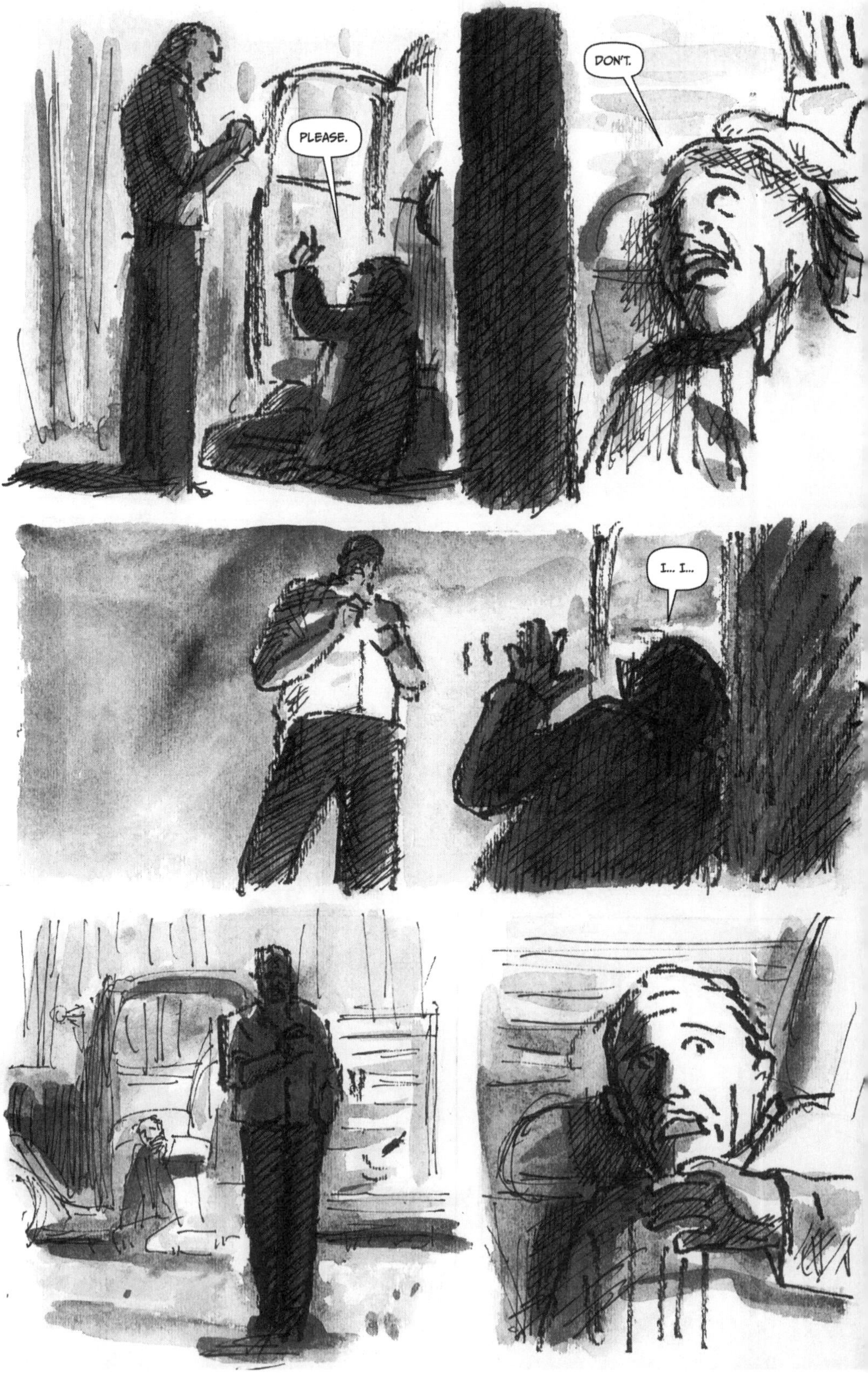
PLEASE.
DON'T.
I... I...

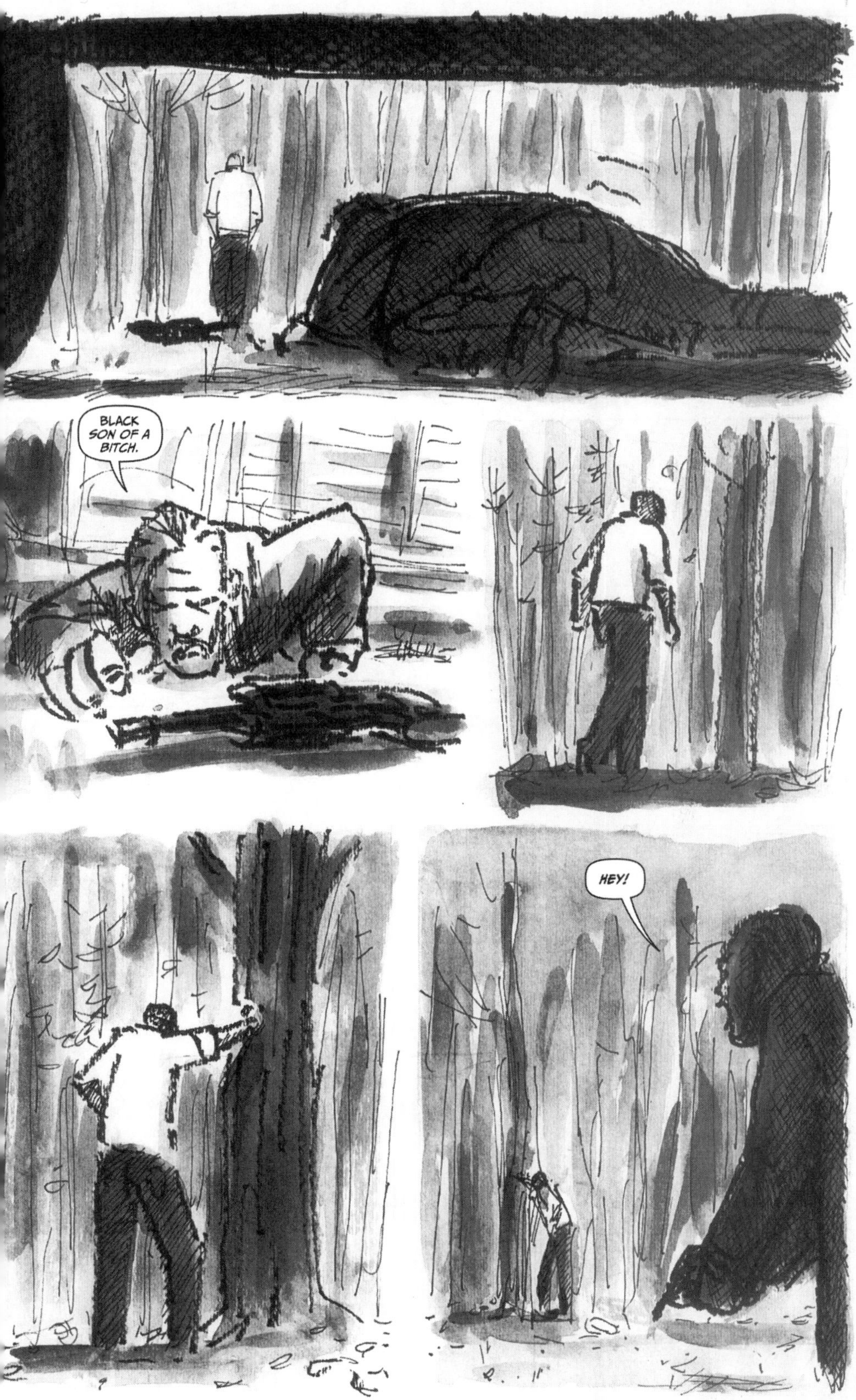
BLACK SON OF A BITCH.
HEY!

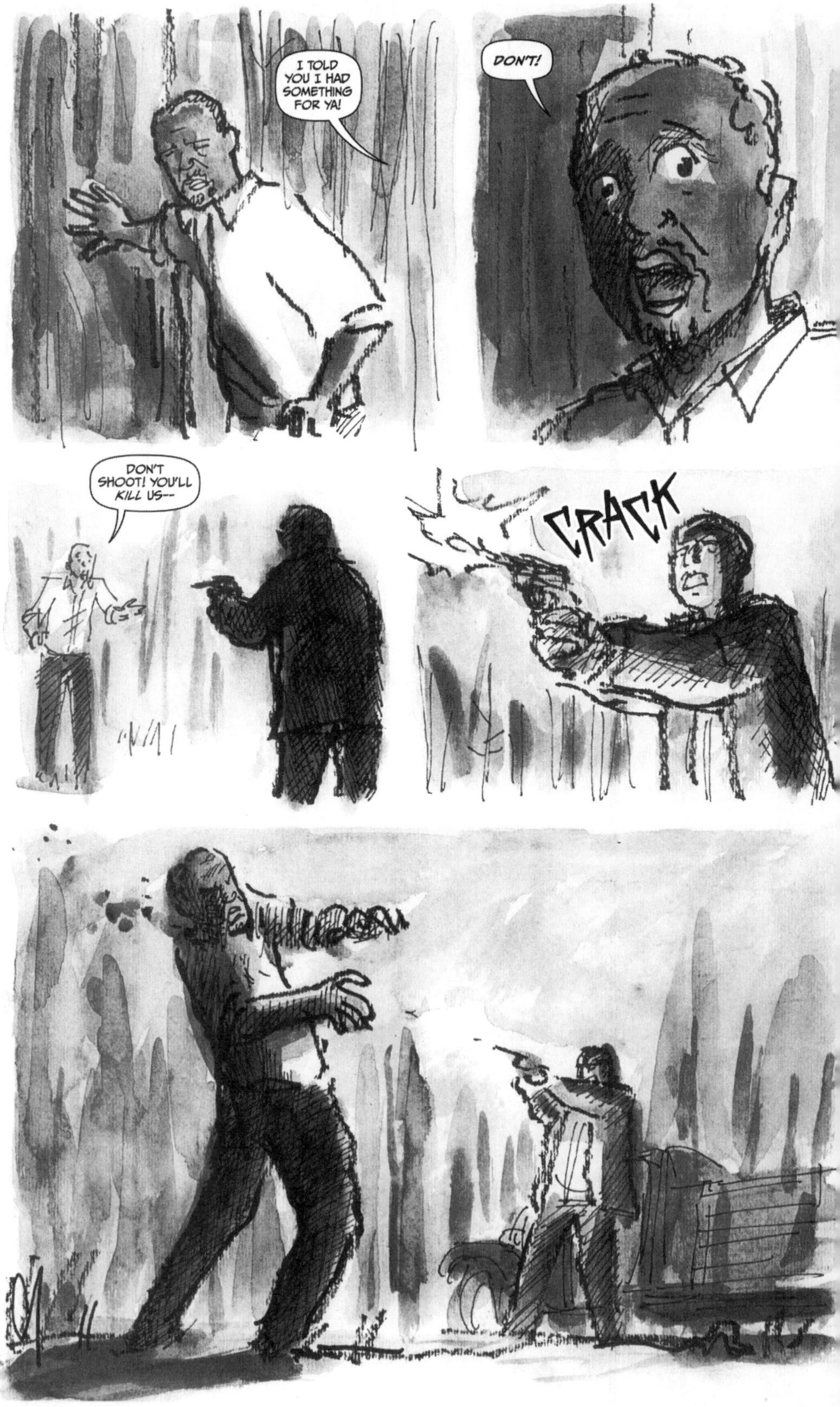

I TOLD YOU I HAD SOMETHING FOR YA!
DON'T!
DON'T SHOOT! YOU'LL KILL US--
CRACK

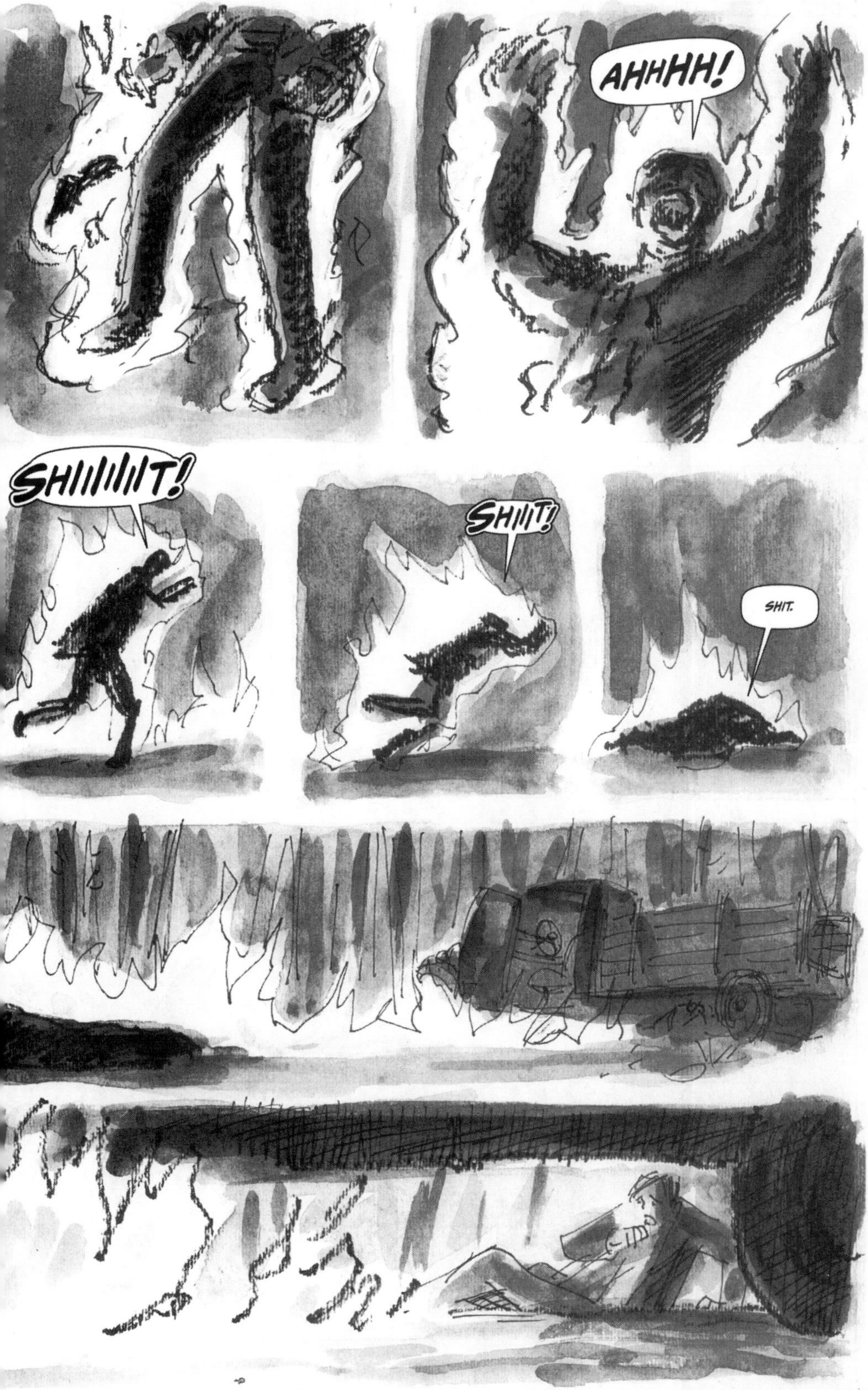
AHHHH!
SHIIIIIIT!
SHIIIT!
SHIT.

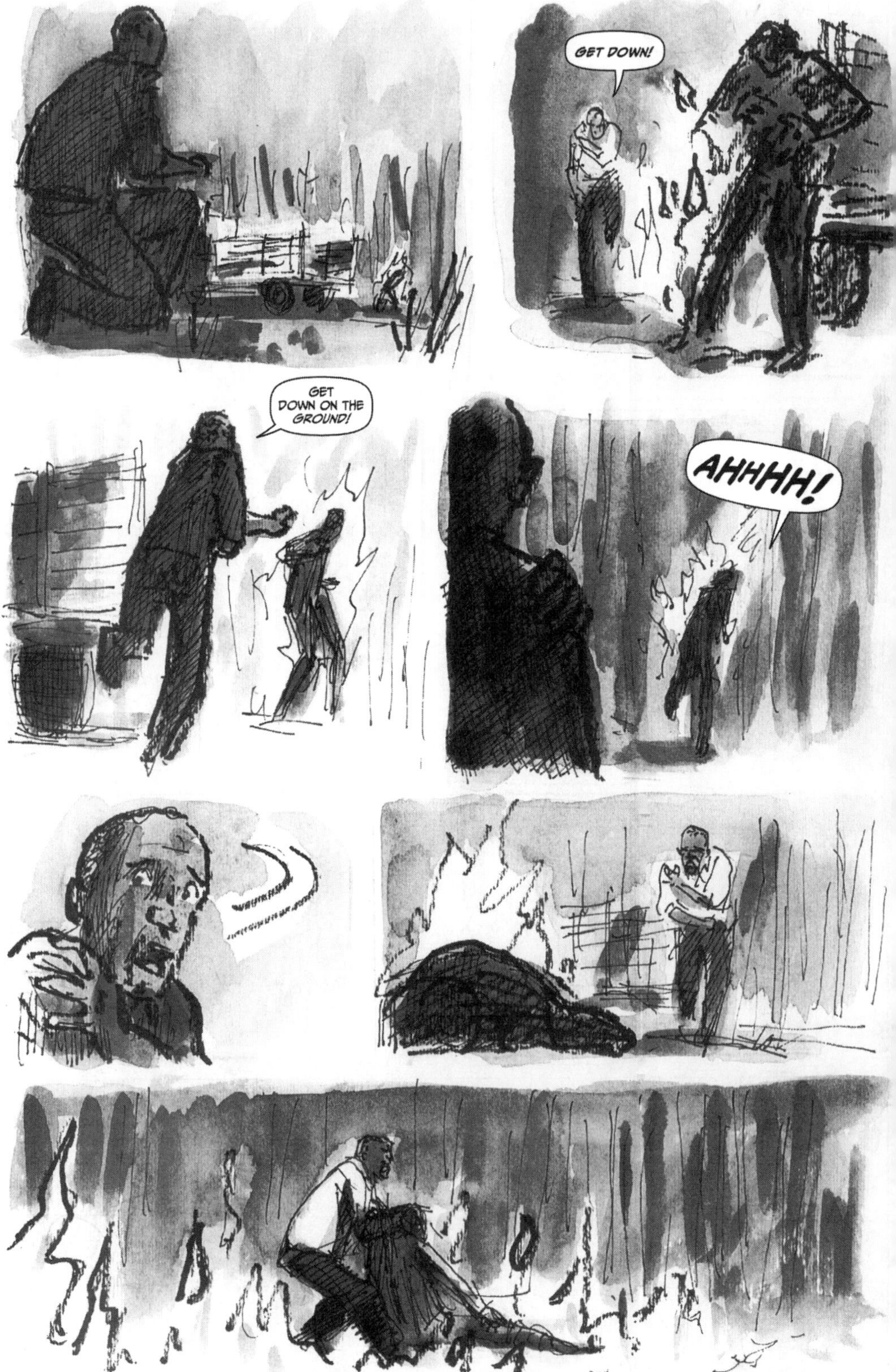
GET DOWN!
GET DOWN ON THE GROUND!
AHHHH!

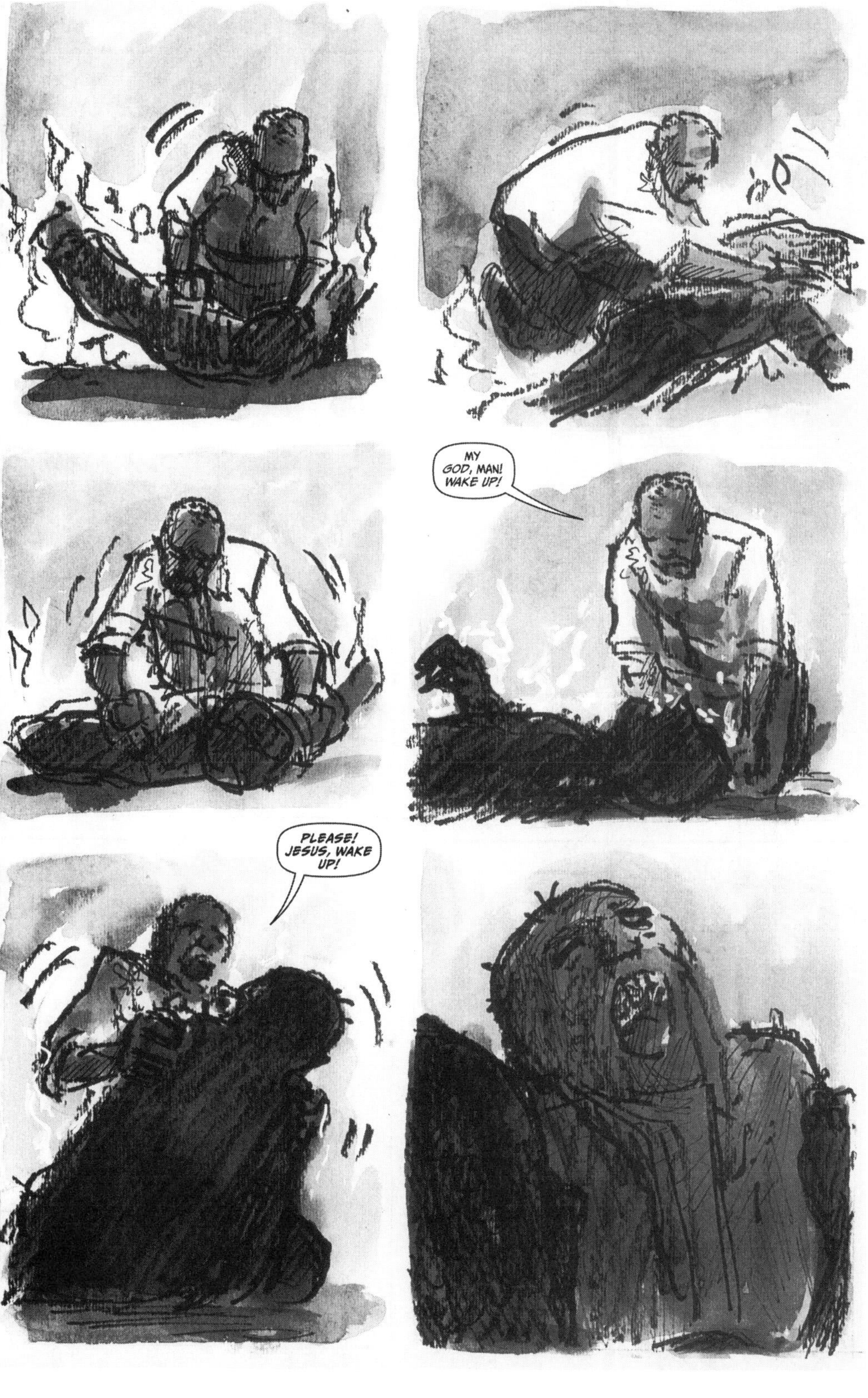
MY GOD, MAN! WAKE UP!
PLEASE! JESUS, WAKE UP!

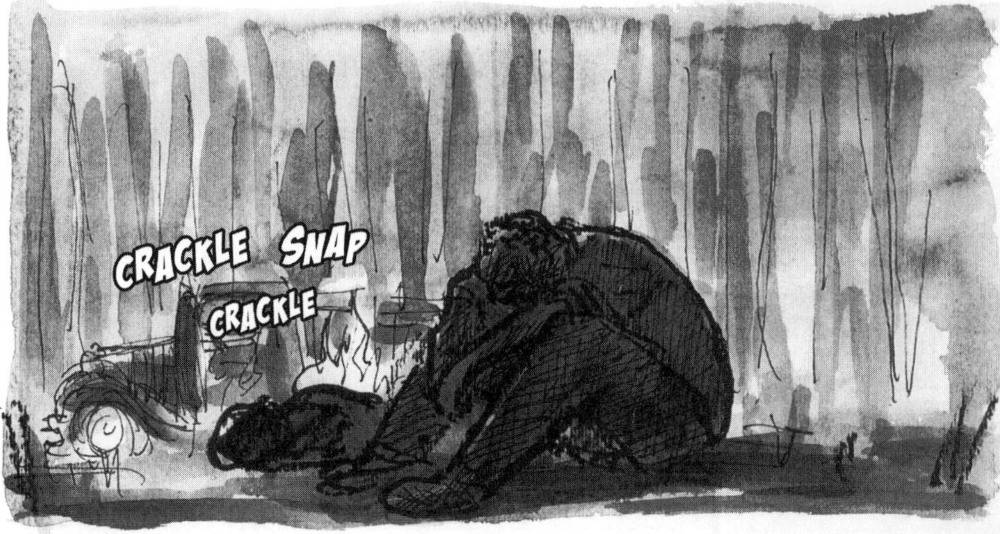
CRACKLE SNAP
CRACKLE
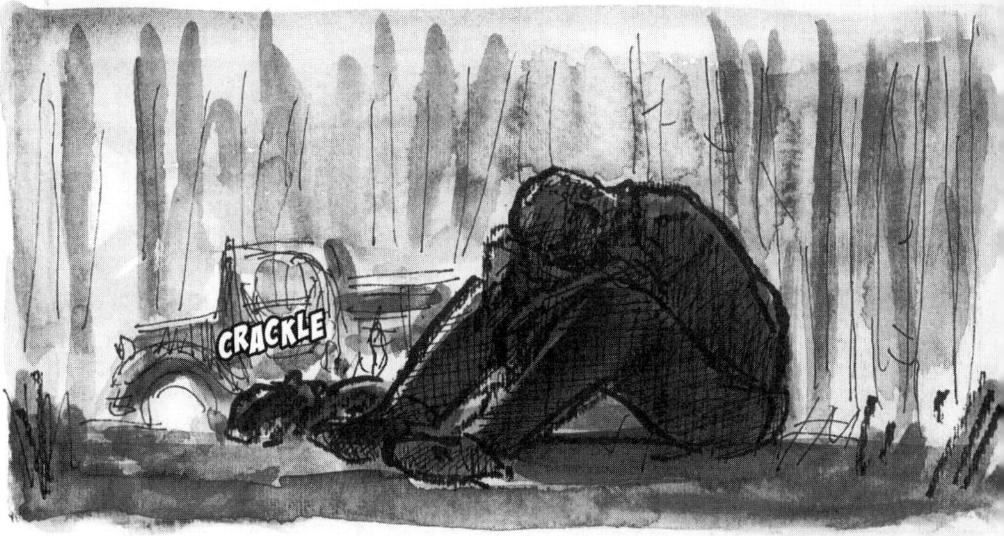
CRACKLE
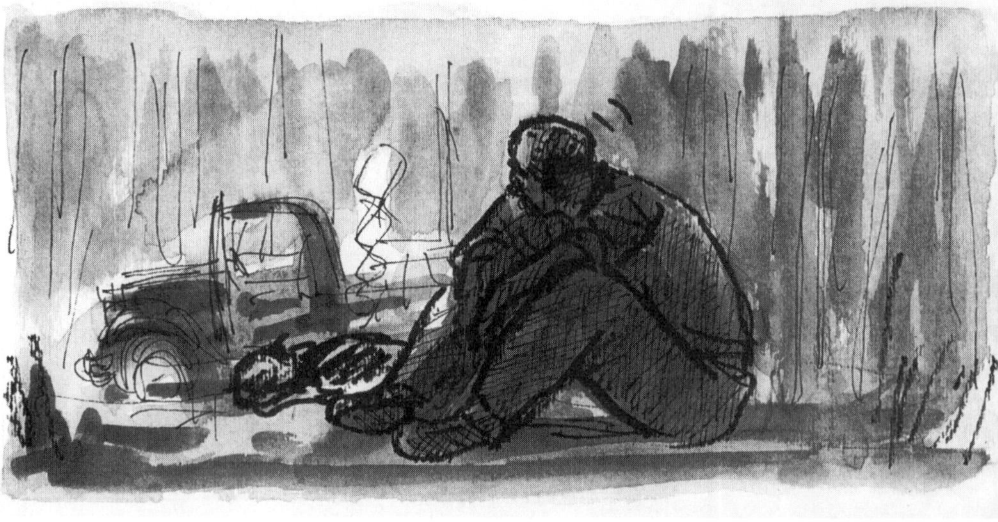

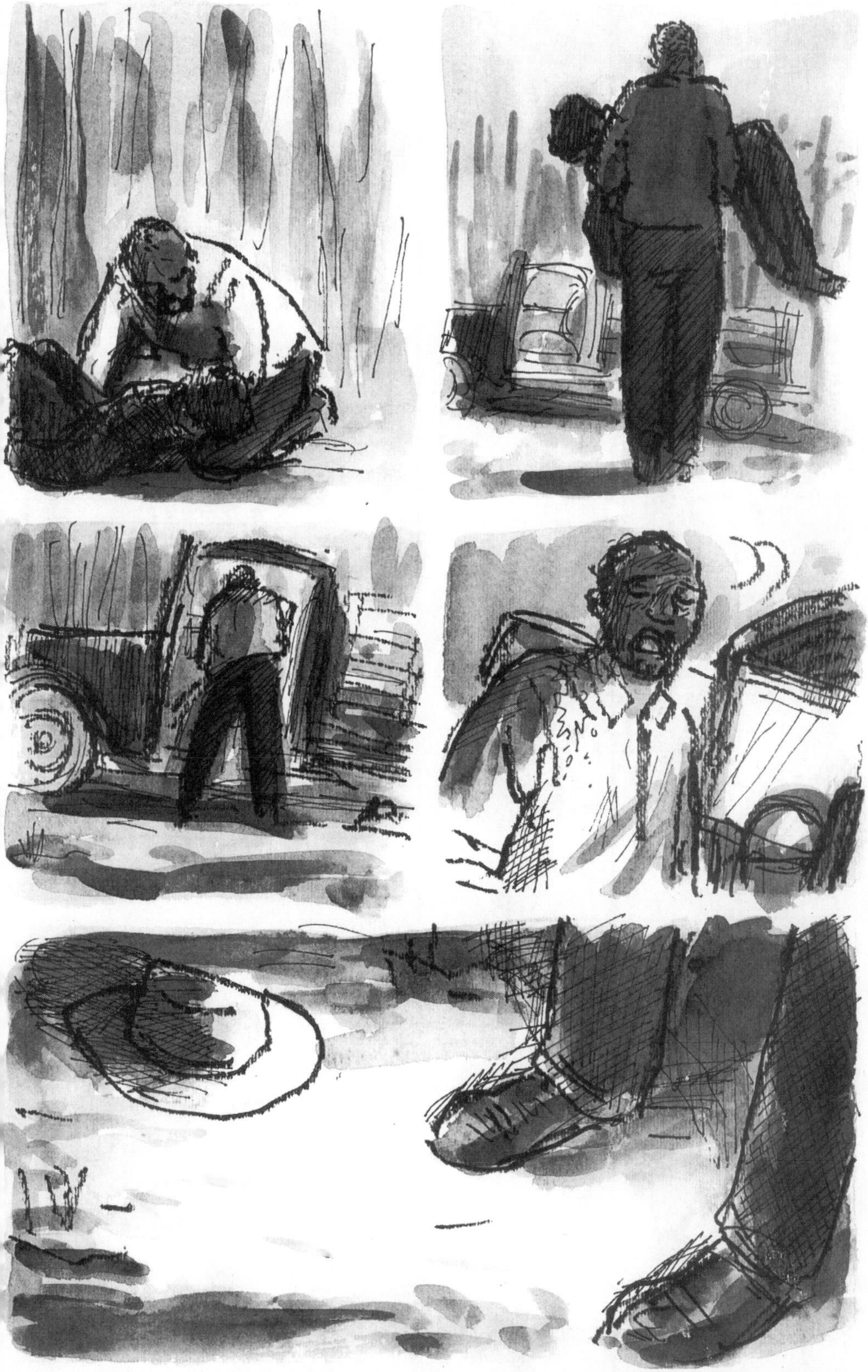

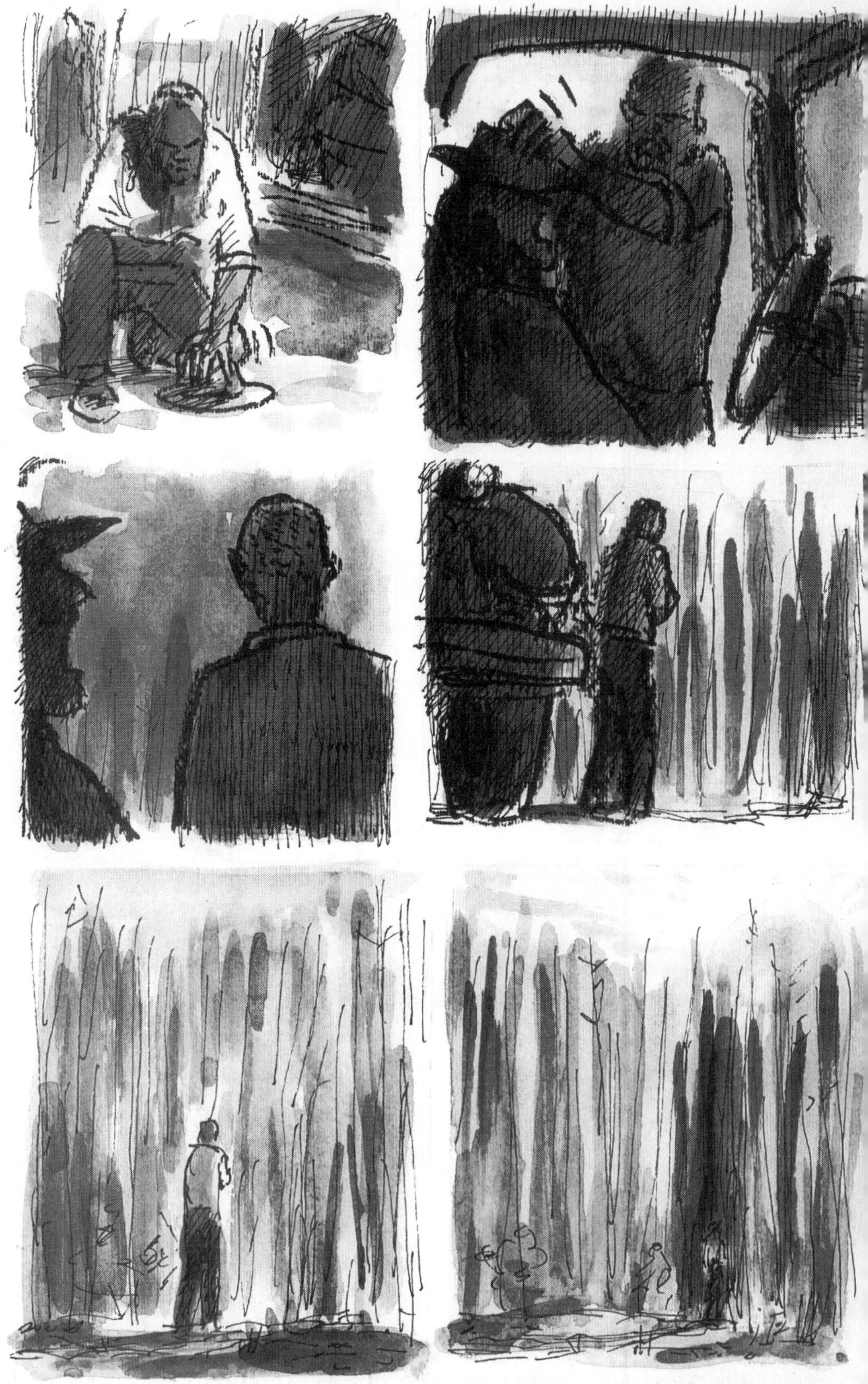

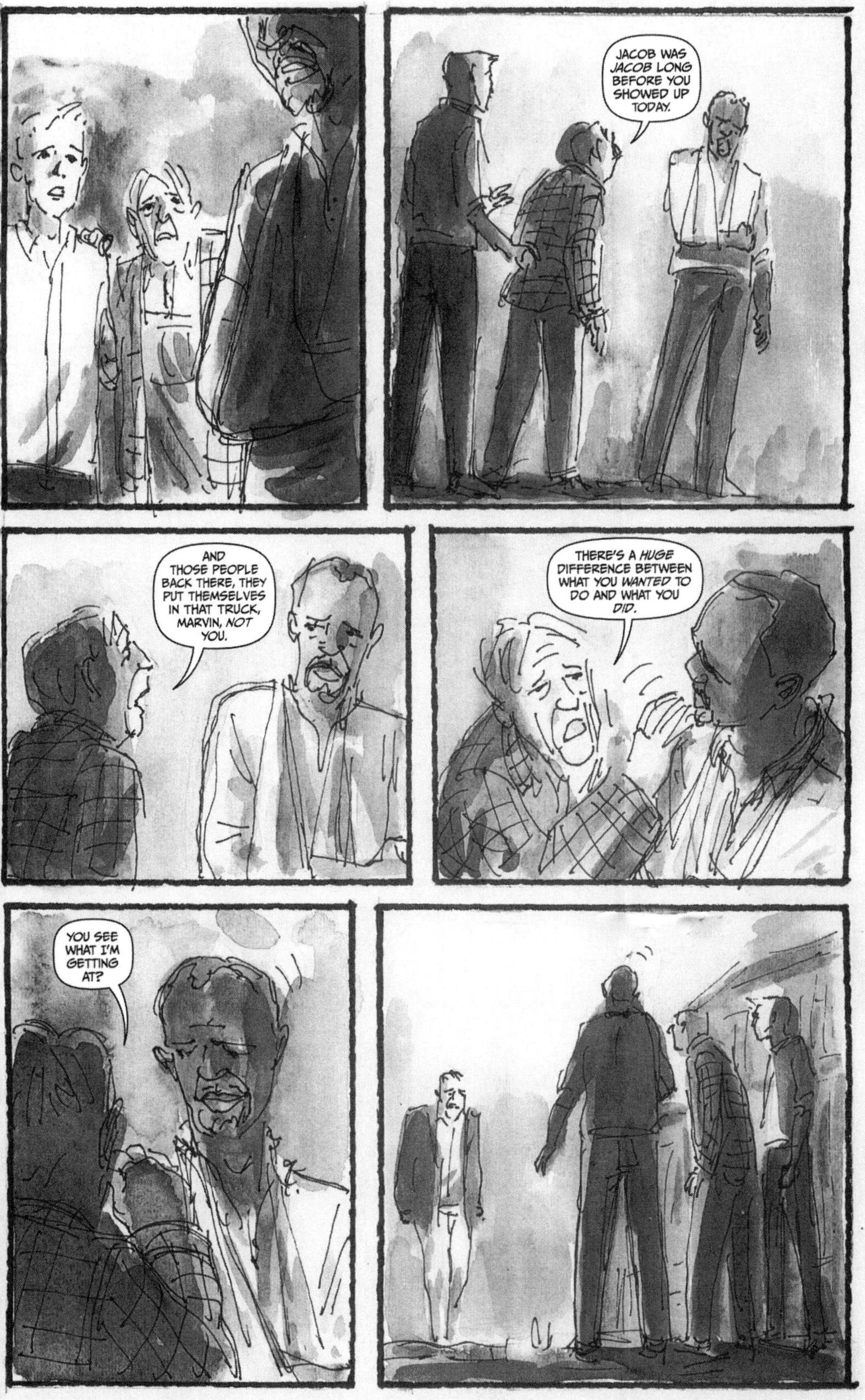
JACOB WAS *JACOB* LONG BEFORE YOU SHOWED UP TODAY.
AND THOSE PEOPLE BACK THERE, THEY PUT THEMSELVES IN THAT TRUCK, MARVIN, *NOT* YOU.
THERE'S A *HUGE* DIFFERENCE BETWEEN WHAT YOU *WANTED* TO DO AND WHAT YOU *DID*.
YOU SEE WHAT I'M GETTING AT?

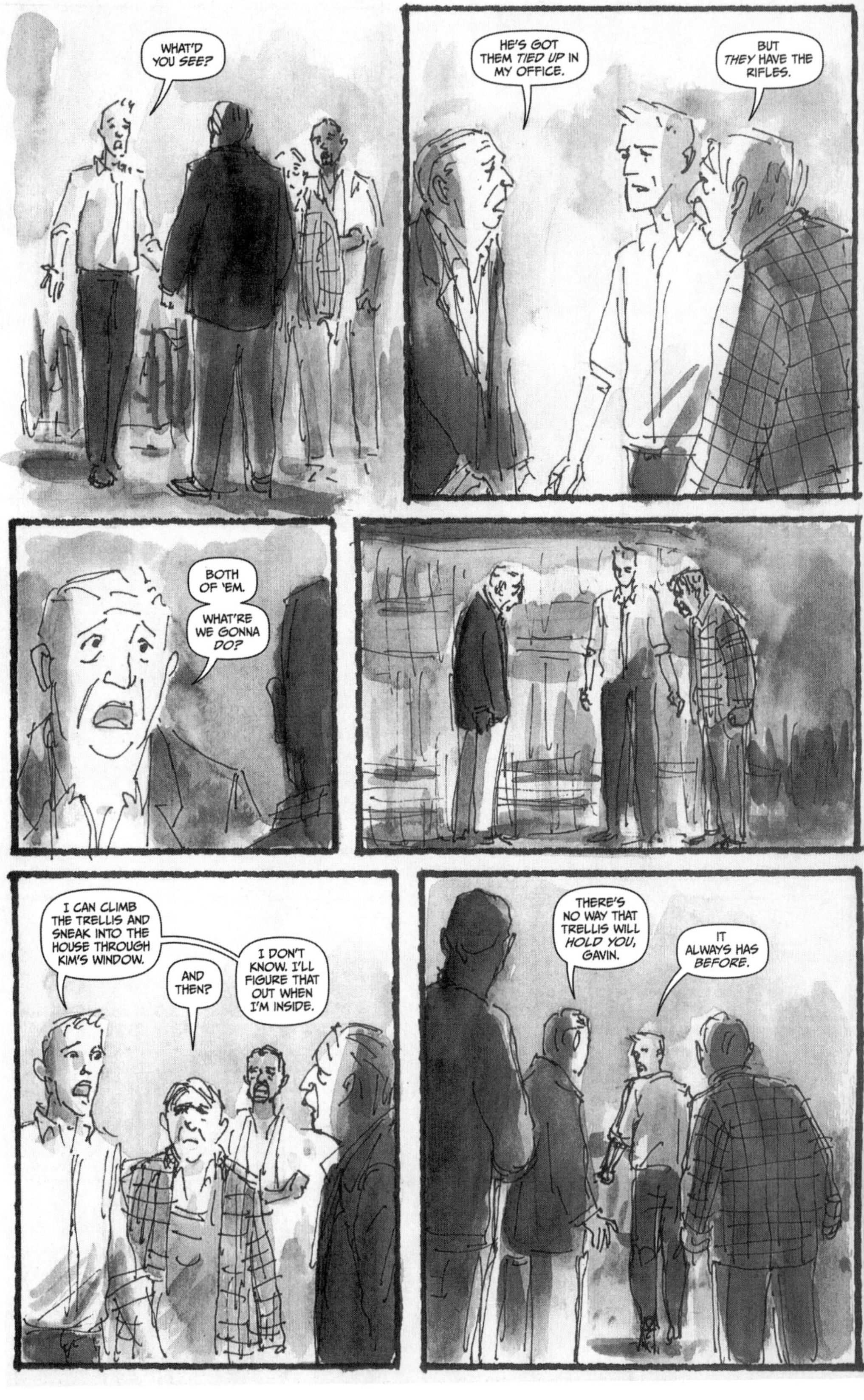
WHAT'D YOU SEE?
HE'S GOT THEM *TIED UP* IN MY OFFICE.
BUT *THEY* HAVE THE RIFLES.
BOTH OF 'EM.
WHAT'RE WE GONNA *DO?*
I CAN CLIMB THE TRELLIS AND SNEAK INTO THE HOUSE THROUGH KIM'S WINDOW.
AND THEN?
I DON'T KNOW. I'LL FIGURE THAT OUT WHEN I'M INSIDE.
THERE'S NO WAY THAT TRELLIS WILL *HOLD YOU*, GAVIN.
IT ALWAYS HAS *BEFORE*.

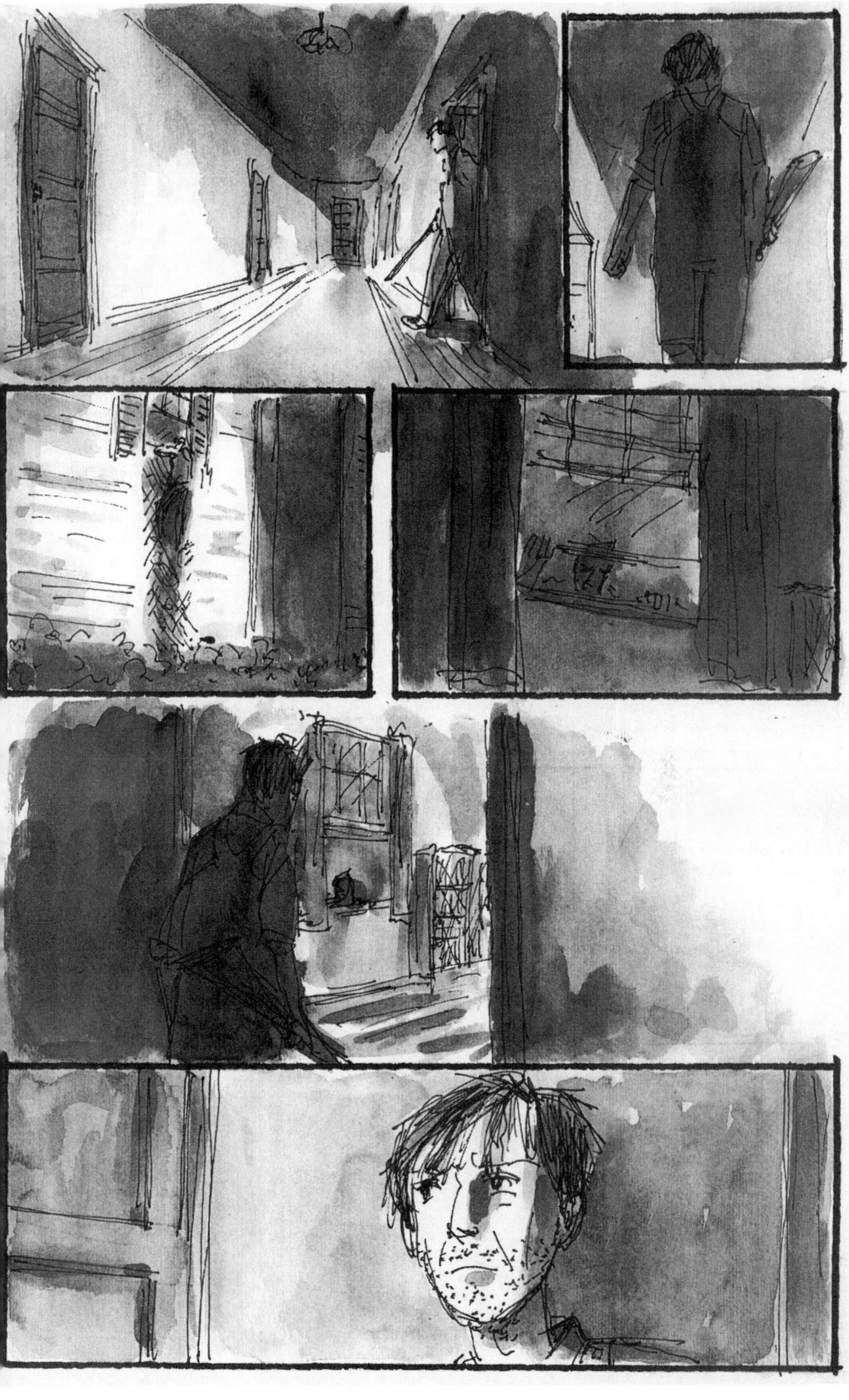

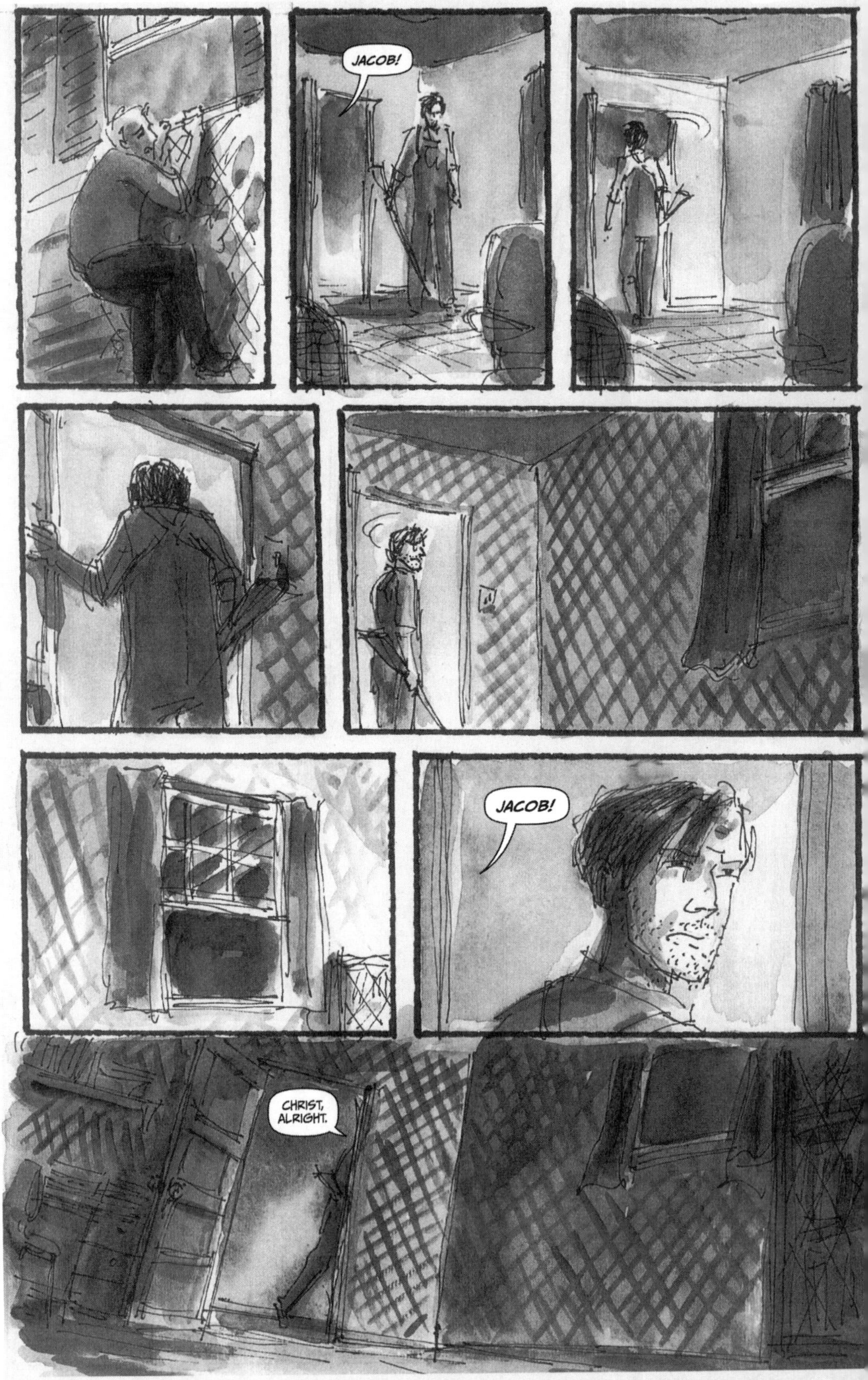
JACOB!
JACOB!
CHRIST, ALRIGHT.

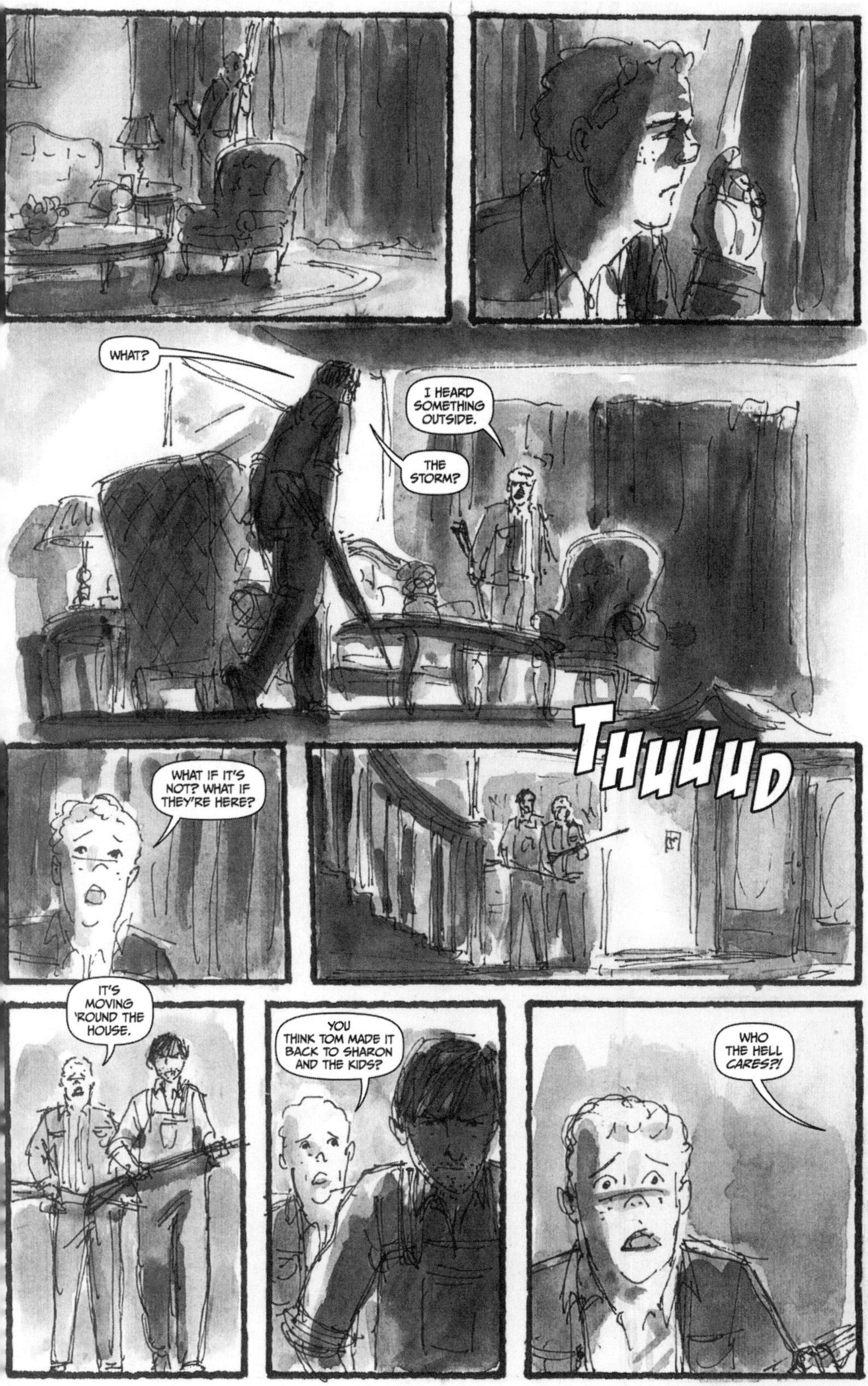
WHAT?
I HEARD SOMETHING OUTSIDE.
THE STORM?
THUUUD
WHAT IF IT'S NOT? WHAT IF THEY'RE HERE?
IT'S MOVING 'ROUND THE HOUSE.
YOU THINK TOM MADE IT BACK TO SHARON AND THE KIDS?
WHO THE HELL CARES?!

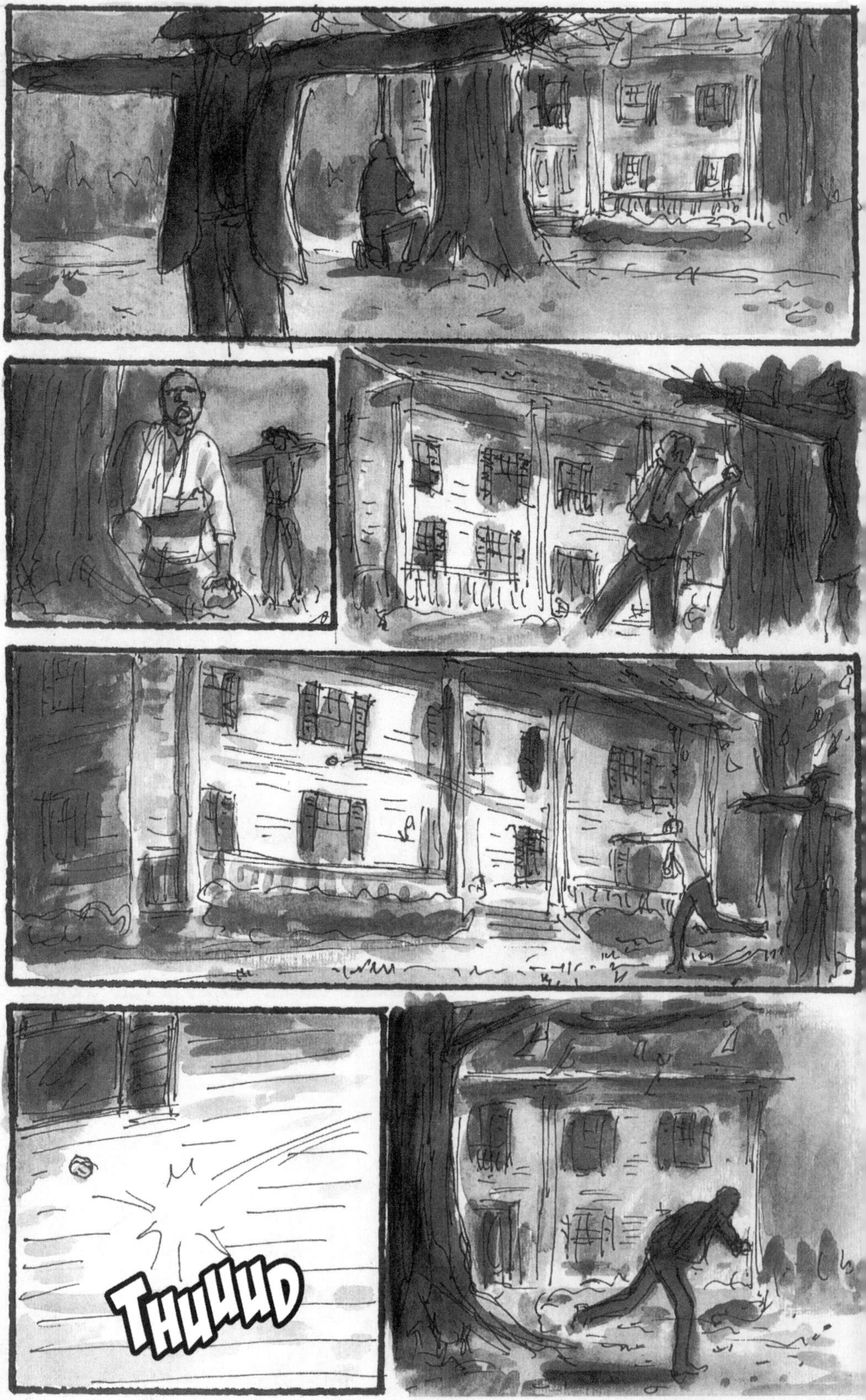
THUUUD

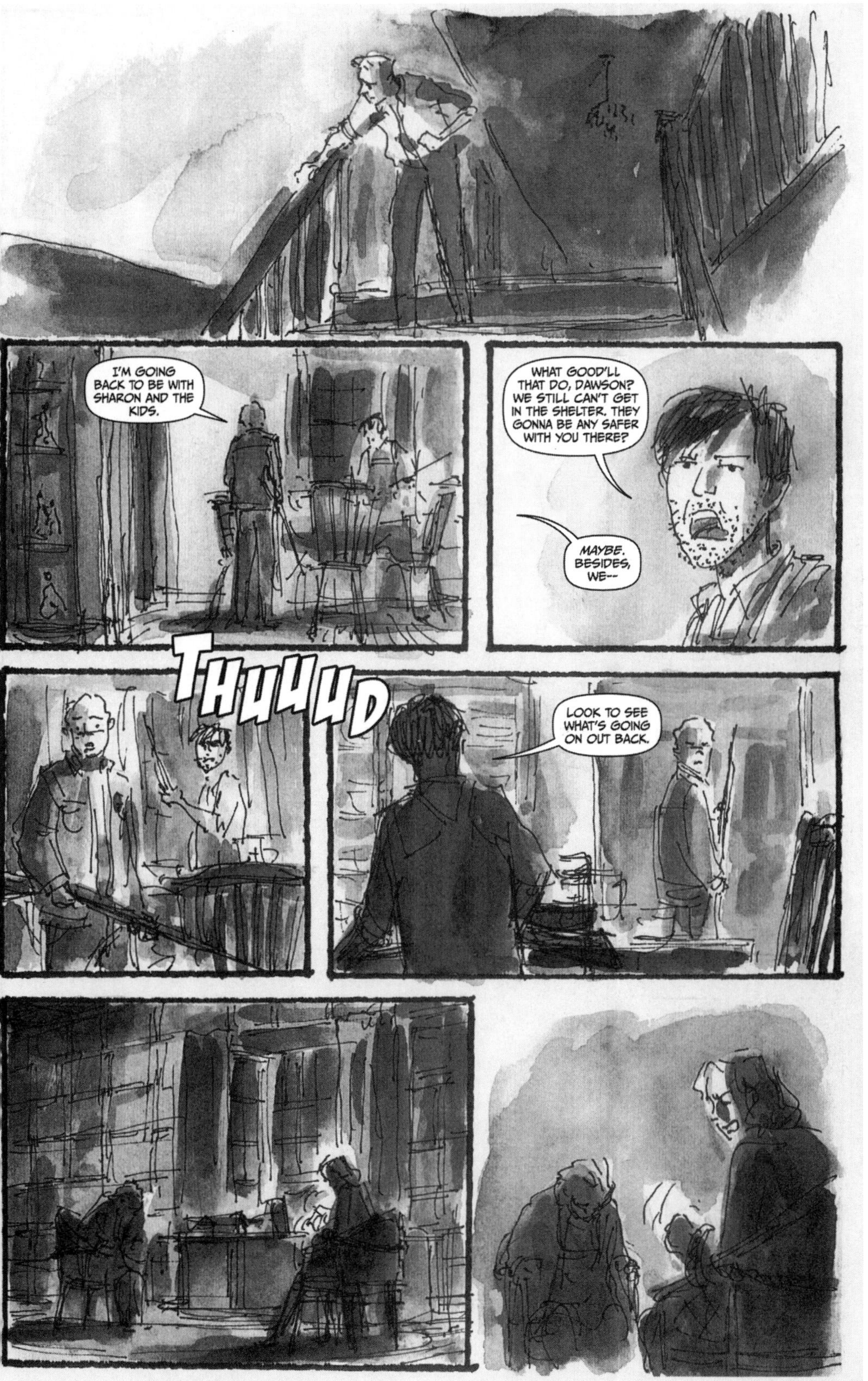
I'M GOING BACK TO BE WITH SHARON AND THE KIDS.
WHAT GOOD'LL THAT DO, DAWSON? WE STILL CAN'T GET IN THE SHELTER. THEY GONNA BE ANY SAFER WITH YOU THERE?
MAYBE. BESIDES, WE--
THUUUD
LOOK TO SEE WHAT'S GOING ON OUT BACK.

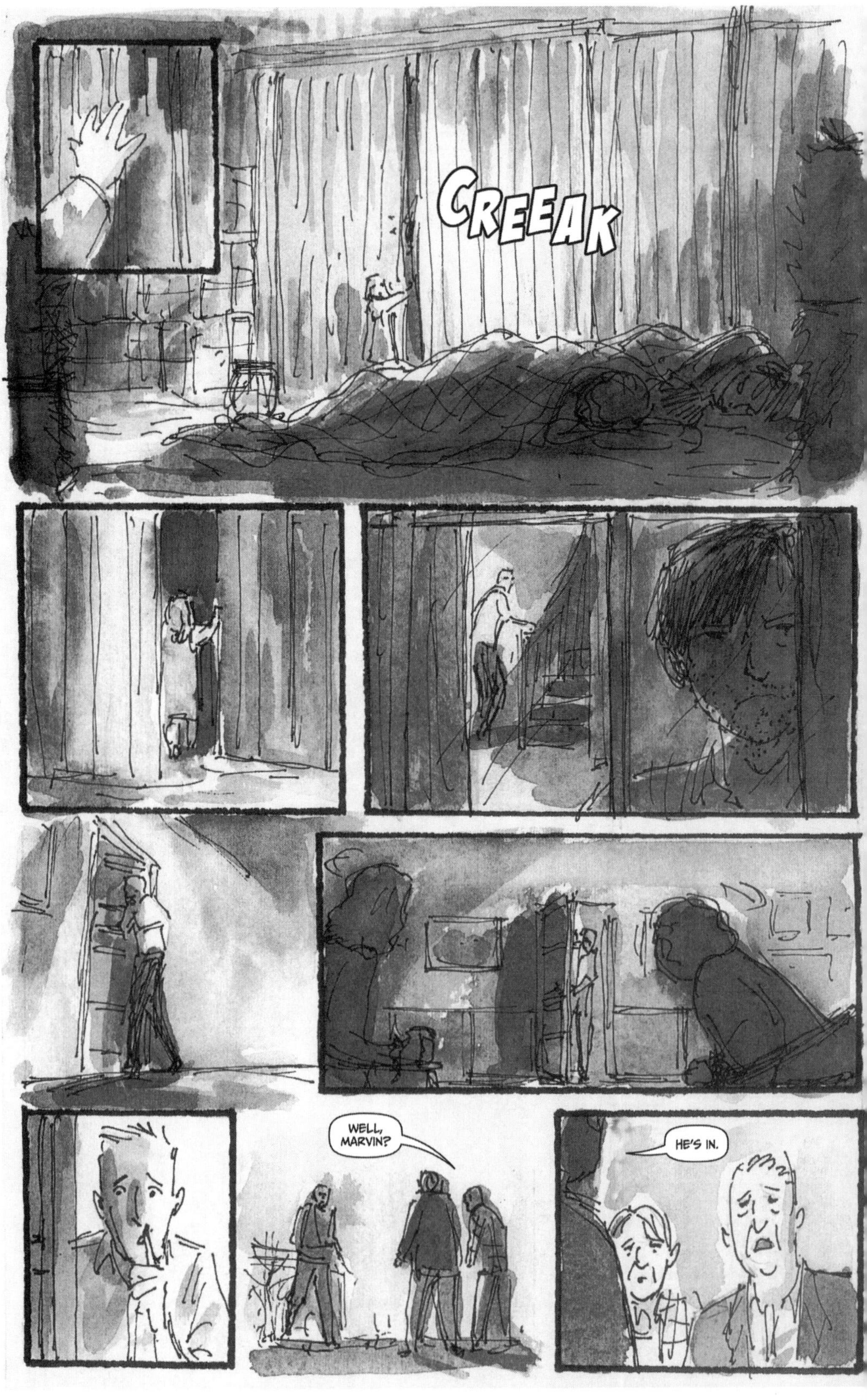
CREEAK
WELL, MARVIN?
HE'S IN.

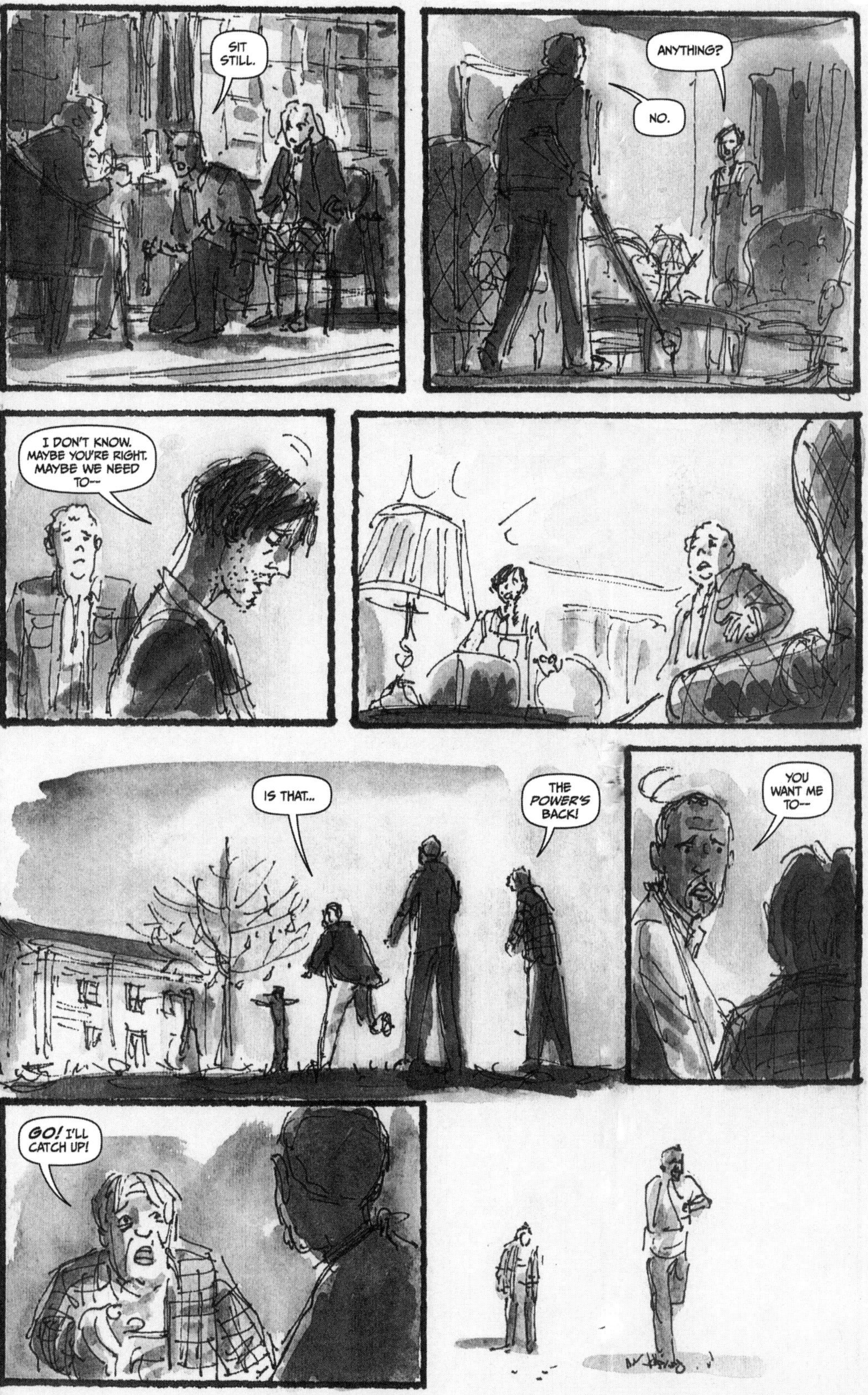
SIT STILL.
ANYTHING?
NO.
I DON'T KNOW. MAYBE YOU'RE RIGHT. MAYBE WE NEED TO--
IS THAT...
THE POWER'S BACK!
YOU WANT ME TO--
GO! I'LL CATCH UP!

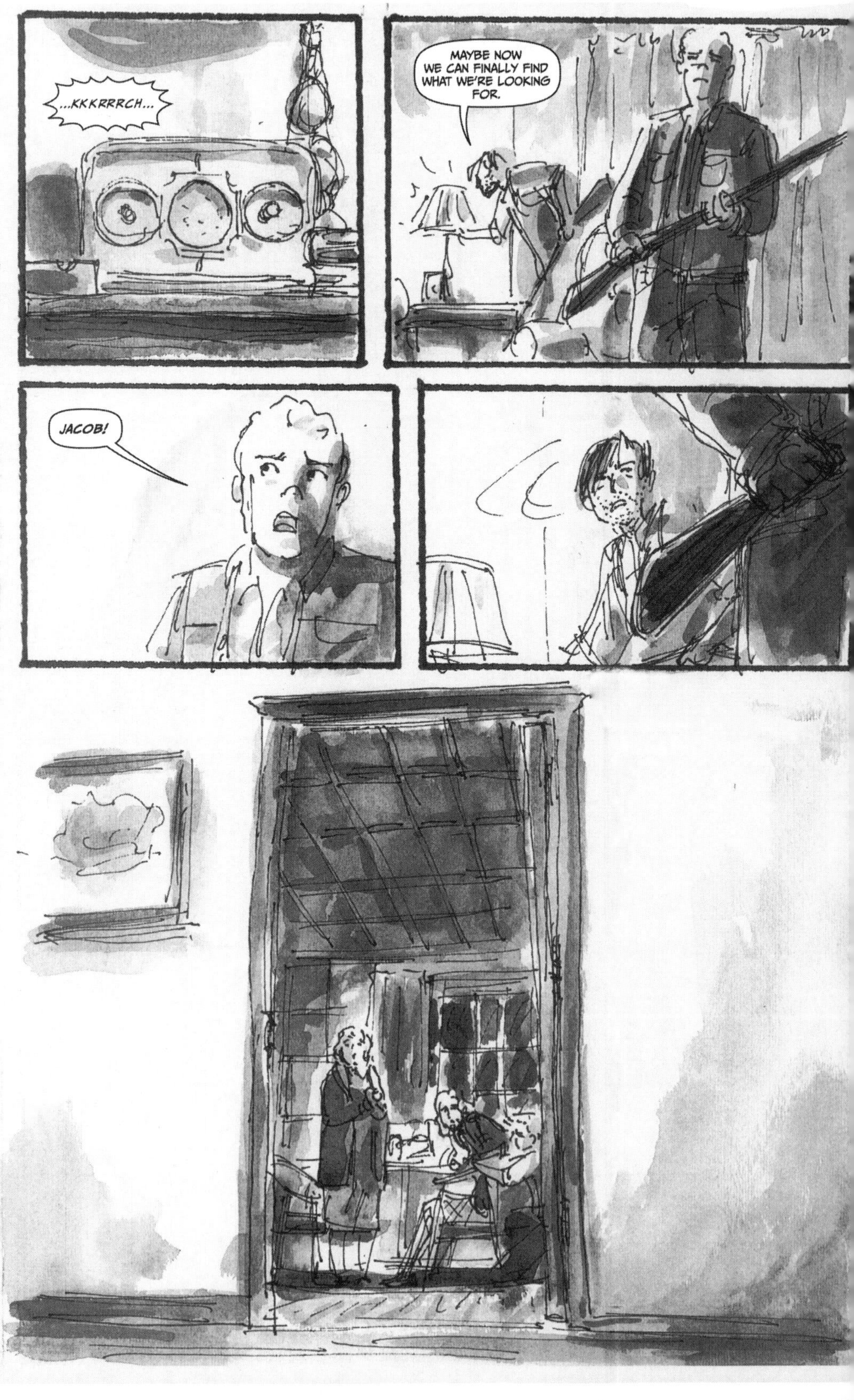
...KKKRRRCH...
MAYBE NOW WE CAN FINALLY FIND WHAT WE'RE LOOKING FOR.
JACOB!

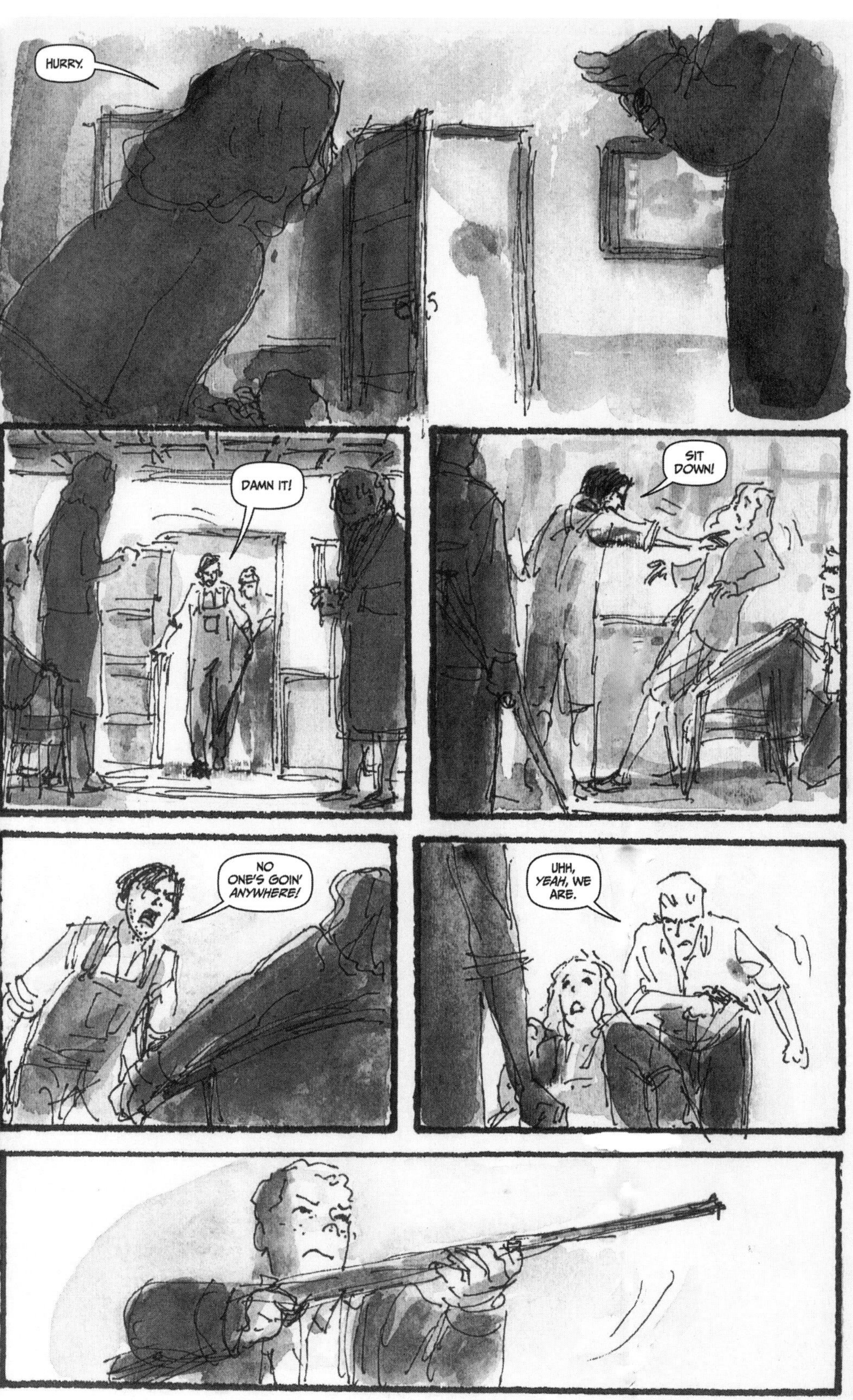
HURRY.
DAMN IT!
SIT DOWN!
NO ONE'S GOIN' *ANYWHERE!*
UHH, *YEAH,* WE ARE.

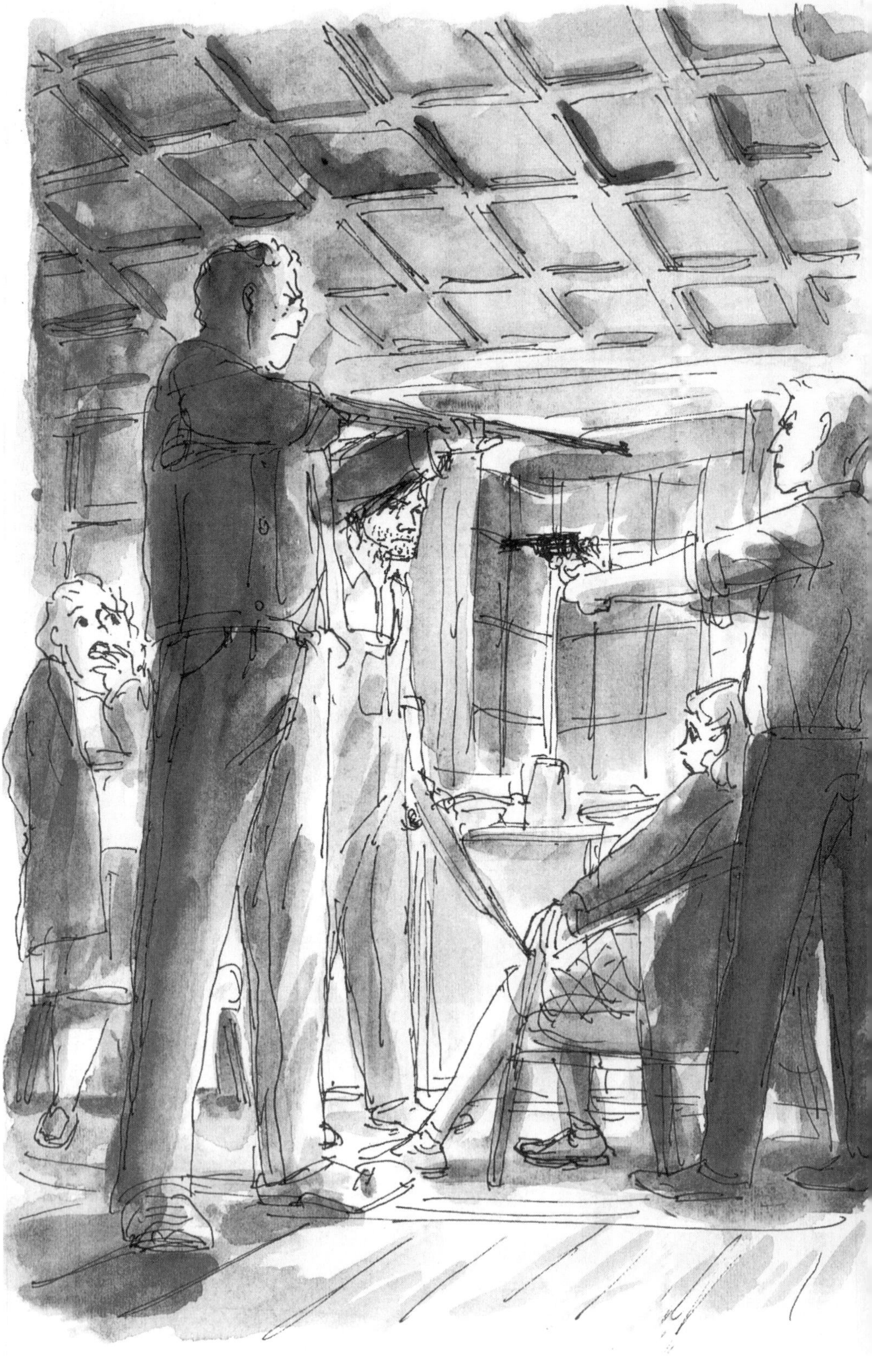

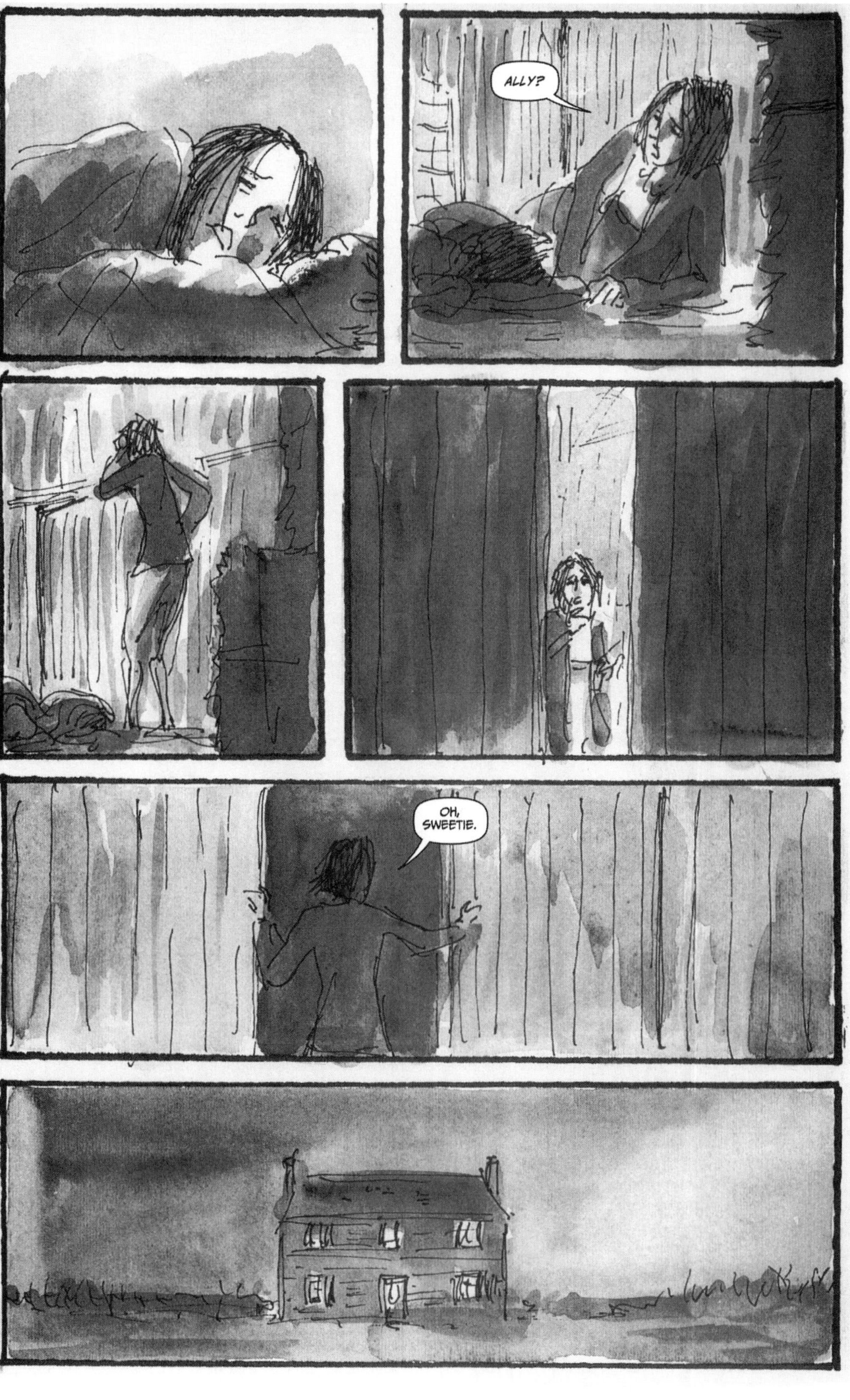
ALLY?
OH, SWEETIE.

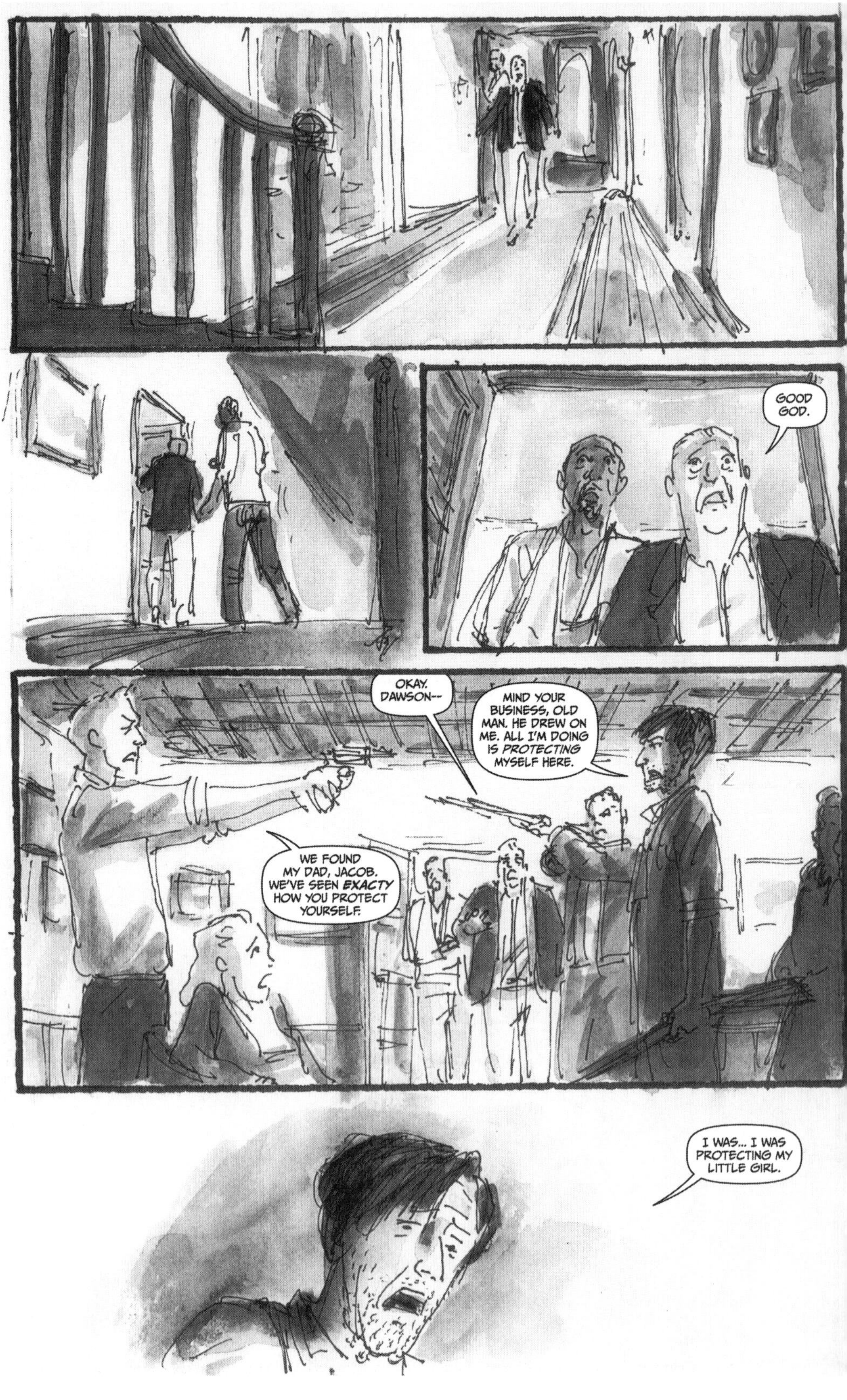
GOOD GOD.
OKAY. DAWSON--
MIND YOUR BUSINESS, OLD MAN. HE DREW ON ME. ALL I'M DOING IS PROTECTING MYSELF HERE.
WE FOUND MY DAD, JACOB. WE'VE SEEN EXACTY HOW YOU PROTECT YOURSELF.
I WAS... I WAS PROTECTING MY LITTLE GIRL.

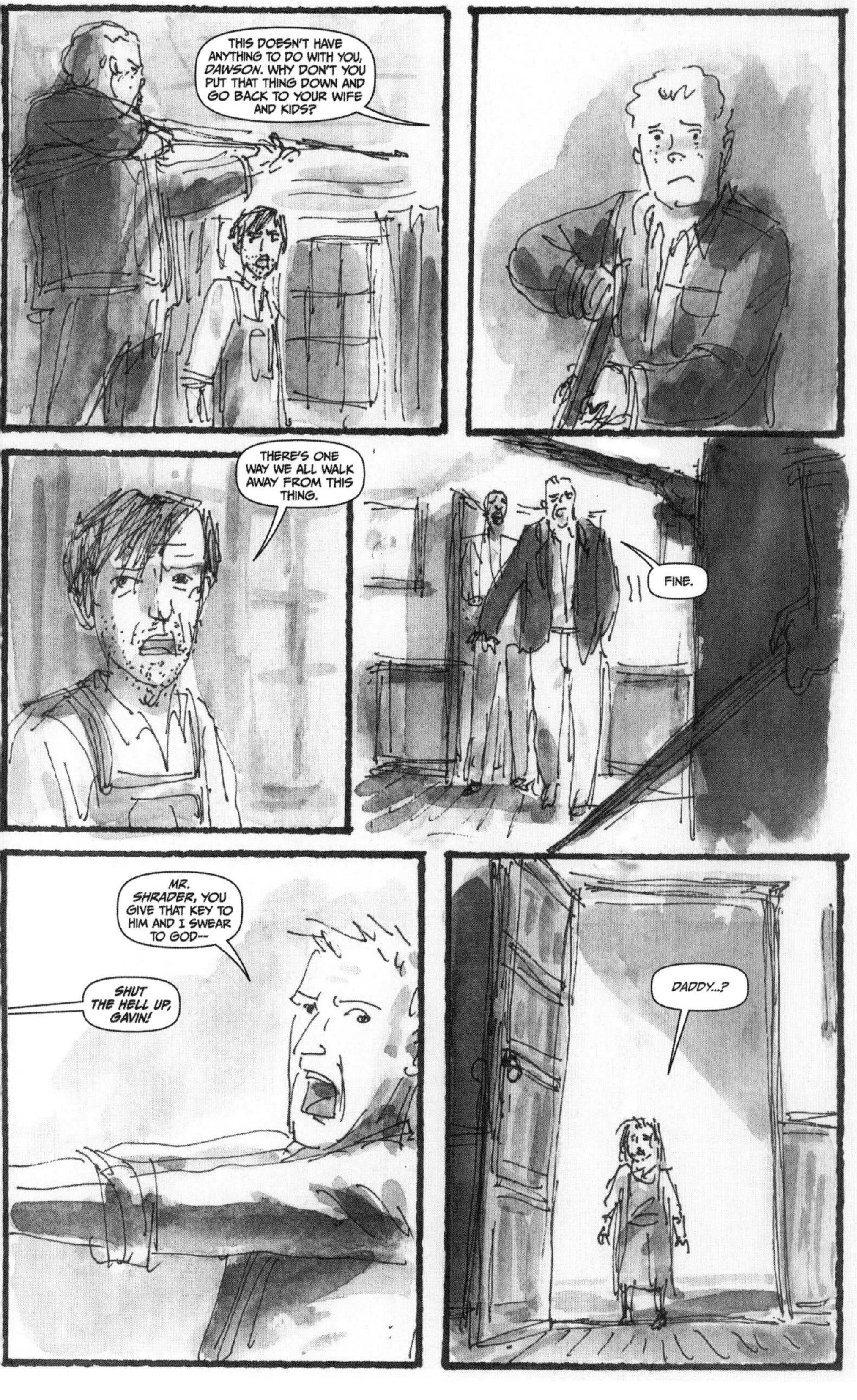
THIS DOESN'T HAVE ANYTHING TO DO WITH YOU, DAWSON. WHY DON'T YOU PUT THAT THING DOWN AND GO BACK TO YOUR WIFE AND KIDS?
THERE'S ONE WAY WE ALL WALK AWAY FROM THIS THING.
FINE.
MR. SHRADER, YOU GIVE THAT KEY TO HIM AND I SWEAR TO GOD--
SHUT THE HELL UP, GAVIN!
DADDY...?

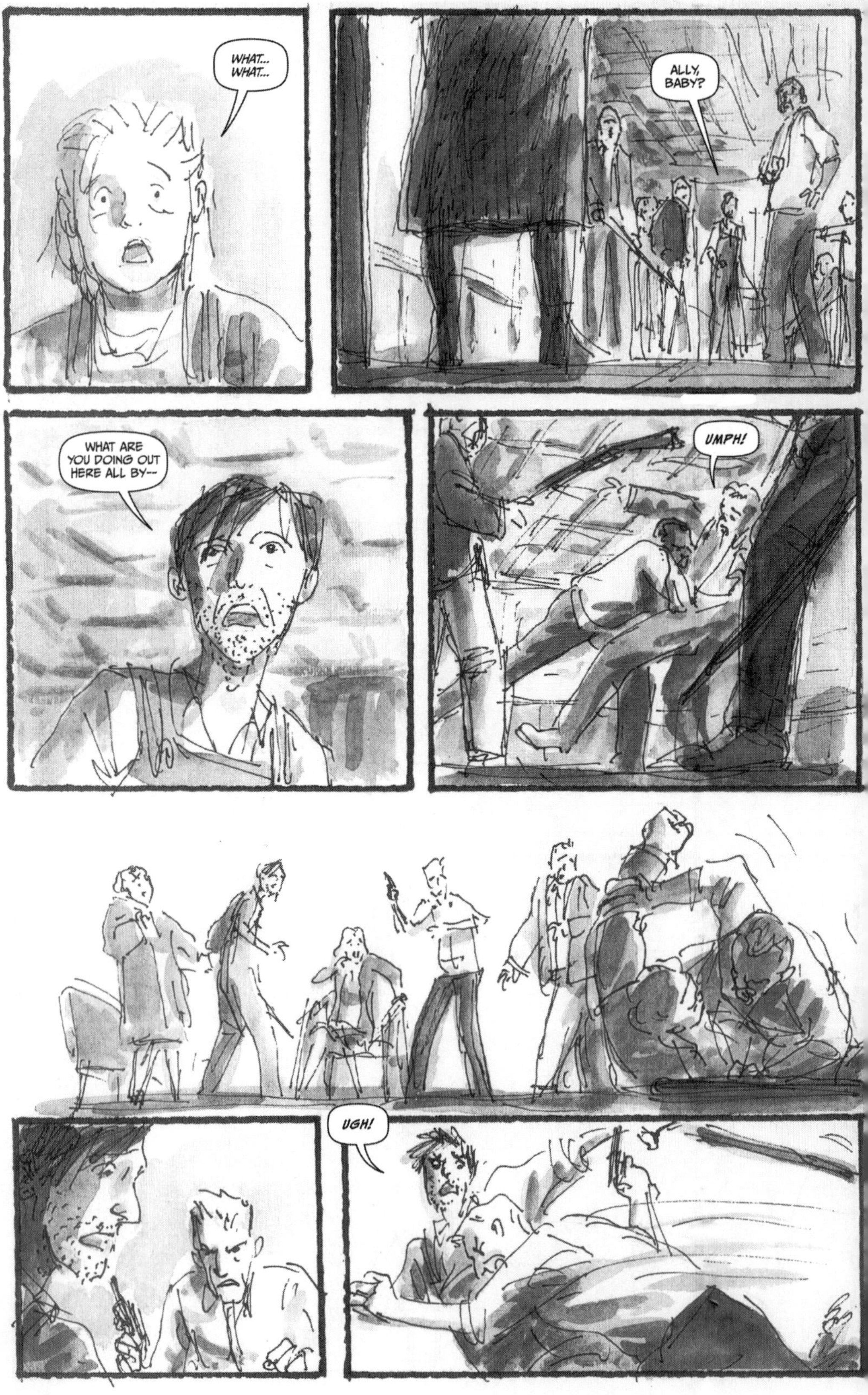
WHAT... WHAT...
ALLY, BABY?
WHAT ARE YOU DOING OUT HERE ALL BY--
UMPH!
UGH!

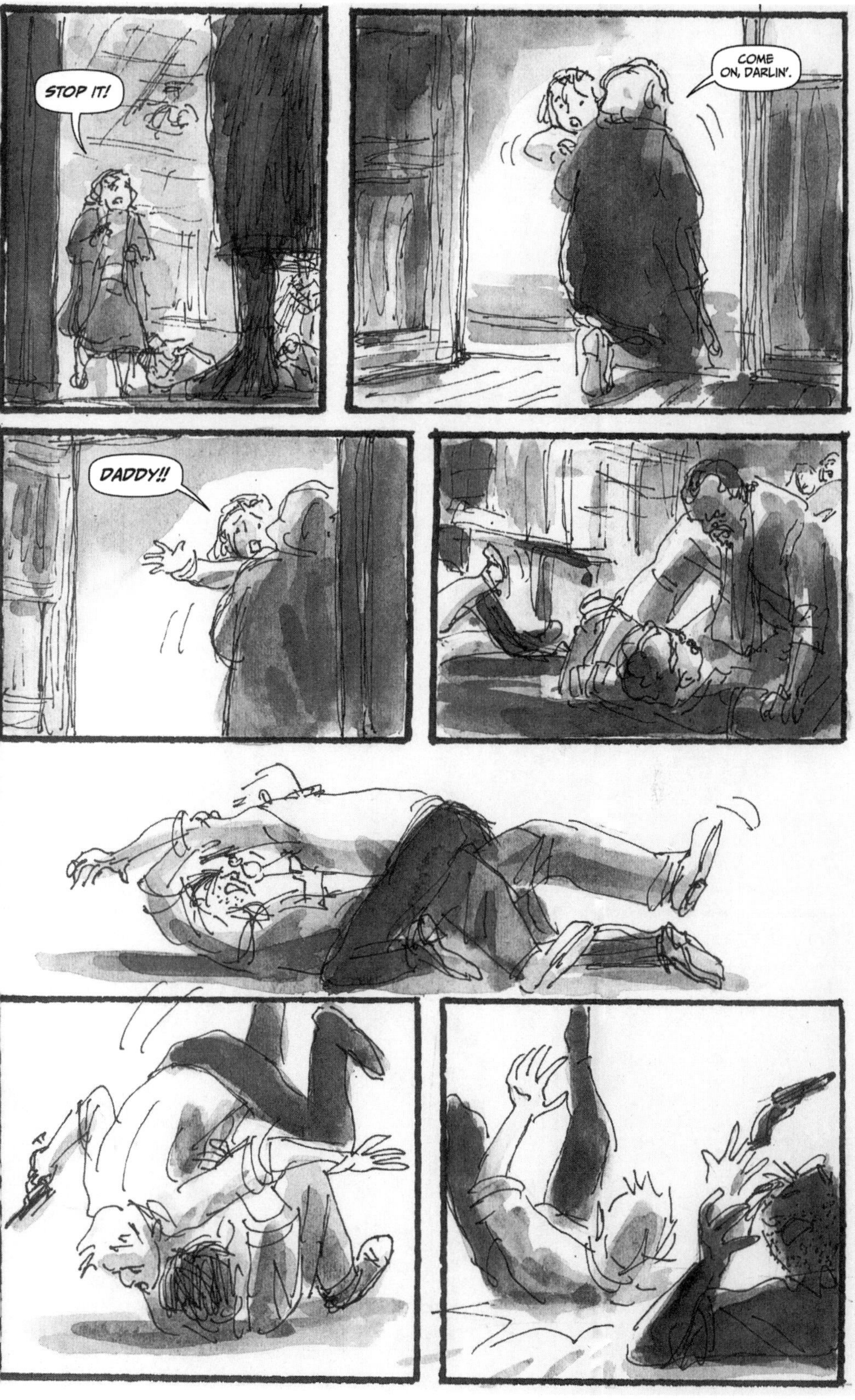
STOP IT!
COME ON, DARLIN'.
DADDY!!

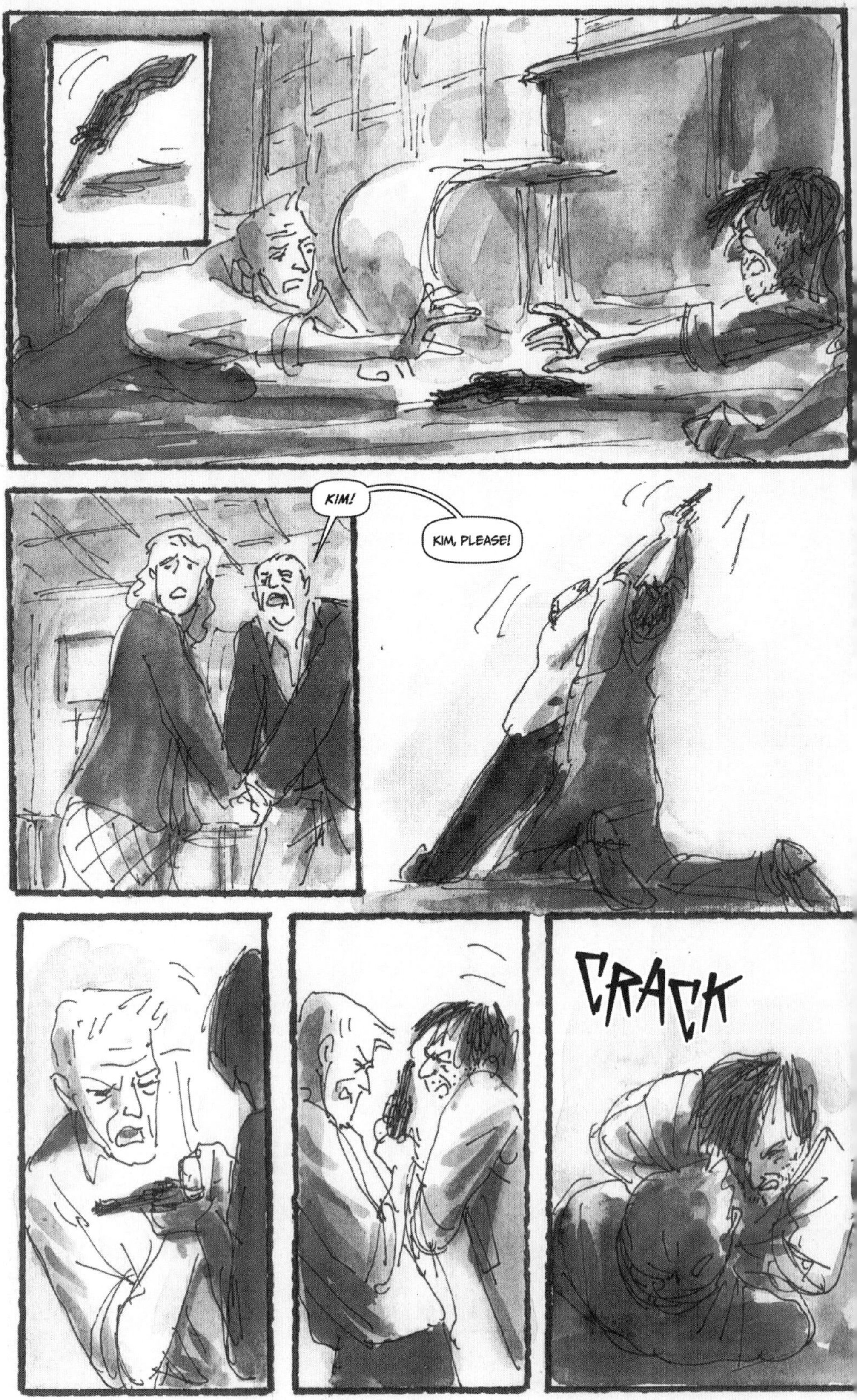
KIM!
KIM, PLEASE!
CRACK

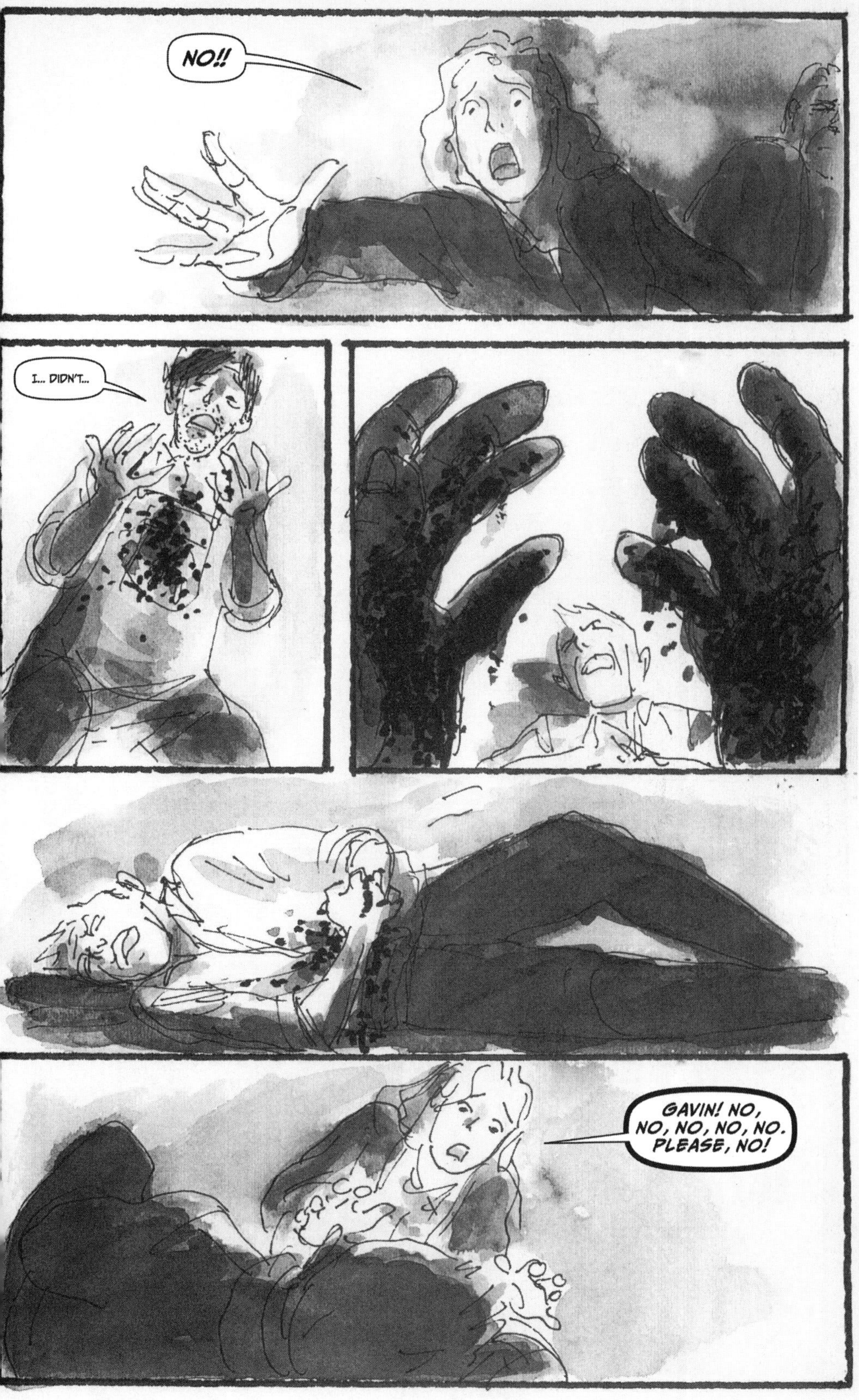
NO!!
I... DIDN'T...
GAVIN! NO, NO, NO, NO, NO. PLEASE, NO!

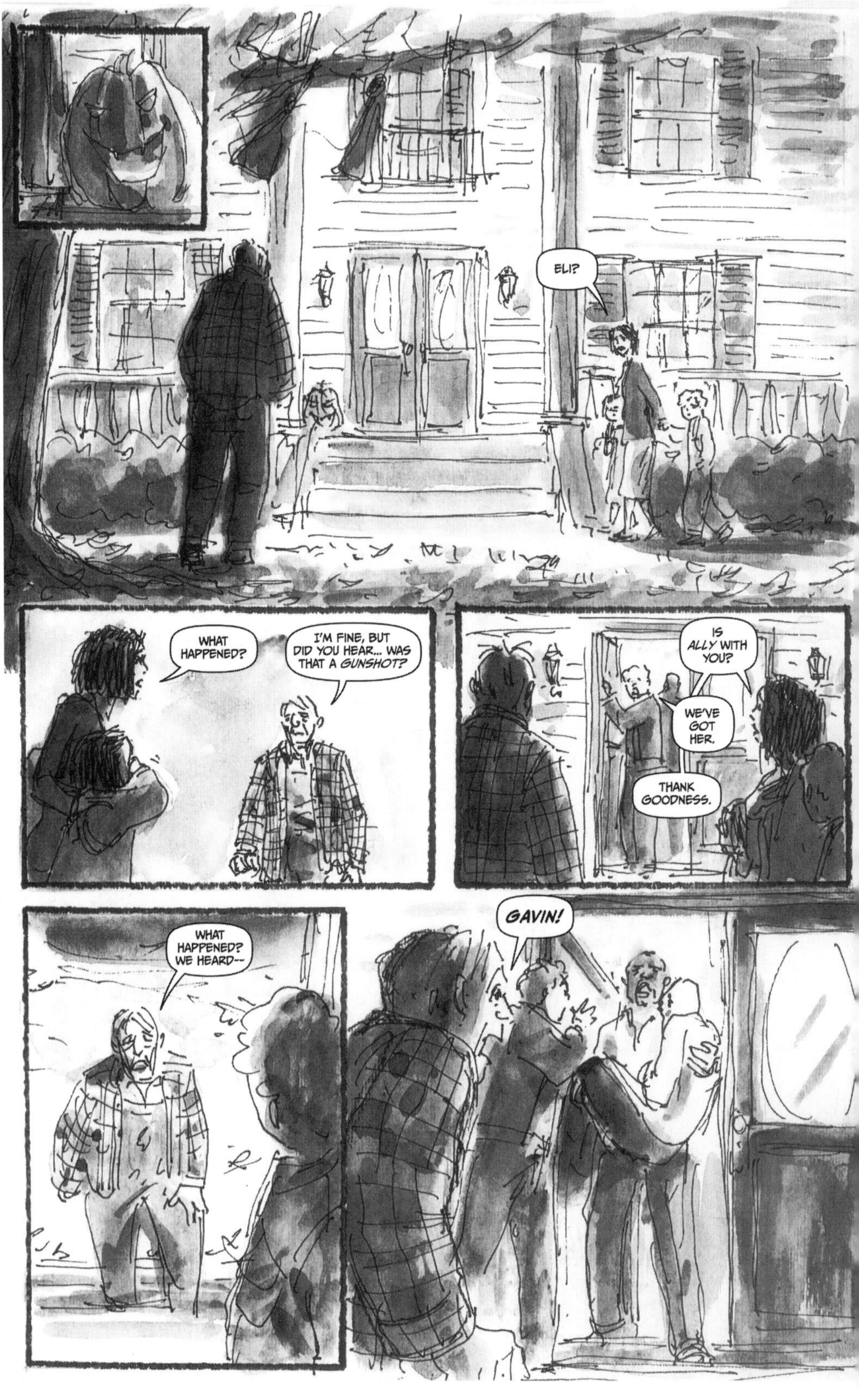
ELI?
WHAT HAPPENED?
I'M FINE, BUT DID YOU HEAR... WAS THAT A GUNSHOT?
IS ALLY WITH YOU?
WE'VE GOT HER.
THANK GOODNESS.
WHAT HAPPENED? WE HEARD--
GAVIN!

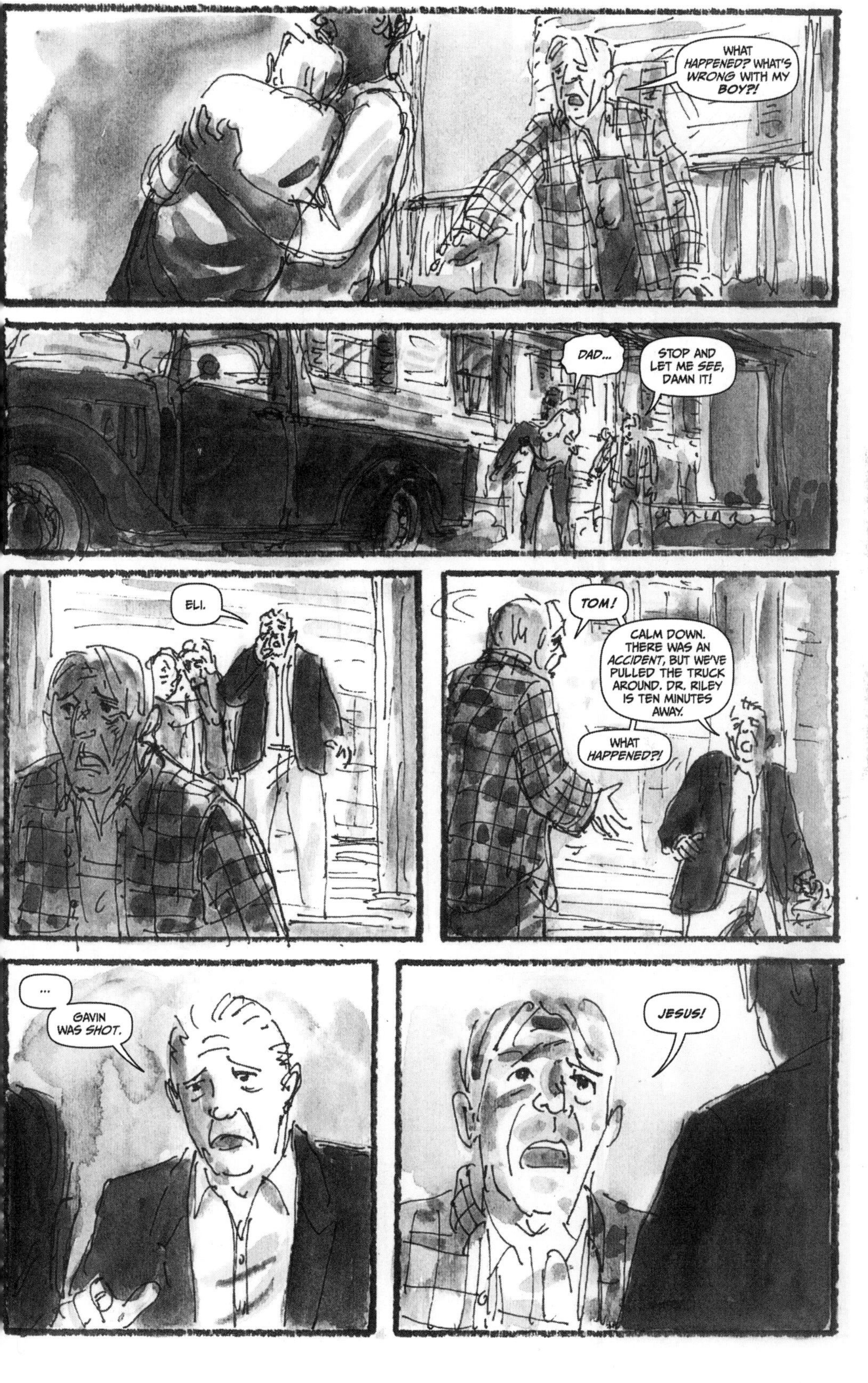
WHAT *HAPPENED?* WHAT'S *WRONG* WITH MY *BOY?!*
DAD...
STOP AND LET ME *SEE,* DAMN IT!
ELI.
TOM!
CALM DOWN. THERE WAS AN *ACCIDENT,* BUT WE'VE PULLED THE TRUCK AROUND. DR. RILEY IS TEN MINUTES AWAY.
WHAT *HAPPENED?!*
...
GAVIN WAS *SHOT.*
JESUS!

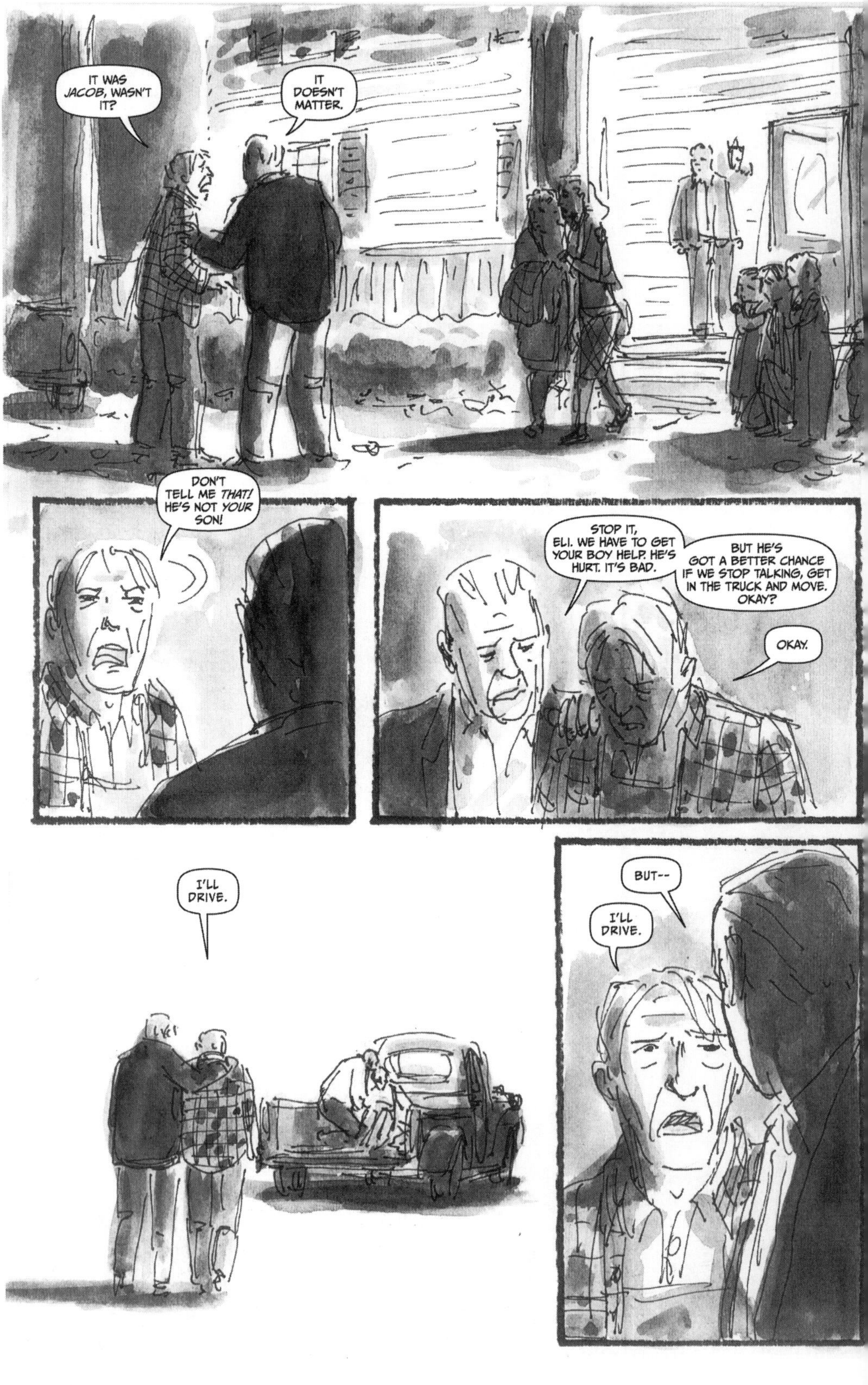
IT WAS JACOB, WASN'T IT?
IT DOESN'T MATTER.
DON'T TELL ME THAT! HE'S NOT YOUR SON!
STOP IT, ELI. WE HAVE TO GET YOUR BOY HELP. HE'S HURT. IT'S BAD.
BUT HE'S GOT A BETTER CHANCE IF WE STOP TALKING, GET IN THE TRUCK AND MOVE. OKAY?
OKAY.
BUT--
I'LL DRIVE.
I'LL DRIVE.

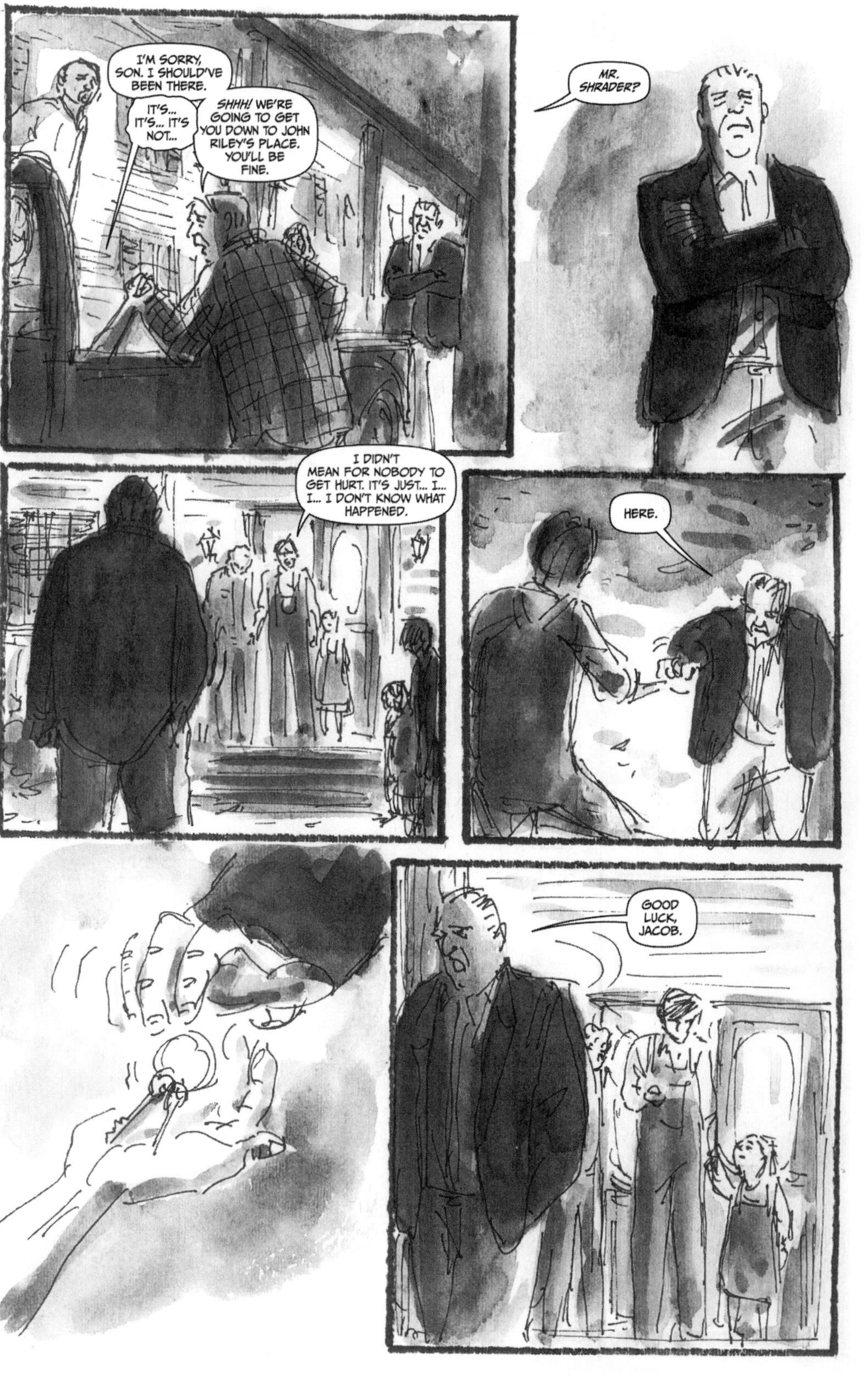
I'M SORRY, SON. I SHOULD'VE BEEN THERE.
IT'S... IT'S... IT'S NOT...
SHHH! WE'RE GOING TO GET YOU DOWN TO JOHN RILEY'S PLACE. YOU'LL BE FINE.
MR. SHRADER?
I DIDN'T MEAN FOR NOBODY TO GET HURT. IT'S JUST... I... I... I DON'T KNOW WHAT HAPPENED.
HERE.
GOOD LUCK, JACOB.

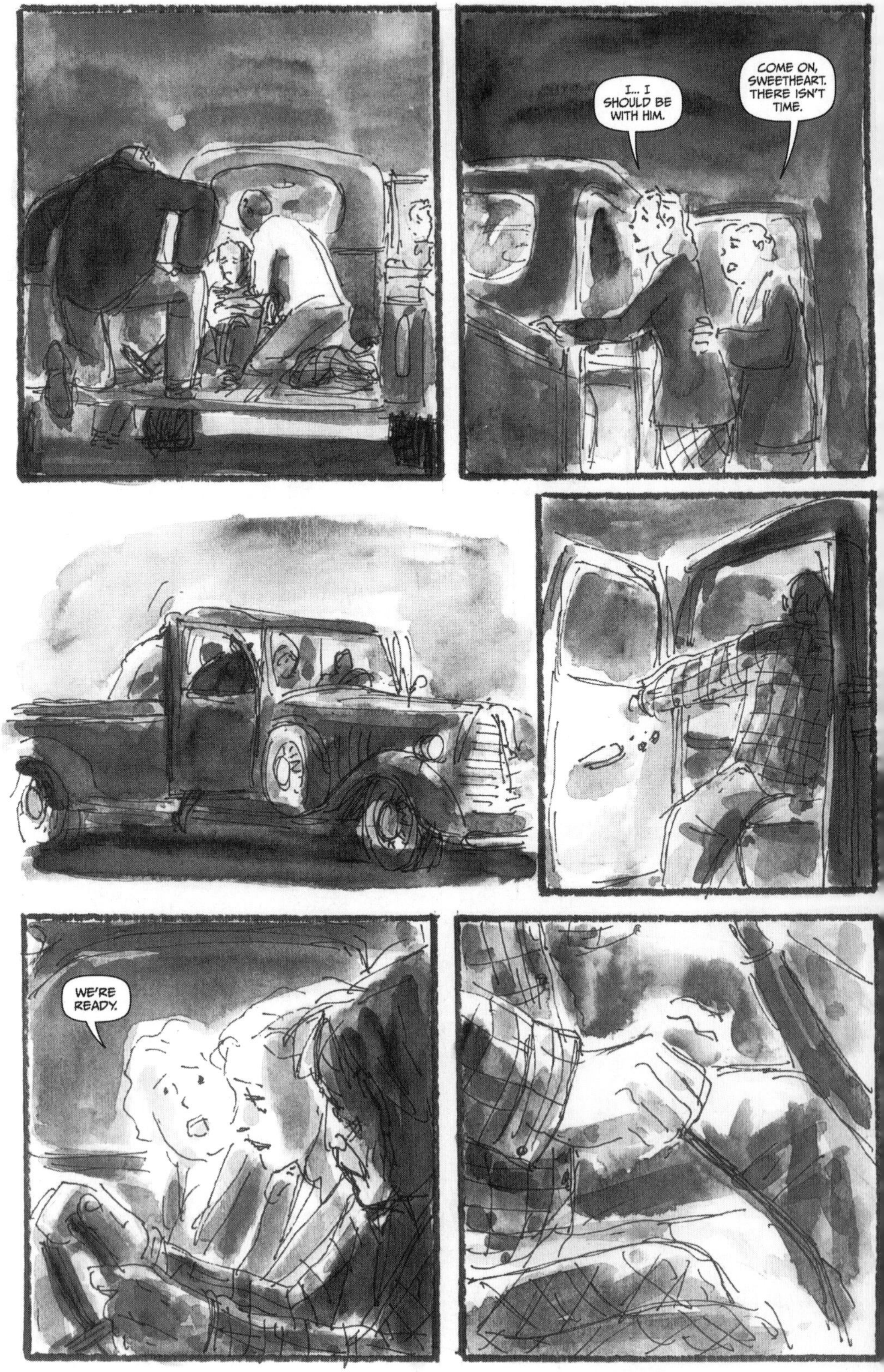
I... I SHOULD BE WITH HIM.
COME ON, SWEETHEART. THERE ISN'T TIME.
WE'RE READY.

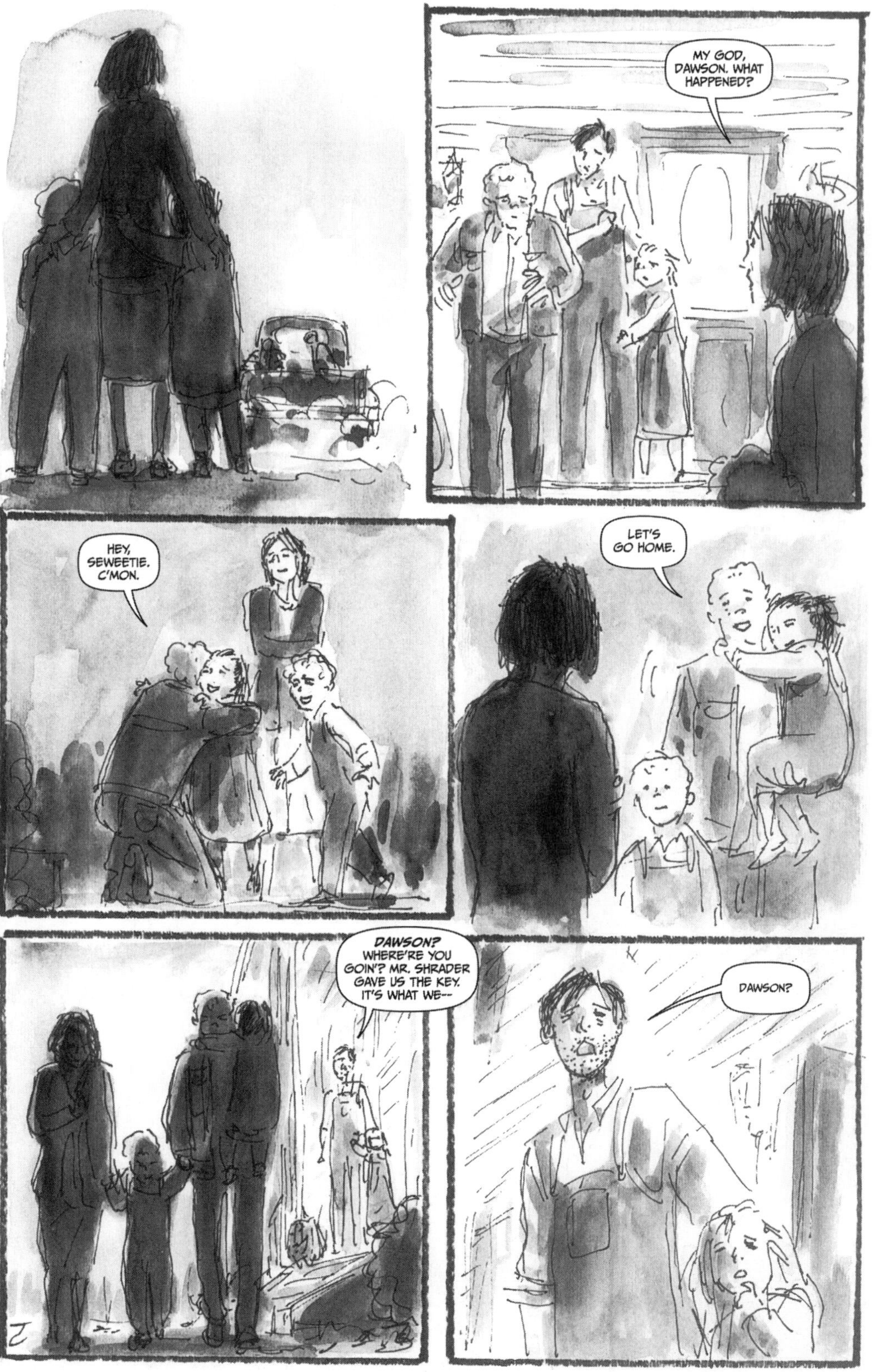
MY GOD, DAWSON. WHAT HAPPENED?
HEY, SEWEETIE. C'MON.
LET'S GO HOME.
DAWSON? WHERE'RE YOU GOIN'? MR. SHRADER GAVE US THE KEY. IT'S WHAT WE--
DAWSON?

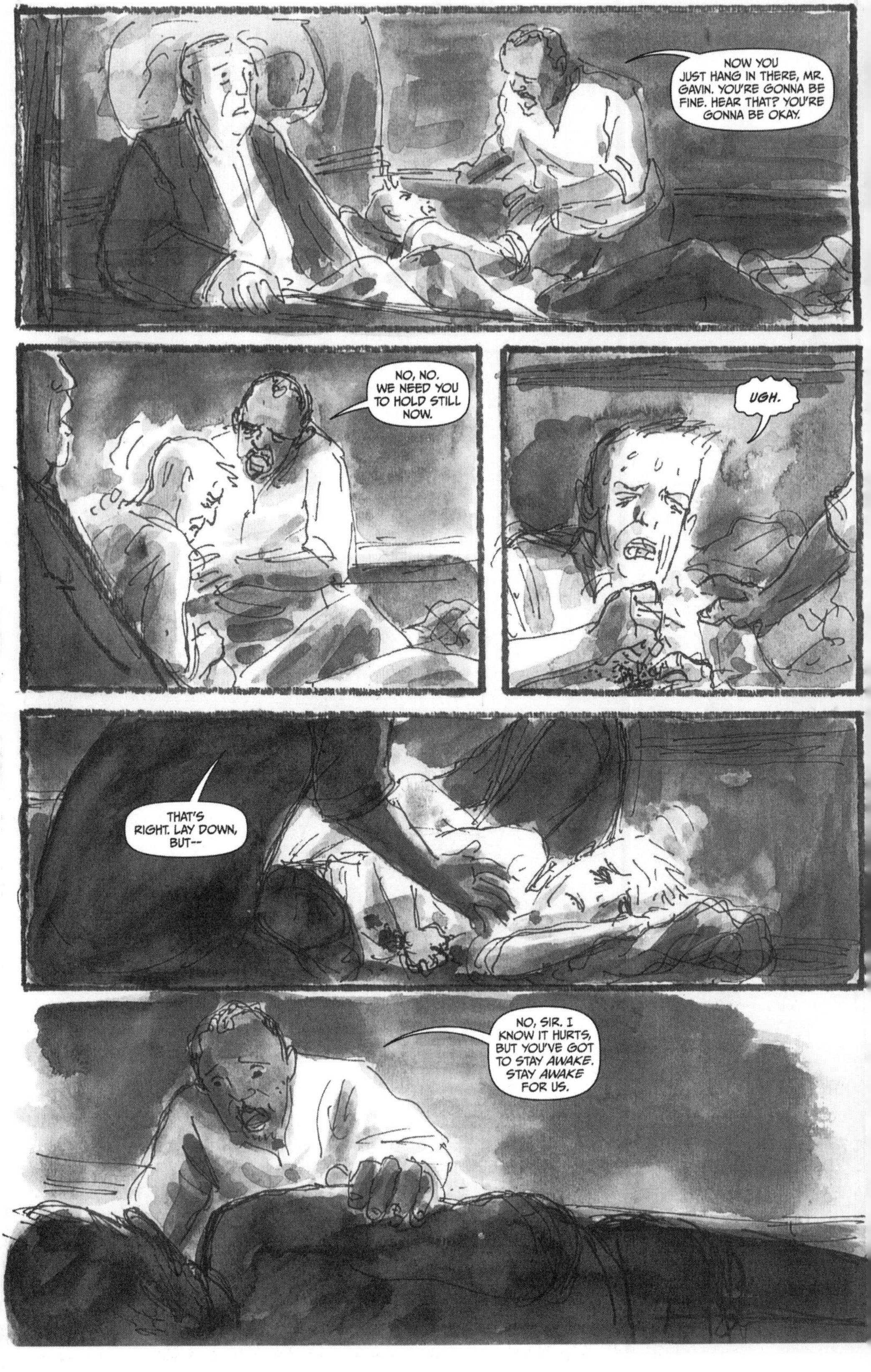
NOW YOU JUST HANG IN THERE, MR. GAVIN. YOU'RE GONNA BE FINE. HEAR THAT? YOU'RE GONNA BE OKAY.
NO, NO. WE NEED YOU TO HOLD STILL NOW.
UGH.
THAT'S RIGHT. LAY DOWN, BUT--
NO, SIR. I KNOW IT HURTS, BUT YOU'VE GOT TO STAY *AWAKE*. STAY *AWAKE* FOR US.

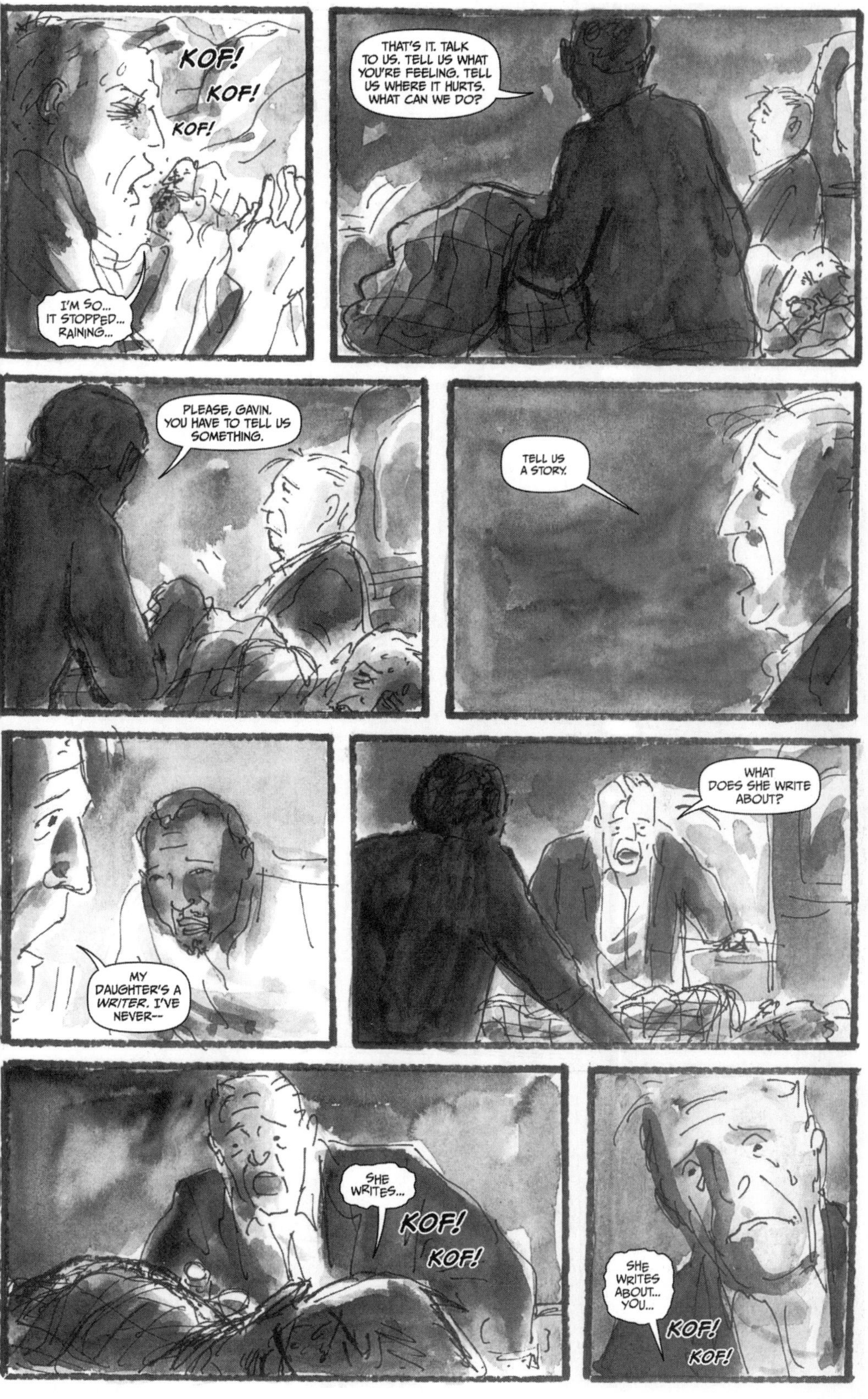
KOF!
KOF!
KOF!
I'M SO... IT STOPPED... RAINING...
THAT'S IT. TALK TO US. TELL US WHAT YOU'RE FEELING. TELL US WHERE IT HURTS. WHAT CAN WE DO?
PLEASE, GAVIN. YOU HAVE TO TELL US SOMETHING.
TELL US A STORY.
MY DAUGHTER'S A WRITER. I'VE NEVER--
WHAT DOES SHE WRITE ABOUT?
SHE WRITES...
KOF!
KOF!
SHE WRITES ABOUT... YOU...
KOF!
KOF!

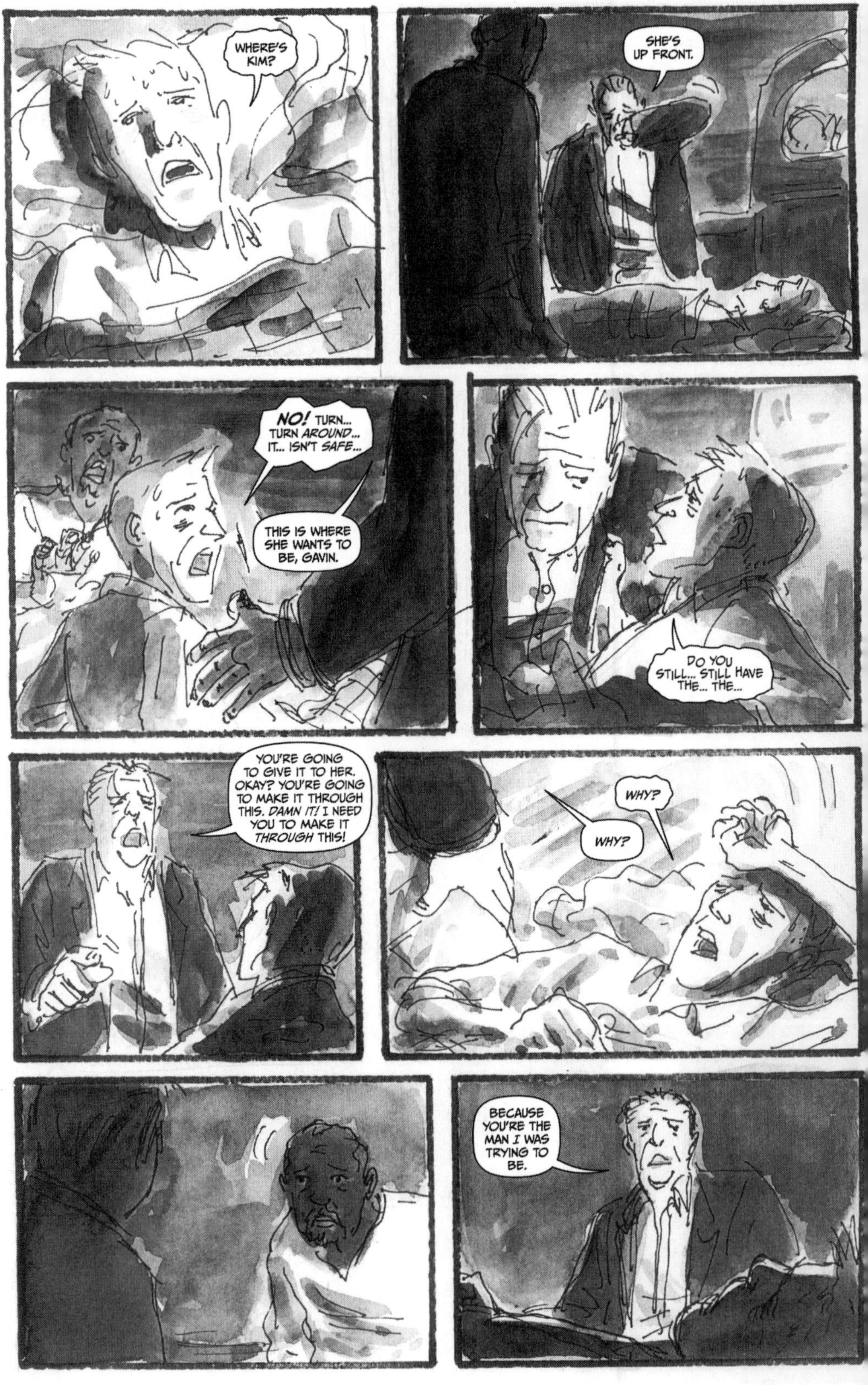
WHERE'S KIM?
SHE'S UP FRONT.
NO! TURN... TURN AROUND... IT... ISN'T SAFE...
THIS IS WHERE SHE WANTS TO BE, GAVIN.
DO YOU STILL... STILL HAVE THE... THE...
YOU'RE GOING TO GIVE IT TO HER. OKAY? YOU'RE GOING TO MAKE IT THROUGH THIS. DAMN IT! I NEED YOU TO MAKE IT THROUGH THIS!
WHY?
WHY?
BECAUSE YOU'RE THE MAN I WAS TRYING TO BE.

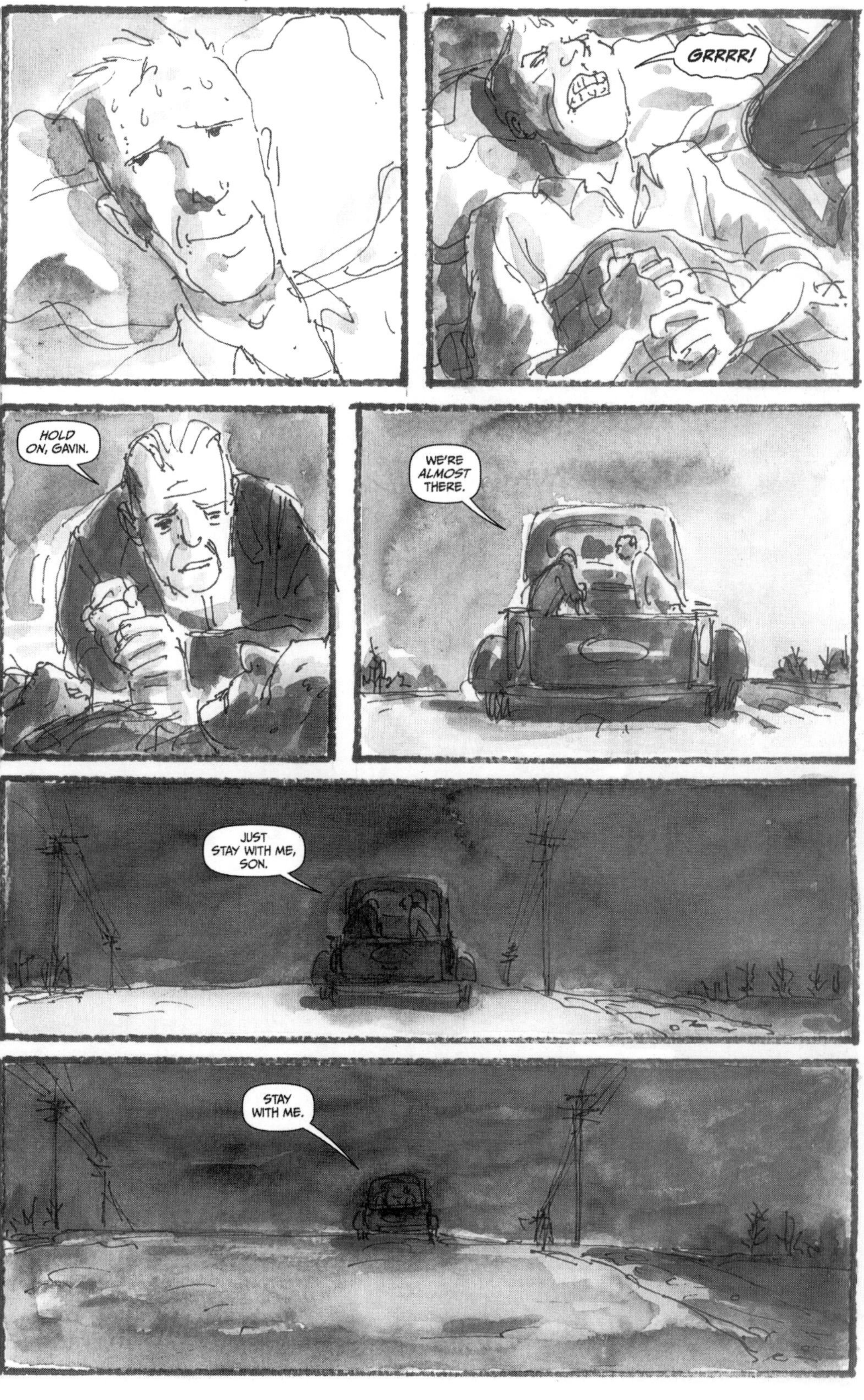
GRRRR!
HOLD ON, GAVIN.
WE'RE ALMOST THERE.
JUST STAY WITH ME, SON.
STAY WITH ME.

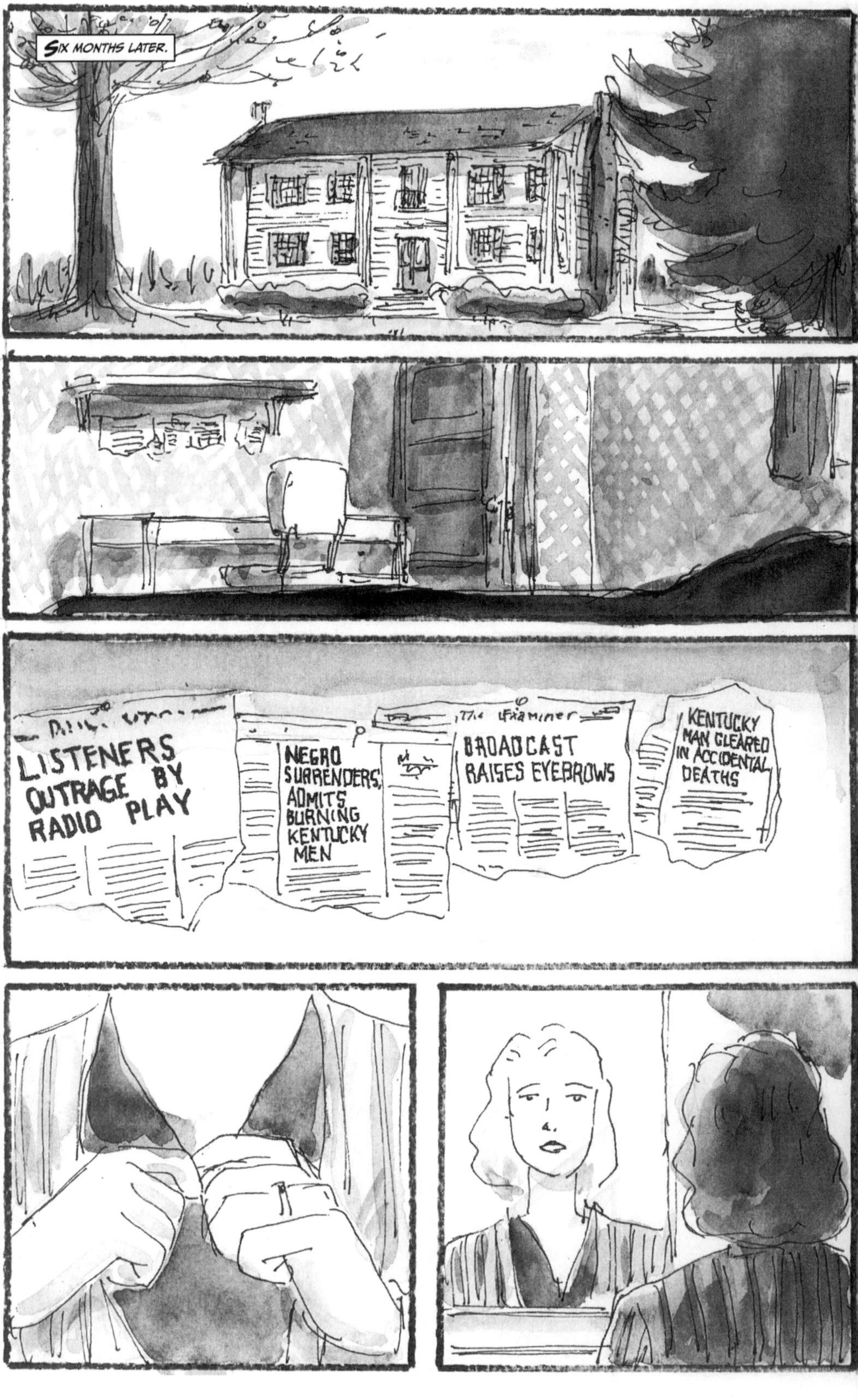
SIX MONTHS LATER.
LISTENERS OUTRAGE BY RADIO PLAY
NEGRO SURRENDERS; ADMITS BURNING KENTUCKY MEN
BROADCAST RAISES EYEBROWS
KENTUCKY MAN CLEARED IN ACCIDENTAL DEATHS

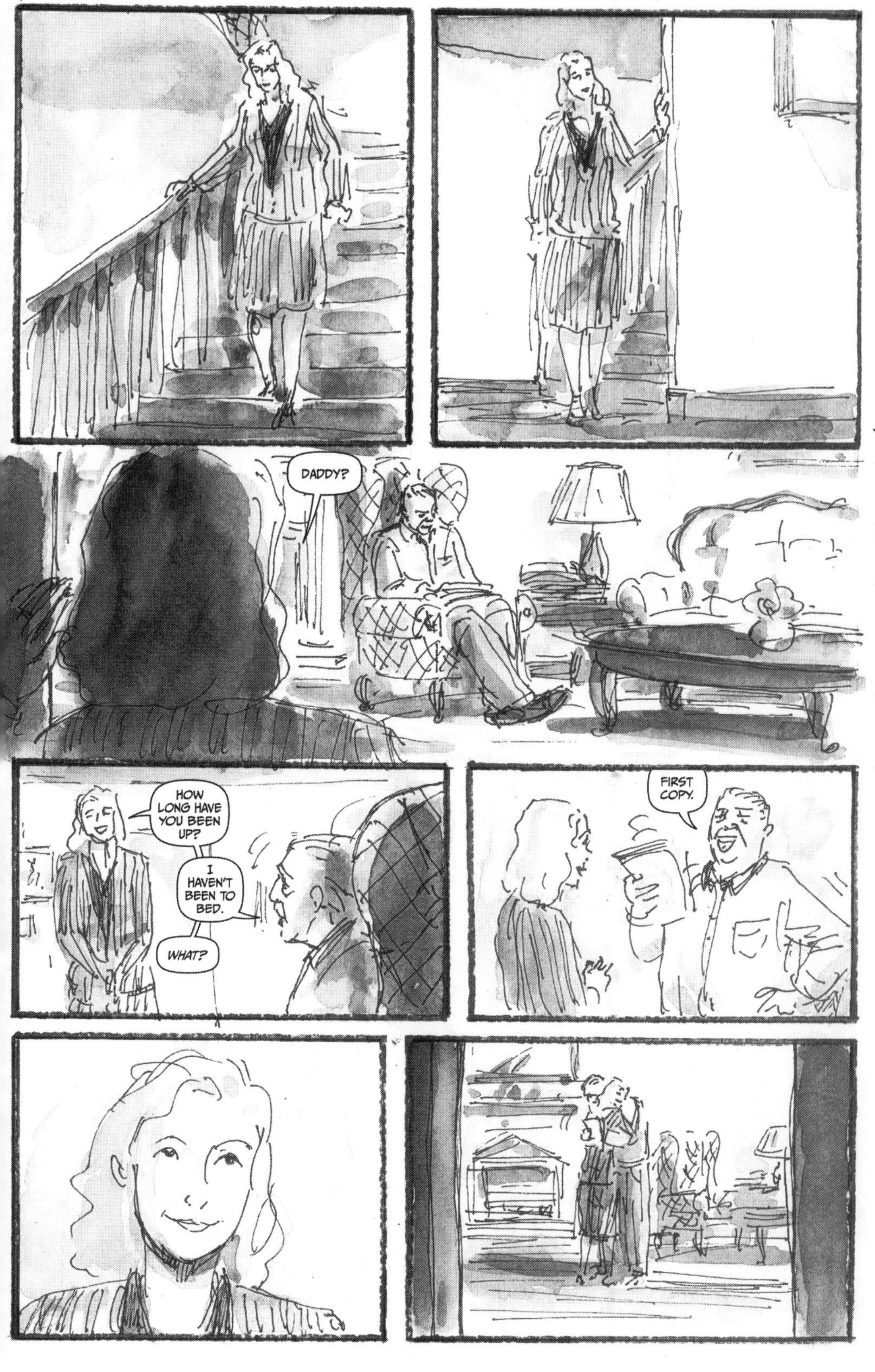
DADDY?
HOW LONG HAVE YOU BEEN UP?
I HAVEN'T BEEN TO BED.
WHAT?
FIRST COPY.

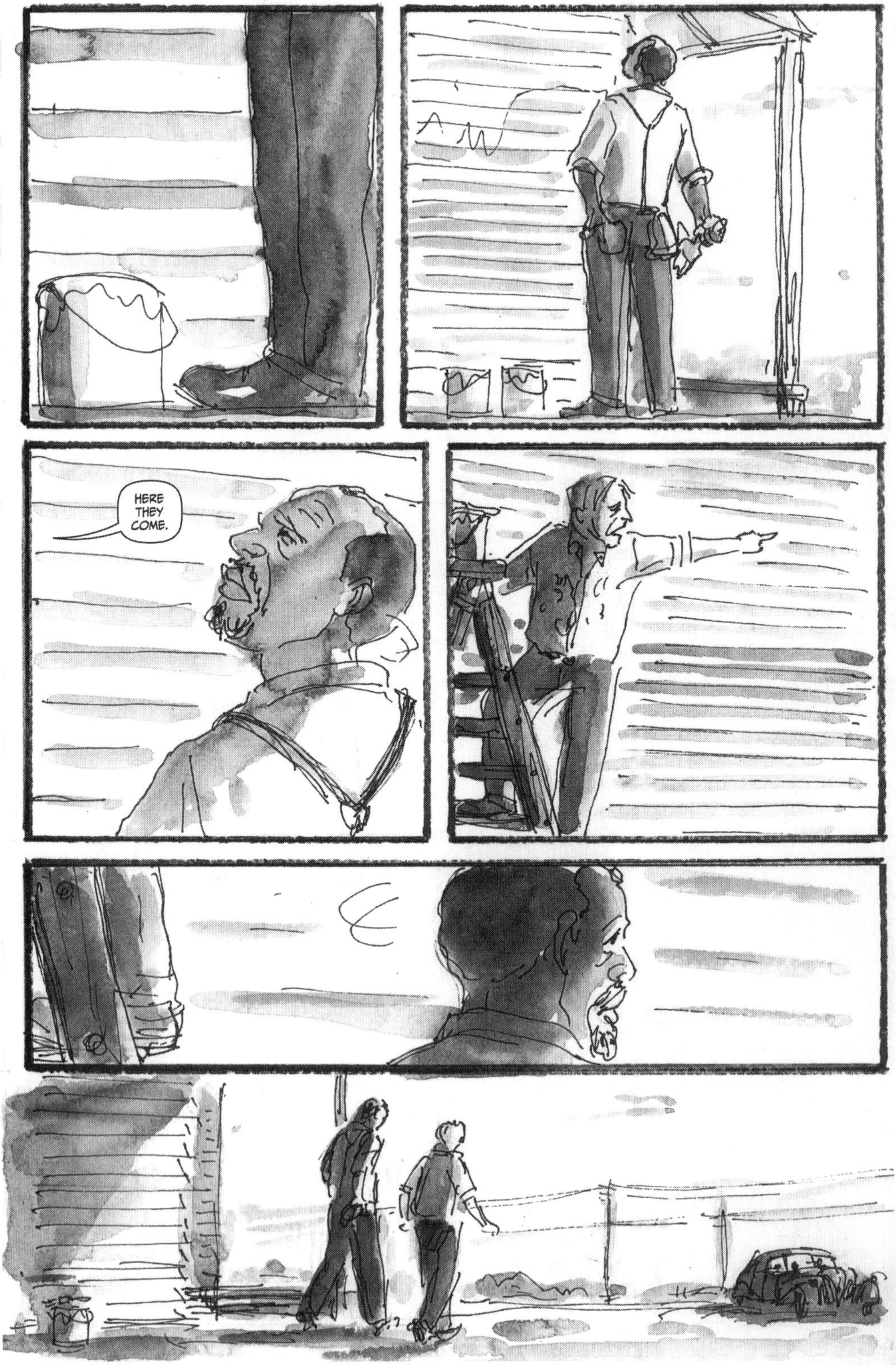
HERE THEY COME.

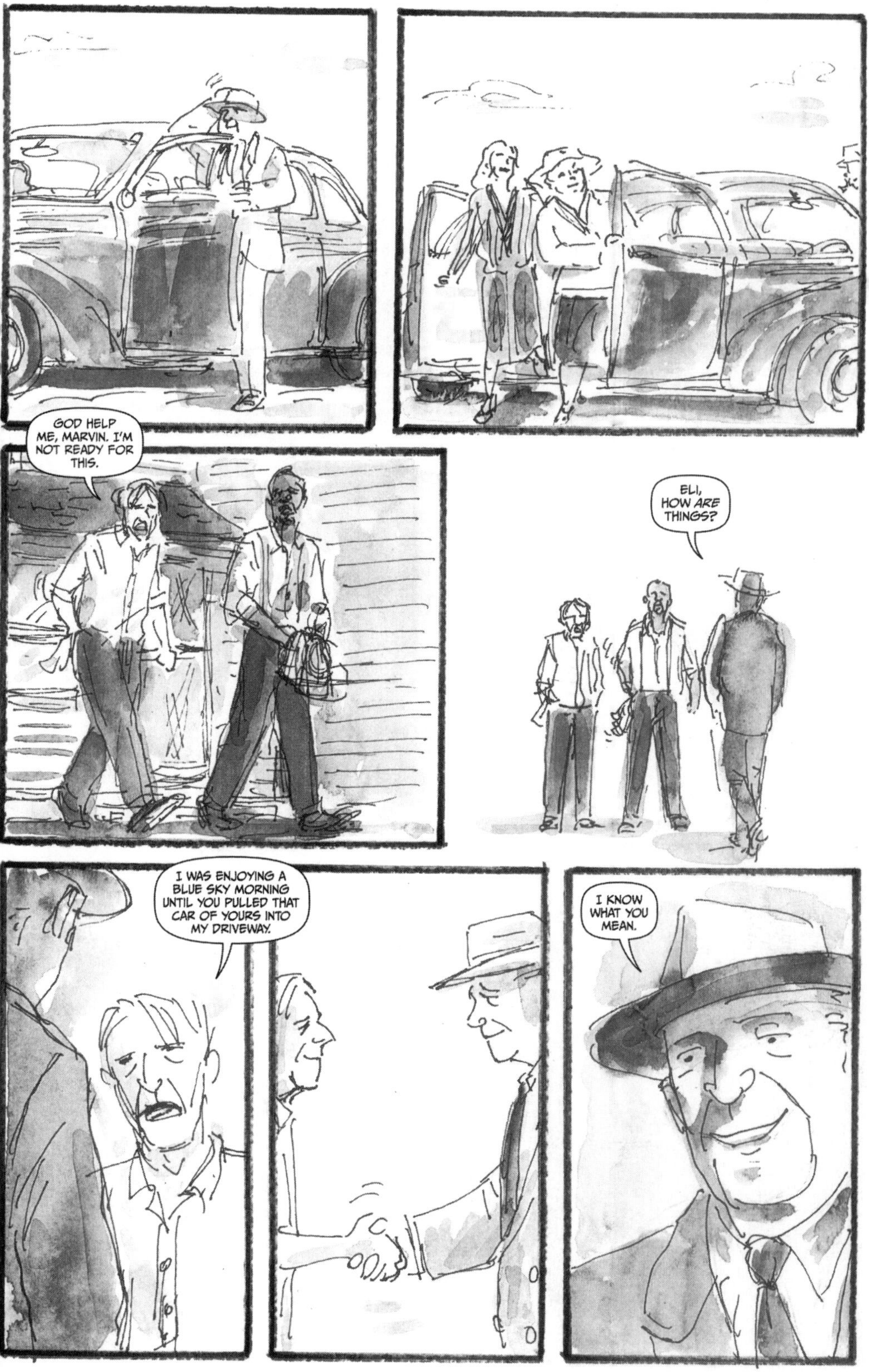
GOD HELP ME, MARVIN. I'M NOT READY FOR THIS.
ELI, HOW *ARE* THINGS?
I WAS ENJOYING A BLUE SKY MORNING UNTIL YOU PULLED THAT CAR OF YOURS INTO MY DRIVEWAY.
I KNOW WHAT YOU MEAN.

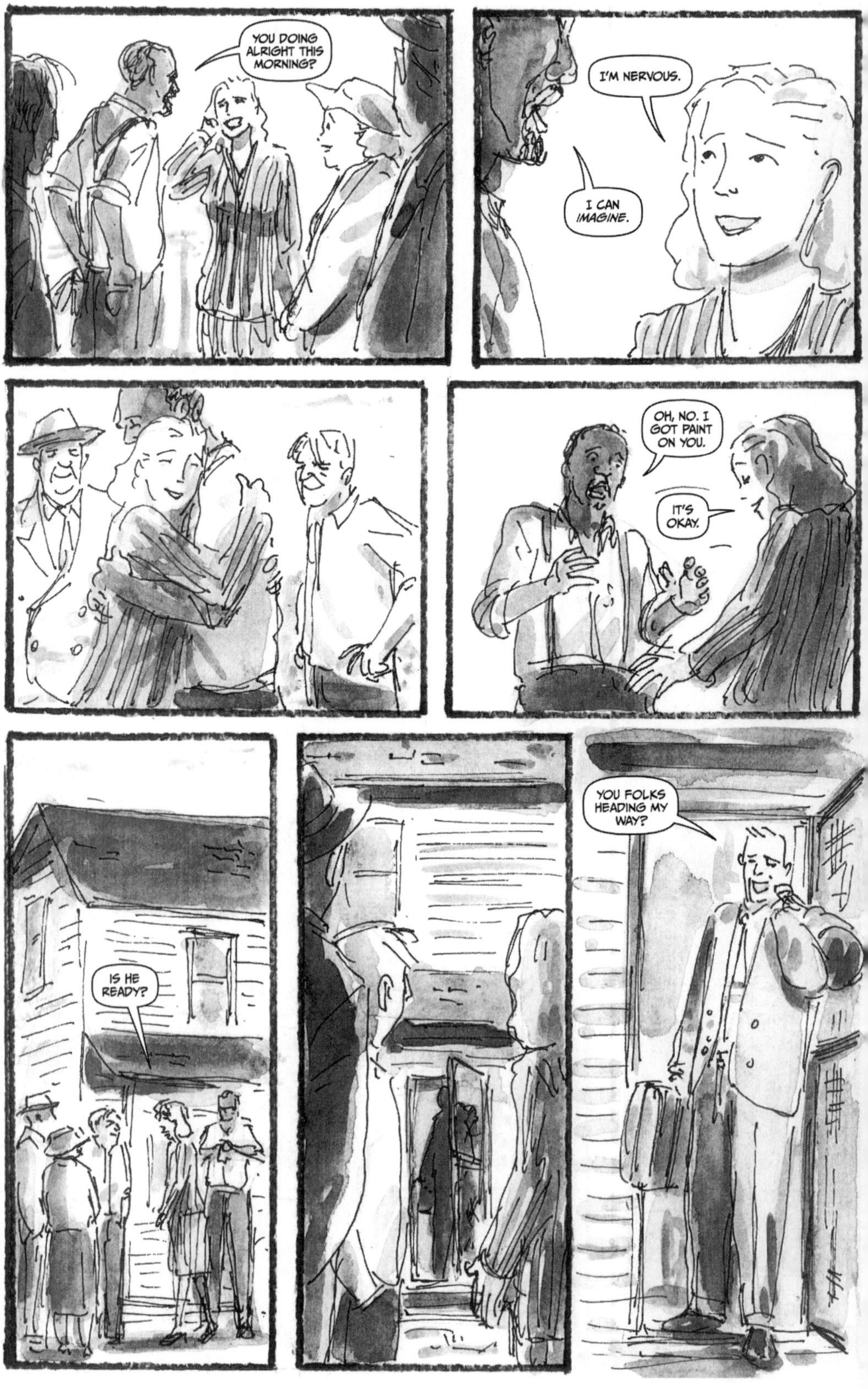
YOU DOING ALRIGHT THIS MORNING?
I'M NERVOUS.
I CAN IMAGINE.
OH, NO. I GOT PAINT ON YOU.
IT'S OKAY.
IS HE READY?
YOU FOLKS HEADING MY WAY?

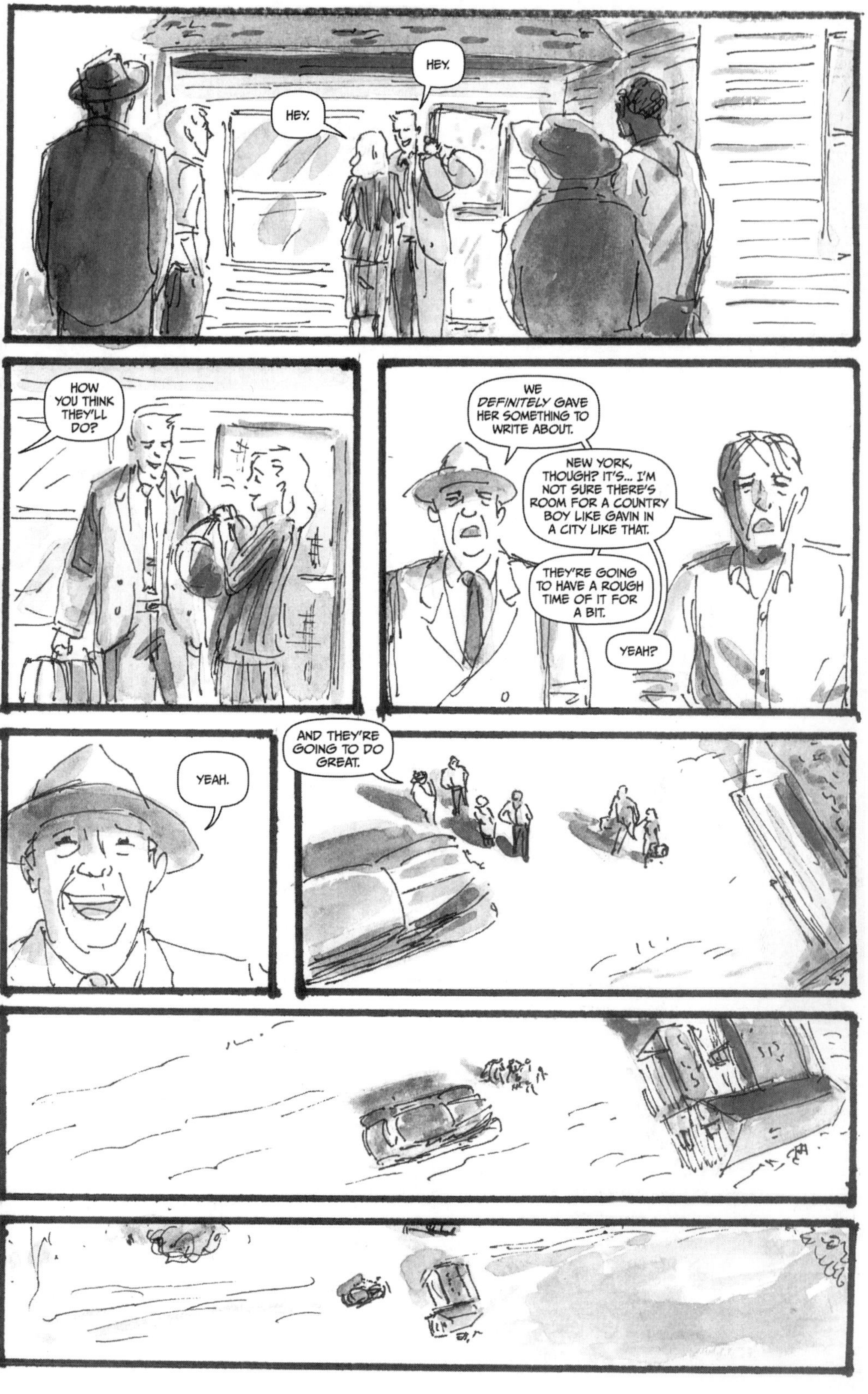
HEY.
HEY.
HOW YOU THINK THEY'LL DO?
WE *DEFINITELY* GAVE HER SOMETHING TO WRITE ABOUT.
NEW YORK, THOUGH? IT'S... I'M NOT SURE THERE'S ROOM FOR A COUNTRY BOY LIKE GAVIN IN A CITY LIKE THAT.
THEY'RE GOING TO HAVE A ROUGH TIME OF IT FOR A BIT.
YEAH?
YEAH.
AND THEY'RE GOING TO DO GREAT.

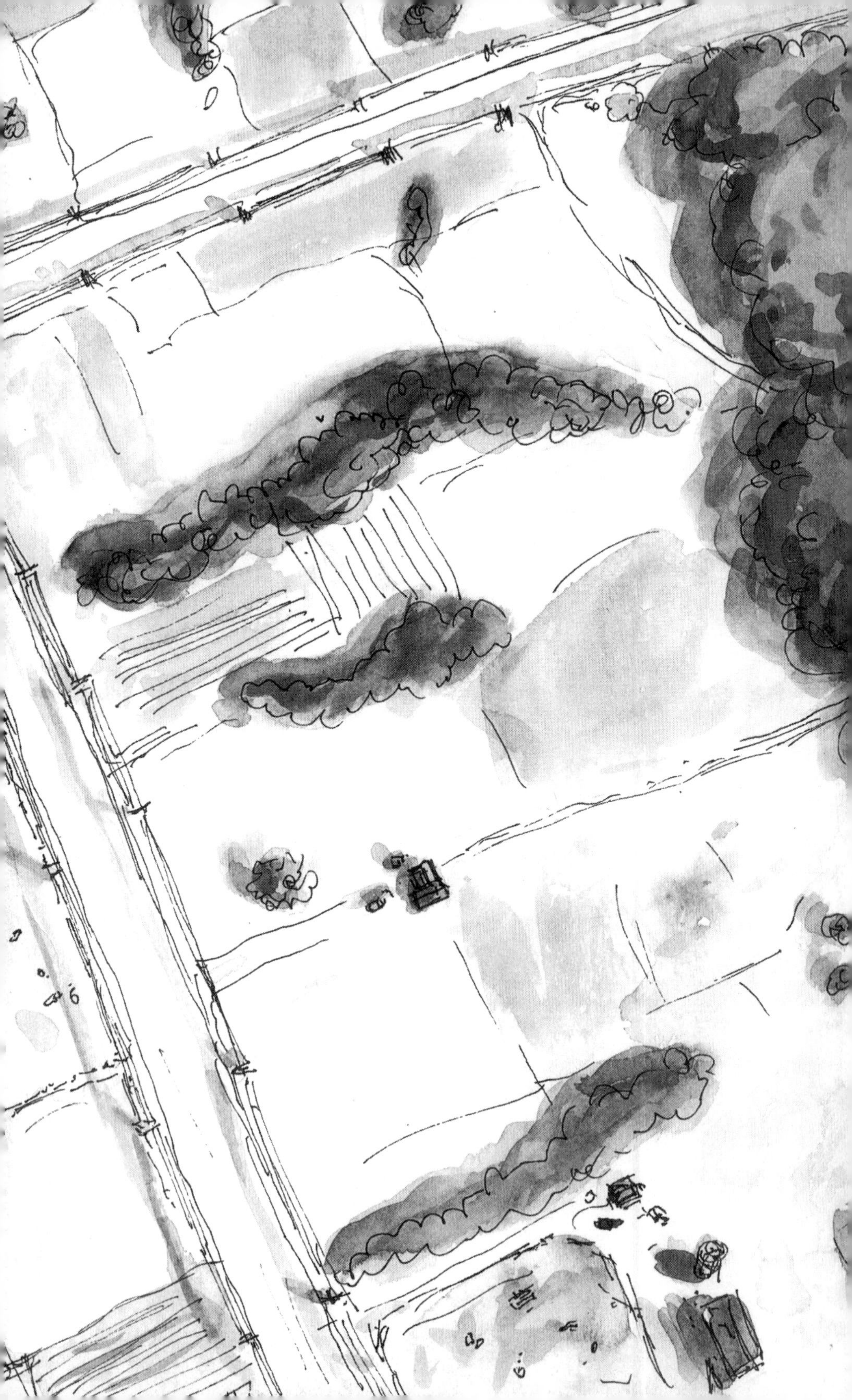

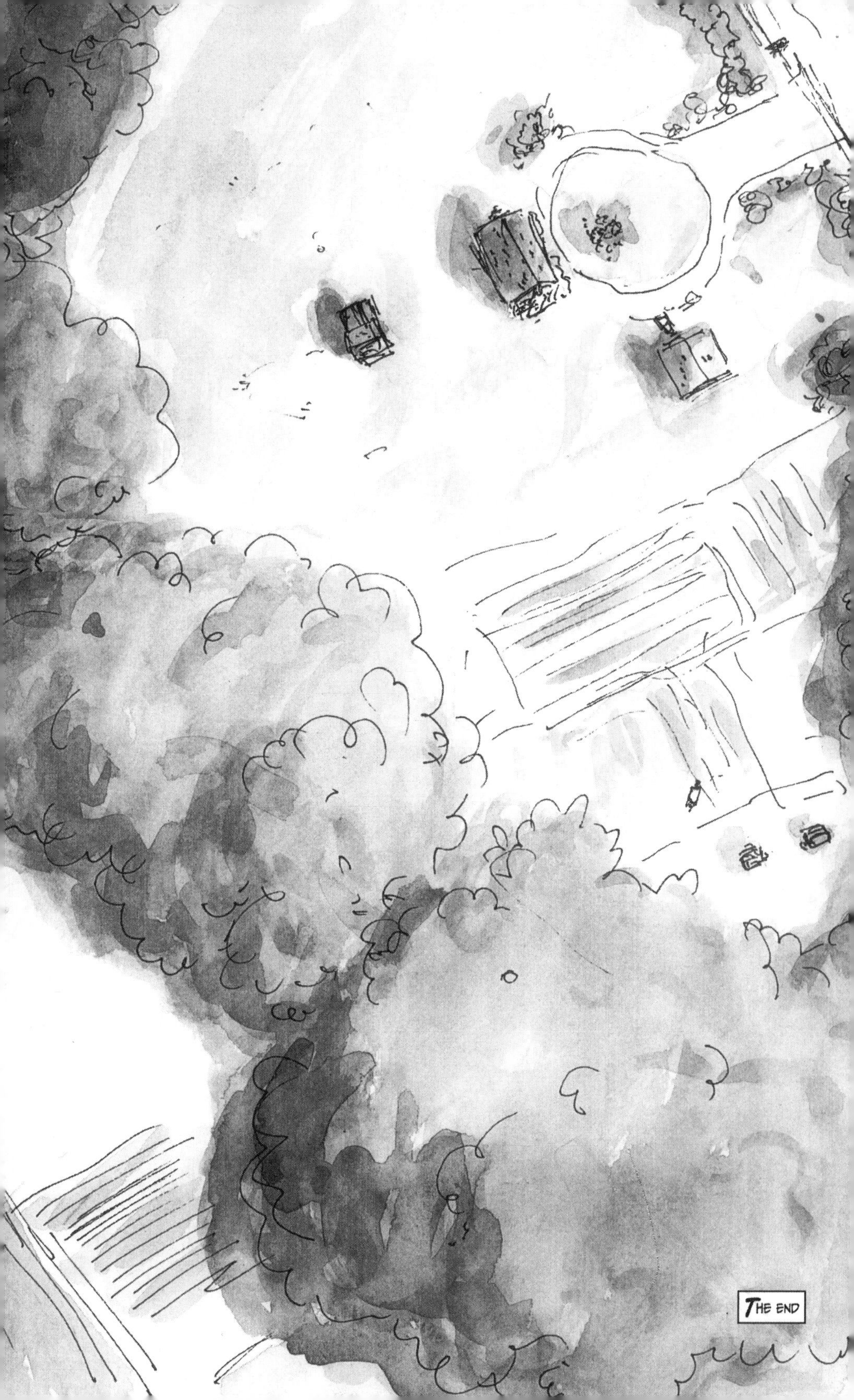
THE END

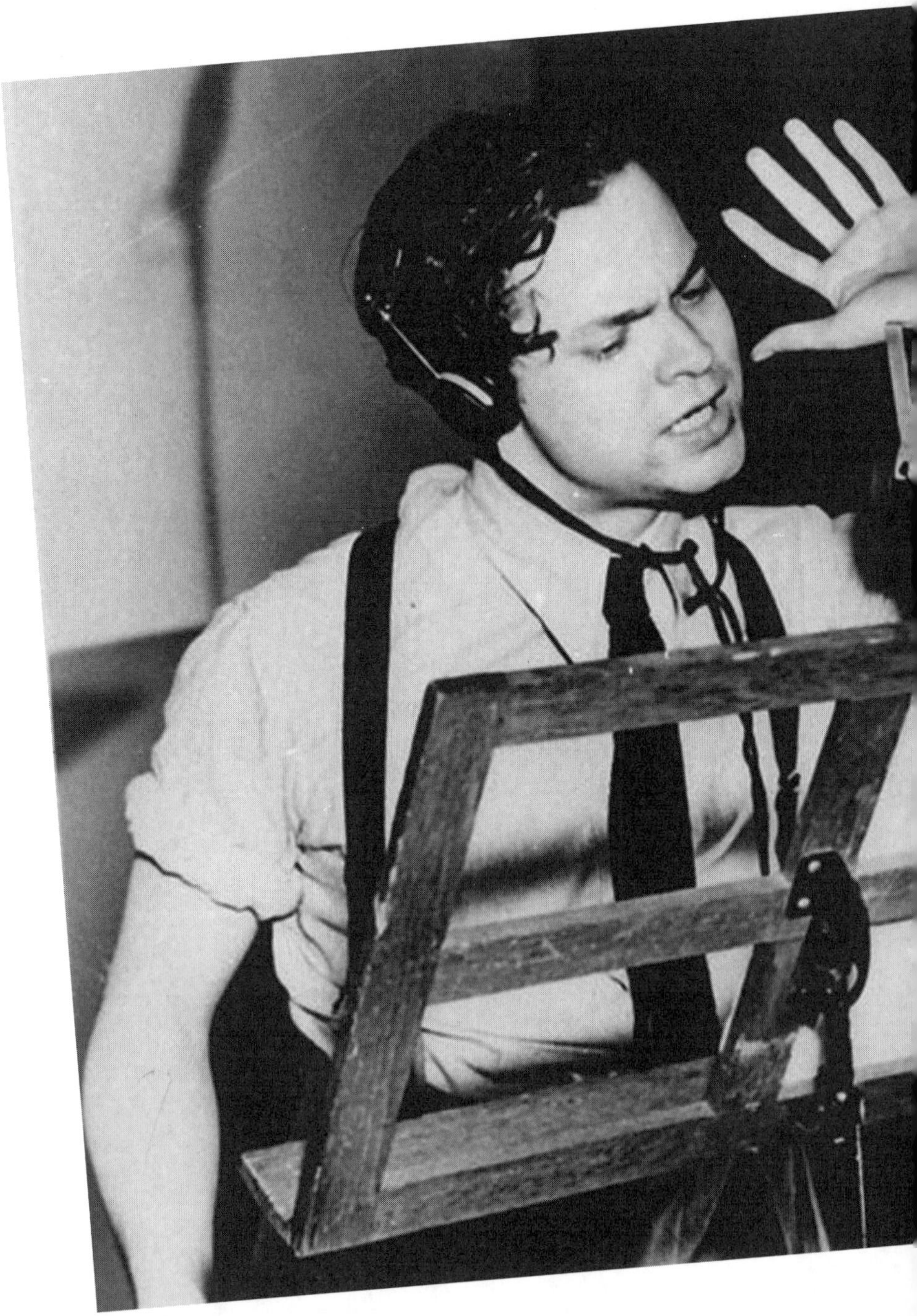

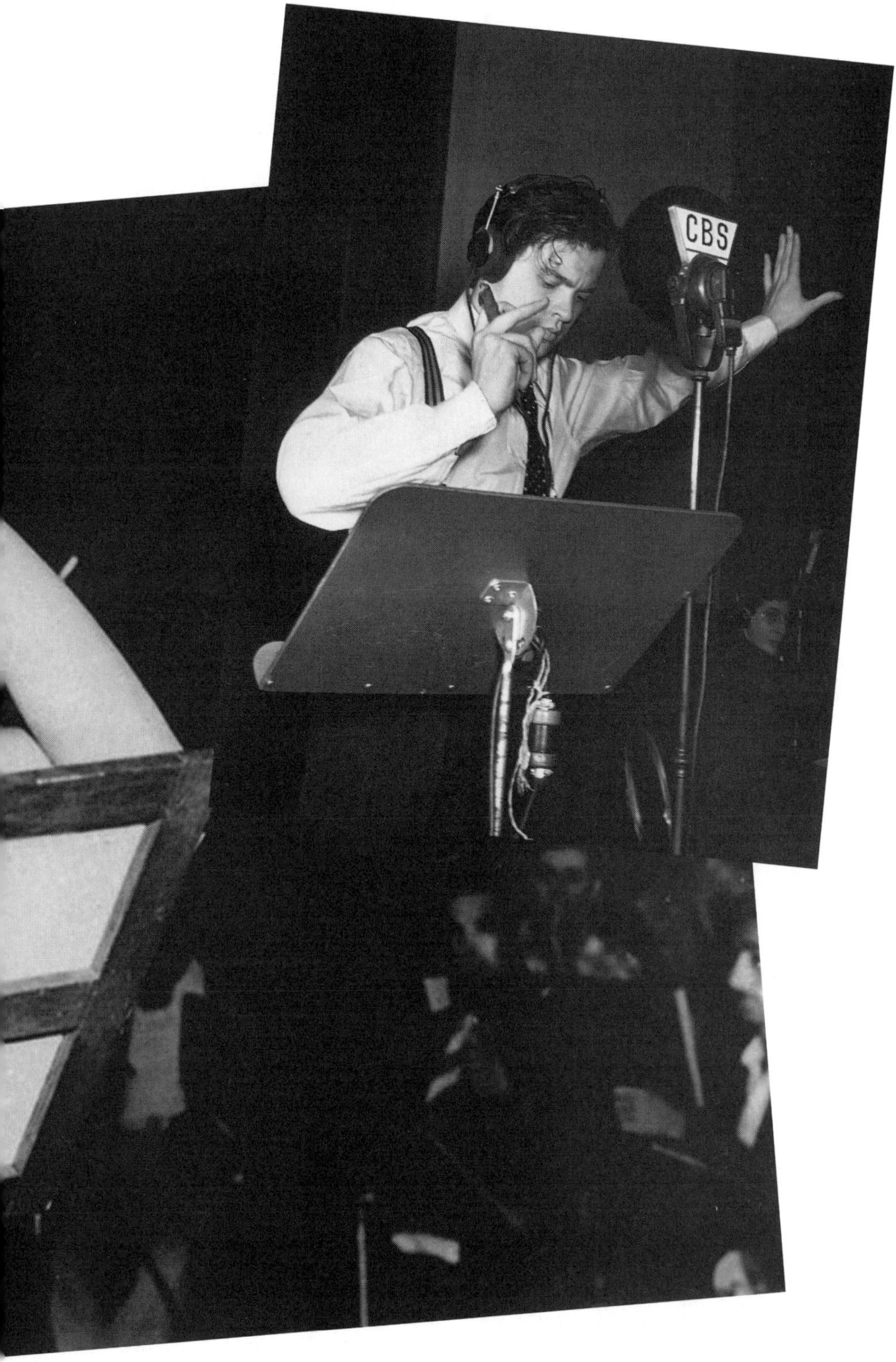
CBS

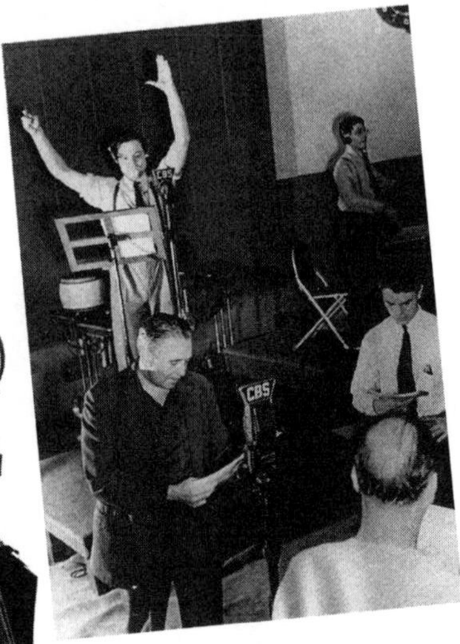

CBS
CBS

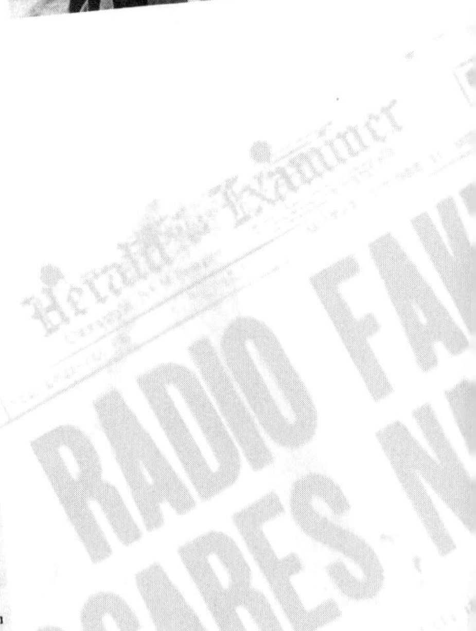

Herald Examiner
RADIO FAK
SCARES N

MAY, 1938

The *Radio* War

Not with bombs, bullets or blood-shed is the present World War raging

and other buildings burning.

BRITAIN SPEEDS RADIO FOR SOUTH AMERICA

Broadcasts Will Start Soon to Combat Harmful Italian and German Propaganda

Wireless to THE NEW YORK TIMES.
LONDON, Feb. 9.—Great Britain is speeding preparations for broad-... South America to ... casts ... man propa-... comba... ganda... feare... and

France, Italy, Germany, Japan, Russia, England and even the United States are intensifying their radio campaigns. Each nation objects to the direct verbal assaults issued against it by the other nations partaking in this feud. The newspaper clipping at the right is only one of hundreds found in the daily press.

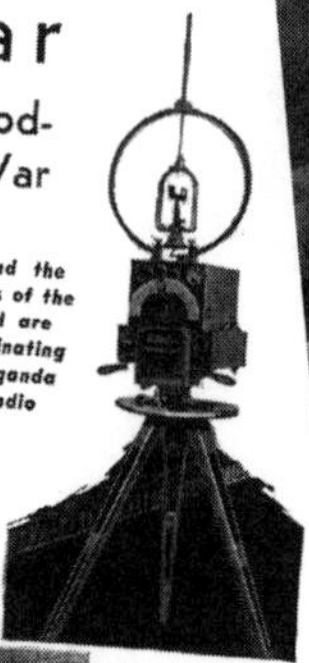

Instead the nations of the world are disseminating propaganda by radio

German police use direction finders of this type to ferret out pirate transmitters with which ousted political parties stimulate rebellion.

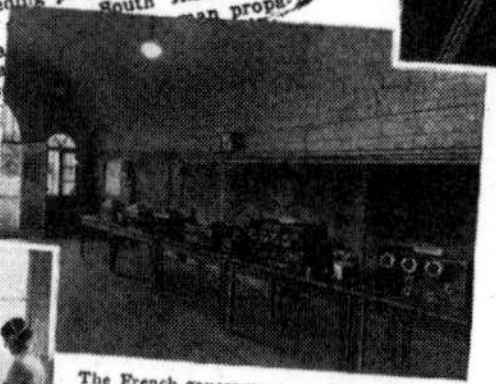

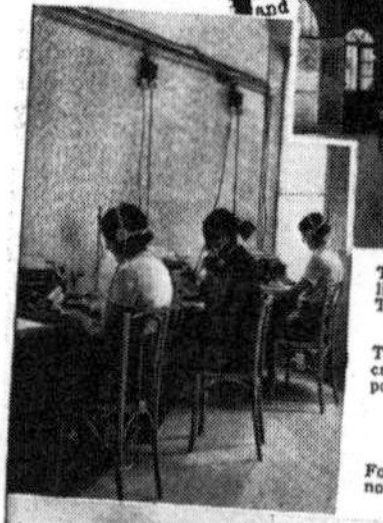

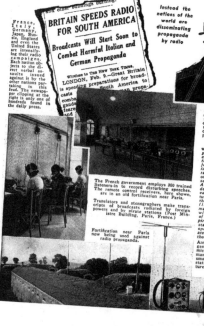

The French government employs 300 trained listeners-in to record disturbing speeches. The remote control receivers, here shown, are in an old fortification near Paris.

Translators and stenographers make transcripts of broadcasts radiated by foreign powers and by pirate stations (Post Ministre Building, Paris, France.)

A battle of words, false reports pro- and anti-government speeches for and against adjoining countries is being waged by radio in all parts of the world. Italy sends radio sets to Africa, England does likewise; and each country disturbs the peace of the other by inflammatory remarks. Meanwhile within the confines of some nations, pirate broadcasting stations are being operated to infuriate listeners against those in power.

Fortification near Paris now being used against radio propaganda.

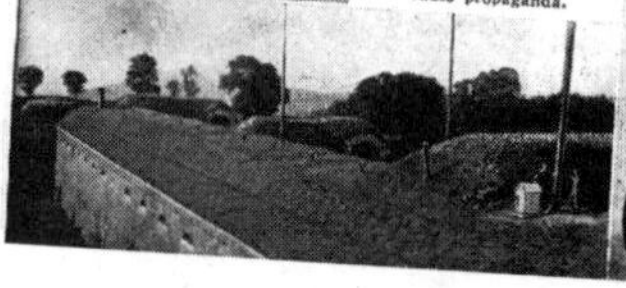

Anti-Nazi propaganda was transmitted within Germany from this small broadcasting station. It was captured by the secret police.

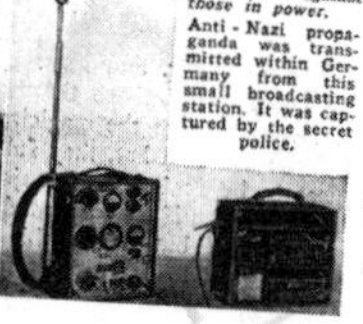

'RENTON EVENING TIMES, TUESDAY, NOVEMBER 1, 1938

FCC Will Study Transcription Of 'War of Worlds' Broadcast

WASHINGTON, Nov. 1 (INS).—Civilization is going to be "de-stroyed" again—so the seven-man Federal Communications Commission can pass judgment.

Some of the commissioners, in-cluding Chairman Fran R. Mc-Ninch, didn't hear the broadcast-ing system's coast-to-coast radio dramatization of H. G. Wells "The War of the Worlds," Sunday night, which apparently caused more fear and excitement among per-sons throughout the land who did not know it was a play, than any other national broadcast.

In response to the commis-sion's request, the CBS today de-livered to McNinch wax discs em-bodying an electrical transcription of the startling realistic broadcast.

The dramatization created a furore among radio listeners who did not hear, or fail to hear, that the realistic news bulletins de-scribing the destruction being wrought in New Jersey and in New York by animal-like crea-tures which landed here from the planet Mars, were all a part of the radio play.

Stating that in his opinion, that "any broadcast that creates such general panic and fear as this one is reported to have done, is, to say the least, regrettable," McNinch reserved judgment until the full commission hears the transcrip-tion of the hour-long fantasy and makes a thorough study.

While complaints against the broadcast continue to pour upon the commission today officials of the broadcasting company and Or-son Welles, star of the "Mercury Theatre of the Air," who wrote the radio adaptation of the fantastic book and played the stellar role, regretted that the play had caused such alarm.

Dies Says Probe to Continue, Scores Administration Abuse

WASHINGTON, Nov. 1 (UP)—Chairman Dies, Democrat, Texas, of the House committee investigat-ing un-American activities, indi-cated today that he would continue his inquiry into subversive activi-ties after denouncing high Admin-istration officials for a "campaign of ridicule" and "torrent of abuse unloosed upon us."

In a radio address last night, Dies defended his hearings and read letters from department heads and Cabinet members who had "refused to comply" with the res-

Ely Pleads For Farmer Suppo

Democrat Senate Nomi Carries His Campaig To Burlington

HACKENSACK, N. J., Nov. 1—William H. J. Ely's "100 per New Deal" campaign for United States Senate neared climax here in his home cou of Bergen where Postmaster G eral James A. Farley is to sp for the Democratic candidate night at the high school.

Campaigning last night at B lington in rural South Jersey, said ex-Senator W. Warren B bour, his Republican oppon was opposed to the direct prim and thus was a "backslider" "one of the most important vances made in our two-party litical system."

"Liberals throughout the co try," Ely said "have clung te ciously to the direct participa by the people in party activ Yet Mr. Barbour, who gives service to liberalism, would this system. His stand in this m ter is merely another example his real backsliding views.

"I am a firm believer in direct primary, and the Democ tic party has for years stood in its defense."

Making a bid for support farmers, Ely said:

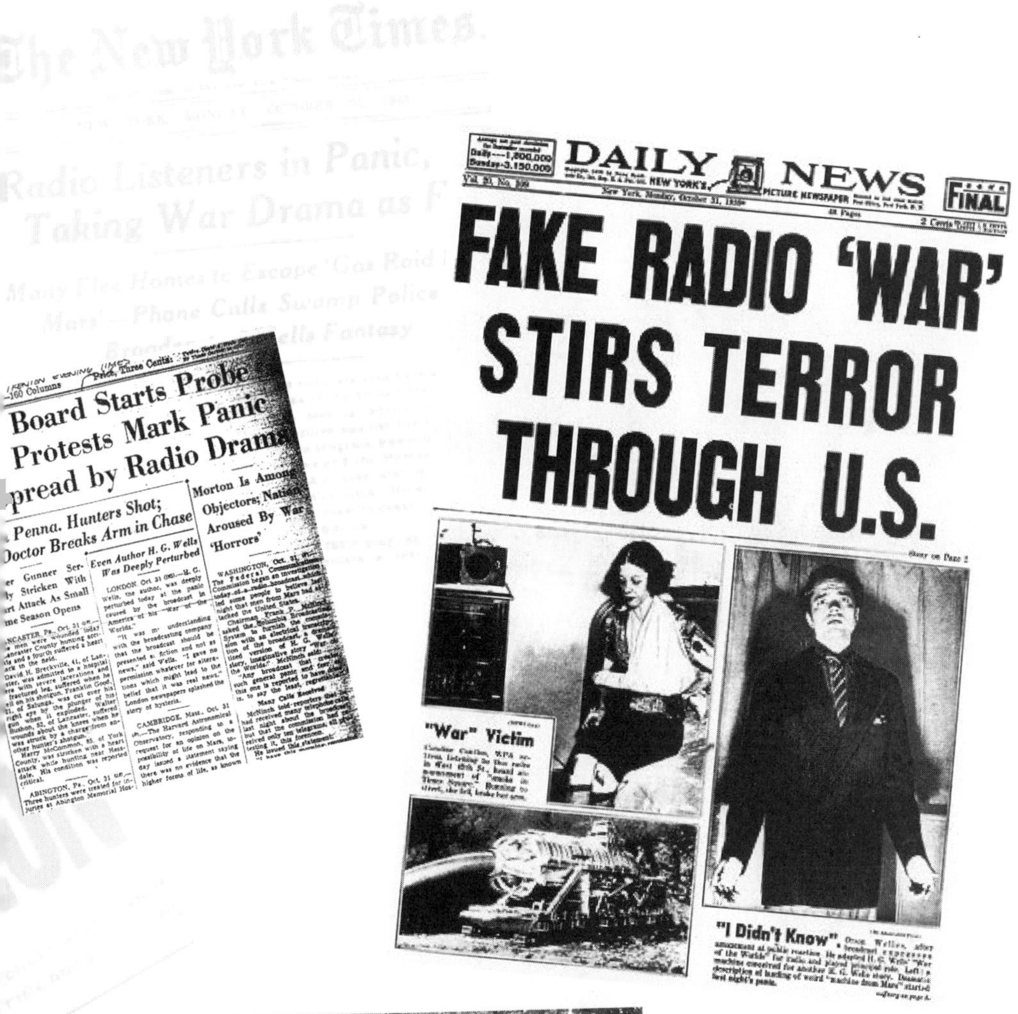

The New York Times.

NEW YORK, MONDAY, OCTOBER 31, 1938

Radio Listeners in Panic, Taking War Drama as F

Many Flee Homes to Escape 'Gas Raid' Mars'—Phone Calls Swamp Police Broadcast Wells Fantasy

TRENTON EVENING TIMES

—160 Columns Price, Three Cents

Board Starts Probe Protests Mark Panic Spread by Radio Drama

Penna. Hunters Shot; Doctor Breaks Arm in Chase

er Gunner Stricken With art Attack As Small me Season Opens

Even Author H. G. Wells Was Deeply Perturbed

LONDON, Oct. 31 —H. G. Wells, the author, was deeply perturbed today at the panic caused by the broadcast in America of his "War of the Worlds."

"It was my understanding with the broadcasting company that the broadcast should be presented as fiction and not as news," said Wells. "I gave no permission whatever for alterations which might lead to the belief that it was real news."

Morton Is Among Objectors; Nation Aroused By War 'Horrors'

WASHINGTON, Oct. 31 — The Federal Communications Commission began an investigation today of a radio broadcast which led some people to believe last night that men from Mars had attacked the United States.

DAILY NEWS

NEW YORK'S PICTURE NEWSPAPER

Daily—1,800,000 Sunday—3,150,000

Vol. 20. No. 109

New York, Monday, October 31, 1938

FINAL

FAKE RADIO 'WAR' STIRS TERROR THROUGH U.S.

Story on Page 2

"War" Victim

"I Didn't Know". Orson Welles, after broadcast, expresses amazement at public reaction. He adapted H. G. Wells' "War of the Worlds" for radio and played principal role. Left: a machine conceived for another H. G. Wells story. Dramatic description of landing of weird "machine from Mars" started last night's panic.

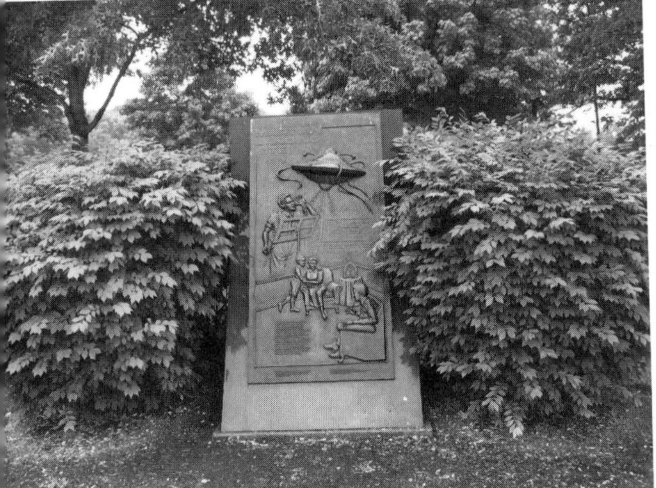

Further Reading

Gosling, John. Waging the War of the Worlds: A History of the 1938 Radio Broadcast and Resulting Panic. (Jefferson, North Carolina: McFarland, 2009.)

Holmsten, Briand and Lubertozzi, Alex. The Complete War of the Worlds. (Naperville, Illinois: Sourcebooks, 2001.)

Koch, Howard. The Panic Broadcast: The Whole Story of Orson Welles' Legendary Radio Show Invasion From Mars. (Boston, Massachusetts: Little, Brown, 1970.)

Deleted Scenes

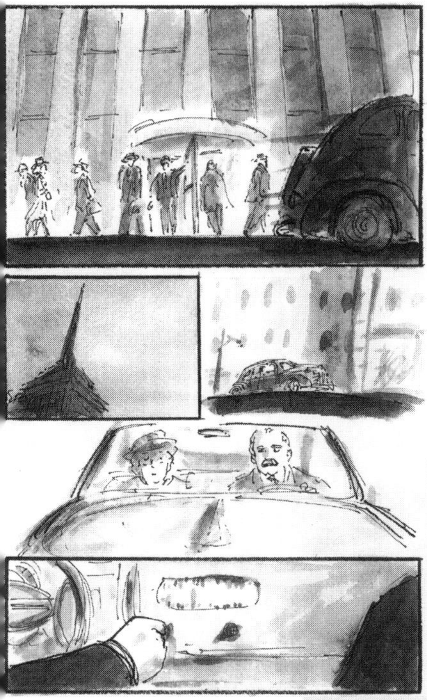

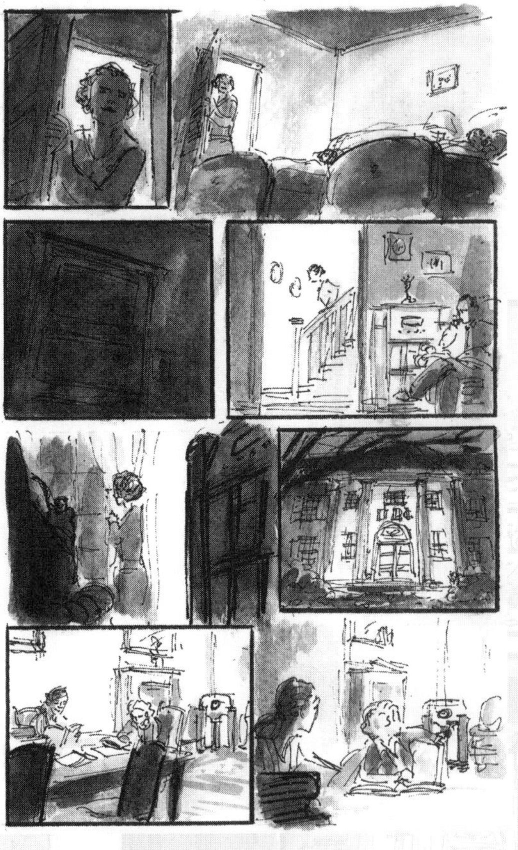

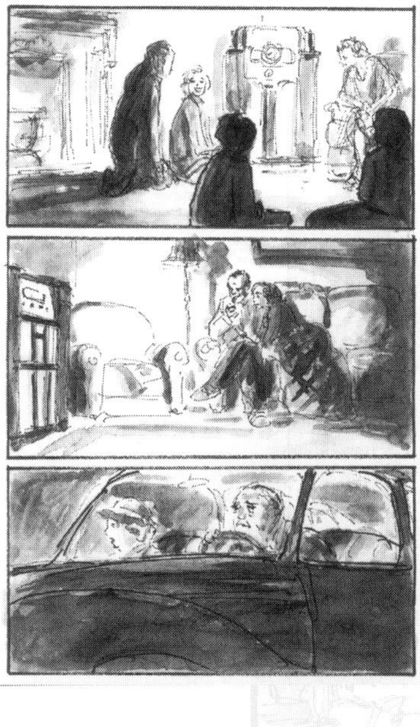

"There were several scenes that didn't make the cut for a number of reasons. These are unlettered, but you can see that not everyone listening on that fateful night responded as those in our story. Some actually enjoyed it."

Character Sketches

"This is probably my favorite step in the creative process. After months of writing an artist comes in and finally breathes life into the characters I've created, moving them from my head and onto the page."

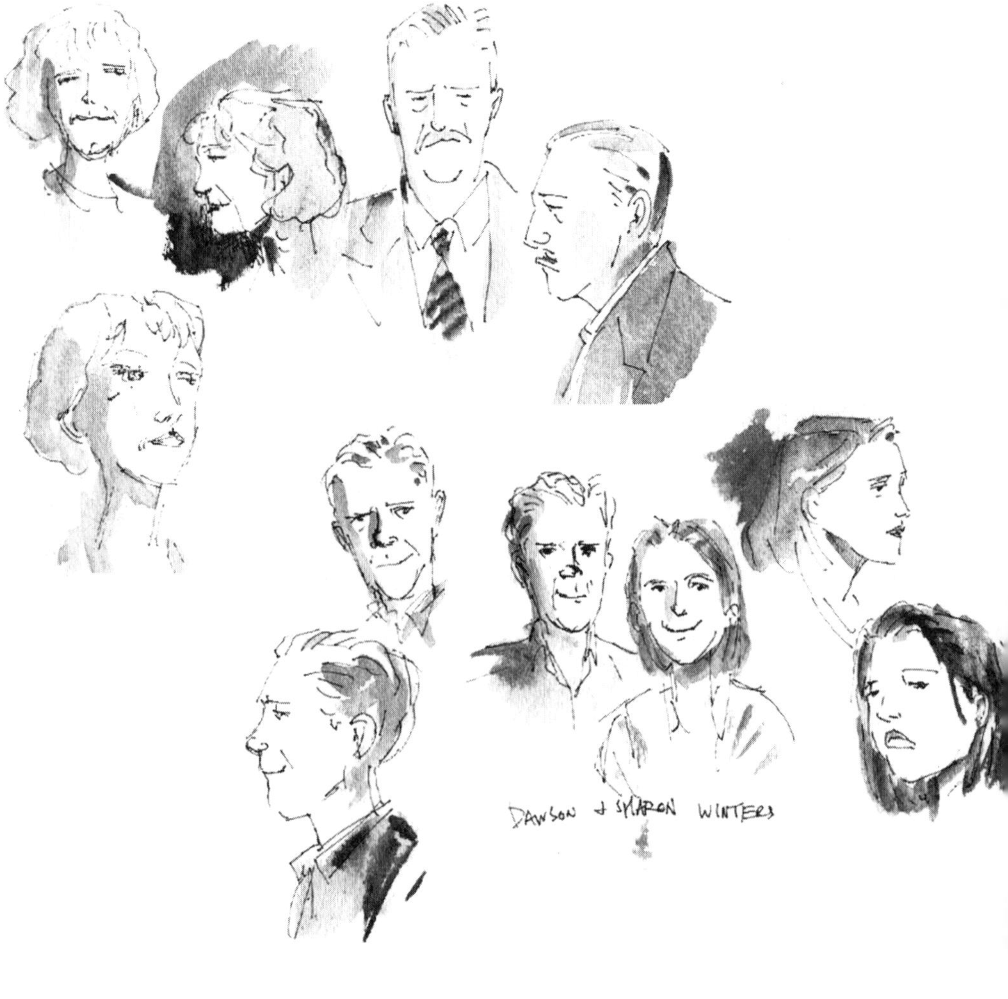
DAWSON & SHARON WINTERS

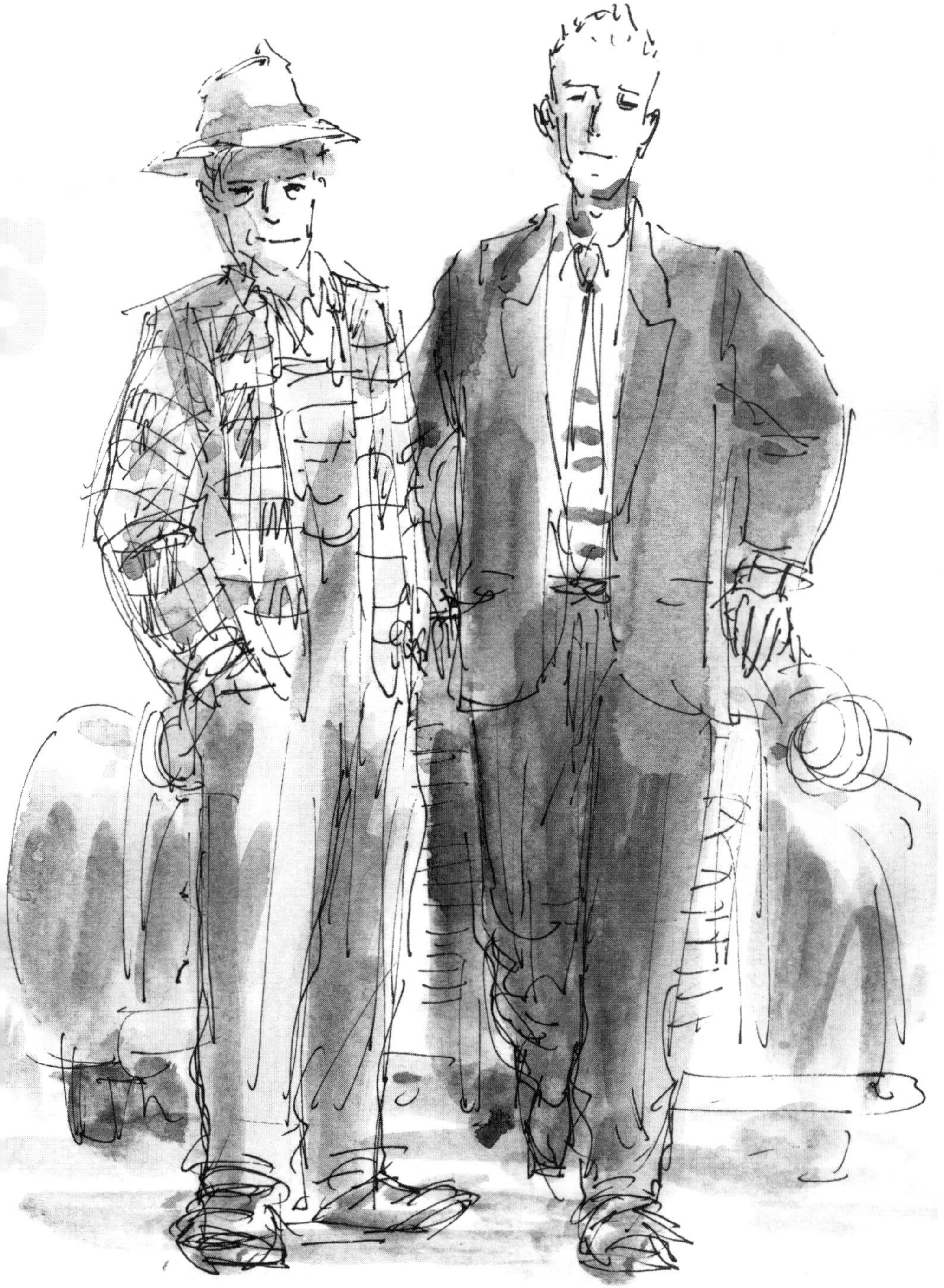

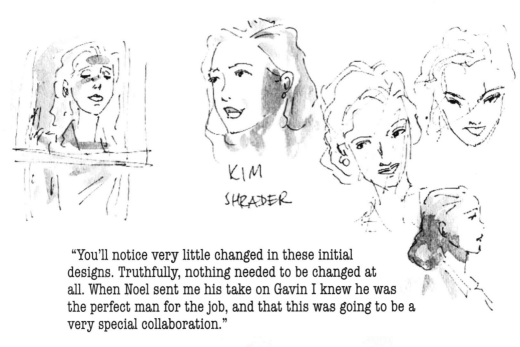

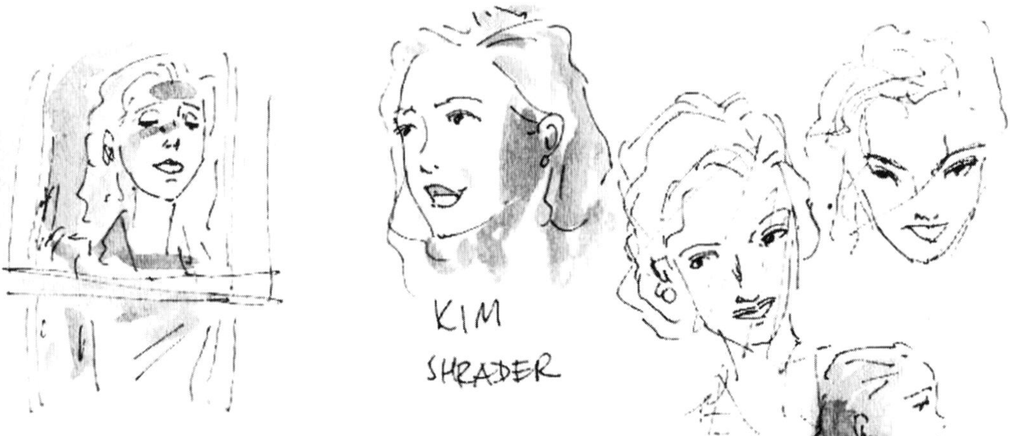
KIM
SHRADER

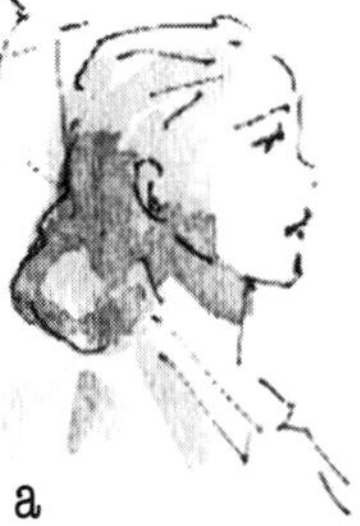

"You'll notice very little changed in these initial designs. Truthfully, nothing needed to be changed at all. When Noel sent me his take on Gavin I knew he was the perfect man for the job, and that this was going to be a very special collaboration."

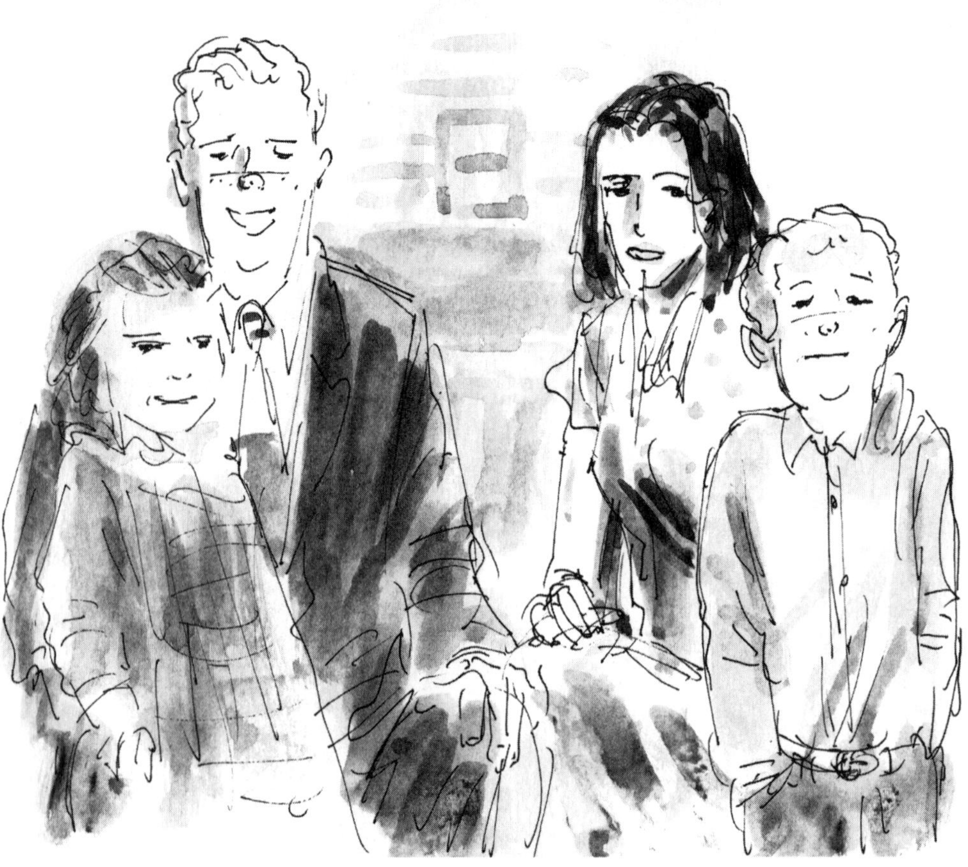

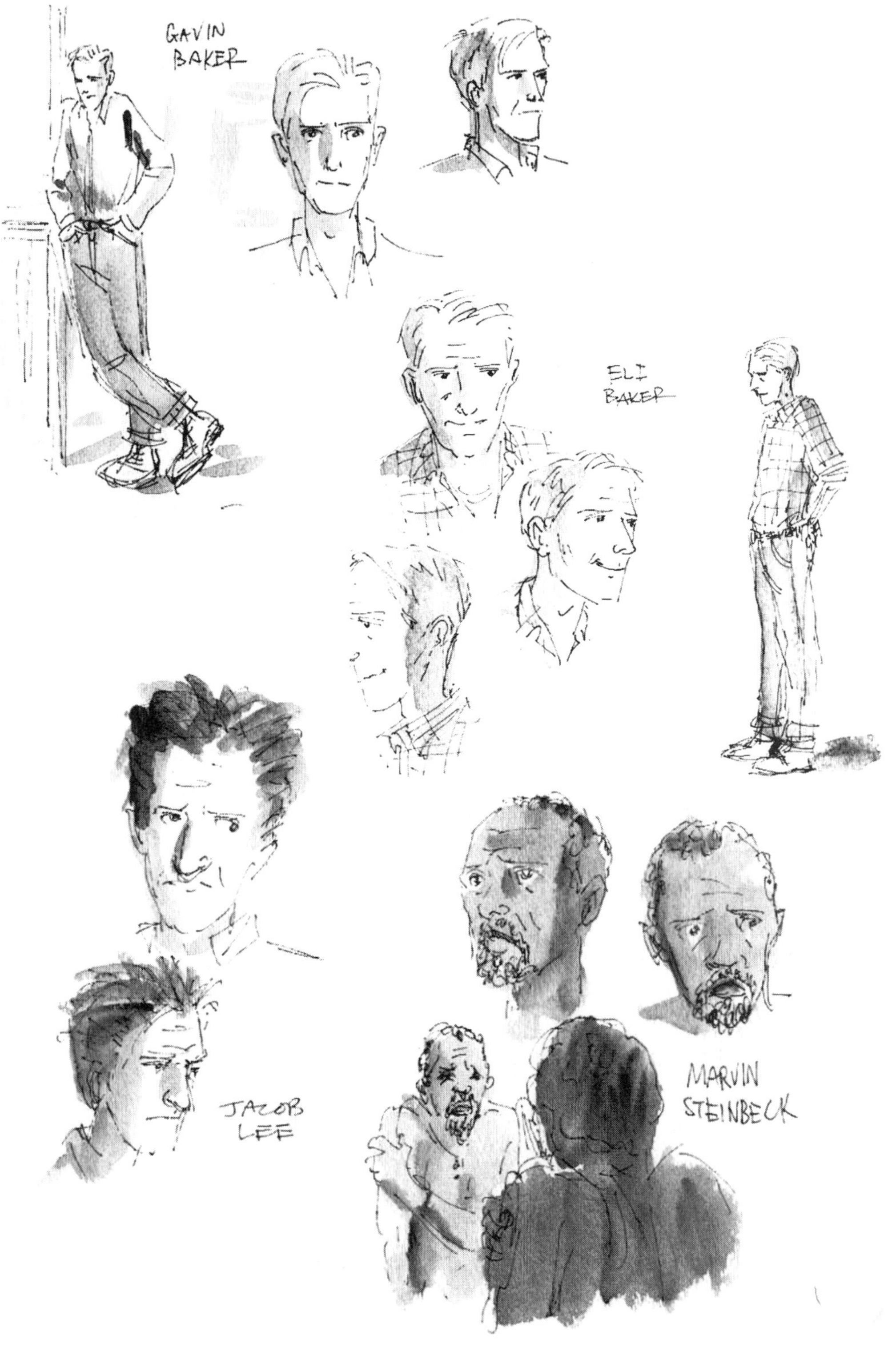
GAVIN
BAKER
ELI
BAKER
JACOB
LEE
MARVIN
STEINBECK

Layouts

"I can't tell you how many times I received a new set of page layouts where Noel had added a few panels I hadn't written or had taken a couple a way. And you know what? He was right every time. I learned so much from Noel about sequential storytelling that by the end of the book he didn't have to change the panel count – I was doing it for him."

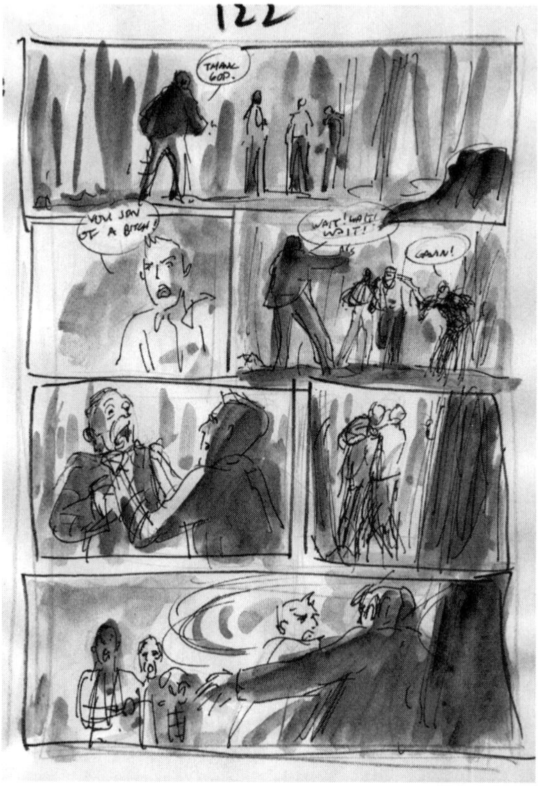
122
THANK GOD.
YOU SON OF A BITCH!
WAIT! WAIT! WAIT!
GAVIN!

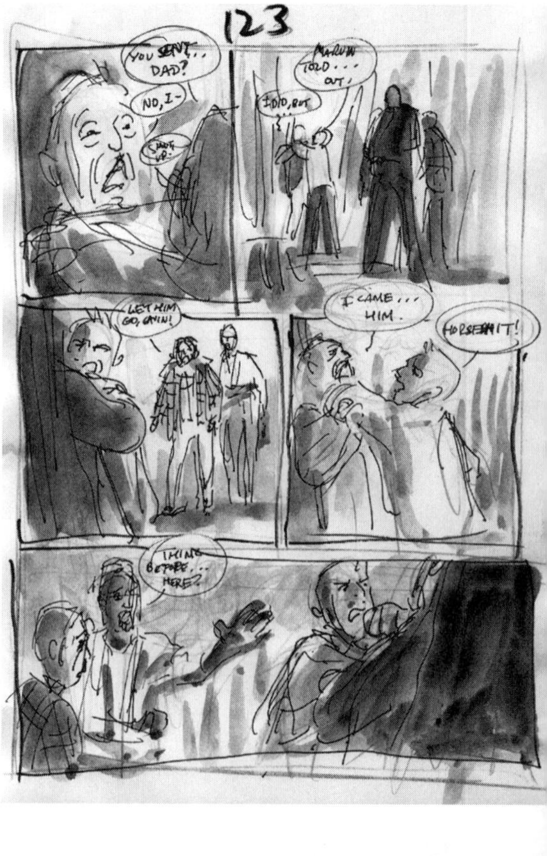
123
YOU SENT... DAD?
NO, I-
SHUT UP.
MARVIN TOLD... OUT.
I DID, BUT...
LET HIM GO, GAVIN!
I CAME... HIM.
HORSESHIT!
THINK BEFORE... HERE?